M000311801

"There is no doubt whatsoever th[...]
the Salvation Army, were remar[...]
and Catherine was a formidable [...]
established convention by preaching in public, something which today is
taken for granted but that was certainly not the case in her day.

"In her work to combat some of the evils of the time such as alcoholism,
poverty and prostitution, her actions were firmly based on a deep faith.
That was her rock. Whatever one might think about her convictions there
is no doubt whatsoever that both she and William were a formidable team
in the fight against some of the evils present in this world. This book reveals
something of her faith and belief. It would, I am sure, be her hope that as
she was inspired by the teaching and life of Christ so others might also be
encouraged in their pilgrimage."

–Terry Waite CBE

"If I could choose a person from history to ask about the essentials of life and
ministry, I would choose Catherine Booth. A woman far ahead of her time,
she blazed a trail and used her gifts in a way that still makes me wide eyed
with wonder. An incredible force for God during her lifetime and a voice
that still echoes His Kingdom come in ours, we would all do well to listen!
Catherine Booth is a prophetic voice that is still speaking of God's boundless
salvation for a world as desperate for good news as ever."

– Danielle Strickland

"Catherine Booth was the co-founder of an international movement which in
25 years reached 100 countries. She fulfilled a heavy preaching schedule in an
era when female voices were rarely heard in the pulpit.

"Catherine Booth from childhood had sought the salvation of others. Later
she pursued her aim by working in the slums, clothing the naked, feeding
the hungry, and helping William grow the Christian Mission to become
The Salvation Army. Throughout she prayed, wrote, encouraged, and spoke,
overcoming her youthful timidity to become a formidable preacher and leader
in 'God's Army'.

In the year when Queen Elizabeth has highlighted 'Service and Duty' I
hope that, through this insightful book by Stephen Poxon, some may find
inspiration from the life of this remarkable lady to 'serve the present age."

– Lord Foster of Bishop Auckland DL DCL

THROUGH THE YEAR WITH

Edited by
Stephen Poxon

MONARCH
BOOKS

Oxford, UK & Grand Rapids, Michigan, USA

Published by
Lion Hudson Limited
Wilkinson House, Jordan Hill Business Park,
Banbury Road, Oxford OX2 8DR, England
www.lionhudson.com

ISBN 978 0 85721 739 4 (hardback)
ISBN 978 0 85721 889 6 (paperback)
e-ISBN 978 0 85721 740 0

First hardback edition 2016
First paperback edtion 2017

A catalogue record for this book is available from the British Library

Printed and bound in the USA, November 2018, LH37

To Mum

Acknowledgments

So many threads combine to make a book that it is with some trepidation I offer these words of acknowledgment; not because I am unwilling to do so (far from it), but because I wonder if I might inadvertently exclude someone who deserves a mention – someone who has helped in one way or another with putting all the threads together. If I miss anyone, I can only hope for forgiveness. No offence is intended.

The staff at Lion Hudson/Monarch have been unfailingly cooperative, patient and helpful. Without their expertise and kindness, this book would never have appeared. I am most grateful to have the privilege of working alongside them.

Likewise, my gratitude extends to those who have (once again) helped me out by allowing me to borrow books that have proved invaluable in my research; representing my spiritual home, The Salvation Army: Major Wendy Goodman, Majors David and Denise Wise, my parents-in-law, Majors Paul and Ena Latham, Eric and Margaret Jerome from The Salvation Army in Luton. Representing my friendships within Methodism: Chris and Mary Bowen. My sincere thanks to you all.

Finally, I say thank you to my wife, Major Heather Poxon, and to my children, Jasmine and Alistair, for granting me hours of uninterrupted time to put these pages together, when they would have been within their rights to claim more from me as husband and father.

I am, I know, indebted to each of you.

Catherine Booth – devoted wife, fiercely proud and protective mother, Wesleyan, Salvationist, scholar, feminist, theologian, eloquent writer, humanitarian, outspoken social campaigner, lecturer, home-maker, advocate of women's rights, friend of the poor, compassionate defender of animal rights, fearless critic of the greedy rich, voluminous letter-writer, pastoral visitor, soul-winner, ardent teetotaller, and co-Founder of The Salvation Army.

Catherine Mumford Booth (1829–90), turned years of ill health to a positive advantage. Confined to bed for long periods as a child and young woman, she used the necessity of enforced rest as an opportunity to read the Bible several times. Thus began a lifelong search for theological truth that would lead her into heartfelt collisions with the established Church, whose lukewarm spiritual life and witness she condemned in forthright terms. Likewise, she pursued personal holiness, which she sought with a ferocity born of her passionate singular devotion to obey the will of God. Naturally intelligent, her commitment to prayerful study served to equip her magnificently for the seemingly endless chain of verbal and literary sparring in which she subsequently engaged.

Desperately concerned that the gospel was for the poor and marginalized (hence her brave visitation to destitute alcoholics and wives whose daily lot was one of poverty and violence), Catherine Booth eschewed any suggestion that such people were beyond the reach of God's love.

Permanently in love with William and regarding his arrival in her life as a definite answer to prayer, she followed his every move as together they explored avenues of ministry – full and comfortable employment with the Methodist New Connexion, unrest within the confines of "ordinary" church life, perilous times of independent ministry in evangelism, before discovering their joint niche and destiny as leaders of The Salvation Army. Her love of God, her husband, and her children was beyond doubt as she held her family together through periods when income was by no means guaranteed. From dressmaking to making do when money was scarce, Catherine Booth supported and encouraged her life-partner throughout unpredictable years of ups and downs. Willing to travel the country for the Kingdom's sake, often undertaking arduous journeys and enduring separations from her loved ones, she regarded all things as loss if she could but win souls for Jesus.

Catherine Booth was a bundle of contradictions. No stranger to controversy, yet somewhat strangely reactive to criticism of The Salvation Army; stern and unyielding in her convictions, yet sufficiently tender-hearted to cry for her children as she prayed for them; progressive in terms of the rights of women in ministry, yet noticeably reluctant to embrace ideas of medical advance; unable to endorse theological points of view that differed from her own, yet deliberately and generously gracious towards adversaries; not blessed with William's qualities of charismatic showmanship and mischievous humour, yet willing to lay her all on God's altar if he would use what she had to offer; gentle and aggressive in turns; scathingly condemning of spiritualism, yet promising to communicate with William from beyond the grave should that prove possible.

Consumed with a love of souls, able to converse with the fashionable wealthy and the downcast poor, the life of Catherine Booth can be likened to a meteor that all-too-briefly flashed across the sky of Christendom. Wearied by duty and remarkably selfless service, that blazing meteor lit up the scene for sixty-one years before her frail body gave way to her Home call.

Her legacy is enormous.

Editing some of Catherine Booth's works has been a challenging privilege, even though I am painfully aware of the fact I have managed to catch and portray but a glimpse of her mind and heart. I am anxious to clarify the fact that many of Catherine Booth's writings appear in several different publications. That is to say, since their original publication, they have been quoted multiple times by authors and biographers, each attempting to relay the story of a unique life. Thus, I have employed quotations immediately from the book or article in which I first encountered them. With apologies to purists, this will explain my use of sources.

S. J. P.

Believe in the Lord Jesus, and you will be saved
(Acts 16:31 *NIV*)

This is one of the most abused texts in the Bible, and one which, perhaps, has been made to do quite as much work for the Devil as for God... To whom does the Holy Spirit say, "Believe on the Lord Jesus Christ, and thou shalt be saved"?[1] Now mark, I answer, NOT to all sinners indiscriminately. And here is a grand mistake... that these words are wrested from their explanatory connexion, and from numbers of other texts bearing on the same subject, and held up independently of all the conditions which must... accompany them.

How can an unawakened, unconvicted, unrepentant sinner believe? As soon might Satan believe. It is an utter impossibility... My dear son... was speaking to a man who was the worse for liquor, and using very improper language; trying to show him the danger of his evil, wicked course... "Oh!" said the man. "It is not by works, it is by faith, and I believe as much as you do."[2] "Yes," said my son, "but what do you believe?" "Oh!" he said, "I believe in Jesus Christ, and of course I shall be saved."

This is a sample of thousands... They believe there was such a man as Jesus, and that he died for sinners, and for them, but as to the exercise of saving faith, they know no more about it than Agrippa or Felix,[3] as is manifest when they come to die, for then these very people are wringing their hands, tearing their hair, and sending for Christians to come and pray with them. If they had believed, why all this alarm and concern on the approach of death? They were only believers of the *head*, and not of the *heart*, that is, they were but theoretical believers... or their faith would have saved them. Now we maintain that is as useless, and as unphilosophical as it is unscriptural to preach "only believe" to such characters.[4]

> God of my head and heart, I offer my whole being to you for a sure and certain salvation. Convict me and confirm me within your saving love. Amen.

1 KJV.
2 Ephesians 2:8.
3 Acts 24, 25, 26.
4 From *Godliness*.

Godly sorrow brings repentance that leads to salvation and leaves no regret, but worldly sorrow brings death

(2 Corinthians 7:10 *NIV*)

It has only been within the last sixty or seventy years that this new gospel has sprung into existence, preaching indiscriminately to unawakened, unconverted, unrepentant sinners… It seems to me, that great injury has been done to the cause of Christ by this wrongly dividing the word of truth,[1] to say nothing of the unphilosophical character of such a course… Christians have not done their duty, and have not discharged their responsibility to these souls when they have told them that Jesus died for them, and that they are to believe in him! They have a much harder work to do, and that is "to open their eyes" to a sense of their danger, and make them by the power of the Spirit realize the dreadful truth that they are *sinners*, that they are sick, and then they will run to the physician. The eyes of the soul must be opened to such a realization of sin, and such an apprehension of the consequences of sin, as shall lead to an earnest desire to be saved *from* sin…

There is not one case in the New Testament in which the Apostles urged souls to believe, or in which a soul is narrated as believing, in which we have not good grounds to believe that these preparatory steps of conviction and repentance had been taken. The only one was that of Simon the sorcerer.[2] He was, as numbers of people are in great religious movements, carried away by the influence of the meeting and the example of those around him, and professed to believe. Doubtless he did credit the fact that Jesus died on the cross. He received the facts of Christianity into his mind, and in that sense he became a believer… and he was baptized. But when the testing time came, as to whose interests were paramount to him, his own or God's, then he manifested the true state of the case, as the Apostle said, "I see thy heart is not right with God;"[3] and nobody is converted whose heart is not right with God![4]

> Lord, these are strong words of challenge. Help me to share a good gospel
> whenever I can, and not to knowingly leave a job half done.
> By your grace, Amen.

---

1   2 Timothy 2:15.
2   Acts 8:9–24.
3   See Acts 8:21.
4   From *Holiness*.

I HAVE APPEARED UNTO THEE FOR THIS PURPOSE,
TO MAKE THEE A MINISTER AND A WITNESS

(Acts 26:16 *KJV*)

Supposing we could blot out from our mind all knowledge of the history of Christianity… from the close of the period described in the Acts of the Apostles, suppose we could detach from our minds all knowledge of the history of Christianity since then, and take the Acts of the Apostles and sit down and calculate what was likely to happen in the world, what different results we should have anticipated, what a different world we should have reckoned upon as the outcome of it all. A system which commenced under such auspices, with such assumptions and professions on the part of the Author (speaking after the manner of men), and producing, as it did, in the first century of its existence, such gigantic and momentous results. We should have said, if we knew nothing of what has intervened from that time to this, that, no doubt, the world where that war commenced, and for which it was organized, would have long since been subjugated, and brought under the power of its great originator and founder! I say, from reading these Acts, and observing the spirit which animated the early disciples, and from the way in which everything fell before them, we should have anticipated that 10,000 times greater results would have followed and, in my judgment, this anticipation would have been perfectly rational and just.

We Christians profess to possess in the gospel of Christ a mighty lever which, rightly and universally applied, would lift the entire burden of sin and misery from the shoulders, that is, from the souls, of our fellow men – a panacea, we believe it to be, for all the moral and spiritual woes of humanity, and in curing their spiritual plagues we should go far to cure their physical plagues also. We all profess to believe this. Christians have professed to believe this for generations gone by… and yet look at the world, look at so-called Christian England… the great majority of the nation utterly ignoring God, and not even making any pretence of remembering him one day in the week.[1]

> God of salvation, assist me, as I ponder these thoughts, to refresh and renew
> my personal commitment to the spread of the gospel. Amen.

---

1 From *Aggressive Christianity.*

SINCE… THE WORLD THROUGH ITS WISDOM DID NOT KNOW HIM,
GOD WAS PLEASED THROUGH THE FOOLISHNESS OF WHAT WAS
PREACHED TO SAVE THOSE WHO BELIEVE

(1 Corinthians 1:21 *NIV*)

Humanity needs a Christ… everywhere and in all ages, men and women have been, and are still, conscious of a strife with evil; not merely physical evil represented by thorns and thistles, but with moral evil – evil in thought, in intention, in action, both in themselves and in those around them. This consciousness of wrong has thrust upon men the realization of their need of help from some extraneous power, or being. In all generations men have seemed to feel that without such help there must be a perishing.

This sense of need has been forced upon men, first, by the failure of their own repeated efforts to help and save themselves. Secondly, by their observation of such fruitless efforts in others. What man or woman who has thought at all, who has not stood on the edge of this human whirlpool, and watched the struggling multitudes as they have risen and sunk, struggling and striving by resolutions, by the embracing of new theories, by taking of pledges, and making new departures, to escape from the evil of their own natures and to save themselves? Who has watched the struggle without realizing the need that some Almighty independent arm should be stretched out to deliver and to save? Who can read history or contemplate the experience of humanity at the present time, without realizing that it needs a Saviour, whatever idea may be entertained as to the kind of Saviour required?

Further, this sense of need is the outcome of the filial instinct born in every human soul, which cries out in the hour of distress and danger to an Almighty Father – a God – a friend somewhere in the universe able to help and to deliver. This instinct is at the bottom of all religions, from that of the untutored savage up to the profoundest philosopher the world has ever produced… crying out for a Christ, a Divine Word, or Logos, a something or somebody who should guide him, taking him up where human reason and philosophy failed him.[1]

Thank you, Father, for shining the brilliant light of Christ into a dark world.

1   From *Popular Christianity.*

Gallio cared for none of those things
(Acts 18:17 *KJV*)

I overheard a conversation between two gentlemen… they were conversing about some person recently dead, and I heard the young man say to the other, "Oh, he had more religion than I have." I thought to myself, *there* is a state of confessed indifference to the subject of religion! I wonder whether that young man is an infidel; I will try to get an opportunity of speaking to him… I found that he professed to believe in God, and the Bible, and Heaven and Hell, as much as I did, and yet he had betrayed in that conversation that he had no religion, and that it was a matter of indifference to him, and I thought, Now this is the state of tens of thousands in this so-called "gospel land"…

These words with respect to Gallio were not spoken directly of his spiritual state, but with respect to matters that affected him more as a magistrate and a ruler; nevertheless, they convey an idea to us of his indifference on great spiritual questions… This is just the position of tens of thousands about us today. They have heard about religion; but they have a notion that it is a system of absurdities, and contradictions, and cant, fit only for half-imbecile minds, that it is no question of theirs, and so dismiss it from their minds – they "care for none of those things"… Who knows what Gallio lost by his indifference? If he had just taken the trouble to enquire into these matters… who knows what the issue might have been both to Gallio and the Church of that time? For anything we know, we might have had an Epistle of Gallio to the Churches! He might have helped to roll along the rising tide of salvation, and been instrumental in the conversion of hundreds of souls; but all this was lost for the want of a bit of trouble![1]

God of opportunity, you try relentlessly to impress us with the importance
of your priorities. Grant me a heart that remains alert to defining moments.
Amen.

[1] From *Life and Death.*

Though I am absent from you in body,
I am present with you in spirit

(Colossians 2:5 *NIV*)

I am very pleased with your letter. It shows a decided improvement. Secondly, I am pleased that you answered all my questions; that was *businesslike*! Thirdly, I am pleased that you are getting on in your soul: this is best of all. Fourthly, I am pleased that you remember us all so lovingly. I am sure we all return your love, and shall be quite as glad to see you as you will be to see us. Papa liked your letter, and thought it worth the postage! We are sorry to hear that you have been poorly. You see it is such a sad loss of time to be in the sick-room. I am sure you have many comforts, considering you are at school; so you must be thankful and make the most of them.

It was a pity you did not know your lesson well the day you wrote to Willie.[1] How was that? I do hope you are industrious, and do not lose time in play and inattention. Remember, Satan steals his marches on us by *littles*. A minute now, and a minute then; be on the lookout, and don't be cheated by him! Your time is flying; one quarter will soon be gone! Do, my boy, work as hard as your health will allow you. I was willing for you to have raw eggs for lunch, but not for tea. One egg at eleven o'clock you may have. I will send a few stamps sometimes for extra letters, but you must do without any *other* extras. Think how hard Willie is working, and he does not even take his pocket money now! I praise the Lord that you are getting on in soul; if you go to him for wisdom and strength he will help you. You remember my text, "The last shall be first."[2] God can bring it to pass; only ask and trust him. All your little trials will soon be over, so far as school life is concerned, and every one of them, if borne with patience, will make you a wise and a better man.[3]

Father of all, touch my heart today with a concern for those
who are absent from home or away from their usual surroundings.
Prompt me towards the ministry of keeping in touch. Amen.

---

1 William Bramwell Booth, the oldest of the Booth children.
2 Matthew 20:16, KJV.
3 From one of Catherine Booth's many letters to her children, written during enforced separations, quoted in *The Life of Catherine Booth The Mother of The Salvation Army, Vol. II*. This may possibly have been written to Ballington.

Those who believed what Peter said were baptized and added to the church that day – about 3,000 in all

(Acts 2:41 *NLT*)

Some have written me this week that they had believed. They had been persuaded into a profession of faith, but no fruits followed. Ah! It was not faith of the heart: it was the faith of the head… and it left you worse than it found you, and you have been groping and grovelling ever since. But do not think that was real faith, and that therefore real faith has failed, but be encouraged to begin again, and *repent*. Try the real thing, for Satan always gets up a counterfeit. Therefore, don't go down in despair because the wrong kind of faith did not succeed. That shall make the real faith of God of none effect – God forbid!

Look at one or two other cases – the 3,000 in a day. Surely this is a Scriptural illustration. Surely no one will call that anti-gospel or legal. What was the first work Peter did? He drove the knife of God's convincing truth into their hearts, and made them *cry out*. He awoke them to the truth of their almost lost and damned condition, till they said, "What must we do to be saved?" They were so concerned, they were so pricked in their hearts, their eyes were so opened to the terrible consequences of their sin, that they cried aloud from the vast multitude, "Men and brethren, what must we do [to be saved]?"[1] He convinced them of sin, and thus followed the order of God… The Eunuch is often quoted as an illustration of faith; but what state of mind was he in? Was he a careless, unconvicted sinner? There he was – and Ethiopian, a heathen; but where had he been? To Jerusalem, to worship the true and living God in the best way he knew and as far as he understood; and then, what was he doing when Philip found him? He was not content with the mere worship of the Temple, whistling a worldly tune on the way back. He was *searching the Scriptures*.[2] He was honestly seeking after God, and the Holy Ghost always knows where such souls are.[3]

Lord, I pray today for those seeking to worship you in spirit and in truth. Amen.

1   Acts 2:37, KJV.
2   Acts 8:26–28.
3   From *Godliness*.

Unless you repent, you too will all perish

(Luke 13:5 *NIV*)

Repentance is an indispensable condition of entering the Kingdom of God. People generally are all at sea on this subject, as though insisting that repentance were an arbitrary arrangement on the part of God. I believe God has made human salvation as easy as his almighty, infinite mind could make it. But there is a necessity in the case that we should repent... It is just as necessary that my feelings be changed and brought to repentance towards God as it is that the wicked, disobedient boy should have his feelings brought back into harmony with his father before he can be forgiven...

If any father has a prodigal son, I ask, how is it that you are not reconciled to your son? You love him intensely. Probably you are more conscious of your love for him than for any other of your children. Your heart yearns over him, you pray for him, you dream of him, your bowels yearn over him.[1] Why are you not reconciled? Why are you obliged to hold him at arm's length and not have him come in and out, and live with you on the same terms as the affectionate, obedient daughter? "Oh!" you say. "The case is different. I cannot. It is not 'I would not', but 'I cannot'. Before that can possibly be the boy's feelings must be changed towards me. He has mistaken notions and thinks I am hard and exacting. I have done all a father could do, but he will go on in defiance of my will"... It is not that God does not love you, sinner, or that the great benevolent heart of God has not, as it were, wept tears of blood over you. It is not that he would not put his loving arms around you this moment if you would only come to his feet... and seek his pardon. He cannot... He dare not and cannot until there is a change of mind in you. You must repent.[2]

God of the prodigal, this day I pray your loving conviction upon those known to me who resist repentance. Speak saving grace to them, Lord. Amen.

---

1   See Genesis 43:30, KJV.
2   From *The Highway of Our God*.

CHILDREN ARE A HERITAGE FROM THE LORD
(Psalm 127:3 *NIV*)

It is because I am so well acquainted with the weight of the trials and duties of maternity that I sympathize so deeply with mothers, and would fain help to lighten their burdens by a little practical advice and instruction… There is not a mother here who would think it right to leave her child to grow up without discipline or training of some kind! Then the question for us to consider is, *what sort* of training does God, and our duty to our children, require from us?…

The first important matter for a parent to settle in her own mind, is this: To whom does this child belong? Is it mine, or is it the Lord's? Surely, this question should not need any discussion, at least by Christian parents! For do we not recognize, even before they are born, that they are peculiarly and exclusively a heritage from the Lord; and when they came into the world, the first effort we put forth was to hold them up and offer them to him? And again, in their christening we acknowledged that they belonged to him, and promised to train them for his glory.[1] Now, the keeping of this one fact before the mind of a mother will be the best guiding principle in training; and it is because Christian parents so often forget whose their children are, that they make mistakes in training them. I say then to you mothers here, settle it in your minds that your child belongs absolutely to God, and not to you – that you are only stewards for God, holding your children to nurse them and train them for him. This responsibility arises… out of the command and ordination of God. Both under the old and new dispensations, the Lord has, in the most emphatic and solemn manner, laid the obligation on parents to train their children for him. He commands it, to whom both parents and children exclusively belong.[2]

> Thank you, Lord, for children, in my family, my neighbourhood, and my church. Bless their parents, Lord, and guide them day by day. Amen.

---

1   The Salvation Army does not perform any ceremonies of christening, but offers ceremonies of dedication or thanksgiving instead, at the discretion of the officer responsible.
2   From *The Training of Children*.

SHOW ME YOUR WAYS, LORD, TEACH ME YOUR PATHS
(Psalm 25:4 *NIV*)

I wish you prayed more and talked less about the matter. Try it, and be determined to get clear and settled views as to your course. Leave your heart before God, and get satisfied in his sight, and then do it, be it what it may. I cannot bear the idea of your being unhappy. Pray do in this as you feel in your soul it will be right. My conscience is no standard for yours... If you come to London, let us be determined to reap a blessed harvest. Let our fellowship be sanctified to our souls' everlasting good. My mind is made up to do my part towards it. I hope to be firm as a rock on some points. The Lord help me. We must aim to improve each other's mind and character. Let us pray for grace to do it in the best way and to the fullest extent possible...

Anyway, don't let the controversy hurt your soul. Live near to God by prayer... You believe he answers prayer. Then take courage. Just fall down at his feet and open your very soul before him, and throw yourself right into his arms. Tell him that if you are wrong you only wait to be set right and, be the path rough or smooth, you will walk in it. Oh, you must live close to God! If you are a greater distance from him than you were, just stop the whirl of outward things, or rather leave it, and shut yourself up with him till all is clear and bright upwards. Do, there's a dear. Oh, how much we lose by not coming to the point. Now, at once, realize your union with Christ, and trust him to lead you through this perplexity. Bless you. Excuse this advice. I am anxious for your soul. If God hears my prayer, he must guide you – he will guide you.[1, 2]

Father, for those who cannot see their way, I pray your clear guidance.
Help those who are praying for direction, whatever the issue. Amen.

1   Written to William Booth during their engagement, at a time when William was unsure whether to remain in the north of England or to consider work in London. He was torn between accepting appointments further afield and remaining close to Catherine. (The Mumfords had moved from Boston, Lincolnshire, England, to London, in 1844. William and Catherine married in 1855.)
2   From *Catherine Booth: A Sketch*.

The righteous care for the needs of their animals
(Proverbs 12:10 *NIV*)

My childish heart rejoiced greatly in the speculations of Wesley and Butler with regard to the possibility of a future life for animals, in which God might make up to them for the suffering and pain inflicted on them here.[1] One incident, I recollect, threw me for weeks into the greatest distress. We had a beautiful retriever, named Waterford, which was very much attached to me. It used to lie for hours on the rug outside my door, and if it heard me praying or weeping, it would whine and scratch to be let in, that it might in some way manifest its sympathy and comfort me. Wherever I went the dog would follow me about as my self-constituted protector – in fact, we were inseparable companions.

One day Waterford had accompanied me on a message to my father's house of business.[2] I closed the door, leaving the dog outside, when I happened to strike my foot against something, and cried out with the sudden pain. Waterford heard me, and without a moment's hesitation came crashing through the large glass window to my rescue. My father was so vexed at the damage done that he caused the dog to be immediately shot. For months I suffered intolerably, especially in realizing that it was in the effort to alleviate my sufferings the beautiful creature had lost its life. Days passed before I could speak to my father, although he afterwards greatly regretted his hasty action, and strove to console me as best he could. The fact that I had no child companions made me miss my speechless one the more.[3, 4]

> Lord of creation, give me a heart that is tender and sensitive,
> respecting life in all its forms, as an act of worship. Amen.

---

1   John Wesley and Bishop Joseph Butler (1692–1752), both of whom taught that animals had souls and would experience life after death. Catherine was greatly influenced by John Wesley and studied Butler's *Analogy of Religion*.
2   John Mumford, a coach builder and itinerant preacher.
3   Catherine Mumford (Booth) had four brothers, but only one, John, grew to adulthood. She spent much of her childhood confined to bed, with spine, lung and heart trouble. Except for a short period at school, she was educated at home by her mother.
4   From *Catherine Booth* by Catherine Bramwell-Booth.

You will seek me and find me when you seek me with all your heart

(Jeremiah 29:13 *NIV*)

Although I was conscious of having given myself up fully to God from my earliest years, and although I was anxious to serve him and often realized deep enjoyment in prayer, nevertheless I had not the positive assurance that my sins were forgiven, and that I had experienced the actual change of heart about which I had read and heard so much. I was determined to leave the question no longer in doubt, but to get it definitely settled, cost what it might. For six weeks I prayed and struggled on, but obtained no satisfaction. True, my past life had been outwardly blameless. Both in public and private I had made use of the means of grace, up to the very limit of my strength, and often beyond the bounds of discretion, my zeal had carried me. Still, so far as this was concerned, I realized the truth of the words:

> *Could my zeal no respite know,*
> *Could my tears for ever flow –*
> *These for sin could not atone.*[1]

I knew, moreover, that "the heart is deceitful above all things and desperately wicked".[2] I was terribly afraid of being self-deceived. I remembered, too, the occasional outbursts of temper when I was at school. Neither could I call to mind any particular place or time when I had definitely stepped out upon the promises, and had claimed the immediate forgiveness of sins, receiving the witness of the Holy Spirit I had become a child of God and an heir of heaven.[3] It seemed to me unreasonable to suppose that I could be saved and yet not know it. At any rate, I could not permit myself to remain longer in doubt regarding the matter. If in the past I had acted up to the light I had received, it was evident I was now getting new light, and unless I obeyed it, I realized that my soul would fall into condemnation.[4]

Rewarding God, please bless those who earnestly seek you this day. Amen.

---

1   From "Rock of Ages" by the Reverend Augustus Toplady (1740–78).
2   Jeremiah 17:9, KJV.
3   Romans 8:16.
4   From *Catherine Booth* by Catherine Bramwell-Booth (probably when Catherine Booth was aged sixteen and experiencing what she described as "a great controversy of soul").

FEAR OF MAN WILL PROVE TO BE A SNARE,
BUT WHOEVER TRUSTS IN THE LORD IS KEPT SAFE
(Proverbs 29:25 *NIV*)

I am persuaded it is the fear of man which shackles you. Do not give place to this feeling. Remember you are the *Lord's servant*, and if you are a faithful one it will be a small matter with you to be judged of man's judgment. Let nothing be wanting beforehand to make what you say helpful, but when you are before the people, try to think only of your own responsibility to him who hath sent you. Try and cast off the fear of man. Fix your eyes simply on the glory of God, and care not for frown or praise of man. Rest not till your soul is fully alive to God. Do assure me, my own dear William, that no want of energy or effort on your part shall hinder the improvement of those talents God has given you.

Could you not provide yourself with a small leather bag or case, large enough to hold your Bible and any other book you may require – pens, ink, paper and a candle? And, presuming that you generally have a room to yourself, could you not rise by six o'clock every morning, and convert your bedroom into a study till breakfast-time? I hope, my dearest love, you will consider this plan, and keep to it, if possible, as a general practice. Don't let little difficulties prevent you carrying it out. You have special need for watchfulness and for much private intercourse with God. My dearest love, beware how you indulge that dangerous element of character, ambition. Misdirected, it will be everlasting ruin to yourself, and perhaps to me also. Oh, my love, let nothing earthly excite it; let not the wish to be great fire it. Fix it on the Throne of the Eternal, and let it find the realization of its loftiest aspirations in the promotion of his glory, and it shall be consummated with the richest enjoyments and brightest glories of God's own Heaven.[1,2]

Thank you, Lord, for Catherine's strong and encouraging counsel to William.
I pray for those who need encouragement and reassurance. Amen.

---

1   From letters Catherine Mumford wrote to William Booth as he travelled from place to place in itinerant ministry. William was plagued by anxiety that he was unsuited to preaching in front of people he regarded as better than himself, and more educated. He worried that his physical appearance wasn't smart enough.
2   From *Catherine Booth: A Sketch*.

January 14th

ONE DAY AS JESUS WAS STANDING BY THE LAKE OF
GENNESARET, THE PEOPLE WERE CROWDING AROUND HIM
AND LISTENING TO THE WORD OF GOD

(Luke 5:1 *NIV*)

Well, bless the Lord! Amidst it all he holds me up and gives me great encouragement. The battle waxes great and hot, but he continues to use "the weak things to confound the mighty".[1] All the glory be to his holy name. Our move to the music hall has proved to be the right step. Both Sunday nights it has been crowded to the ceiling, 3,000 people in at least, and a very large majority of them men. The crowd in the street has been such that outer doors have had to be fastened, and it has been all that two policemen could do to keep order. The attention inside has been profound – as orderly as a regular congregation – and in the judgment of our friends the word has been with mighty power.

Sunday night week, twenty-eight souls came forward for salvation, and there were numbers of convicted souls all over the place. Last Sabbath not so many came out, but I believe quite as much execution for eternity was done. On Tuesday night I had a smaller hall, holding about 700, and we were crowded through the ante-rooms and down the stairs, and sixteen or eighteen cases, some of them the finest fellows it was ever my privilege to see at a penitent-form. Tomorrow night I am to have the Baptist chapel, lent for the occasion, which will hold 1,000 people. I doubt not we shall be full. Oh, for power to break down every stubborn heart in the place! Pray for me. No one knows how I feel. I think I never realized my responsibility as I did on Sunday night. I felt really awful before rising to speak. The sight almost overwhelmed me. With its two galleries, its dome-like roof and vast proportions, when crammed with people it presents a most imposing appearance. The top gallery is ten or twelve seats deep in front, and it was full of men; such a sight as I never witnessed on any previous occasion.[2, 3]

Father, we long for such times again, when thousands gather to hear the gospel.
We pray for Holy Spirit revival. Amen.

---

1   See 1 Corinthians 1:27, KJV.
2   Written to William and Catherine Booth's friend, Mrs Billups, regarding campaign meetings held in Portsmouth in 1873. Music halls in close proximity to brothels and drinking dens were chosen deliberately as venues. Mr and Mrs Billups became friends with the Booths in Cardiff.
3   From *Catherine Booth The Mother of The Salvation Army, Vol. II.*

OUR STRUGGLE IS... AGAINST THE POWERS OF THIS DARK WORLD AND
AGAINST THE SPIRITUAL FORCES OF EVIL IN THE HEAVENLY REALMS
(Ephesians 6:12 *NIV*)

I believe that the old arch-enemy has done in this dispensation what he did in former ones – so far circumvented the purposes of God, that he has succeeded... in retarding the accomplishment of God's purposes and keeping the world thus largely under his own power and influence... by deceiving God's people. He has always done so. He has always got up a caricature of God's real thing, and the nearer he can get it to be like the original the more successful he is. He has succeeded in deceiving God's people... He has for the Church, nearly as a whole, to receive what I call an "Oh, wretched man that I am" religion![1] He has got them to lower the standard which Jesus Christ himself established in this book [the Bible] – a standard, not only to be aimed at, but to be attained unto – a standard of victory over sin, the world, the flesh, and the Devil, real, living, reigning, triumphing Christianity! Satan knew what was the secret of the great success of the early disciples. It was their wholehearted devotion, their absorbing love to Christ, their utter abnegation of the world. It was their utter absorption in the salvation of their fellow men and the glory of their God. It was an enthusiastic religion that swallowed them up, and made them willing to become wanderers and vagabonds on the face of the earth – for his sake to dwell in dens and caves, to be torn asunder, and to be persecuted in every form.[2]

It was this degree of devotion, before which Satan saw he had no chance. Such people as these, he knew, must ultimately subdue the world. It is not in human nature to stand before that kind of spirit, that amount of love and zeal, and if Christians had only gone on as they began long since, the glorious prophecy would have been fulfilled. The kingdoms of this world would have become the kingdoms of our Lord and of his Christ.[3, 4]

Lord Jesus, strengthen your Church as we listen for the victor's song. Amen.

1 Romans 7:24.
2 Hebrews 11:38.
3 Revelation 11:15.
4 From *Aggressive Christianity*.

Jesus was speaking to the crowd

(Matthew 12:46 *NLT*)

One Sabbath I was passing down a narrow, thickly populated street on my way to chapel, anticipating an evening's enjoyment for myself, and hoping to see some anxious ones brought into the Kingdom, when I chanced to look up at the thick rows of small windows above me, where numbers of women were sitting, peering through at the passers-by, or listlessly gossiping with each other. It was suggested to my mind with great power, "Would you not be doing more service and acting more like your Redeemer, by turning into some of those houses, speaking to these careless sinners, and inviting them to the service, than by going to enjoy it yourself?" I was startled; it was a new thought, and while I was reasoning about it, the same inaudible interrogator demanded: "What efforts do Christians put forth, answerable to the command, '*compel them to come in, that my house may be filled*'?"[1]

This was accompanied by a light and unction which I knew to be divine. I felt greatly agitated. I felt verily guilty. I knew that I had never thus laboured to bring lost sinners to Christ; and, trembling with a sense of my utter weakness, I stood still for a moment, looked up to Heaven, and said: "Lord, if thou wilt help me, I will try," and without stopping further to confer with flesh and blood, turned back and commenced my work. I spoke first to a group of women sitting on a doorstep; and what that effort cost me, words cannot describe; but the Spirit helped my infirmities,[2] and secured for me a patient and respectful hearing with a promise from some of them to attend the house of God. This much encouraged me; I began to taste the joy which lies hidden under the cross, and realize, in some faint degree, that it is more blessed to give than to receive.[3] With this timely, loving cordial from my Master, I went on to the next group who were standing at the entrance of a low, dirty court.[4]

Thank you, Lord, that your gracious enabling is ours just for the asking.
Keep me alert today to gospel opportunities, even in streets and shops. Amen.

1 Luke 14:23, KJV.
2 Romans 8:26.
3 Acts 20:35.
4 From *Catherine Booth* by W. T. Stead.

WHERE THE SPIRIT OF THE LORD IS, THERE IS FREEDOM
(2 Corinthians 3:17 *NIV*)

I can never forget the agony I passed through. I used to pace my room till two o'clock in the morning; and when, utterly exhausted, I lay down at length to sleep, I would place my Bible and hymn book under my pillow, praying that I might wake up with the assurance of salvation. One morning, as I opened my hymn book, my eyes fell upon the words:

> *My God, I am Thine! What a comfort divine!*
> *What a blessing to know that my Jesus is mine!*[1]

Scores of times I had read and sung these words, but now they came home to my inmost soul with a force and illumination they had never before possessed. It was as impossible for me to doubt it as it had before been for me to exercise faith. Previously, not all the promises in the Bible could induce me to believe; now, not all the devils in Hell could persuade me to doubt. I no longer hoped that I was saved; I was certain of it. The assurances of my salvation seemed to flood and fill my soul. I jumped out of bed and, without wanting to dress, ran into my mother's room and told her what had happened. Till then I had been very backward in speaking even to her upon spiritual matters. I could pray before her, and yet could not open my heart to her about my salvation. It is a terrible disadvantage to people that they are ashamed to speak freely to one another upon so vital a subject. Owing to this, thousands are kept in bondage for years, when they might easily step into immediate liberty and joy. I have myself met hundreds of persons who have confessed to me that they had been church members for many years without knowing what a change of heart really was, and without having been able to escape from this miserable condition of doubt and uncertainty to one of assurance and consequent satisfaction.[2]

Lord of liberty, place your releasing touch upon my heart, mind and tongue,
so that I am not deprived of any blessing. Thank you. Amen.

---

1   Charles Wesley (1707–78).
2   From *Catherine Booth The Mother of The Salvation Army, Vol. I.*

NOR IS THERE MALE AND FEMALE, FOR YOU ARE ALL ONE IN CHRIST JESUS

(Galatians 3:28 *NIV*)

The wife may realize as blissful and perfect a oneness with her husband as though it [the curse] had never been pronounced. For while the semblance of it remains, Jesus has beautifully extracted the sting by making love the law of marriage, and by restoring the institution itself to its original sanctity. What wife would not be careful to reverence a husband, who loves her as Christ loves his Church? Surely the honour put upon woman by the Lord, both in his example and precepts, should make his religion doubly precious to her and render his sanctuary her safe refuge from everything derogatory or insulting to her nature! Oh, that Christians at heart would throw off the trammels of prejudice, and try to arrive at the truth of this subject! Oh, that men of noble soul and able intellect would investigate it, and then ask themselves and their compeers, *why* the influence of woman should be so underestimated...

If it be only partially true that those who rock the cradle rule the world, how much greater is the influence wielded over the mind of future ages by the *mothers* of the next generation than by all the young men living! Vain, in my opinion, will be all the efforts to impregnate minds generally with noble sentiments and lofty aspirations, while the mothers of humanity are comparatively neglected, and their minds indoctrinated from the schoolroom, the press, the platform, and even the pulpit, with self-degrading feelings and servile notions of their own inferiority! Never till woman is estimated and educated as man's equal – the literal "she-man" of the Hebrew – will the foundation of human influence become pure or the bias of mind noble and lofty! Oh, that the Church generally would enquire whether narrow prejudice and lordly usurpation has not something to do with the circumscribed sphere of woman's religious labours, and whether much of the non-success of the gospel is not attributable to the restrictions imposed upon the operations of the Holy Spirit in this as well as other particulars![1]

Lord, on contentious subjects, may your people arrive at their conclusions with careful study, Christ-like courtesy, and consideration. Amen.

---

1   From *Catherine Booth* by Catherine Bramwell-Booth.

A HAPPY MOTHER OF CHILDREN

(Psalm 113:9 *NIV*)

My dearest mother: I thank you very sincerely for your kind, nice, long letter, and especially as I know what an effort it is for you to write. Don't fear for a moment that I should think you indifferent to my comfort. How could I possibly think it, with so many proofs to the contrary? If I ever indulged any hard thoughts, it has been my sin, for which I need the forgiveness of God: it has been prompted by the same spirit which has too often led me to *"charge God foolishly"*.[1] But so far from this feeling being the offspring of my calmer moments and better judgment, it is only the effects of an evil heart full of unbelief, an impetuous will, and a momentary loss of common sense, for I know and *firmly believe* that God will do all things well.[2] Let us trust in him.

I thank you for your very kind and seasonable advice. I do pray and read the Scriptures with Maria, and she prayed aloud the other day, the first time she has ever done so in anybody's presence. I hope the work is begun; if not I tremble for her. But charity *hopeth* all things – believeth all things.[3] I have had a deal of talk to her about election and Christian perfection, the last of which she would not admit to be possible. I never felt clearer light on these points than now. Oh, the depth of the riches and the wisdom of God! If I am able, I shall go next Sunday to class in the afternoon, and Maria is going with me to see what a class-meeting is like. Her church holds Calvinistic doctrines. I went to her chapel once, but could not receive all I heard, though I believe the minister was a true Christian.[4]

Thank you, Lord, for Christian mothers and their lasting influence. Amen.

---

1   Job 1:22, KJV.
2   Mark 7:37.
3   1 Corinthians 13:7, KJV.
4   From *The Life of Catherine Booth The Mother of The Salvation Army, Vol. I.*

Start children off on the way they should go
(Proverbs 22:6 *NIV*)

Napoleon once said that "the great want of France was mothers" and I am afraid we may say to a greater extent than ever before in our history, that the great want of England is mothers – right-minded, able, competent, Christian mothers, who realize their responsibility to God and to their children, and who are resolved at all costs and sacrifices to discharge it…

This responsibility arises out of our ability for the task. We are able to train our children in the way they should go, or God would not have enjoined it upon us. He required every father and mother in Israel to train their children for him – he admitted of no exception, no excuse; and in the New Testament it is assumed as a first duty with believers to train up their children "in the nurture and admonition of the Lord".[1] The training God requires is a moral training – the inspiring of the child with the love of goodness, truth, and righteousness, and leading him to its practice and exercise in all the duties and emergencies of life. Now, any parent, however poor, unlearned, or occupied, can do this, if only she has the grace of God in her heart, and will take the trouble. Training a child in the way he should go does not necessarily imply a scholastic training. All parents have not the power to educate their children, nor to do much for them temporally; they cannot put them in a position to get much of this world's goods, but these things are not included in the right training. A child may be trained for the highest moral and spiritual development without these; and, where there is natural ability, for the highest mental development also. This is abundantly established in the histories of some of our great men. We know what kind of homes some of them were trained in, what humble parentage some of them had, but, nevertheless, they were trained in the way they should go.[2]

> Lord, I thank you for good parents, but I pray today for children whose parents are not interested in their progress or development. Help them, Lord. Amen.

---

1 Ephesians 6:4, KJV.
2 From *Practical Religion*.

Awake thou that sleepest, and arise from the dead, and Christ shall give thee light

(Ephesians 5:14 *KJV*)

God has taken endless trouble with some of you. He has knocked you about to try to awaken you but you would not be roused. He has got your head round sometimes, and made you face the problems of the future; but, as quick as ever you could, you have turned it back the other way; you *would* not look, you are *wilfully* ignorant. Mind, it won't make damnation any easier! You will be woke up by-and-by, never to go to sleep again. If you once get to *Hell*, there is no sleeping there; indifference is the last thing that will ever visit that dark, black abode!

You can shut your eyes now. Oh! Yes, against the glorious Sun of Righteousness[1] himself; you can turn your head away, and refuse to see: but you will never go to sleep any more, when once you are awaked for the last time. May God wake you *now*! "Awake, thou that sleepest, and arise from the dead…" You *can* do it, or he would not bid you do it. It is *your* work to arise. God will make you stand, and keep you going when you are up. "Arise from the dead, and *Christ shall give thee light*." Will you awake tonight? Will you face right round? Will you let the light of the eternal world come streaming on your spiritual eyeballs? Will you look? If you will only look, you will be saved; if you go to sleep again, Christ himself cannot save you. The Lord help you to wake up!… A lady said to me, "How have you managed to get your children converted so early?" "Oh!" I said. "*I have been beforehand with the Devil.* I have not allowed my children to become preoccupied with the things of this world, *before* I have got the seed of the Kingdom well in. I have taken time by the forelock and cheated his Satanic Majesty out of his opportunities!"[2]

Gracious God, I praise you as the Great Awakener, the lover of souls.
Thank you for that mysterious moment when you woke me up to the
realities of life and death. Keep me from dozing! Amen.

---

1   Malachi 4:2.
2   From *Life and Death.*

The world and its desires pass away,
but whoever does the will of God lives forever

(1 John 2:17 *NIV*)

I said to a gentleman… once, "Have you settled this matter?" He said, almost grinning in my face with vexation, "No, I have not. The fact is, I have no time to think about religion." He was very much annoyed that he had been *made* to think about it for three-quarters of an hour. I said, "You will have to find time one day; how shall you manage that? Death won't ask your leave; don't you think it would be wise to find a bit of time to prepare for it?"

Preoccupied – full of other things. People tell us in our "anxious meetings",[1] "I am so busy," or "I am set on this or on the other." And, alas, alas! While they are running hither and thither, the reckoning day comes; death overtakes them; bronchitis, or fever, or apoplexy, or accident comes, and they are gone! They never thought they would be damned, they never intended such a thing. They! Not likely, with all their light and opportunities. Oh, dear, no. But they were preoccupied, they did not see wither they were going. Satan took care to keep them too busy to look God, and death, and judgment, and eternity in the face. We read that there are something like 350 people killed in the streets of London every year.[2] How is that? Oh! They tell us it is through preoccupation of mind. Here is a gentleman walking to his office… he is not thinking of the hansom or the omnibus close by; he is wondering whether that ship has come in, what he shall make by that cargo, or by that scheme he is negotiating; he forgets he is in the midst of danger, when on comes the hansom, and *he is killed*. He was *preoccupied*. That preoccupation led to his destruction. Oh, what an illustration of people on the platform of time![3]

Lord of time and eternity, please keep interrupting my life,
keeping me close to you day by day. Prompt me and check me, I pray. Amen.

---

1   After the fashion of the evangelist Charles Finney (1792–1875). During his altar calls, Finney called "anxious" sinners to the front of the congregation, to sit on an "anxious bench", there to receive prayer or to be preached to directly. The Salvationist equivalent is known as the mercy seat; a place of prayer.
2   Circa. 1883.
3   From *Life and Death*.

GREATER IS HE THAT IS IN YOU, THAN HE THAT IS IN THE WORLD
(1 John 4:4 *KJV*)

I observed a woman standing on an adjoining doorstep, with a jug in her hand. My divine teacher said: "Speak to that woman." Satan suggested: "Perhaps she is intoxicated"; but after a momentary struggle I introduced myself to her by saying: "Are the people out who live on this floor?", observing that the lower part of the house was closed. "Yes," she said, "they are gone to chapel"; I thought I perceived a weary sadness in her voice and manner. I said: "Oh, I am so glad to hear that; how is it that you are not gone to a place of worship?" "Me," she said, looking down upon her forlorn appearance, "I can't go to chapel, I am kept at home by a drunken husband. I have to stop with him to keep him from the public house, and I have just been fetching him some drink." I expressed my sorrow for her, and asked if I might come in and see her husband. "No," she said, "he is drunk; you could do nothing with him now." I replied: "I do not mind his being drunk, if you will let me come in; I am not afraid; he will not hurt me." "Well," said the woman, "you can come in if you like; but he will only abuse you." I said: "Never mind that," and followed her up the stairs.

I felt strong now in the Lord and in the power of his might, and as safe as a babe in the arms of its mother. I realized I was in the path of obedience, and I feared no evil[1]... I found a fine, intelligent man, about forty, sitting almost double in a chair, with a jug by his side, out of which he had been drinking. I leaned on my Heavenly Guide for strength and wisdom, love and power, and he gave me all I needed. He silenced the demon, strong drink, and quickened the man's perceptions to receive my words.[2]

God of grace, you are for the alcoholic in his or her distress.
In your mercy, use your people to reach out in love and compassion. Amen.

---

1   Psalm 23:4.
2   From *Catherine Booth* by W. T. Stead.

Deborah, a prophet, the wife of Lappidoth, was leading Israel at that time

(Judges 4:4 *NIV*)

I believe that one of the greatest boons to the race would be woman's exaltation to her proper position, mentally and spiritually. Who can tell its consequences to posterity? If what writers on physiology say be true, and experience seems to render it unquestionable, what must be the effects of neglect of mental culture and the inculcation of frivolous, servile, and self-degrading notions into the minds of the *mothers* of humanity. Oh, that which next to the plan of salvation endears the Christian religion to my heart is what it has *done*, and is *destined* to do, for my own sex. And that which excites my indignation beyond anything else is to hear its sacred precepts dragged forward to favour degrading arguments. Oh, for a few more Adam Clarks[1] to dispel the ignorance of the Church. Then should we not hear reasoning against holy and intelligent women opening their mouths for the Lord in the presence of the Church.

Whenever you have to argue with such, just direct them to read the three following passages and Clark's comment on the first two: Exodus 15 c. 20–22 v; Judges 4 c. from the 4 v.; and Second Chronicles 34 c. from the 21 v. On the first he says the same word in the original is used in reference to *Moses* and the other prophets, and therefore Miriam was as truly inspired, and that she was chosen and constituted joint leader of the *people*. We have the express word of God for it, viz. Micah 6 c. 4 v.... Clark says that Deborah seems to have been supreme as well in *civil* matters and spiritual. "She *judged* Israel." The same term is used to denote the functions of the regular judges. She appointed Barak as general of the armies as well as declared God's will for him, and Barak most unhesitatingly recognized her authority.[2, 3]

Father, may we only ever use the Bible to speak of you and your love,
never to judge or belittle anyone. May we always minister with respect. Amen.

---

1 Adam Clark(e) (1760 or 1762–1832), a Methodist theologian chiefly remembered for his commentary on the Bible which took him forty years to complete and which was a primary Methodist theological resource.
2 Judges 4:14.
3 From *Catherine Booth* by Catherine Bramwell-Booth.

HOLD ON TO WHAT IS GOOD

(1 Thessalonians 5:21 *NIV*)

He [Satan] gradually lowered the standard of Christian life and character, and though, in every revival, God has raised it again to a certain extent, we have never got back to the simplicity, purity, and devotion set before us in the Acts of the Apostles and the Epistles... Satan knew that he must get Christians down from the high pinnacle of wholehearted consecration to God. He knew that he had no chance till he tempted them down from that blessed vantage ground, and so he began to spread those false doctrines, to counteract which John wrote his epistles, for, before he died, he saw what was coming, and sounded down the ages: "Little children, let no man deceive you: he that doeth righteousness is righteous, even as he is righteous. He that committeth sin is of the devil; for the devil sinneth from the beginning. For this purpose the Son of God was manifested, that he might destroy the works of the devil."[1] The Lord revive that doctrine! Help us afresh to put up the standard!

Oh! The great evil is that dishonest-hearted people, because they feel it condemns them, lower the standard to their miserable experience. I said, when I was young, and I repeat it in my mature years, that if it sent me to Hell I would never pull it down. Oh! That God's people felt like that. There is the glorious standard put before us. The power is proffered, the conditions laid down, and we can all attain it if we will; but if we will not – for the sake of the children, and for generations yet unborn, do not let us drag it down, and try to make it meet our little, paltry, circumscribed experience. Let us keep it up. This is the way to get the world to look at it. Show the world a real, living, self-sacrificing, hard-working, toiling, triumphing religion, and the world will be influenced by it; but anything short of that they will turn round and spit upon![2]

Lord, for the sake of your Church today, remember and
honour Catherine Booth's prayers for revival. Amen.

---

1   1 John 3:7–8, KJV.
2   From *Aggressive Christianity*.

Write down the revelation
(Habakkuk 2:2 *NIV*)

This has been an especially good day for my soul. I have been reading the life of Mr William Carvosso.[1] Oh, what a man of faith and prayer was he! My expectations were raised when I read the book. I prayed for the divine blessing upon it, and it has been granted. My desires after holiness have been much increased. This day I have sometimes seemed on the verge of the good land. Oh, for mighty faith! I believe the Lord is willing and able to save me to the uttermost. I believe the blood of Jesus Christ cleanses from all sin. And yet there seems something in the way to prevent me from fully entering in. But today I believe at times I have had tastes of perfect love. Oh, that these may be droppings before an overwhelming shower of grace. My chief desire is holiness of heart. This is the prevailing cry of my soul. Tonight "Sanctify [me] through thy truth: thy word is truth"![2] Lord, answer my Redeemer's prayer.

I see this full salvation is highly necessary in order for me to glorify my God below and find my way to heaven. For "without [holiness] no man shall see the Lord"![3] My soul is at times very happy. I have felt many assurances of pardoning mercy. But I want a clean heart. Oh, my Lord, take me and seal me to the day of redemption…

This has been a good day to my soul. This morning I felt very happy, and held sweet communion with my God. I feel very poorly, and excessively low, but I find great relief in pouring out my soul to God in prayer. Oh, I should like to leave this world of sin and sorrow, and go where I could not grieve my Lord again![4]

> Lord of my life, thank you for this written record of Catherine Booth's spiritual experience, as evidence of your hand upon her life. Thank you for your guiding hand upon me too, as today I reflect on the years of your goodness. Amen.

---

1 William Carvosso (1750–1834), an early Wesleyan leader in Cornwall, England.
2 John 17:17, KJV.
3 Hebrews 12:14, KJV.
4 From *The Life of Catherine Booth The Mother of The Salvation Army, Vol. I.*

THE SPIRIT GOD GAVE US DOES NOT MAKE US TIMID, BUT GIVES US POWER, LOVE AND SELF-DISCIPLINE

(2 Timothy 1:7 *NIV*)

I felt much depressed in mind… and was not expecting anything particular, but as the testimonies proceeded I felt the Holy Spirit come upon me.[1] It seemed as if a voice said to me: "Now, if you were to go and testify, you know I would bless it to your own soul as well as to the people!" I gasped again, and said in my heart: "Yes, Lord, I believe thou wouldst, but I cannot do it!" I had forgotten my vow.[2] A moment afterwards there flashed across my mind the memory of the time when I had promised the Lord that I would obey him at all costs. And then the voice seemed to ask me if that was consistent with that promise. I almost jumped up and said, "No, Lord, it is the old thing over again. But I cannot do it!" I felt as though I would sooner die than speak. And then the Devil said, "Besides, you are not prepared. You will look like a fool, and will have nothing to say." He made a mistake. He overreached himself for once. It was this word that settled it. "Ah!" I said. "This is just the point. I have never yet been willing to be a fool for Christ.[3] Now I will be one!" Without stopping another moment, I rose up from my seat and walked down the aisle. My dear husband thought something had happened to me, and so did the people. We had been there two years, and they knew my timid, bashful nature. He stepped down, and asked me, "What is the matter, my dear?" I replied, "I want to say a word!" He was so taken by surprise that he could only say, "My dear wife wishes to speak!" and sat down. For years he had been trying to persuade me to do it. Only that very week he had wanted me to go and address a little cottage meeting of some twenty working people, but I had refused.[4]

Lord of our emotions, you are sympathetic to our fears and timidity.
I pray today for anyone struggling to overcome any kind of scared reluctance
or nervous panic, whatever their situation. Amen.

---

1   During a service in Gateshead, north-east England, where William Booth was preaching. This story has merged into Salvationist folklore as a pivotal moment in the Army's recognition and promotion of female ministry.
2   Catherine Booth had publicly advocated the right of women to speak for God, but struggled with her bashfulness and timidity. As a teenager, she vowed to commence public speaking if the Lord helped her.
3   1 Corinthians 4:10.
4   From *Catherine Booth: A Sketch*.

I PRAY THAT YOU MAY ENJOY GOOD HEALTH AND THAT ALL MAY GO WELL
WITH YOU, JUST AS YOU ARE PROGRESSING SPIRITUALLY

(3 John 1:2 *NIV*)

There is a meeting of the Evangelical Alliance in the Town Hall this evening. If I feel able, I think of going, but I shall not stop late. I wish I could see you, though I shall be sorry to come home just yet. The change is most agreeable to my feelings. It is like a new world to me… Oh, I love the sublime in nature! It absorbs my whole soul, I cannot resist it, nor do I envy those who can. There is nothing on earth more pleasing and profitable to me than the meditations and emotions excited by such senses as I witness here. I only want those I love best to participate my joys, and then they would be complete. For though I possess a share of that monstrous ugly thing called selfishness in common with our human race, yet I *can* say my own pleasure is always enhanced by the pleasure of others, and always embittered by their sorrows. Thanks be to God, for it is by his grace I am what I am. Oh, for that fullness of love which destroys self and fills the soul with Heaven-born generosity.

Brighton is very full of company. Many a poor invalid is here strolling about in search of that pearl of great price – health. Some, like the fortunate diver, spy the precious gem, and hugging it to their bosoms, return rejoicing in the possession of real riches. But many, alas, find it not, and return only to bewail their misfortune. Whichever class I may be amongst, I hope I shall not have cause to regret my visit. If I find not health of body, I hope my soul will be strengthened with might, so that if the outward form should decay, the inward may be renewed day by day.[1] I should like to spend another week or two here… There are bills in all directions announcing the loss of gold watches, seals, keys, brooches, boas, etc., and offering rewards according to the value of the article but, alas, I have not been fortunate enough to find a mite yet![2, 3]

Father, today I pray for those who are ill, physically or mentally. Likewise, for
those who care for them; loved ones, friends and health care workers. Amen.

---

1   2 Corinthians 4:16.
2   From a letter Catherine wrote to her mother, when she was spending a few weeks in Brighton for change and rest, on doctor's advice. 1847 or 1848.
3   From *Catherine Booth* by Catherine Bramwell-Booth.

He will turn the hearts of the parents to their children, and the hearts of the children to their parents
(Malachi 4:6 *NIV*)

The most disastrous consequence of this young man's sin [the prodigal son] fell upon himself. We read that he came to be in want – the natural and inevitable consequence of having spent all. The spending time was soon over; it yielded little pleasure, and that transitory. It was, doubtless, a goodly possession that youth took away from his father's house, but it was soon gone. And no sooner was it gone than "there arose a famine in the land". As the old adage says, "Troubles never come alone", and something generally happens when the substance is gone. How terrible this young man's circumstances! Alone, in a strange land, forsaken by his merry companions, of whom, doubtless, he had plenty while the substance lasted; but, when the money goes, away go such companions, like rats from a sinking ship. There is many a poor forlorn wretch tonight dying in an attic or cellar without a single friend.

A man's all is soon spent; his life, privileges, talents, opportunities, soon lost – and lost for ever. And then how *long, and bitter, and dreadful, the want* which ensues! We read that to this young man's want no man ministered – "no man gave unto him". Alas! No creatures *can*, if they would, minister to the sinner's spiritual destitution. In vain must he cry to the world, the flesh, or the Devil to satisfy the wants of his hungry soul. They one and all reply, "It is not in me." There is nothing in the pleasures of sense or the antidotes of Satan that will meet the wants of famished souls. What bitter reflections must have filled his mind! Can you not imagine that you see him sitting on a stone, amid the husks and filth of the swine-yard, ruminating on his past life, thinking of his folly and wickedness, and wondering whether if he were to go back his father would receive him? Happily, these reflections led him to *resolution*. How many take the first step! They think and ponder and promise and intend, but they *don't make up their minds*. Not so this young man. He says, "I will arise".[1,2]

Heavenly Father, I pray for those away from loving homes, those in sad circumstances, and those frightened of returning. Bless them. Amen.

---

1   From a series of sermons preached in Portsmouth, England, circa. 1873. This one is based upon Luke 15:11–20.
2   From *Catherine Booth The Mother of The Salvation Army, Vol. II.*

IN THE LORD WOMAN IS NOT INDEPENDENT OF MAN,
NOR IS MAN INDEPENDENT OF WOMAN

(1 Corinthians 11:11 *NIV*)

I despise the attitude of the English Press towards woman. Let a man make a decent speech on any subject, and he is lauded to the skies. Whereas, however magnificent a speech a woman may make, all she gets is, "Mrs So-and-so delivered an earnest address"! I don't speak for myself. My personal experience, especially outside London, has been otherwise. But I do feel it keenly on behalf of womankind at large, that the man should be praised, while the woman, who has probably fought her way through inconceivably greater difficulties in order to achieve the same result, should be passed over without a word! I have tried to grind it into my boys that their sisters were just as intelligent and capable as themselves. Jesus Christ's principle was to put woman on the same platform as man, although I am sorry to say his Apostles did not always act up to it…

That woman is, in consequence of her inadequate education, generally inferior to man intellectually, I admit. But that she is naturally so… I see no cause to believe. I think the disparity is as easily accounted for as the difference between woman intellectually in this country and under the degrading slavery of heathen lands. No argument, in my judgment, can be drawn from past experience on this point, because the past has been false in theory and wrong in practice. Never yet in the history of the world has woman been placed on an intellectual footing with man. Her training from babyhood, even in this highly favoured land, has hitherto been such as to cramp and paralyze, rather than to develop and strengthen, her energies, and calculated to crush and wither her aspirations after mental greatness rather than to excite and stimulate them. And even where the more directly depressing influence has been withdrawn, the indirect and more powerful stimulus has been wanting.[1,2]

Lord of all, help us each to respect and encourage each other's ministries,
looking beyond gender and nurturing one another's gifts. Amen.

---

1   Partly from a letter written by Catherine Mumford to her pastor, Dr David Thomas (Congregational), in response to one of his sermons. Dr Thomas was to offer William Booth the opportunity of becoming a Congregationalist minister.
2   From *Catherine Booth The Mother of The Salvation Army, Vol. I.*

Today, if you hear his voice, do not harden your hearts
(Hebrews 13:7 *NIV*)

The other morning, as I went through the City, I said to a friend who was with me, "Look at the men streaming along, look how they go, how energetic they are, how intent; you can see what is going on in many of their minds." I said, "If we could only get people as much concerned about God, eternity, and the salvation of the world, as these men are about their earthly affairs, what might not be done? If you were to speak to them about eternity, they would think it an impertinence, that you should dare to intrude religion upon them at such a time, when they are so full of other things: and on they go, and there is scarcely a week passes but brings us the intelligence of some suddenly gone into eternity. The day dawned on them most unexpectedly, perhaps in the height of their prosperity, when God said [in Luke 12:20, KJV], 'Thou fool, this night thy soul shall be required of thee'"…

It would be very foolish to expose yourself to any great temporal loss or suffering, if by a little forethought and consideration it might be averted. Suppose you were afflicted with some terrible disease, which by the use of judicious means might be arrested, and your life be saved; but when your friends warn you and counsel you to seek medical aid, you say, "I don't care about my lungs or my liver; here are these books, I must attend to them; here is this shop, this building; I cannot stop to think of my body"; and on you go, indifferent to the consequences. What folly; your friends would say, "He is mad," and truly you would prove yourself to be so. "Ah," you say. "There are no people so foolish as that." No, perhaps not in temporal things; but, alas! There are thousands of such "fools" spiritually. How the Devil laughs at such people! What chuckling they have over them down below![1]

Lord of eternity, please bring to mind the names of those I know who procrastinate spiritually, so that I may have the privilege of praying for them today. Hurry them along into the Kingdom. Amen.

1 From *Life and Death.*

OPEN THEIR EYES AND TURN THEM FROM DARKNESS TO LIGHT,
AND FROM THE POWER OF SATAN TO GOD,
SO THAT THEY MAY RECEIVE FORGIVENESS OF SINS

(Acts 26:18 *NIV*)

Will you stop? Will you give your soul a chance? Will you make a bit of time to think about your dying bed, and the judgment bar? Will you stop in your chase after riches, position, learning, pleasure? Will you pull yourself up, as a rational being ought, and face about, and look God and eternity in the face? Oh! Will you? Would to God I could make you! Would to God I could come and put my arms around you, and entreat you, with tears and prayers, to stop and think! If you will only stop and think, *you will be saved.* It is not in human nature to go into Hell with the full realization of the danger. If you will not think now, remember, I beseech you, that you will have to spend eternity in thinking.

Oh, how wicked in the sight of angels, and all holy intelligences, thus to murder your soul for want of a little thought! Oh, how wicked to circumvent the purposes of God, and help the Devil to damn the world, when a little thought and consideration would have prevented it! Oh, what a *monster of wickedness you are* to be thus *indifferent*! What an example to set to all created beings! What a strengthening of the hands of all the wicked! What a vile murderer you are in the estimation of angels, and even of devils, for they can see the heinousness of your conduct, whether you see it or not! You are worse than an infidel, for you are more inconsistent. He does not profess to believe in a God; but you profess to believe in one, and yet take no notice of him. He professes to believe there is no Hell or Heaven; you profess to believe in both, and yet you are plunging down to Hell; your sin is more monstrous than infidelity. You are saying, "I care for none of these things." I say, this indifference is the height of folly, and the extreme of wickedness. May God help you to see it![1]

Lord, these are astonishingly strong words. Please impart in me a similar
passion for souls as this, so that I may think more about eternity than what
others may think of what I say. Amen.

1   From *Life and Death.*

As the deer longs for streams of water, so I long for you, O God
(Psalm 42:1 *NLT*)

I had had the strivings of God's Spirit all my life, since I was about two years old. My dear mother has often told me how she went upstairs to find me crying, and when she questioned me, I said I was crying because I had sinned against God. Thank the Lord, I do not say this boastingly. I have good cause to be ashamed that I was so long before I fully gave myself up; but all through my childhood I was graciously sheltered by a watchful mother from outward sin and, in fact, brought up as a Christian. When I came to be between fifteen and sixteen when, I believe, I was thoroughly converted, the great temptation of Satan to me was this: "You must not expect such a change as you read of in books. You have been half a Christian all your life. You always feared God. You must content yourself with this."

Oh! How I was frightened! It must have been the Spirit of God that taught me. I was frightened at it. I said: "No, no. My heart is as bad as other people's, and if I have not sinned outwardly I have inwardly." I cried to God to show me the evil of my heart, and said: "I will never rest till I am as thoroughly and truly changed, and know it, as any thief, or any great outward sinner."

I went on seeking God in this way for six weeks, often till two o'clock in the morning, wrestling, and I told the Lord I would never give up, if I died in the search, until I found God, and I did find him, as every soul does, when it comes to him in that way.[1] I cried for nothing on earth or Heaven, but that I might find him whom my soul panted after, and I did find him, and you can find him.[2]

Lord, you graciously reward those who seek you. Please bless and touch those who earnestly search for you this day, revealing your goodness. Amen.

---

[1] See Genesis 32.
[2] From *Catherine Booth* by W. T. Stead.

YOUR WORD IS A LAMP FOR MY FEET, A LIGHT ON MY PATH

(Psalm 119:105 *NIV*)

I have been reading of late the New Testament with special reference to the aggressive spirit of Primitive Christianity, and it is wonderful what floods of light come upon you when you read the Bible with reference to any particular topic on which you are seeking for help. When God sees you are panting after the light, in order that you may use it, he pours it in upon you. It is an indispensable condition of receiving light that you are willing to follow it. People say they don't see this and that, no, because they do not wish to see. They are not willing to walk in it and, therefore, they do not get it; but those who are willing to obey shall have all the light they want.

It seems to me that we come infinitely short of any right and rational idea of the aggressive spirit of the New Testament saints. Satan has got Christians to accept what I may call a namby-pamby, kid-glove kind of system of presenting the gospel to people. "Will they be so kind as to read this tract or book, or would they not like to hear this popular and eloquent preacher? They will be pleased with him quite apart from religion." This is the short of half-frightened, timid way of putting the truth before unconverted people, and of talking to them about the salvation of their souls. It seems to me this is utterly antagonistic and repugnant to the spirit of the early saints: "Go ye… and preach the gospel to every creature;"[1] and again the same idea – "Unto whom now I send thee."[2] Look what is implied in these commissions. It seems to me that no people have ever yet fathomed the meaning of these two divine commissions. I believe The Salvation Army have come nearer to it than any people that have ever preceded them. Look at them. Would it ever occur to you that the language meant, "Go and build chapels and churches and invite the people to come in, and if they will not, leave them alone"?[3]

> Lord of light, grant me insight into your ways, and what I may do
> in your service. Grant me, too, your enabling grace. Amen.

1   Mark 16:15, KJV.
2   Acts 26:17, KJV.
3   From *Aggressive Christianity*.

A MAN WILL LEAVE HIS FATHER AND MOTHER AND BE UNITED TO
HIS WIFE, AND THE TWO WILL BECOME ONE FLESH
(Matthew 19:5 *NIV*)

Who can wonder that marriage is so often a failure, when we observe the ridiculous way in which courtship is commonly carried on? Would not *any* partnership result disastrously that was entered into in so blind and senseless a fashion?

Perhaps the greatest evil of all is *hurry*. Young people do not allow themselves time to know each other before an engagement is formed. They should take time and make opportunities for acquainting themselves with each other's character, disposition, and peculiarities before coming to a decision. This is the great point. They should on no account commit themselves until they are fully satisfied in their own minds, assured that if they have a doubt beforehand it generally increases afterwards. I am convinced that this is where thousands make shipwreck and mourn the consequences all their lives.

Then again, every courtship ought to be based on certain definite principles. This, too, is a fruitful cause of mistake and misery. Very few have a definite idea as to what they want in a partner, and hence they do not look for it. They simply go about the manner in a haphazard sort of fashion, and jump into an alliance upon the first drawings of mere natural feeling, regardless of the laws which govern such relationships… Each of the parties ought to be satisfied that there are bound to be found in the other such qualities as would make them friends if they were of the same sex. In other words there should be a congeniality and compatibility of temperament. For instance, it must be a fatal error, fraught with perpetual misery, for a man who has mental gifts and high aspirations to marry a woman who is only fit to be a mere drudge, or for a woman of refinement and ability to marry a man who is good for nothing better than to follow the plough, or look after a machine.[1]

> My prayer today, Lord, is for those contemplating marriage; may your Spirit
> guide them with wisdom and clarity of mind. Bless their joy and optimism.
> Amen.

---

1   From *Catherine Booth* by Catherine Bramwell-Booth.

WOE TO ME IF I DO NOT PREACH THE GOSPEL!
(1 Corinthians 9:16 *ESV*)

If I were asked to put into one word what I consider to be the greatest hindrance to the success of divine truth, even when spoken by sincere and real people, I should say *stiffness*. Simplicity is indispensable to success, *naturalness* in putting the truth. It seems as if people, the moment they come to religion, put on a different tone, a different look and manner – in short, become unnatural...

Oh, if we could get more of the spirit of prayer into those who love God! Few understand it at all. I always find an exact proportion in the results to the spirit of intercession I have had beforehand. That is why I like to be alone in lodgings...

They say the sinners here will "bide some bringing down".[1] Well, the Lord can do it. They tell me, too, that I am immensely popular with the people. But *that* is no comfort unless they will be saved... God made you responsible, not for delivering the truth, but for getting it in – getting it home, fixing it in the conscience as a red-hot iron, as a bolt, straight from his throne; and he has given you also the *power to do it*; and if you do not do it, *blood* will be on your skirts. Oh, this genteel way of putting the truth! How God hates it! "If you please, dear friends, will you listen? If you please, will you be converted? Will you come to Jesus? Shall we read just this, that, and the other?" No more like apostolic preaching than darkness is like light.[2, 3]

Lord of the Church, you have gifted some people with the ability to preach.
Thank you for their skill and dedication. Bless and inspire them as they work to
convey your truths, especially through barren patches. Amen.

---

1   Portsmouth, a Naval town on the south coast of England, where Catherine held a preaching campaign.
2   From Catherine's notes and lectures on preaching.
3   From *Catherine Booth: A Sketch*.

A GOSSIP BETRAYS A CONFIDENCE;
SO AVOID ANYONE WHO TALKS TOO MUCH
(Proverbs 20:19 *NIV*)

Being so much alone in my youth, and so thrown on my thoughts and those of the mighty dead as expressed in books, has been helpful to me. Had I been given to gossip, and had there been people for me to gossip with, I should certainly never have accomplished what I did. I believe gossip is one of the greatest enemies to both mental and spiritual development. It encourages the mind to dwell on the superficial aspect of things and the passing trivialities of the hour.

There are very few people who have either the capacity or inclination to converse on deep and important questions. And therefore, if you mix much with them, you are obliged to come to their level and talk their twaddle. This you cannot do, except perhaps now and then as a recreation, without it having a reflective evil effect on the mind. I should think that, as a rule, if we knew the lives of persons whose mental attainments are of a superior character, we should find that they are men and women who have been very much thrown upon their own resources, and cut off from others, either by choice or by their circumstances. In confirmation of this, one has only to note the ordinary conversation at a dinner table, or in a railway carriage, to observe how little *substance* there is in it. As a rule there is not a word spoken of an elevating or useful tendency in the whole conversation, and indeed it is commonly the case that nothing has been said which might not just as well, or better, have been left unsaid... I have every reason to be glad that I never read a single novel in my young days. Indeed I could count on my fingers the number I have read throughout my life, and I do not believe the little I gained from those I did read was worth the expenditure of time.[1,2]

Lord, you have given the gift of time. Thank you for my hours and days.
Help me to use that gift wisely and well, taking time to be holy. Amen.

1   As a child and a teenager, Catherine Mumford was confined to bed for long periods of time, with health problems. She devoted this enforced time of rest to reading theological books and the Bible, which she had read eight times by the age of twelve.
2   From *The Life of Catherine Booth The Mother of The Salvation Army, Vol. I.*

BE YE NOT UNEQUALLY YOKED TOGETHER WITH UNBELIEVERS
(2 Corinthians 6:14 *KJV*)

As quite a young girl I early made up my mind to certain qualifications which I regarded as indispensable to the forming of any engagement[1]... I was determined that his religious views *must* coincide with mine. He must be a sincere Christian; not a nominal one, or a mere church member, but truly converted to God. It is probably not too much to say that so far as professedly religious people are concerned, three-fourths of the matrimonial misery endured is brought upon themselves by the neglect of this principle. Those who do, at least in a measure, love God and try to serve him, form alliances with those who have no regard for his laws, and who practically, if not avowedly, live as though he had no existence. Marriage is a divine institution, and in order to ensure, at any rate, the highest and most lasting happiness, the persons who enter into it must first of all themselves be in the divine plan. For if a man or woman be not able to restrain and govern their own natures, how can they reasonably expect to control the nature of another? If his or her being is not in harmony with itself, how can it be in harmony with that of anybody else?

Thousands of Christians, women especially, have proved by bitter experience that neither money, position, nor any other worldly advantage has availed to prevent the punishment that invariably attends disobedience to the command, "Be not unequally yoked together with unbelievers"... I knew that I could never respect a fool, or one much weaker mentally than myself. Many imagine that because a person is *converted*, that is all that is required. This is a great mistake. There ought to be a similarity or congeniality of *character* as well as of grace. As a dear old man once said, "When thou choosest a companion for life, choose one with whom thou couldst live without grace, lest he lose it!"[2]

Thank you, Father, for the beautiful idea and gift of marriage.
Bless and help married couples, especially those who are working through
problems at the moment. Impart your peace and counsel. Amen.

---

1   Catherine Mumford listed those qualities she would like in any future husband, making this a matter of prayer. She wanted a husband who was a minister, was tall and, preferably, called William!
2   From *Catherine Booth The Mother of The Salvation Army, Vol. I.*

HE GOT UP AND WENT TO HIS FATHER.
BUT WHILE HE WAS STILL A LONG WAY OFF, HIS FATHER
SAW HIM AND WAS FILLED WITH COMPASSION FOR HIM

(Luke 15:20 *NIV*)

Alas! How many of God's prodigals… resolve and *re-resolve*, but never *act*. This young man puts his resolution into *action*. He starts on the journey. No doubt, he had many a struggle with himself on the road, and many a struggle with the Devil. Methinks as he got halfway, hungry and weary, I see him leaning his back against a tree and going through one of those mental conflicts. The possibility of his father being dead, or if alive, unable to receive him, angrily and reproachfully shutting the door in his face, would rise before him. Satan would suggest, "What impudence for you to think of going home after having treated the old man as you have done – breaking his law, wasting his money, and bringing yourself into this disgraceful and dilapidated condition. How dare you think of it! It is adding insult to injury. You had better turn back, or try and get a situation somewhere up in this neighbourhood."

But the prodigal's eyes were opened; he was looking towards his father's house, and his heart was melting with repentance, and longing to be reinstated in his father's love. And so, plucking up his courage, he starts again, supporting himself as best he can on his weary route. As he comes within view of the old homestead, the familiar scenes of his childhood are too much for him, and he stands almost paralyzed with grief! We will leave him there for a minute, and go seek his father. I don't suppose the father was looking out for him; but, as is customary in the East, he was probably walking on the roof of his house in the cool of the day and, as on many a former occasion, he thought of his long-lost son – for, though he was a prodigal, he *was his lad still*! It might be that he had some strange presentiment or foreboding, as we sometimes have when anything uncommon is about to happen. How natural that he should gaze over the expanse of country across which his son has gone.[1,2]

Father, what a lovely word picture we see here, of your mercy and compassion towards us. Thank you that you run to embrace us. Amen.

---

1   From one of Catherine's Portsmouth sermons. It is estimated that at least 600 people were converted during her campaign there.
2   From *Catherine Booth The Mother of The Salvation Army, Vol. II.*

HE RAN TO HIS SON, THREW HIS ARMS ROUND HIM AND KISSED HIM

(Luke 15:20 *NIV*)

As he looks, he sees a speck in the distance: a vague curiosity compels his gaze; he looks as if into vacancy until the figure draws nearer, when something in the form or the gait strikes him, and he says to himself, "Can this be my boy coming back?" Then he chides himself, and says, "What a foolish old man I am! Because I dreamed of him last night, or have felt this strange foreboding, should I expect him to come?" And he takes his eyes away, and breathes another prayer, added to hundreds offered before: "O Lord, my God, grant that I may see my prodigal boy before I die!"

He takes another round on the roof, and returns to the same spot, and as he looks again he perceives the figure has come nearer, and his eyes are glued, as it were, to that form; the eye of affection is quick of recognition. He says, "Can it be? It is like him – it must be – God is going to answer my prayers – *it is, it is my long-lost boy!*"

He makes the best of his way down, and then, as fast as his aged limbs will carry him, he runs to assure himself. It is years since he ran like that, but love inspires him with strength and makes his feet like hinds' feet.[1] Away he goes over the lawn and through the adjoining meadow! The prodigal, too, has been thinking as he draws nearer; and when he lifts up his eyes and beholds his father, he runs to meet him; they rush into each other's arms, and his father falls upon his neck with the kiss of reconciliation. He waits not to hear the boy's confession: the best proof of his repentance is that he is *here at home* again.[2]

Father, there are some lovely phrases in today's reading, all of which describe your love and grace, albeit inadequately. Thank you for this parable. Amen.

---

1 Psalm 18:33.
2 From *Catherine Booth The Mother of The Salvation Army, Vol. II.*

GO YE INTO ALL THE WORLD,
AND PREACH THE GOSPEL TO EVERY CREATURE

(Mark 16:15 *KJV*)

If you set your servant to do something for you, and said, "Go and accomplish that piece of business for me," you know what it would involve. You know that he must see certain persons, running about the city to certain offices and banks, and agents, involving a great deal of trouble and sacrifice; but you have nothing to do with that. He is *your servant*. He is employed by you to do that business, and you simply commission him to "Go and do it". What would you think if he went and took an office and sent out a number of circulars inviting your customers or clients to come and wait on his pleasure, and when they chose to come, just to put your business before them? No, you would say, "Ridiculous". Divesting our minds of all conventionalities and traditionalisms, what would the language mean? "Go ye!" To whom? "To every creature." Where am I to get at them? Where they are.

"Every creature." This is the extent of your commission. Seek them out; run after them, wherever you can get at them. "Every creature" – wherever you find a creature that has a soul – there go and preach the gospel to him. If I understand it, *that* is the meaning and the spirit of the commission. And then again, to Paul, he [God] says, "Unto whom now I send thee, To open their eyes, and to turn them from darkness to light, and from the power of Satan unto God".[1] They are asleep – go and wake them up. They do not see their danger. If they did, there would be no necessity for you to run after them. They are preoccupied. Open their eyes, and turn them round by your desperate earnestness and moral suasion and moral force; and, oh! What a great deal one man can do for another, it makes me tremble to think! "Turn them from darkness to light, and from the power of Satan unto God."[2]

Thank you, Lord, for your unending love of souls, and the planned urgency
with which you organize things so that people may hear the gospel.
Help me to play my part in your plan of salvation. Amen.

---

1 Acts 26:18, KJV.
2 From *Aggressive Christianity*.

JESUS... SAID UNTO HIM, "VERILY, VERILY, I SAY UNTO THEE,
EXCEPT A MAN BE BORN AGAIN, HE CANNOT SEE THE KINGDOM OF GOD"

(John 3:3 *KJV*)

We meet with a great many people... who seem to have a general notion of their obligation to serve God, and a desire to do so. They feel that they are not right – are not quite what they ought to be, and would like to be if they were going to die; and they desire to be so. They are sincere, so far as they go; but they seem to have no definite idea of that experience which is necessary in order to make them right; they do not understand how they are to be saved.

Nicodemus seems to have been one of this class; he seems to have come to the Saviour with these general sort of notions. I dare say he thought he was a pretty good man; but he wanted to be a better one. There was the same dissatisfaction, the same disquiet in his soul that there is in every human soul till it finds God, and which nothing else can ever satisfy; because God has made us for himself, and until we find the end of our being, we can never rest; we are like Noah's dove, wandering hither and thither and finding no rest for the soles of our feet.[1] It was just so with Nicodemus. He wanted something. He had heard of this teacher; nay, he had probably heard him speak, and felt that he was a teacher come from God; and like a great many other Nicodemuses since, he felt the words of the teacher to be true; but he had a great many "ifs" and "buts" about it. He wanted to hear more, and so he sought a private interview, no doubt thinking that he could bring out his own personal difficulties, and get more light in that way; and begins in a way which would lead us to think that he expected that Jesus would enter into an elaborate conversation as to the orderings and method of his outward life; but Jesus stopped him right in the middle of his introduction with a doctrine that utterly confounded him.[2]

Thank you, Lord Jesus, that we may approach you at any time for a "private interview" in prayer. Thank you that we may always bring our deepest concerns to you in confidence and trust. Amen.

1 Genesis 8:8–9.
2 From *Life and Death*.

IT IS THE LORD CHRIST YOU ARE SERVING

(Colossians 3:24 *NIV*)

It may be well to explain that we understand religious aggressive effort to be *that interference on the part of Christians with the thoughts and actions of ungodly men which the Bible shows to be necessary in order to secure their present and eternal well-being.* We Christians see around us everywhere men and women under the influence of false ideas, given up to selfish indulgences and evil practices, which enslave their faculties and render real happiness impossible to them, either in this life or in that which is to come. Now, religious aggressive effort implies measures taken for their deliverance from these evil habits, and from the bondage of Satan, and the actual bringing of these souls into the liberty, power, and blessedness of the family of God. It is, in short, a holy warfare, prosecuted under the direction and power of the Holy Spirit, to bring men from darkness to light, from the power of Satan unto God...

The very nature of Christianity renders this aggressive effort incumbent on all Christians. Not only are there many passages directly enforcing this duty, but it is assumed as a fundamental principle, underlying the whole economy of grace, that the truly regenerate will be benevolently active for the good of others. A desire to save the lost seems to be a divinely inspired impulse in the soul of every real child of God, as it were a holy instinct, in which the disciple ever resembles his master, and the servant his lord. I am aware that there is a great deal of professed Christianity in these days which lacks this lineament of the divine likeness, and makes so much of faith that love is deemed almost superfluous. An inspired apostle, however, declares that there is something greater even than faith, which is charity, and though we have a faith that will remove mountains, if we have not charity it profiteth us nothing.[1,2]

Lord, an awareness of your love clearly brings responsibilities. Cause me to look upon those responsibilities as privileges in your service. Amen.

[1]   1 Corinthians 13, KJV.
[2]   From *Practical Religion.*

Wine is a mocker, strong drink a brawler
(Proverbs 20:1 *ESV*)

The use of intoxicating drinks as a beverage is the cause and strength of a very large proportion of the wickedness, crime, vice, and misery which exist around us… The time is fast passing in which there has existed a difference of opinion amongst the wise and good, as to the real character of these drinks. The baneful harvest of crime and misery which their consumption has entailed on us as a nation has opened the eyes of almost every thinking and patriotic mind to the fact that the drink, not the abuse of it, but the drink itself, is an evil thing, in very truth a "mocker", the product of Satanic art and malice… We might adduce overwhelming evidence that strong drink is the natural ally of all wickedness. Unquestionable statistics have been produced which show that its stimulus is essential to the plotting and commission of almost every kind of villainy. The gambler seeks it to aid him in the craft and cunning by which he lures his victim on to financial ruin. The seducer has recourse to its deceptive power to pave the way for his cruel licentiousness. The burglar braces his courage and hardens his conscience by its exhilarating fumes. The harlot drowns in the intoxicating cup her sense of shame, and from it gathers strength to trample out the deepest, tenderest instincts of womanhood. The murderer is powerless to strike the fatal blow till maddened by its infernal stimulus. In short, all classes and sizes of criminals unite to testify, "By the influence of drink we are what we are," and missionaries, Bible-women,[1] chaplains, gaolers, magistrates, and judges, say, "Amen" to their testimony. We have no hesitation in affirming that strong drink is Satan's chief instrumentality for keeping the masses of this country under his power. If the foregoing propositions are correct – Christians are bound to aggress on the kingdom of Satan, and if strong drink constitutes one of the mightiest forces of that kingdom, then it follows inevitably that to be successful in an aggressive effort Christians must deal with the drink.[2, 3]

May it be, Father, that your people hold fast to personal standards. Amen.

---

1 Bible women were local missionaries (sometimes feminist political activists) engaged in ministry to women. Often, they were employed by wealthier women keen to support evangelism in working-class neighbourhoods.
2 From *Practical Religion*.
3 Catherine had pledged never to marry a man who was not a total abstainer from alcohol, and persuaded William of her conviction. Her views, shaped by John Wesley's teaching, laid the foundations of The Salvation Army's teetotal stance. She was a supporter of temperance movements.

THE ONLY OBLIGATION YOU HAVE IS TO LOVE ONE ANOTHER
(Romans 13:8 *GNT*)

There were... certain rules which I formulated for my married life, before I was married or even engaged. I have carried them out ever since my wedding day, and the experience of all these years has abundantly demonstrated their value.

The first was never to have any secrets from my husband in anything that affected our mutual relationship, or the interests of the family. The confidence of others in spiritual matters I did not consider as coming under this category, but as being the secrets of others, and therefore not my property. The second rule was, never to have two purses, thus avoiding even the temptation of having any secrets of a domestic character. My third principle was that in matters where there was any difference of opinion, I would show my husband my views and the reasons on which they were based, and try to convince in favour of my way of looking at the subject. This generally resulted either in his being converted to my views, or in my being converted to his, either result securing unity of thought and action.

My fourth rule was, in cases of difference of opinion never to argue in the presence of the children. I thought it better even to submit at the time to what I might consider as mistaken judgment, rather than have a controversy before them. But of course when such occasions arose, I took the first opportunity for arguing the matter out. My subsequent experience has abundantly proved to me the wisdom of this course.[1]

Lord, thank you for faith that is practical and relevant to day-to-day life.
Keep my Christianity grounded in the realities of business and family matters
so that my life on earth may be of some heavenly use. Amen.

1   From *The Life of Catherine Booth The Mother of The Salvation Army, Vol. I.*

As newborn babes, desire the sincere milk of the word
(1 Peter 2:2 *KJV*)

I am fond of tracing the analogy which in many instances exists between the economy of the natural and spiritual worlds, and I think to all who love and seek out the ways of the Lord, this must be an ever-interesting and profitable exercise. I think, too, there are truths and principles of extensive application and great practical importance often deducible from it…

What are the considerations indispensable to the preservation and growth of the natural babe?… 1) An adequate supply of congenial aliment. 2) A pure and invigorating atmosphere. 3) A careful cleansing away of all impurities. 4) Freedom from undue restraint in the exercise of its faculties. Between these conditions and those necessary to the preservation and progress of spiritual life, there appears to me a striking and beautiful analogy. The first and most important want of the babe in Christ is unquestionably congenial aliment; it needs to be fed with "the sincere milk of the word". Deprived of this, there is no chance of life, to say nothing of growth. How important, then, that the character of the ministry should be suited to the wants of the new-born soul, "the sincere milk of the word", that which is felt to be *real*. Words without heart will chill the very life-current of a young believer. It must be that which has been *tasted* and handled of the Word of Life. The spiritual babe will soon pine away under mere theoretical teaching. It must be sustaining, and in order to [obtain] this the milk must be pure, unmixed with either diluting or deleterious doctrines. It must be congenial to the cravings of a spiritual appetite, and capable of being assimilated by a spiritual nature. It must be direct and practical. The babe, under its teachings, must learn how to walk in all the ordinances and statutes of the Lord blameless – how to apply the principles of action laid down in his word to the daily occurrences of life.[1, 2]

> Father, I pray for those who teach Bible truths; pastors, teachers
> and Sunday school leaders. Give them clarity and conviction. Amen.

Cont/…

1 From a letter Catherine Mumford wrote to the Editor of *Methodist New Connexion Magazine*, 1854.
2 From *The Life of Catherine Booth The Mother of The Salvation Army, Vol. I.*

Grow in the grace and knowledge of our Lord
(2 Peter 3:18 *NIV*)

Cont/…

Then comes the second scarcely less important condition – a pure and invigorating atmosphere. Not more surely will the sprightly infant born in some pent-up garret, which for generations has been impregnable to the pure air of heaven, pine and die, than will the spiritual babe introduced into the death-charged atmosphere of some churches. So far from it being a matter of surprise that so many converts relapse into spiritual death, it appears to me a far greater wonder that so many survive under the influence of the noxious atmosphere into which they are often forced.

Let the spiritual infant, born amidst the genial influences of a genuine revival, and just awakened to a sense of the importance and reality of eternal things, be transplanted to a church in which the tide of holy feeling has been rolled back by a flood of worldliness, formality, and indifference, and what a shock his spiritual nature must sustain! Nay, suppose him introduced into some class-meeting where there are professors of ten, twelve, or twenty years' standing, who ought to be far ahead of him in the joy and strength of the Lord, but whose everlasting complaint is "my leanness, my leanness," and this always in the same key – the key of doubt, who can estimate the freezing, paralyzing effects of such an atmosphere? What can be expected but misgiving, anxiety, and relaxation in duty? Oh, if the Church would indeed be the nursery of the future kings and priests of her God, she must awake up from her lethargy and create an atmosphere of warm and holy feeling, pure and unfeigned love, incessant and prevailing prayer, and active untiring effort for souls! Then may she hope that the converts born under special outpourings of the Spirit will grow and thrive, and in due time arrive at the stature of men and women in Christ.[1,2]

> What a lovely responsibility it is to care for new converts.
> Lord of the Church, keep your people alert to this crucial duty. Amen.

Cont/…

---

1   From a letter Catherine Mumford wrote to the Editor of *Methodist New Connexion Magazine*, 1854.
2   From *The Life of Catherine Booth The Mother of The Salvation Army, Vol. I.*

GROWING IN THE KNOWLEDGE OF GOD

(Colossians 1:10 *NIV*)

Cont/...

The third condition of physical life and health is the cleansing away of impurities. The infant, though truly a living and healthy child, is too feeble and ignorant to remove what would be injurious to itself and render it offensive to others, and therefore some maternal and loving hand must come to its help. Is there no analogy in this respect between the natural and spiritual babe? Has the latter no injurious habits to be pointed out and overcome; no false views to be corrected; no mistaken conduct to be rectified; no unholy tendency to be subdued; and is it not generally too feeble and ignorant to understand its errors and to correct them? Then does it not need the careful pruning of experienced and loving Christians, the tender watchfulness of fathers and mothers in Christ, that its life be not sacrificed or its spiritual nature depressed? It is as great a mistake to expect perfection in the spiritual babe as it would be to expect maturity of strength and intellect in the natural. If indeed it were born perfect, of what force the injunction, "*Go on* to perfection!"[1] and why the precaution to give milk unto babes rather than strong meat?[2] There may be heterogeneous substances to be cleansed away, and some unseemly blemishes to be removed, where the germ of true spiritual life has been deposited. But let not nursing fathers and mothers be discouraged on that account. Rather let them learn of the heavenly husbandman how to hasten the pruning process and develop the hidden life. There is yet another condition in which the analogy between the natural and spiritual seems even more striking and complete, namely, that of freedom from undue restraint in the use of the faculties. Thank Heaven, the days of ignorance with reference to the operation of natural law are fast passing away, and mothers and nurses are learning that health and vigour are attendants on freedom and exercise. Would that the Church generally would make, and act upon, the same discovery.[3, 4]

Father, assist your Church as it welcomes and nurtures newcomers. Amen.

Cont/...

1   See Hebrews 6:1.
2   1 Corinthians 3:2; Hebrews 5:12.
3   From a letter Catherine Mumford wrote to the Editor of *Methodist New Connexion Magazine*, 1854.
4   From *The Life of Catherine Booth The Mother of The Salvation Army, Vol. I.*

One of those listening was a woman...
named Lydia... a worshipper of God

(Acts 16:14 *NIV*)

Cont/...

If religion consists in doing the will of God, what an anomaly is an inactive Christian! Yet there are multitudes in this our day professing to be Christians, who do absolutely nothing for the salvation of souls, or the glory of God... The babe in Christ must be made to feel his individual untransferable responsibility. He must be taught that labour is the law of life, spiritual as well as natural... Methodism, beyond almost any other system, has recognized the importance of this principle, and to this fact doubtless owes much of its past success; but has it not in some measure degenerated in this respect, at least with regard to its employment of female talent?

There seems in many societies a growing disinclination among the female members to engage in prayer, speak in love feasts, band meetings, or in any manner bear testimony for their Lord, or to the power of his grace. And this false God-dishonouring timidity is too fatally pandered to by the Church, as if God had given any talent to be hidden in a napkin... Why should the swaddling bands of blind custom, which in Wesley's days were so triumphantly broken, and with such glorious results thrown to the moles and the bats, be again wrapped around the female disciples of the Lord Jesus? Where are the Mrs Fletchers[1] and the Mrs Rogers[2] of our churches now, with their numerous and healthy spiritual progeny? And yet who can doubt that equal power in prayer and the germ of equal usefulness of life exist in many a Lydia's heart, smothered and kept back though it may be... I would warn our societies against drifting into false notions on this subject. Let the female converts be not only allowed to use their newly awakened faculties, but positively encouraged to exercise and improve them. Let them be taught of their obligations to work themselves in the vineyard of the Lord... Oh! That the Church would excite its female members.[3, 4]

I pray for the members of my own church, Lord, that we may all be led to grow in our faith. Help us to fan our gifts and skills into flame. Amen.

[1] Mary Fletcher (1739–1815), the first female preacher authorized by John Wesley to preach.
[2] Hester Ann Rogers (1756–1794), friend and housekeeper of John Wesley, Methodist class leader and writer.
[3] From a letter Catherine Mumford wrote to the Editor of *Methodist New Connexion Magazine*, 1854.
[4] From *The Life of Catherine Booth The Mother of The Salvation Army, Vol. I.*

DO NOT FORSAKE YOUR MOTHER'S TEACHING

(Proverbs 1:8 *NIV*)

I hope you will show yourself to be a true son of your mother, and a consistent disciple of the Lord. Very much depends on you as to the ease and comfort of managing the little ones. Do all you can. Be forbearing where only your own feelings or comfort are concerned, and don't raise unnecessary difficulties; but where their obedience to us or their health is at stake, be firm in trying to put them right.

I am pleased that Mr W puts such confidence in you; but do not be puffed up by it. Remember how weak you are, and ask the Lord to save you from conceit and self-sufficiency. Try to be fair and just in all dealings with the boys – i.e. do not be hard on a boy whom you may not happen to like so well as another; but be fair, and treat all alike when left in charge.

You are under a mistake to suppose that sacrificing your recreation time will help you in the end. It will not. Cramming the mind acts just in the same way as cramming the stomach. It is what you digest well that benefits you, not what you cram in. So many hours spent in study, and then relaxation and walking, will do your mind much more good than "all work, and no play". Now mark this. Do not be looking so much at what you *have* to do as to what you are *doing*. Leave the future (you may spend it in Heaven), and go steadily on doing today's work in today's hours, with recreation in between to shake the seed in. One step well and firmly taken is better than two with a slip backwards. Poor human nature seems as though it must go to extremes – either all or none, too much or too little, idleness, or being killed with work! May the Lord show you the happy medium.[1, 2]

> Lord, this day bless all mothers who do their best for their children.
> I pray for mums. Amen.

---

1 Catherine Booth wrote to her children with advice on looking after their siblings when she wasn't at home, and instruction on how to act when they were chosen to be school monitors.
2 From *Catherine Booth: A Sketch*.

I AM REMINDED OF YOUR SINCERE FAITH, WHICH FIRST LIVED
IN YOUR GRANDMOTHER LOIS AND IN YOUR MOTHER EUNICE AND,
I AM PERSUADED, NOW LIVES IN YOU ALSO

(2 Timothy 1:5 *NIV*)

"They have put their children into the movement," people say. Yes, bless God! And if we had twenty, we would do so. But I stand here before God, and say that it is all from the same motive and for the same end – the seeking and saving of the lost. But, I ask, how comes it to pass that these children all grow up with this one ambition and desire? Is not this the finger of God? Some of our critics don't find it so easy to put their children where they want them to be! Could all the powers of earth give these young men and women the *spirit* of this work, apart from God?

Some of you know the life of toil, self-sacrifice, and devotion this work entails. What could bring our children to embrace it without a single human inducement such as influences other young people the world over?

As spirits are not finely touched but to fine issues, so surely God hath fashioned their souls for the work he wants them to do; and though all the mother in me often cries, "Spare them!", my soul magnifies the Lord, because he hath counted me worthy of such honour.[1, 2, 3]

Thank you, Lord, for William and Catherine's resolve to encourage
church attendance and involvement in their children.
Draw alongside all Christian parents who try to do likewise,
especially in an age of competing interests. Amen.

---

1   Luke 1:46.
2   William and Catherine Booth succeeded to quite an exceptional degree in persuading their children to reject "worldly" pleasures in favour of spiritual interests and church activities. Criticism arose that undue prominence within The Salvation Army was given to their family. Although such criticism was largely superficial, Catherine found it exasperating that people should disapprove of their desire, as Christian parents, to ensure that matters of faith and belief were a family affair.
3   From *The Life of Catherine Booth The Mother of The Salvation Army, Vol.II.*

LET YOUR CONVERSATION BE GRACIOUS AND ATTRACTIVE
(Colossians 4:6 NLT)

The General was a fine old man. His colloquial, unpretentious way of talking could not fail to produce an impression.[1] Why is it that in speaking about religion a stilted and unnatural style should be so commonly in vogue? The stirring tones, the flashing eye, the eager gesture which emphasize conversation regarding every theme – why should these be banished from the pulpit?

If I were asked to put into one word what I consider to be the greatest obstacle to the success of divine truth, even when uttered by sincere and real people, I should say *stiffness*. Simplicity is indispensable to success; *naturalness* in putting the truth. It seems as if people the moment they come to religion assume a different tone, a different look and manner – in short, become unnatural. We want sanctified humanity, not sanctimoniousness. You want to talk to you friends in the same way about religion as you talk about earthly things. If a friend is in difficulties, and he comes to you, you do not begin talking in a circumlocutory manner about the general principles on which men can secure prosperity, and the sad mistakes of those who have not secured it; you come straight to the point, and, if you feel for him, you take him by the buttonhole, or put your hand in his, and say, "My dear fellow, I am very sorry for you; is there any way in which I can help you?" If you have a friend afflicted with a fatal malady, and you see it, and he does not, you don't begin to descant on the power of disease and the way people may secure health, but you say, "My dear fellow, I am afraid this hacking cough is more serious than you think, and that nasty flush on your cheek is a bad sign. I am afraid you are ill. Let me counsel you to seek advice." That is the way to speak to people about earthly things. Now just do exactly so about spiritual things.[2]

> Lord, take my everyday conversations and season them with salt, so that the ordinary words I speak may resonate with charming truth. Amen.

1 Catherine Booth had listened to General Neal Dow, a guest speaker at the 1874 Conference of the Christian Mission (the forerunner of The Salvation Army). General Dow (1804–97), soldier and politician, was the author of the first prohibitive legislation against alcohol in the United States.
2 From *Catherine Booth The Mother of The Salvation Army, Vol. II.*

I URGE... THAT PETITIONS, PRAYERS, INTERCESSION AND THANKSGIVING
BE MADE... FOR KINGS AND ALL THOSE IN AUTHORITY
(1 Timothy 2:1-2 *NIV*)

The special sphere for The Salvation Army is no doubt what are termed the dangerous classes, and that there is great need for some such agency recent events make but too manifest. The inability of the authorities to cope with the ruffianly element even in the metropolis, the proposed addition of 500 to the police force, the attempt to blow up one of the government offices,[1] and the escape of the offenders, together with the continual discovery of plots, and outbursts of ruffianism vented on others besides the members of The Salvation Army,[2] ought to wake everybody to the necessity for something being done. The fact that there is a vast mass of our population entirely untouched by any civilizing or Christianizing influences, left to the mercy of socialist and infidel leaders, daily increasing in numbers and lawlessness, and fast learning the power of combination and organization, is enough to alarm all thoughtful people as to the lookout ahead of us. You know as well as I do that in France and Germany the steady advance of socialist opinions threatens the orderly government, and menaces the existence of any government at all. The discovery of the Black Hand Associations in Spain,[3] which openly avow the most terrible principles of the socialist theory, may be taken as an indication of the extent to which these opinions must be spreading in countries where there is next to no restriction put on the advocacy of *any* principles whatsoever. In Switzerland, the reputed home of freedom, the propagation of the gospel is alone put under close inspection... while the murder of the rich and the division of their property is allowed to be advocated in public meetings! In the United States we all know how the destruction, not only of public property, but of vessels and life, has been openly advocated and arranged for, for years gone by.[4]

God of the world, whatever our personal political differences, may your people
always unitedly rise up against injustice wherever it is encountered. Amen.

1   An attempt by Fenians to blow up government offices in Westminster (15 March 1883). Fenians were dedicated to the establishment of an independent Irish Republic, under the auspices of the Irish Republican Brotherhood.
2   Members of The Salvation Army were frequently exposed to violent attacks, especially from "The Skeleton Army" whose recruits came largely from the drinking classes opposed to Army teetotalism.
3   A violent anarchist group interested in defending the rights of peasants and agricultural workers. Spanish police cracked down on their activities a matter of months before Catherine Booth gave this lecture.
4   From *The Salvation Army in Relation to the Church and State*.

YOU SHOULD NOT BE SURPRISED AT MY SAYING, "YOU MUST BE BORN AGAIN"

(John 3:7 *NIV*)

Except anyone be born again, he *cannot* – mark the term; it is not *shall not*, but *cannot* – enter into the Kingdom of God.[1] This new birth is a necessity of the case, as if the Saviour had said to Nicodemus, "You are a purely natural man; you live a merely natural life, actuated by natural instincts, hopes and aspirations; whereas my Kingdom is a spiritual Kingdom, and its subjects are spiritual people, actuated by holy motives, holy desires and purposes; therefore it is indispensable that this great change should take place in you before you can become a member of my Kingdom. You must be born again."

And, in answer to the surprise of Nicodemus, he says, "Marvel not, neither reject this doctrine because you cannot comprehend it, for you encounter quite as great mysteries every day of your life; for instance, 'The wind bloweth where it listeth, and thou hearest the sound thereof, but canst not tell whence it cometh, and whither it goeth'.[2] This is a great mystery, yet you know the wind does blow because you see its results and you feel its power. It is just so with the operations of the Spirit; we see its results and feel its power, and know that we are under its influence." It would seem that under the surprise there was lurking some repugnance in the mind of Nicodemus to this doctrine, which is so obnoxious to human pride, self-sufficiency, and morality. Nicodemus betrays his utter ignorance of spiritual truth by the question, "How can a man be born when he is old?" [John 3:4, KJV] Now, mark, I want you who are anxious about your soul, to note this: the Saviour here lays down a definite experience, which he declares all must pass through; no matter what a man may be, or what he may do, or what he may believe, if he have not this experience, "he *cannot* enter into the Kingdom of God."[3]

> Sometimes, Lord Jesus, your words seem hard to swallow.
> Help me to bend my will to yours, allowing you to dissolve anything of self
> that may stand in the way. Be my barrier-breaker. Amen.

1   See John 3:5.
2   John 3:8, KJV.
3   From *Life and Death*.

JESUS… SAID UNTO HIM, VERILY, VERILY, I SAY UNTO THEE,
EXCEPT A MAN BE BORN AGAIN, HE CANNOT SEE THE KINGDOM OF GOD

(John 3:3 *KJV*)

There is not a glorified spirit in heaven nor a sanctified saint on earth who has not passed through it. Some may have experienced it in childhood, and therefore not have a very distinct recollection of the time; but every saint *has* experienced it…

I want you carefully to mark the terms used by the Saviour here… Mark, the Saviour does not say, "Except a man be born, he cannot enter into the Kingdom of God" – for everybody is born – but, "Except a man be born *again*." In another place this change is called "the regeneration of the Spirit" – mark, not generation, but *regeneration*. The soul existed before; but it is to be regenerated by the Holy Ghost – that is, the old soul is born into a new life. Again, this change is spoken of as being "renewed in the spirit of our minds". The same idea, you see – that what previously existed shall be renewed, transformed, and changed in character. In another place this change is spoken of as having the "heart purified", in another as having it circumcized, and in another as having it washed, cleansed, etc.… this new birth is not a new creation in the sense of having a new soul, or a new something apart from ourselves introduced into us, to live alongside the old unrenewed wicked heart till death, when I suppose, in such a case, one would have to go to Hell and the other to Heaven! No; neither the Saviour nor the Bible teaches any such nonsense, but they teach that this new birth is a renewal of the old soul, making the man himself a new creature in Christ Jesus;[1] hence the figure used by our Lord truly illustrates his meaning, seeing that the natural birth is not a new creation, but the introduction of something previously created into a new life. Just so the soul, when it is born again, is introduced into a new life.[2]

Thank you, Father, for the lovely opportunity of a new life – a fresh start to savour. Help me to make the most if it, moment by moment. Amen.

---

1   2 Corinthians 5:17.
2   From *Life and Death*.

THE SON OF MAN CAME TO SEEK AND TO SAVE THE LOST
(Luke 19:10 *NIV*)

Some people seem to think that the Apostles laid the foundations of all the churches. They are quite mistaken. Churches sprang up where the Apostles had never been. The Apostles went to visit and organize them after they had sprung up, as the result of the work of the early laymen and women going everywhere and preaching the word. Oh! May the Lord shower upon us in this day the same spirit! We should build chapels and churches... we should invite the people to them; but do you think... we should rest in this, where three parts of the population utterly ignore our invitations and take no notice whatever of our buildings and our services? *They will not come to us.* That is an established fact. What is to be done? They have souls. You profess to believe that as much as I do, and that they must live for ever. Where are they going? What is to be done?...

When all the civil methods have failed; when the genteel invitations have failed; when one man says that he has married a wife, and another that he has bought a yoke of oxen, and another that he has bought a piece of land – then does the Master of the feast say, "The ungrateful wretches, let them alone!"? No. He says, "Go out into the highways and hedges, and compel them to come in, that my house may be filled. I will have guests, and if you can't get them in by civil measures, use military measures. Go and compel them to come in."[1] It seems to me that we want more of this determined, aggressive spirit. Those of you who are right with God – you want more of this spirit to thrust the truth upon the attention of your fellowmen. People say, you must be very careful, very judicious. You must not thrust religion down people's throats... What! Am I to wait until an unconverted, godless man *wants* to be saved before I try to save him?[2]

Father, recreate in me a deep compassion that will care and care again. Amen.

---

1 Luke 14:15–23; here, verse 23 quoted from the KJV.
2 From *Aggressive Christianity*.

Rivers of Waters Run Down Mine Eyes,
Because They Keep Not Thy Law
(Psalm 119:136 *KJV*)

Am I to let my unconverted friends and acquaintances drift down quietly to damnation, and never tell them about their souls, until they say, "If you please, I want you to preach to me!"? Is this anything like the spirit of early Christianity? No. Verily, we must *make* them look – tear the bandages off, open their eyes, make them bear it, and if they run away from you in one place, meet them in another, and let them have no peace until they submit to God and get their souls saved. This is what Christianity *ought* to be doing in this land, and there are plenty of Christians to do it. Why, we might give the world such a time of it that they would get saved in very *self-defence*, if we were only up and doing, and determined that they should have no peace in their sins…

I would we were all like David. "Rivers of water ran down his eyes because men kept not the Law of God." But you say, "We cannot all hold services." Perhaps not. Go as you like. Go as quietly and as softly as the morning dew. Have meetings like the Friends, if you like.[1] Only do it. Don't let relatives, and friends, and acquaintances die, and their blood be found on your skirts![2] I shall never forget the agony depicted on the face of a young lady who once came to see me. My heart went out to her in pity. She told me her story. She said, "I had a proud, ungodly father, and the Lord converted me three years before his death, and, from the very day of my conversion, I felt I ought to talk to him, and plead, and pray with him about his soul, but I could not muster. I kept intending to do it, and intending to do it, until he was taken ill. It was a sudden and serious illness. He lost his mind, and died unsaved," and she said, "I have never smiled since, and I think I never shall any more."[3]

Holy Spirit, place those names on my heart of people for whom I can pray and to whom I may witness. Show me who and show me how. Amen.

---

1 The Religious Society of Friends (Quakers).
2 Jeremiah 2:34.
3 From *Aggressive Christianity*.

JESUS SAW THE HUGE CROWD... AND HE HAD COMPASSION ON THEM
(Mark 6:34 *NLT*)

The state of the masses in our own country is to me a cause of daily, hourly grief and apprehension. Since coming more in contact with them, I have found their condition to be so much worse than anything I had previously conceived, that I have often felt confounded, disheartened, and almost paralyzed. I have seen many hundreds of thousands of the lower classes gathered together during the last two or three years, and have often said to myself, is it possible that these are our fellow-countrymen in this end of the nineteenth century in this so-called Christian country? Perhaps hundreds of men in one crowd such as one would be afraid to meet on a dark evening, bearing in their persons, in their eyes, in their countenances, in their conceive, [a] kind of mischief, and only wanting the match of some political or other disturbances to give vent to the bitterness and malignity which they seem to feel against everybody either better or more prosperous than themselves.

I have said to my husband on such occasions, oh that we could get our rulers to look on these multitudes – our ministers, our philanthropists, our intelligent Christian gentlemen and merchants! They could not sit still in indifference. They would recognize the necessity for operating upon, and at any rate trying to civilize this outlying mass of heathenism, lawlessness, and vice. I wish that... strangers to these facts would come to some of our open-air gatherings or to some of our meetings even round about London, just to form their own judgment – to the Eagle, [for] instance[1] – stand outside or some in, and Sunday night, and get a seat on the platform, where you can see the people, and you will gather something of their utterly sunken, reckless, godless condition.[2]

Give me too, Lord, a heart of compassion, moved at the impulse of love. Amen.

---

1   The Eagle Tavern, a public house in Hackney, North London. It was rebuilt as a music hall in 1825, then sold to The Salvation Army in 1883 for use as a Salvation Army hall. The tavern appears in the nursery rhyme "Pop goes the weasel".
2   From *The Salvation Army in Relation to the Church and State*.

IT IS NOT FOR KINGS... TO DRINK WINE, NOT FOR RULERS TO CRAVE BEER

(Proverbs 31:4 *NIV*)

Even heathen chiefs, the heads of savage tribes, have sent us words that "it is of no use to send them the Bible, if at the same time we send them strong drink". Alas! That Christians have been so slow to learn the power of this *mitrailleuse* of Hell but, thank God, some of them are beginning to appreciate it at last, and these are crying, what is to be done? How shall we deal with the drink? We answer, in the name of Christ and humanity, deal with it as you do with all other Satan-invented, Christ-dishonouring, soul-ruining abominations. Wash your hands of it at once, and for ever! And give a united and straightforward testimony to the world that you consider it an enemy of all righteousness and the legitimate offspring of Satan!

I submit that there is no other way for Christians to deal with strong drink. All other ways have been tried and have failed. *The time has come for Christians to denounce the use of intoxicating drinks as irreligious and immoral*; and God Almighty will put immortal renown on those of his servants who are sufficiently true, and brave, and self-sacrificing first to run the gauntlet of earth and Hell in doing this. "They shall be had in everlasting remembrance",[1] and counted amongst the greatest benefactors of their race. We contend that the attempt to make what is termed the moderate use of strong drink consistent with a profession of religion has signally and ignominiously failed; and the common sense of mankind is turning upon those who have made it with this most pertinent question: How can that which produces all this crime and misery be a good thing? And if it be an evil thing, how can it be moderately used? This question comes with overwhelming force to those who stand forth as labourers for the spiritual benefit of mankind.[2]

Lord of humanity, I pray for anyone trapped by alcohol today; addicted and struggling. I ask you to help them and anyone who ministers to them. Amen.

1   See Psalm 112:6, KJV.
2   From *Practical Religion*.

HE THAT LOVETH PLEASURE SHALL BE A POOR MAN:
HE THAT LOVETH WINE AND OIL SHALL NOT BE RICH

(Proverbs 21:17 *KJV*)

We rejoice over thousands... rescued, redeemed, saved; but our rejoicing is always counterbalanced by grief for those who are not saved... There are yet thousands who are leaving their wages... every Saturday night at the public house instead of taking them home to the wife and children. There are thousands who are thus spending their days and squandering their opportunities and abusing their capacities in all manner of debauchery and sin, instead of improving them for the good of their families and for the good of the nation; and we feel that all we can do, great as some people think it, and too much in a hurry as other people think we are, is as nothing in comparison with the overwhelming necessity.

Frequently in meetings in the mining districts and other parts, where wages used to be high, as many as five and six men in succession will give something like the following testimony, "Friends, you all know me," and there is a general nod of recognition, "for so many years I earned so much money. I received every Saturday night" – some will say £4, some £3, and some £2, and so on; and they will tell you that they left regularly every Saturday night of their lives £3 out of the £4 at the Black Eagle[1] or the White Swan,[2] or some place of the kind, and took home £1 or 10s.[3] to the starving wife and children; or they earned £2, spent £1 10s., and took home 10s., according to the different grades they occupied.[4]

Father of families, my prayers today are for those whose family units are torn
apart by alcohol-induced poverty; bestow sanity, sobriety, and salvation.
Bless those who offer help and support. Amen.

---

1   A popular public house in Brick Lane, Spitalfields, east London. Possibly the venue referred to, although this reference may well be generic.
2   High Street, Shadwell, east London.
3   Pre-decimal; twenty shillings equalled one pound.
4   From *The Salvation Army in Relation to the Church and State*.

You, Lord, took up my case; you redeemed my life
(Lamentations 3:58 *NIV*)

Another most important evidence of improvement in morality is the number of unfortunate women reclaimed through our agencies. So greatly does God use the Army to this class that at this moment one of our most pressing needs is a temporary home for the reception of the lady portion of them, until we can fit them for some useful occupation. With the poorer class we find but little difficulty because, as a rule, some of our dear people take them to their homes, procure for them some sort of decent clothing, and set them going in charring, washing, sewing, or some way of obtaining a living. We have numbers of instances of poor girls having been saved and restored to comparatively respectable positions without having been removed from the neighbourhood of their former sinful career! Some of the stories of girls being sent home to heartbroken parents are touching in the extreme, if only we had the time to write them.

Crowds come to the meetings and hear about God, eternity, Heaven, and Hell; and their own consciences are awakened, so that *they are afraid* to run the same lengths in sin. They see in the improved appearance, clothing, and family life of the converts how much more rational and profitable it is to spend their money in supporting their families than in drink and debauchery. Thus whole counties are being reawakened and influenced towards morality and reform. Another important national result of Salvation Army influence is a great diminution in the consumption of strong drink! We have thousands of converted drunkards in our ranks, who for years have spent the chief of their earnings at the public house. Of course this leads to great deterioration of public house property. We know as a fact that numbers of houses which used to do roaring businesses are now on the verge of ruin; and we know also that their masters attribute this state of things to the influence of The Salvation Army, and they should be the best judges.[1,2]

> Lord, you have indeed "taken up our case", whether we are destitute, drunk, or otherwise in need of your gracious touch. We're all seeking the same Saviour.
> Amen.

---

1 The Salvation Army was deeply unpopular with public house landlords and breweries. Their loss of income when drunkards were converted was significant, often resulting in organized violent opposition.
2 From *The Salvation Army in Relation to the Church and State*.

You came to visit me

(Matthew 25:36 *NIV*)

You will not be surprised… to hear me say that I esteem this work of house-to-house visitation next in importance to the preaching of the gospel itself. Who can tell the amount of influence and power which might be brought to bear on the careless, godless inhabitants of our large towns and cities – nay, on our whole nation if all real Christians would only do a little of this kind of work! The masses of the people look upon Christians as a separate and secluded class, with whom they have no concern and possess nothing in common. They watch them go past their houses to their various places of worship with utter indifference or bitter contempt; and, alas! Has there not been too much in our past conduct calculated to beget this kind of feeling, much of Pharisaic pride and selfish unconcern? If the zeal of the Lord's house had eaten us up,[1] if we had realized more fellowship with Christ in his sufferings,[2] if we had understood the meaning of his words, "compel them to come in",[3] if we had been baptized with Paul's spirit, when he could almost have wished himself accursed from Christ for his brethren's sakes,[4] should we not have gone out amongst the people as our Master did, by the roadside and into their houses, to have spoken to them the "words of this life", to have persuaded, implored, and compelled them to come in? Alas, we are verily guilty! Nor has it been in many instances for want of light, or for want of the leadings of the Holy Spirit; but it has been for want of obedience, and because of our pride, or shame, or fear. O that, with all who read this, the time past might suffice to have walked after the flesh in this matter! Oh that from this hour you… would set yourself individually to this work; you can do it.[5]

Lord Jesus, you were well known for popping in to people's houses,
gracing their homes with your presence and your counsel.
Grant me that same spirit that I too may visit well. Amen.

---

1   Psalm 69:9, KJV.
2   Philippians 3:10, KJV.
3   Luke 14:23, KJV.
4   Romans 9:3, KJV.
5   From *Aggressive Christianity*.

I AM SLOW OF SPEECH AND TONGUE
(Exodus 4:10 *NIV*)

However weak, timid, or "slow of speech", he says, "I will be with thy mouth, and teach thee what thou shalt say"[1] and "it shall be given you in that same hour what ye shall speak".[2] All that is needful is for you to give yourself up to the leadings of the Spirit. Lean on him for all you want (lack). He will inspire you with the constraining love, the melting sympathy, the holy zeal, and the mighty faith alone necessary for the task... There are teeming thousands who never cross the threshold of church, chapel, or mission hall, to whom all connected with religion is as an old song, a byword, and a reproach. They need to be brought into contact with a living Christ in the characters and persons of his people. They want to see and handle the Word of Life in a living form. Christianity must come to them embodied in men and women who are not ashamed to eat "with publicans and sinners";[3] they must see it looking through their eyes, and speaking in loving accents through their tongues, sympathizing with their sorrows, bearing their burdens, reproving their sins, instructing their ignorance, inspiring their hope, and wooing them to the fountain opened for sin and uncleanness. Dear reader, here is a sphere for you! You have long wished to do something for your "blessed, blessed Master". Here is work, boundless in extent, and momentous beyond an angel's power to conceive. For it, you need no human ordination, no long and tedious preparation, no high-flown language, no towering eloquence; all you want is the full baptism of the Spirit on your heart, the Bible in your hand, and humility and simplicity in your manner. Thus equipped, you will be mighty through God to the pulling down of strongholds.[4] You will find your way to many a heart long since abandoned by hope and given up to despair; and in the great day of account you shall have many a sheaf as the result of your labour, and the reward of your self-denial.[5, 6]

> Lord, it is a wonderful thing that you use the trembling and the timid in your great work. We are but channels only, but what channels in your hands!

---

1   Exodus 4:12, KJV.
2   Matthew 10:19, KJV.
3   Matthew 9:11, KJV.
4   See 2 Corinthians 10:4, KJV.
5   See Psalm 126:6.
6   From *Aggressive Christianity*.

ENABLE YOUR SERVANTS TO SPEAK YOUR WORD WITH GREAT BOLDNESS
(Acts 4:29 *NIV*)

For ten years of my Christian life, my life was one daily battle with the cross – not because I wilfully rejected, as many do, for that I never dared to do. Oh no! I used to make up my mind I would, and resolve and intend, and then, when the hour came, I used to fail for want of courage. I need not have failed. I now see how foolish I was, and wrong...

God forced me to begin to think and work. I was obliged, and I did it with four little children, the eldest then four years and three months old.[1] It looked an inopportune time, did it not, to begin to preach? It looked as though the Lord must have made a mistake. However, he gave me grace and strength, and enabled me to do it; and while I was nursing my baby, many a time I was thinking of what I was going to say next Sunday, and between times noted down with a pencil the thoughts as they struck me. And then I would appear sometimes, with an outline scratched in pencil, trusting in the Lord to give me the power of his Holy Spirit; and I think I can say that from that day he has never allowed me to open my mouth without giving me signs of his presence and blessing. Don't you see that while the Devil kept me silent, he kept me comparatively fruitless; now I have ground to hope and expect to meet hundreds in glory, whom God has made me instrumental in saving. The Lord dealt very tenderly with me; giving me great encouragement, but some things were dreadful to me at first. I would not go into pulpits until the people demanded it. And the first time I saw my name on a wall! I shall never forget the sensation. Then my dear husband said, "When you gave yourself to the Lord, did you not give him your name?"[2]

> For those reluctant to preach, Lord, and for those easily intimidated,
> I pray that you would bestow this sort of courage and enabling.
> By the same token, surround them with encouragers. Thank you, Lord. Amen.

---

1   Bramwell Booth was born on 8 March 1856.
2   From *Catherine Booth* by W. T. Stead.

From childhood you have been acquainted with the sacred writings

(2 Timothy 3:15 *ESV*)

I used to take my eldest boy on my knee from the time he was about two years old, and tell him the stories of the Old Testament in baby language, and adapted to baby comprehension, one at a time, so that he thoroughly drank them in, and also the moral lessons they were calculated to convey. When between three and four years old, I remember once going into the nursery, and finding him mounted on his rocking horse, in a high state of excitement, finishing the story of Joseph to his nurse and baby brother, showing them how Joseph galloped on his live "gee-gee", when he went to fetch his father to show him to Pharaoh.[1] In the same way we subsequently went through the history of the Flood, having a Noah's ark which was kept for Sabbath use; making the ark itself the foundation for one lesson, Noah and his family of another, and the gathering of the animals of a third, and so on until the subject was exhausted.[2] When my family increased, it was my custom before these Sabbath lessons to have a short lively tune [and] a short prayer, in which I let them all repeat before me, sentence by sentence, asking the Lord to help us to understand his word and bless our souls, and so on. After the lesson another short prayer, and then another tune or two. After this they would adjourn to the nursery, where frequently they would go through the whole service again, the eldest being the preacher. When baby was asleep, their nurse[3] would read interesting infantile stories to the elder ones, or teach them suitable bits of poetry by letting them all repeat it together after her. Thus the Sabbath was made a day of pleasure as well of instruction and improvement. I never allowed my children to attend public services till they were old enough to take some interest in them.[4]

Lord Jesus, you came to us as a child, full of fun and energy. Impart afresh that sense of wonderment and innocence, especially when life leaves us jaded. Amen.

---

1   See Genesis 47.
2   See Genesis 6–8.
3   Women such as Catherine Booth established communities of volunteer nurses to visit impoverished communities; coming daily to clean houses, bring in clean washing, cook meals, and wash children. These nurses also dispensed advice on religion and housekeeping. The Booths retained their own children's nurse.
4   From *Practical Religion*.

I SAW SOME NAIVE YOUNG MEN,
AND ONE IN PARTICULAR WHO LACKED COMMON SENSE
(Proverbs 7:7 *NLT*)

I could not tell you what I have felt when visiting some of our large provincial towns – manufacturing towns such as Leicester or Nottingham. I am often received by friends living at a distance from the halls used for our services on Sunday, so that on my way to them I have to pass through many streets. This gives me an opportunity of observing the character of the population I meet; and in these towns on a summer's evening I have met thousands of the youth of both sexes, ranging, say, from fourteen to twenty years of age, rushing away to seek their Sunday evening's enjoyment in the fields or wherever they listed, screaming at the top of their voices, pushing one another off and on the pavement, frequently using most offensive, if not positively blasphemous and obscene language.

In our large gatherings I have also taken particular notice of the youths and of the girls, and what strikes me as the most appalling feature of all is the utter recklessness they manifest with regard to any kind of authority or of superior influence. It is quite a common thing for these boys and girls to say to our officers, when they speak to them about their duty towards their parents, or their duty towards their God, "What do I care!" and to laugh in their faces, saying, "I don't believe in your God." Tens of thousands of our youth are in this condition. There seems to be nothing back in their minds on which to rest any appeal, on which to put the lever by which you are to civilize, refine and exalt them… In bygone generations *this was not the case.* You may call it superstition; but that is preferable to no recognition of any authority beyond and above the individuals themselves and their own wild and lawless passions. There was something back in the mind which ministers and philanthropists and teachers could appeal to, and get some sort of response; but now we seem to have to create this.[1]

Father, for those who devote their time to coming alongside young people,
I pray your blessing and help; youth club leaders, teachers and youth pastors.
Amen.

---

1   From *The Salvation Army in Relation to the Church and State.*

THOUGH THE FIG-TREE SHOULD NOT BLOSSOM, AND THERE BE
NO FRUIT ON THE VINES, THOUGH THE YIELD OF THE OLIVE SHOULD FAIL
AND THE FIELDS PRODUCE NO FOOD... YET I WILL EXULT IN THE LORD,
I WILL REJOICE IN THE GOD OF MY SALVATION

(Habakkuk 3:17–18 *NASB*)

It must be manifest, I think, in every spiritual and thoughtful Christian that there is a great want somewhere in connection with the preaching of the gospel, and the instrumentalities of the Church at large. That there are many blessed exceptions I joyfully and gladly admit. No one hails them with greater gladness than I do. That there are blessed green spots here and there in the wilderness is quite true, and when these are gathered together and descanted on in articles, they look very nice, and we are apt to take the flattering unction to our souls that things are not so bad after all; but, when we come to travel the country over and find how few and far between those green spots are, and hear what a tide of lamentation and mourning reaches us all round the land as to the deadness, coldness, and dearth of Christian churches, we cannot help feeling that there is a great want somewhere! This is not only my opinion, but it is almost universally admitted, that with the enormous expenditure of means, the great amount of human effort, the multiplication of instrumentalities during the past century, there has not been a *corresponding result*.

People say to me, on every band, "We have meetings without number, services, societies, conventions, conferences, but what becomes of them all, *comparatively*?" And I may just say here that numbers of ministers and clergymen, in private conversation, admit the same thing. In fact, none are more ready to admit this comparative lack of results than many dear spiritual ministers. They say, when talking with us behind the scenes – "Yes, it is a sad fact. I think I preach the truth. I pray about it. I am anxious for results, but alas! Alas! The conversions are but few and far between." And then, not only are those conversions few, but in the mass of instances superficial.[1]

> Lord, for those times when we are discouraged, when our best efforts seem
> to achieve little or nothing, encourage us. Keep our heads up. Amen.

---

1   From *The Holy Ghost*.

GROW IN THE GRACE AND KNOWLEDGE OF OUR LORD

(2 Peter 3:18 *NIV*)

If those who have carefully read the word of God will think for a moment, they will remember having found two distinct classes of passages depicting, or bearing on, different stages of Christian experience. One class, referring more particularly to an important initiatory or backslidden stage of experience; the other class, and far the most numerous, referring to a rejoicing, triumphing, progressive experience, giving to its possessors' victory over the world, the flesh and the Devil, and fitting them for the inheritance of the saints in light.

With respect to those texts which recognize or depict the lower grade of experience, I want to remark that they are exceedingly few in number, and either in themselves or by their immediate context show that they are by no means taken as denoting a state either safe for the believer or satisfactory to God. Persons in this state of soul are spoken of as "partially carnal" – as "babes in Christ". As "foolish, having begun in the spirit expecting to be made perfect by the flesh"... As "having left their first love". As being "lukewarm".[1] Such terms can only be applied, either to those who are in the first stages of Christian life, or to those who have lost much of what they once possessed. They doubtless apply in many instances to those who have been converted, but who through want of light or of obedience to the light they had are only partially sanctified, and who are conscious of themselves in certain dispositions, purposes, motives and feelings [that] spring up within them which they know to be incompatible with the law and will of God, and with the mind of Christ. In many cases such souls deplore and bewail those roots of bitterness, for in spite of all sophistical reasonings in the world, an enlightened soul can never feel contented or happy or satisfied while conscious of anything contrary to the will of God.[2]

Father God, as we grow in our spiritual experience, grant us grace throughout.
Let nothing turn us back from the Calvary track. Amen.

1   1 Corinthians 3:1; Galatians 3:3; Revelation 2:4; Revelation 3:16 (all scriptures KJV).
2   From *Holiness*.

MARCH 10TH

A GREAT ROAD WILL GO THROUGH THAT ONCE DESERTED LAND.
IT WILL BE NAMED THE HIGHWAY OF HOLINESS

(Isaiah 35:8 *NLT*)

I often thank God that people's religious instincts are too strong for their beliefs, and batter to pieces their false creeds. People demonstrate this in their letters from all parts of the kingdom. They talk of it to us when we converse with them. They come to us poor Salvation Army people, and I take it as a great compliment – no, I take it as a grand proof that we are on the right track, that these hungering, thirsting souls, including ministers and leading friends in churches, after coming to our meetings or reading our books, say, "You have something that we have not." They don't mind about stooping to enquire of such lowly people. They say, "I want to get into this secret. If there is anything I can learn I am willing to sit at the feet of any sweep or tinker in order to learn it." These souls are longing after deliverance and, in spite of what false theologies or creeds teach them, their intuitions tell them that it must be the will of God that they should be delivered from that which is hateful to God, and that they should be wholly conformed to his will, therefore they go searching after the light and, thank God, many find and rejoice in it.

Others try to find rest on the lower level of experience by continually dwelling on those portions of the word of God which depict or recognize it; but I would have you note that there is scarcely a single text in which the experience of a partial sanctification is recognized with which there is not coupled injunctions, commands or exhortations to go on further to realize the fullness of the blessing of the gospel of Christ, such as, "leaving the first principles... let us go on to perfection."[1] "When for the time ye ought to be teachers, ye have need that one teach you again which be the first principles of the oracles of God."[2] Again, "Following after holiness, without which no man shall see the Lord", and "following on to know the Lord."[3, 4]

Holy God, help me to understand and embrace holiness. Amen.

---

1   See Hebrews 6:1, KJV.
2   Hebrews 5:12, KJV.
3   See Hebrews 12:14, KJV.
4   From *Holiness*.

Turn away from all your offences
(Ezekiel 18:30 *NIV*)

Be honest. That is what God wants – that you be honest. "Oh," says he, "why cover ye my altar with tears, and bring your vain oblations? Just be honest, and I will be honest with you and bless you; but while you come before me and weep and profess, and bring the halt, and the maimed, and the blind, a curse be upon you." He looks at you afar off. Be honest. Repentance is not mere sorrow for sin. You may be ever so sorry, and all the way down to death be hugging on to some forbidden possession, as was the young ruler. That is not repentance. Neither is repentance a promise that you will forsake sin in the future. Oh! If it were, there would be many penitents… There is scarcely a poor drunkard that does not promise, in his own mind, or to his poor wife, or somebody, that he will forsake his cups. There is scarcely any kind of a sinner that does not continually promise that he will give up his sin, and serve God, but he does not do it.

Then what is repentance? Repentance is simply renouncing sin – turning round from darkness to light – from the power of Satan unto God.[1] This is giving up sin in your heart, in purpose, in intention, in desire, resolving that you will give up every evil thing, and do it now. Of course, this involves sorrow, for how will any sane man turn himself round from a given course into another, if he does not repent having taken that course? It implies, also, hatred of sin. He hates the course he formerly took, and turns round from it. He is like the prodigal, when he sat in the swine-yard amongst the husks and the filth, he fully resolved, and at last he acts. He went, and that was the test of his penitence! He might have sat resolving and promising till now, if he had lived as long, and he would never have got the father's kiss, the father's welcome, if he had not started; but he went.[2, 3]

> Father, show me those things that need to be discarded –
> in thought, word, or deed – then grant me strength to discard them.
> Help me to choose and cherish all things good. Amen.

---

1 Acts 26:18.
2 Luke 15.
3 From *Godliness*.

GOD IS ABLE TO DO WHATEVER HE PROMISES
(Romans 4:21 *NLT*)

People say, "I have not the power to repent." Oh! Yes, you have. That is a grand mistake. You have the power, or God would not command it. You can repent. You can this moment lift up your eyes to Heaven, and say, with the prodigal, "Father, I have sinned, and I renounce my sin."[1] You may not be able to weep – God nowhere requires or commands that; but you are able, this very moment, to renounce sin, in purpose, in resolution, in intention. Mind, don't confound the renouncing of the sin, with the power of saving yourself from it. If you renounce it, Jesus will come and save you from it. Like the man with the withered hand – Jesus intended to heal that man. Where was the power to come from to heal him? From Jesus, of course. The benevolence, the love, that prompted that healing, all came from Jesus; but Jesus wanted a condition. What was it? The response of the man's will; and so he said, "Stretch forth thy hand."[2] If he had been like some of you, he would have said, "What an unreasonable command! You know I cannot do it – I cannot." Some of you say that; but I say you can, and you will have to do it, or you will be lost. What did Jesus want? He wanted that "I will, Lord," inside the man – the response of his will. He wanted him to say, "Yes, Lord" and, the moment he said that, Jesus supplied strength, and he stretched it forth, and you know what happened.

Don't look forward, and say, "I shall not have strength"; that is not your matter – that is his. He will hold you up; he is able, when you once commit yourself to him.

Now then, say, "I will." Never mind what you suffer – it shall be done. He will pour in the oil and balm. His glorious, blessed presence will do more for you in one hour, than all your struggling, praying, and wrestling have done all these weary years.[3]

> Thank you, Lord, for a love that will not let me go. Thank you for your enabling power, overriding my willpower. Thank you for the speed of your grace. Amen.

1   Luke 15.
2   Luke 6:10, KJV.
3   From *Godliness*.

SEEK THE KINGDOM OF GOD ABOVE ALL ELSE

(Matthew 6:33 *NLT*)

We are constantly meeting with persons in perplexity as to how far they may participate in worldly amusements without compromising their Christian profession… attending or assisting at concerts, penny readings, and gatherings of a similar though more private and social character… Is it *lawful* and secondly, is it *expedient* for Christians either to provide or attend such entertainments as penny readings,[1] concerts, private theatricals, and the like?… What saith the Scriptures? "For thou art an holy people unto the LORD thy God; the LORD thy God hath chosen thee to be a special people unto himself, above all the people that are upon the face of the earth." "And ye shall be holy unto me: for I the LORD am holy, and have severed you from other people, that ye should be mine." "Be not conformed to this world; but be ye transformed by the renewing of your mind, that ye may prove what is that good, and acceptable, and perfect, will of God." "If ye were of the world, the world would love his own: but because ye are not of the world… therefore the world hateth you." "For all that is in the world… the lust of the eyes, and the pride of life, is not of the Father, but is of the world." "Wherefore come out from among them, and be ye separate, saith the Lord, and touch not the unclean thing; and I will receive you. And will be a Father unto you, and ye shall be my sons and daughters, saith the Lord Almighty." "Whosoever therefore will be the friend of the world is the enemy of God."[2] We presume that all Christians attach some meaning to such passages as these; but one says they do not apply to this worldly custom, and another says they do not apply to that, until, as in the case of the Mahometan pig, the whole is swallowed away.[3, 4]

> What a complex subject this is, Lord! One person's charity
> raffle ticket is another person's sin! Help me not to judge, but to
> quietly decide what is right for me in my own walk with you. Amen.

---

1   Musical entertainments for which the price of admission was one penny.
2   Deuteronomy 7:6; Leviticus 20:26; Romans 12:2; John 15:19; 1 John 2:16; 2 Corinthians 6:17–18; James 4:4 (all KJV).
3   Probably a reference to a satirical poem – "Mohametan Pig" – written in 1792. It discusses which parts of a pig may be eaten, the moral of the story being that if several different people agree to eat several different parts, then eventually the entire animal will be consumed, though no one is held responsible for actually eating a pig.
4   From *Godliness*.

THE HEARTS OF THE PEOPLE ARE FICKLE
(Hosea 10:2 *NLT*)

We might cite the testimony of Scripture, and quote numbers of passages which directly or indirectly assert that the heart of man is deceitful above all things, and desperately wicked.[1] We might also refer to the history of our race – a history written in blood and watered by tears; but we prefer to come to experience. What does your own heart say? Ah, there is the difficulty. You readily admit that a portion of the race is depraved; and if the Saviour had confined his declaration to the openly wicked and profane, you would admit its necessity. But when he declares that everyone must be born again or he cannot enter his Kingdom,[2] you perceive this declaration includes you, and those whom you love; and your heart says, I was never a drunkard, or immoral, or profane; I never wronged anybody. I have always led a good, respectable, moral life, therefore I don't see why I should be classed with reprobates of creation, and be required to go through a change which may be very necessary for them.

My friends, it was to one of your class exactly that our Saviour declared this necessity. Nicodemus was respectable, and moral, and withal a religious man in his way, a master in Israel; and yet Jesus assures him over and over again that neither he nor anyone can enter his Kingdom without this new birth. You see this change is to take place in *the heart*, not merely in the life; and your heart is as bad as anybody else's!... The restraints of Providence, such as kind friends, education, Christian influence, and other causes, have modified your outward life – not because your heart is any better. But for those restraints you would have been as wicked as many around you.[3]

> Lord, we do not always like to admit our need of heart surgery, yet we know
> that every move you make is founded upon love. Help us to be willing patients;
> accepting your diagnosis and allowing you to impart your healing grace. Amen.

---

1 Jeremiah 17:9, KJV.
2 John 3:7.
3 From *Life and Death*.

RETURN TO ME WITH ALL YOUR HEART
(Joel 2:12 *NIV*)

Though you are not outwardly wicked, have you not sufficient evidence of the sinfulness of your heart in other directions? For instance: you are conscious that you have no true religion. You don't even profess to have. You practise none of the duties or exercises of religion. You have never truly repented of and forsaken sin. You don't even truly pray and habitually read God's word. You are not even striving to love God with all your heart, and your neighbour as yourself.[1] No; you live in indifference towards God, and in the rejection of both his law and gospel. What further proof can you require of the depravity of your heart than this? But, further, you know not only that you have no true religion, but also that there is much in your heart that is opposed to God. You entertain hard and dishonouring thoughts of God. Your heart often rebels against his government, in order to meet your own evil propensities; and your rebellious will often sets itself in open defiance of his purposes. You know that God commands you to repent… and to forsake sin – asks for your heart and your love – and requires you to form your plans and purposes with respect to his will and glory. But you systematically ignore both, and form them with reference to your own ease, pleasure, gain, or ambition. With all your boasted morality, you have thought, and felt, and desired, and done many things for which your own heart has condemned you, and which you would not confess… I ask you why you have thus thought and acted contrary to the dictates of your conscience. Because your heart is depraved, alienated from God, and committed to self and Satan. Therefore, you see how this heart-depravity unfits you for the Kingdom of God. The true service of God is obedience prompted by love. "If ye love me, keep my commandments."[2] "Why call ye me, Lord, Lord, and do not the things [that] I say?"[3, 4]

This day, Lord, I pray for anyone known to me who is resistant to your pleading
voice; that your relentless love would melt that resistance. Amen.

1   Mark 12:30–31.
2   John 14:15, KJV.
3   Luke 6:46, KJV.
4   From *Life and Death*.

SEEK THE PEACE AND PROSPERITY OF THE CITY
(Jeremiah 29:7 *NIV*)

The work of The Salvation Army tends to benefit the State, because we teach the universal brotherhood of man. Peace and goodwill to all men, even to enemies, is a fundamental with us; and we utterly repudiate the possibility of being right with God while doing wrong to man! Consequently, we have numberless instances of long-standing quarrels and animosities being healed, and the parties brought reconciliation and amity. Quite a number of husbands who had forsaken their wives and families have gone back to them, clothed and in their right minds, and are now filling good situations, their families living in peace and comfort. Further, everyone who has been rescued from ignorance and debauchery is made to feel his or her responsibility for those whom he [or she] has left still in the sinks of iniquity. The precepts of Jesus Christ as to all men being our brethren, irrespective of their condition, are resuscitated and clothed in living acts before the eyes of our soldiers every day of their lives; they are taught that all personal considerations, such as ease, comfort, gain, reputation, and associates, are to be made subservient, or, if need be, relinquished, for the salvation of their fellow men! I could give you numbers of illustrations as to how this teaching is taking effect. We have many officers who have given up lucrative situations with pensions or other future advantages attached; others who have relinquished flourishing little businesses with tempting prospects; some amongst our women who have given up comparatively luxuriant homes, others who have refused offers of marriage involving good prospects and a life of comparative ease, in order to devote themselves body and soul to this work of rescuing the ignorant and the lost! Perhaps the most significant illustration, however, is the fact that we have hundreds of mothers all over the land with no ambition than to train their children so that they shall be saviours of men; many of these mothers, themselves have only been picked out of sinks of iniquity a few months, or two, three, or four years ago.[1]

Lord, today I pray for those who work hard to improve communities and to have a positive impact in their neighbourhood. God bless altruism!

---

1   From *The Salvation Army in Relation to the Church and State.*

March 17th

I will remember the deeds of the Lord
(Psalm 77:11 *NIV*)

I had such a view of his love and faithfulness on the journey from Wellingborough[1] that I thought I would never doubt again about anything. I had… such a precious season with the Lord that the time seemed to fly. As the lightning gleamed around I felt ready to shout: "The chariot of Israel, and the horsemen thereof."[2] Oh, how precious it is when we see, as well as believe; but yet more blessed to *believe* and *not see*. Lord, work this determined, obstinate, blind, unquestioning, unanswering faith in me… As I looked at the waving fields, the grazing sheep, and flashing sky, a voice said in my soul: "Of what oughtest thou to be afraid; am I not *God*? Cannot I supply thy little, tiny needs?" My heart replied: "It is enough, Lord, I will trust thee; forgive my unbelief."[3]

That promise was one given me in a great crisis of my life, when I was passing through one of those occasions when it seemed as if I were going to leave all and lose all. It looked at the time too great to be true. I did not even understand it. The Lord said to me, with one of those inner voices which some of you know and recognize as his voice, "I will make thee a mother of nations." I put it away. I did not understand it. I said it was too good and great to be true; but, behold! It is accomplished, and he has proved his faithfulness even to one who has been so comparatively unworthy, and unfaithful in many respects, but who always, by his grace, has kept his Kingdom and his interests first.[4, 5]

Teach me, Lord, to record your deeds of goodness towards me; this will
support me and bolster my faith when times are tough. Help me to remember
in the dark that which you have taught me in the light. Amen.

1   Northamptonshire, England.
2   2 Kings 2:12, KJV.
3   See Mark 9:24.
4   Catherine Booth was in the habit of keeping a journal when she travelled, or when she felt God speaking to her at various times. She was an advocate of Christians developing the skill or recognizing the voice of God "speaking from the invisible".
5   Quoted in *Catherine Booth* by W. T. Stead.

GIVE US AID AGAINST THE ENEMY
(Psalm 60:11 *NIV*)

I have only a minute or two; but, lest you should think I don't sympathize with you, I send a line. You ask, did I ever feel so? Yes, I think just as bad as any mortal *could* feel – *empty*, inside and out, as though I had nothing human or divine to aid me, as if all Hell were let loose upon me. But I have generally felt *the worst before the best results*, which proves it was Satanic opposition. And it has been the same with many of God's most honoured instruments. I believe nearly all who are truly called of God to special usefulness pass through this buffeting.

It stands to sense, if there is a Devil, that he should desperately withstand those whom he sees are going to be used of God. Supposing *you* were the Devil, and had set your heart on circumventing God, how would you do it but by opposing those who were bent on building up his Kingdom? He hopes to drive you from the field by blood and fire and vapour of smoke. But our Captain fought and won the battle for us, and we have only to hold on long enough, and victory is sure. "Courage!" your Captain cries. "Only be thou strong, and of good courage, and I will be with thee, and teach thee what to say."[1] "He hath chosen the weak things."[2] He has not *made shift with them* – taken them because there were no others. No! He hath *chosen* them. Will he ever forsake them, and thus make himself a laughing stock for Hell? Never! Will he ever let the Devil say, "Ah, ah! He chose this weak one, and then let him fail"? No, no, no![3]

Come to my aid, Lord, when the battle between good and evil is hard.
I pray for those who feel attacked and discouraged.
Grant them fresh strength and victory. Amen.

1   From Joshua 1:9, KJV.
2   See 1 Corinthians 1:27, KJV.
3   From *Catherine Booth: A Sketch*.

Loud beat the horses' hoofs with the galloping
(Judges 5:22 ESV)

I have not been out today, in consequence of feeling stiff and poorly from the effects of an accident which befell me on Friday. And when I have described it I am sure you will join me in praising God that I am no worse. William has wanted me and the children to go to Sheriff Hill[1] ever since the special services there commenced, but we put it off to the last. On Friday, however, we all went to the concluding services. Mr Scott brought a very nice conveyance and his own pony to fetch us. We went in safety and comfort, enjoyed the meeting, and were coming home at about half-past six. Through a little oversight, however, it was found we could not have the same conveyance for return, but only a gig belonging to one of our friends. So, fortunately, I sent the nurse home on foot with the baby,[2] a young woman accompanying her. William delayed going into the meeting to pack us off all right. Young Scott was driving, Willie[3] sat in the middle, and I with Ballington[4] on my knee, all muffled and cloaked, next to him. The moment we were all in I felt we were too light on the horse's back, but did not say anything for fear of being thought ridiculous. We had not gone many yards, however, before I was sure we were not safe, and I said to Mr Scott, "Oh, dear! I feel as though we were slipping backwards!" I had hardly got the words out of my mouth when the pony, frightened by the rising of the shafts, set off, and we were all thrown out behind. I fell flat on the back of my head with Ballington on top of me... William and all Mr Scott's family still stood watching us when it happened, and of course flew to our assistance... I was greatly shaken and nearly all the sense knocked out of me, but I trust no harm was done. I feel better this evening. Is it not a mercy that I am able to write to you?[5, 6]

Lord, guide our journeys, and those of our loved ones. Bless those who travel today, near or far, especially in dangerous places. Amen.

1   A suburb of Gateshead, England, where the Booths worked with the Methodist Connexion.
2   Katie (born September 1858).
3   William Bramwell (born March 1856).
4   Born July 1857.
5   From *Catherine Booth* by Catherine Bramwell-Booth.
6   From a letter Catherine Booth wrote to her parents in 1858.

NOW IS THE TIME OF GOD'S FAVOUR, NOW IS THE DAY OF SALVATION
(2 Corinthians 6:2 *NIV*)

When men are seen to be wrong, it must be very desirable to get them right. And what is conversion but a process by which those who are wrong are put right? As for the method by which it takes place, or the length of time it occupies, I have always been puzzled to understand why persons who believe in conversion at all should object either to the employment of any reasonable means, or to the speed with which they operate. Here is a man who has developed a fixed habit of evil-doing, of falsehood, impurity, drunkenness, or some other sin. The great end in view is to persuade him to abandon his evil course, and surely the sooner you can persuade him to do so the better... Supposing a friend is about to adopt some mistaken course, you ply him with the best arguments you can command, and the more quickly these take effect the better you are pleased. You praise his candour and say, "This man is not only open to conviction, but acts spontaneously upon the light he has received." You do not think any the worse of him, because of the readiness with which he has accepted the truth. Nor do you for a moment imagine that he must go through a long preparatory process, before he can act upon his convictions. Why then in the religious world should the exactly similar phenomenon be doubted, simply on account of its suddenness? Surely it should be even less a subject of surprise, when we remember that the special operation of the Spirit of God is to convict of sin[1] and to present the most momentous motives and sentiments that can be laid before the human mind, in favour of its abandonment. The idea is, I know, that owing to its suddenness the change will not be permanent. But this is a mistake. The permanence of a conversion is not determined by the gradual process which produces it, or by the speed with which it is accomplished, but by its reality.[2, 3]

Father, you are perfectly capable of granting the grace of instant conversion –
thank you. Be with those who receive such a lovely blessing; guide them,
guard them. Surround them with good mentors. Amen.

---

1   John 16:8.
2   From *The Short Life of Catherine Booth The Mother of The Salvation Army*.
3   Catherine Booth reflecting on criticism of "sudden conversions". Critics of the Booth's ministry were concerned that such conversion experiences were merely transient.

AS FOR ME AND MY HOUSEHOLD, WE WILL SERVE THE LORD
(Joshua 24:15 *NIV*)

I heard from William this morning. They had a triumphant day on Sunday; the chapel packed, and upwards of forty cases at night, some of them very remarkable ones. He will finish up at Hull on Thursday, and come here on Friday for a week's rest previous to commencing the services at Sheffield. I anticipate his coming much.

It is such a splendid country. As I rambled out in the green lanes this morning, hemmed in on every side by fields of golden corn, in which the reapers are busy in all directions, and surrounded by the most lovely scenery of hill and dale, wood and garden, I did wish you, my dear mother, could come and spend a fortnight with me. As for Hull, I would much prefer Brixton, and our *bit of garden*, to the great majority of its homes. It is like being in fairyland here, after being there, though I had every kindness and attention heart could desire. But you know how precious fresh air is to me at all times, or I would not be a voluntary exile from my beloved husband, even for a week. Bless him! He continues all I desire.

I am glad you changed the boots. Fudge about paying me! I should think you wore an extra pair out in running up and down stairs after me, when I located my troublesome self at Brixton last. Whether or not, it is all right.

We are to have apartments at Sheffield. You cannot think with what joy I anticipate being to ourselves once more. It will seem like being at home, sweet home. For though I get literally oppressed with kindness, I must say I would prefer home, where we could sit down together at our own little table, myself the mistress and my husband the only guest.[1,2,3]

> Father, thank you for the gifts of home and family.
> May I never take these for granted. Amen.

---

1   William Booth enjoyed great success as an itinerant evangelist in Yorkshire, England. The Methodist Annual Conference had appointed him to this special role.
2   From a letter Catherine wrote to her mother in 1855, shortly before the Booths married. Catherine was unwell, and stayed in Caistor, Lincolnshire, England, to rest.
3   From *Catherine Booth The Mother of The Salvation Army, Vol. I.*

IT IS GOOD NOT TO EAT MEAT OR DRINK WINE OR
DO ANYTHING THAT CAUSES YOUR BROTHER TO STUMBLE

(Romans 14:21 *ESV*)

Our Lord taught his disciples to pray to be kept out of temptation; and again and again we are warned and enjoined to keep ourselves out, and on this condition all his promises of grace and deliverance are suspended. God has nowhere promised to keep the man who needlessly and for the sake of his own indulgence runs into temptation. How fearful, then, the responsibility of those Christians who tell the reclaimed inebriate, aye, who tell any man, "You may safely tamper with the drink! You may play with this fire of Hell, and trust in God to keep you from being burnt." Alas! How do such counsellors unwittingly play the part of Satan in his cunning approaches to our Lord: "Cast thyself down: for it is written, He shall give his angels charge concerning thee; and in their hands they shall bear thee up, lest at any time thou dash they foot against a stone." Oh, that all our brethren and sisters would ever bear in mind the memorable answer: "Thou shalt not tempt the Lord thy God".[1] But not only is abstinence valuable, nay, indispensable, in order to *preserve those rescued out of the power of this great destroyer, but it is equally valuable to prevent others from falling into it.* We all profess to believe that prevention is better than cure; seeing, then, that strong drink is proved to be the most dangerous foe to perseverance in righteousness, and the most potent cause of declension, inconsistency, and apostasy, ought not Christians to strive, both by example and precept, to warn the young, the weak, and the inexperienced from touching it? Can any man answer for the consequences of putting a bottle to his neighbour's mouth, be it ever such a *small* one, or ever such a *genteel* one? God has recorded his curse against the man who does this, and thousands of hoary-headed parents, broken-hearted wives, and weeping, blighted children groan their Amen to the dreadful sentence![2]

Lord, I pray today for those enslaved by addictions. I pray too for
those agencies reaching out to help. Help me to think carefully about
how my own actions may influence others. Amen.

---

1   Matthew 4:6–7 KJV.
2   From *Catherine Booth The Mother of The Salvation Army, Vol. II.*

THE LORD IS NOT... WANTING ANYONE TO PERISH

(2 Peter 3:9 *NIV*)

Supposing a plague were to break out in London, and suppose that the Board of Health were to meet and appropriate all the hospitals and public buildings they could get to the treatment of those diseased, and suppose they were to issue proclamations to say that whoever would come to these buildings should be treated free of cost, and every care and kindness bestowed on them and, moreover, that the treatment would certainly cure them; but, supposing the people were so blind to their own interests, so indifferent and besotted that they refused to come and, consequently, the plague was increasing and thousands dying, what would you in the provinces say? Would you say, "Well, the Board of Health have done what they could, they deserve to perish; let them alone!"? No, you would say, "It is certainly very foolish and wicked of the people, but these men are in a superior position. They understand the matter. They know and are responsible for the consequences. What in the world are they going to do? Let the whole land be depopulated? No! If the people will not come to them, they must go to the people, and force upon them the means of health, and insist that proper measures should be used for the suppression of the plague..."

Men are preoccupied, and it is for us to go and force it upon their attention. Remember, you can do it. There is some *one soul* that you have more influence with than any other person on earth – some soul, or souls. Are you doing all you can for their salvation? Your relatives, friends, and acquaintances *are* to be rescued. Thank God! We are rescuing the poor people all over the land by thousands. There they are, to be looked at, and talked with, and questioned – people rescued from the depths of sin, degradation, and woe – saved from the worst forms of crime and infamy; and if he [Jesus] can do that, he can save your genteel friends, if only you will go to them desperately and determinedly.[1]

Saving God, I invite you to bring to mind those for whom I can pray today.
Would you inspire me in my witness, and lead me? Amen.

---

1 From *Aggressive Christianity.*

WOE TO YOU WHEN EVERYONE SPEAKS WELL OF YOU

(Luke 6:26 *NIV*)

Opposition! It is a bad sign for the Christianity of this day that it provokes so little opposition. If there was no other evidence of it being wrong, I should know it from that. When the Church and the world can jog along comfortably together, you may be sure there is something wrong. The world has not altered. Its spirit is exactly the same as it ever was, and if Christians were equally faithful and devoted to the Lord, and separated from the world, living so that their lives were a reproof to all ungodliness, the world would hate them as much as it ever did. It is the *Church* that has altered, *not* the world. You say, "We shall be getting into endless turmoil." Yes! "I came not to bring peace on the earth, but a sword."[1] There would be uproar. Yes: and the Acts of the Apostles are full of stories of uproars. One uproar was so great that the Chief Captain had to get Paul over the shoulders of the people, lest he should have been torn in pieces.[2] "What a commotion!" you say. Yes: and, bless God, if we had the like now we should have thousands of sinners saved.

"But," you say, "see what a very undignified position this would bring the gospel into." That depends on what sort of dignity you mean. You say, "We should always be getting into collision with the powers that be, and with the world, and what very unpleasant consequences would result." Yes, dear friends, there always have been unpleasant consequences to the flesh, when people were following God and doing his will. "But," you say, "wouldn't it be inconsistent with the dignity of the gospel?" It depends from which standpoint you look at it. It depends upon what really constitutes the dignity of the gospel. What does constitute the dignity of the gospel? Is it human dignity, or is it divine? Is it earthly, or is it heavenly dignity? It was a very undignified thing, looked at humanly, to die on the cross between two thieves.[3]

Lord Jesus, you were willing to lay down your dignity for my sake; please help
me to do the same for yours. Thank you for your willingness. Amen.

---

1   See Matthew 10:34.
2   Acts 21:35.
3   From *Aggressive Christianity*.

MOSES WROTE

(Deuteronomy 31:22 *NIV*)

12 May 1847: I felt very ill in the train, but could lie down when I felt faint. My mind was kept calm, and while passing through some tunnels I thought, should any accident happen amidst this darkness and hurry me into eternity, shall I find myself in Glory? And I felt I could say, even here, "Lord, if it were thy will to take me, I could come, but how unworthy I am."...

14 May 1847: This morning while reading *Roe's Devout Exercises of the Heart*[1] I was much helped and enabled to give myself afresh into the hands of God, to do and suffer all his will. Oh, that I may be made useful to this family... help me to display the Christian character... I find much need of watchfulness and prayer, and I have this day taken up my cross in reproving sin... Lord, follow with the conviction of thy Spirit all I have said... Oh, to be a Christian indeed and to love thee with all my heart is my desire. I do love thee, but I want to love thee more, I want to enjoy thee more...

15 May 1847: I was much blessed this morning at private prayer particularly in commending my dear parents into the hands of God. I sometimes get into an agony of feeling while praying for my dear father. O my Lord, answer prayers and bring him back to thyself.[2]

16 May 1847: I went to chapel... though I felt very poorly and my cough was very troublesome, which gave rise to wandering thoughts. At night I could not venture to chapel again but spent the time reading to my dear aunt and the person in the house... I hope the Lord will make me useful here. I think the restitution of my health is not the only reason I am here. My dear aunt is in trouble about one of her children who is not a comfort to her.[3, 4]

Lord, thank you for your loving interest in every detail of our lives.
Thank you that our concerns are your concerns too. Help me to remember this.
Amen.

---

1   *Mrs Rowe's* (not Roe's) *Devout Exercises of the Heart* (1738). Catherine Booth was often heavily influenced by books she read, taking notes and incorporating their teachings into her life.
2   Catherine's father had been a devout Methodist, but spent several years out of fellowship with the Lord.
3   Catherine Mumford kept a diary while convalescing. This was part of her personal pursuit of holiness.
4   From *Catherine Booth* by Catherine Bramwell-Booth.

TO THE ANGEL OF THE CHURCH IN EPHESUS WRITE... I KNOW YOUR
DEEDS, YOUR HARD WORK AND YOUR PERSEVERANCE... YET I HOLD THIS
AGAINST YOU: YOU HAVE FORSAKEN THE LOVE YOU HAD AT FIRST

(Revelation 2:1–4 *NIV*)

Is not this message to these Ephesian Christians equally applicable to multitudes in our day, who are serving him with much zeal and patience; but they have left their first love, and are, notwithstanding all their outward professions and labour, backsliders in heart? Some of you start at the use of such a phrase, and you say, "But these Ephesians were not backsliders." Not in the general acceptation of the term, but in the estimation of their Lord they were backsliders in heart. They had partially fallen, partially gone from that wholehearted service which once they rendered him, and without which all outward works, however worthy or zealous, will not suffice. I fear that after this manner the great majority of Christians are backsliders. I have conversed with numbers up and down this land, and many who have occupied prominent positions in Christian churches, who have confessed that they were secret backsliders, having lost much that they once enjoyed, and walking far less carefully than they once did. Taking these as representatives of others in similar circumstances I say, I cannot but fear that a very large majority of professing Christians have, like these Ephesian converts, left their first love. I have no doubt that there are many of this class here this morning, and I desire to speak especially to these... Let me entreat you, my dear friends, to open your hearts to the reception of the truth. Forget the feeble instrumentality through which it comes, and if it commends itself to your consciences as God's truth, let it have its full weight upon your hearts. If you are right, it will do you no harm to examine yourselves. It will establish you and help you "to assure your hearts before him".[1] And if you are not right, who can tell the importance of making the discovery in time, while there is opportunity and grace offered by which you may be made right? I beseech you be honest with yourselves and with God.[2]

Search me, Lord, and know my heart today.

---

1   See 1 John 3:19, KJV.
2   From *Practical Religion*.

DEMAS HAS DESERTED ME BECAUSE HE LOVES THE THINGS OF THIS LIFE
(2 Timothy 4:10 *NLT*)

Some professors seem to regard nothing as worldly which is not absolutely devilish, such as profanity, blasphemy, or obscenity. But the Scriptures carefully and clearly distinguish between the two. They prohibit Christians conforming to the world in all the habits and usages of daily life. They are not to *talk* like the world, in the way of foolish jesting, "swelling words," "insincere speech," &c. But, on the contrary, their conversation is to "be seasoned with salt, meet to administer grace to the hearers".[1] It is to be "pure, proceeding from a good (not a doubtful) conscience".[2] It is to be "in Heaven, from whence we look for the appearing of our Lord Jesus Christ".[3] The Scriptures prohibit Christians *dressing* like the world. "Whose adorning let it not be that outward adorning of plaiting the hair, and of wearing of gold, or of putting on of apparel" (1 Peter iii. 3 [KJV]). "In like manner also, that women adorn themselves in modest apparel, with shamefacedness and sobriety, *not* with braided hair, or gold, or pearls, or costly array; But (which becometh women professing godliness) with good works" (1 Tim. ii. 9–10 [KJV]). "Moreover the LORD saith, Because the daughters of Zion are haughty, and walk with stretched forth necks and wanton eyes, walking and mincing as they go… *Therefore* the LORD will smite with a scab the crown of the head of the daughters of Zion" (Isa. iii. 16–17). We commend this whole chapter to the consideration of all whom it may concern, and we would suggest that as the Lord Jehovah regarded the dress of those Israelitish women as a sign of their backslidden condition, and thought it sufficiently important to be recorded by his holy prophet, it may be well for us to consider how far the same signs are manifest amongst us in our day. The Scriptures prohibit Christians singing the songs of the world, for they expressly enjoin that when they are merry or glad they are to sing psalms and make melody in their heart unto the Lord.[4]

In my life, Lord, be glorified.

1   See Colossians 4:6.
2   See 1 Timothy 1:5.
3   See Philippians 3:20.
4   From *Practical Religion*.

FOR GOD IS NOT A GOD OF DISORDER
(1 Corinthians 14:33 *NIV*)

We must have forms and methods, and the more intelligently planned and the more wisely adapted, the better they will succeed. Haphazard, fitful, unorganized, unreliable action fails everywhere, no matter how good the cause in which it is engaged. You never trust to this kind of action in business. If you want to accomplish anything, you call your heads of departments together, and plan how it is to be done; you set the best man to the best post, and make him responsible for carrying out your arrangements. Well might the Saviour say, "The children of this world are in their generation wiser than the children of light."[1] I wonder how long that will remain true. I wonder when the children of light will rise up and say, "Is this a necessity? Are we born to the heritage of fools? Are we forced to hinder the chariot car of progress? Must we always be in the background? Can we not learn wisdom from the children of this world? And if this glorious gospel is what we all profess to believe… can we not put forth more thought, more effort, and more care to bring it to bear upon men?" Men act on these lines with respect to the affairs of this world. When they want to excavate a tunnel, make a railway, lay a telegraph cable, they don't talk about it for generations in a vague, sentimental way, but lay their plans and set to work to accomplish the thing. If any businessman were to talk and act as many Christians do he would be set down as having a screw loose… You may have known a young man full of vague notions of how he is going to get rich. He is going to make a fortune. He is quite sure he can accomplish it… He has grand notions of how it is to be done. A wise businessman says to him, "That is not the way. You will have to begin at the bottom of the ladder and climb slowly. You will not do it by building castles in your airy brain… You will have to concentrate your mind."[2, 3]

> Take my plans and let them be, touched and polished by your wisdom.
> Take my ideas and develop them as you prefer. Amen.

---

1   Luke 16:8, KJV.
2   From a lecture in response to criticisms that The Salvation Army applied business methods to spiritual matters in terms of its strategy and organization.
3   From *Catherine Booth The Mother of The Salvation Army, Vol. II.*

You are the salt of the earth
(Matthew 5:13 *NIV*)

When in Darlington one of the Fry family[1] took the chair for me at a select meeting at the Livingstone Hotel, and told us that he had been drawn to look at the work in consequence of thirty men having applied to be admitted into their evening school to be taught to read, within a few months, who had been converted in Army meetings. Similar facts have transpired all over the country, in many instances, flourishing night or Saturday afternoon schools have been formed exclusively by our converts. The circulation of our Army organs, *The War Cry* and *Little Soldier*, is now 450,000 per week, besides thousands of copies of other Army publications, showing the great desire for religious reading amongst our people; and it must be borne in mind that The Salvation Army has created this constituency for the most part out of the class whose previous readings consisted in the *Sunday News*, or the Penny Dreadfuls.[2]

A further result of the Army's work bearing upon the State, is the improved temporal condition of large numbers of the people. This is manifested in the *better homes*, which, as soon as possible, they secure for themselves. The General has always said: "Let us *make the man*, and he will soon find himself a home, both temporal and spiritual." And so it has proved, for in some of the large towns and cities, where we have three, four, or six corps, the denizens of whole neighbourhoods have migrated to better ones, furnishing their little homes by degrees; thus putting themselves altogether in better conditions, and commencing, for the first time in their lives, something like family and social life. The money of these people being diverted from the public house and spent in necessary furniture, clothing, and wholesome food, of course brings increase and prosperity to all legitimate trades. This has been so marked in many towns that the little tradesman have quite hailed the formation of a corps in their neighbourhoods; I could give you some amusing illustrations of this, but time forbids.[3]

Lord of the Church, help the church I belong to, to make a
positive impact locally. Guide us in such ways. Amen.

---

1 Possibly Theodore or Francis Fry. Theodore Fry was Liberal Member of Parliament for Darlington, England, and made baronet.
2 Cheap storybooks (comics) aimed at the working classes. They were full of sensational stories and sometimes featured ghosts and ghouls.
3 From *The Salvation Army in Relation to the Church and State*.

Love the Lord your God with all your heart and with all your soul and with all your strength and with all your mind

(Luke 10:27 *NIV*)

One of the worst signs of our times is the little respect which children seem to have for their parents… How has this come to pass? Did these children leap all at once from the restraints and barriers of parental affection and authority? Oh no, it has been the result of the imperceptible growth of years of insubordination and want of proper discipline – the gradual loss of parental influence until they have thrown it off altogether, and resolved to do as they pleased. Hence the terrible exhibitions we have of youthful depravity, lawlessness, and rebellion. Well, I think I hear some mother say: I see, I feel my responsibility, and I long to train my children in the way they should go, but *How am I to do it?*… Let us look at the meaning of the word "Train". It does not mean merely to *teach*. Some parents seem to have the notion that all they have to do in training their children aright is to *teach them*; so they cram them with religious sentiment and truth, making them commit to memory the Catechism, large portions of Scripture, a great many hymns, and so on… which may all be done without a single stroke of real training such as God requires, and such as the hearts of our children need. Nay, this mere teaching, informing the head without interesting or influencing the heart, frequently drives children off from God and goodness, and makes them *hate*, instead of love, everything connected with religion. In the early part of my married life, when my dear husband was travelling very much from place to place, I was frequently thrown into the houses of leading families in churches for three or four weeks at a time, and I used to say to myself, "How is it that these children seem frequently to have a more inveterate dislike for religion and religious things than the children of worldly people who make no profession?" Subsequent observation and experience has shown me the reason. It is because such parents inform the head without training the heart.[1]

> Lord, may my experience of your love and grace easily and frequently
> travel between my head and my heart, so that neither is lacking. Amen.

---

1   From *Practical Religion*.

I GO TO PREPARE A PLACE FOR YOU
(John 14:2 *ESV*)

Another of the joys of the Kingdom is the communion of saints – the very sight of each other makes real saints happier; and interchange of thought, and feeling, and desire fills them with unspeakable joy. They realize that oneness with each other for which the Saviour prayed, "That they all may be one, as we are one."[1] But nothing is more irksome to the unconverted than intercourse with real saints; in fact, they cannot endure it, and always run away from it when possible. Sinners find their happiness here in eating and drinking, reading novels, dress, business, going to concerts, theatres, etc., from which, to say the least, God is shut out. Unconverted people would be wretched without these and kindred occupations and amusements. But the Kingdom of God provides occupations and joys of an entirely different character. Therefore, for the sinner to enter into these he must be born again.

Further, this depravity unfits man for the enjoyment of the Kingdom of God on high. If the joys of Heaven consisted of a continuation of the employments of earth, then sinners would be happy there. But Heaven is a holy place, prepared for holy things, whose employment will be to serve God continually: They "serve him day and night in his temple".[2] Their happiness will consist in their perfect love and complete obedience to his will. The multitude which John saw, who had on white robes – emblematical of the purity of their hearts – had been washed and made white in the blood of the Lamb.[3] Sinner, would you like to appear in such a place, surrounded by those beings, with your unchanged, selfish, worldly heart? Supposing God would let you enter, do you think you would feel at home there? Are you prepared for the enjoyments of Heaven? No; verily, if you were admitted, you would seek the first opportunity to escape. The light of that glorious abode would be more intolerable to you than the darkness of Hell itself. Why? Because your heart would be out of harmony with it all, and you would stand self-revealed before that glorious company.[4]

God of Heaven, fit my heart for my eternal home. Mould me. Amen.

---

1   See John 17:22, KJV.
2   Revelation 7:15, KJV.
3   Revelation 6:11; 7:14.
4   From *Life and Death*.

APRIL 1ST

HE FELL TO THE GROUND AND HEARD A VOICE SAY TO HIM,
"SAUL, SAUL, WHY DO YOU PERSECUTE ME?"

(Acts 9:4 *NIV*)

Despisest thou the riches of his goodness? Will you give up despising him? Will you come to his feet?... Will you say: "It is enough, Lord"?...

Oh, if I were to stand here till tomorrow afternoon, I should occupy the time in telling you of awful cases that have come under my own observation, of people who have despised his goodness. There is a day coming when God says: "I will say, Behold, ye despisers, and wonder and perish."[1] Now is the accepted time...[2]

A man who kept a public house came to a meeting, and was deeply affected. Some of the friends gathered round him, and tried to persuade him to stop to the prayer meeting. He had been convicted many a time before. He knew all about it, and he knew the soul-ruining traffic in which he was engaged. God pulled him up, and arrested him once more – made him think, and feel, and tremble. Friends said, "Stop, and give up your business, and give yourself to God"; but he shook his head and went away. He said, "No, not this time." He despised. He died the next Thursday, raving, and without a ray of hope. He despised the riches of his goodness. I was just getting up to speak in a large theatre, when a Bible-woman at work in the town said: "I want to tell you something. There was a woman hearing you last Sunday who was deeply affected. She wept and trembled, and we tried to persuade her to give her heart to God. She said she couldn't then, but she would come another time. She died on Thursday without hope, and was buried on Friday." She despised his goodness.[3, 4]

Lord, in your mercy, keep me faithful in prayer for those who
procrastinate regarding spiritual matters. Please hear my prayers
and please do not give up on them. Amen.

---

1   See Habakkuk 1:5, KJV.
2   2 Corinthians 6:2, KJV.
3   Extracts from one of Catherine Booth's sermons.
4   From *Catherine Booth* by W. T. Stead.

THROUGH THE YEAR WITH CATHERINE BOOTH   99

The Lord is good to those whose hope is in him
(Lamentations 3:25 *NIV*)

The Devil sets such innocent-looking traps – *spiritual* traps – to catch young people! Ah, he is a serpent still! Beware of his devices, and always cry to God for wisdom and strength of will to put down all foolish tampering. You are born for greater things. God may want you to be a leader in some vast continent, and you will want a companion and a counsellor – a "helpmeet".[1] The original word means "*a help corresponding to his dignity*". This is the meaning given by the best expositors.

Oh, what wisdom there is even in the *words* which God has chosen to express his ideas! "Corresponding to his dignity"! Yes, and no man ever takes one below this mark who does not suffer for it; and, worse still, generations yet unborn have to suffer also. Mind what God says, and keep yourself till that one comes. A wrong step on this point, and you are undone. Oh, the misery of an unsuitable match! It is beyond description. I could tell you tales of woe that are now being enacted… I have seen too much of life, and know too much of human nature, to have much confidence in promises given under such circumstances. For my own part, I made up my mind when I was but sixteen that I would not have a man, though a Christian, who should offer to become even an abstainer for my sake. I felt that such a promise would not afford me ground for confidence afterwards. And do not we see enough all around us to show that unless people adopt things on principle, because they see it to be right, they soon change? Look at the folks who promise to give up tobacco and dress, for the sake of getting into berths; how soon it evaporates! No, my lad, wait a bit. "Couldst thou not watch with me one hour?"[2] Jesus lived a single life for your sake all the way through. Can you not live so till he finds you one after your own heart?[3]

God of love, I pray for those contemplating relationships and marriage;
guide their thoughts. I pray too, for those who are single and
hoping to meet a partner. Bless them. Amen.

---

1 Genesis 2:18, KJV.
2 See Mark 14:37, KJV.
3 From *Catherine Booth: A Sketch*.

Many waters cannot quench love
(Song of Solomon 8:7 *NIV*)

The highest happiness I can wish to my beloved children is that they may realize as thorough a union in heart and mind, and as much blessing in their married life, as the Lord has vouchsafed to us in ours.

If he will do this for them I will be content, so far as they are individually concerned. But I covet for them that, where I have been the mother of hundreds of spiritual children, she may be the mother of thousands, and I covet for my son that, whereas the Lord has blessed his father to the salvation of thousands, he may bless him to tens of thousands! I gave him to God for this when he was born. If you want to know how to get your children saved, and to make the God of Abraham, Isaac, and Jacob the God of your *families*, I can only recommend to you the way which has succeeded with mine.

Yes, I believe I did give my son fully to the Lord, and I covenanted that I would, as far as my light and ability went, to train him for God alone; that I would ignore this world's prizes and praises, and that he should be, as far as I could make him, a man of God...

[God says] "You must put me first, and leave me to choose their earthly destiny. Choose my Kingdom first. Give them wholly and solely to me, and train them for me, and leave me to choose their inheritance and fix the bounds of their habitations."[1]

Lord of love and marriage, today I pray for married couples,
especially those who need some extra help with their relationship. Amen.

1 Part of a speech Catherine Booth gave at the wedding of her son, Bramwell. From *Catherine Booth* by F. de L. Booth-Tucker

Sanctify them through thy truth: thy word is truth
(John 17:17 *KJV*)

Oh! What a great deal of talk we have about the truth, and not any too much. I would not yield to any man or woman in this audience in my love for this Bible. I love this word, and regard it as the standard of all faith and practice, and our guide to live by; but it is not enough of itself. The *great want* is not the truth, for you see facts would contradict this theory. If it were the truth, then there would be no lack at this day, compared with other times, because we never had so much of the truth. There never was so much preaching of the truth, or such a wide dissemination of the word of God, yet, comparatively, where are the results? – further, not only as to *quantity*, but as to *quality* I am discouraged.

Not only are there comparatively few conversions, but a great many of these are of a questionable kind. We should not only ask are people converted, but what are they converted to? What sort of saints are they? Because, I contend, you had far better let a man alone in sin than give him a sham conversion and make him believe he is a Christian when he is nothing of the kind. So you see we must look after the quality as well as the quantity, and I fear we have an awful amount of spurious production, and it behoves us – and I will, for one, if I were to be crucified for it tomorrow – be true to what the Spirit of God has taught me on this point; I will never pander to things as they are for the fear of the persecution which follows trying to put them right. God forbid!… The lack is not the *truth*. There will be thousands of sermons preached today – the truth, and nothing but the truth. Nobody will pretend to say they were not in perfect keeping with the word of God; and yet they will be perfect failures, and nobody will know it better than they who preach them![1, 2]

> Lord Jesus, you are the truth. May my pursuit of biblical truth be also my pursuit of your presence in my life. I pray for preachers of your truth, and for those who hear their sermons; may your word live in us all. Amen.

---

1   Genesis 2:18, KJV.
2   From *The Holy Ghost.*

YOU WILL RECEIVE POWER WHEN THE HOLY SPIRIT COMES ON YOU;
AND YOU WILL BE MY WITNESSES

(Acts 1:8 *NIV*)

I was talking… with a good man, who said: "Ah! Yes, I have not seen a conversion in my church for these two years." Now what was the reason? There *was* a reason, and I am afraid many might say the same. Yet there are the unconverted. They come to be operated upon. Take a church where there is a congregation of, say, 800 or 1,000, suppose with a membership of 200 or 300. What becomes of the 500 or 700 unbelievers, who come and go, Sunday after Sunday, like a door on its hinges, neither better nor worse? – nay, God grant it might be so, but they are worse. They get enough light to light them down to damnation, but they do not get enough power to lift them into salvation. *What* is the matter? There must be something wrong. Will you account for it? It ought to be accounted for! It ought not to be so. God is not changed. Surely he is as anxious for the salvation of men as he ever was. Human hearts are not changed; they are neither better nor worse; they are depraved, vile, devilish – just the same. The gospel is exactly the same power it ever was, rightly experienced, lived, and preached. It is still the power of God unto salvation. Then what is the matter? The truth is preached. The people hear it, and yet they remain as they were. Where is the lack?…

The great want is power… This power is as distinct, and definite, and separate a gift of God as was this book, as was the Son, or any other gift which he has given us! It is distinctly recognized… as a distinct and definite gift accompanying the efforts of those who live on the conditions on which God can give it to them. We cannot explain this gift, but it is the power of the Holy Spirit of God in the soul of the speaker accompanying his word, making it cut and pierce to the "dividing asunder of soul and spirit".[1,2]

Powerful God, touch me, and touch your Church, with fresh power for this day.
I pray for churches to be powerhouses that will touch and change lives. Amen.

1   Hebrews 4:12, KJV.
2   From *The Holy Ghost*.

IF ANYTHING IS EXCELLENT OR PRAISEWORTHY –
THINK ABOUT SUCH THINGS

(Philippians 4:8 *NIV*)

We find that it is no uncommon thing for entertainments to be held in private drawing rooms and in rooms connected with churches and chapels, over which ministers and leading men in churches preside, at which Shakespearian readings are given, with extracts from the works of the most popular and worldly novelists, and the same songs sung as are echoed and applauded in the public house and the dancing-room... First, are they not *professedly* worldly? Do they not savour of the world, all of the world, and of the world only? Were not the authors of the things said and sung at such entertainments thoroughly Christless men, and some of them professed infidels? Second, are not these the songs and sentiments which worldlings have always claimed as their own? Are they not sung in their ballrooms, theatres, and casinos? And is not this proof enough that they are congenial to their tastes, and in keeping with their spirit? Third, such songs, recitations, and performances have no reference whatever to God, righteousness, or eternity. God is not only "not in all their thoughts",[1] but he is not in any of them, therefore they must be thoroughly worldly. Fourth, the spirit of such amusements is manifestly adverse to the dignity, gravity, and usefulness of the Christian character. What are its effects? Lightness, foolish jesting, a false estimate of creature delights, obtuseness to spiritual things, and frequently uproarious merriment and godless mirth. We put it to any Christian who has ever allowed himself to take part in such amusements, whether these are not their inevitable and bitter fruits, and whether he has not found their spirit to be utterly antagonistic to the spirit of Christ? We have heard many backsliders in heart attribute their declension to mingling in such scenes of folly and frivolity, and we never met with one whom we had reason to believe had been renewed in the spirit of his mind who could say he could enter into them without condemnation.[2]

Lord of my choices, I pray for your gentle guidance in my decisions;
how I spend my leisure time, what I watch on television, how I choose to relax.
Thank you for moments of rest and recreation. Amen.

---

1   See Psalm 10:4.
2   From *Practical Religion*.

WHOEVER WALKS WITH THE WISE BECOMES WISE
(Proverbs 13:20 *ESV*)

A further gain to the State through the influence of the Army is a greatly improved morality… "A little leaven leaveneth the whole lump."[1] In this way a few truly converted men and women in a factory, a shipyard, or a mine have such a civilizing and reforming influence on the others that we have some of the most wonderful testimonies from employers of labour on this point. Only the other day, the General was in a town where the master of a shipyard had given this testimony to one of our captains: "This yard used to be a perfect Hell, but now it is comparatively like Heaven." (There were some 3,000 men employed.) "We have no swearing now, and it is all the influence of The Salvation Army."

We have many testimonies from managers of mines to the same effect. Instead of the miners spending their little spare time at their dinner hour in… gambling, in many cases they hold prayer meetings; and instead of the ears of the managers being assailed by oaths and blasphemies, Salvation Army songs salute them on every hand. Mayors, magistrates, and police in numbers of instances bear witness to the same results with respect to their spheres of observation. The same fact also leaks out when our converts are telling their stories. They will say, "I used to be troubled weeks or months before I got saved. I used to follow the procession[2] and then stop outside; but at last I came inside, I gave up the public house and my evil companions, I only got drunk now and then," that is when he was overcome by the persuasions of his companions. In many cases they abandon the drink and their immoral associates long before they take the final step and commit themselves to the high standard which we put before them. You can see by this how the teaching and the influence of the converts affect the population round about them.[3]

> Lord, I might not have opportunity to influence thousands at a time,
> but I do want to be useful where I am, day by day, for Jesus' sake. Amen.

---

1   Galatians 5:9, KJV.
2   Probably a Salvation Army march led by musicians and timbrellists, leading to an Army hall where a meeting would be held.
3   From *The Salvation Army in Relation to the Church and State*.

"NOT BY MIGHT NOR BY POWER, BUT BY MY SPIRIT," SAYS THE LORD ALMIGHTY

(Zechariah 4:6 *NIV*)

Oh! What numbers of people have come to me who have been at work in different directions, in churches, as ministers, elders, deacons, leaders, Sabbath-school teachers, tract distributors, and the like, confessing that they had been for more or less lengthened periods, and had seen comparatively little result. They say, "Do you think this is right? Do you think I ought to go on?" Go on, assuredly, but not in the same track… They are without this endowment of power, and they see no result… Go on, most decidedly, but seek a fresh inspiration. There is something wrong, or you would have seen some fruit for your labour – not all the fruit. God does not give to any of us to see it all; but we do see enough to assure us that the Holy Ghost is accompanying our testimony. God's people have always done that when they worked in conformity with the conditions on which the power can be given… "Ye shall receive power after that the Holy Ghost is come upon you."[1] "You shall be endued with," – not the truth, not faith… but, "Ye shall be endued with power… which all your adversaries shall not be able to gainsay or resist."[2] Though they may stone you, as they did Stephen, they shall be cut in their hearts, and made to feel the power of your testimony.[3] Now, this is how I account for the want of results – the want of the direct, pungent, enlightening, convicting, restoring, transforming power of the Holy Ghost; and I care not how gigantic the intellect of the agent, or how equipped from the school of human learning. I would rather have a Hallelujah Lass,[4] a little child, with the power of the Holy Ghost, hardly able to put two sentences of the Queen's English together, to come to help, bless and benefit my soul than I would the most learned divine in the kingdom without it.[5]

> Lord, if we, your people, have not your Spirit, then we might as well pack up and go home. Endue your Church afresh for these days, I pray. Pour out your gracious Holy Spirit upon our lives, touching us with ancient power. Amen.

---

1   Acts 1:8, KJV.
2   See Luke 24:49; Luke 21:15, KJV.
3   Acts 6 and 7.
4   "Hallelujah Lasses" were usually single, female Salvation Army officers engaged in slum work or public house "reclamation" ministry.
5   From *The Holy Ghost*.

When Priscilla and Aquila heard him [Apollos],
they invited him to their home and explained to him
the way of God more adequately

(Acts 18:26 *NIV*)

Whether the Church will allow women to speak in her assemblies can only be a question of time; common sense, public opinion, and the blessed results of female agency will force her to give us an honest and impartial rendering of the solitary text on which she grounds her prohibitions. Then, when the true light shines and God's words take the place of man's traditions, the Doctor of Divinity who commands women to be silent when God's Spirit urges her to speak will be regarded much the same as we should regard an astronomer who should teach that the sun is the earth's satellite. As to the obligation devolving on woman to labour for her Master, I presume there will be no controversy. The particular sphere in which each individual shall do this must be dictated by the teachings of the Holy Spirit and the gifts with which God has endowed her. If she has the necessary gifts, and feels herself called by the Spirit to preach, there is not a single word in the whole book of God to restrain her, but many, very many to urge and encourage her. God says she shall do so, and Paul prescribed the manner in which she shall do it, and Phoebe,[1] Junia,[2] Philip's four daughters,[3] and many other women actually did preach and speak in the primitive churches. If this had not been the case, there would have been less freedom under the new than under the old dispensation, a greater paucity of gifts and agencies under the Spirit than under the law, fewer labourers when more work to be done. Instead of the destruction of caste and division between the priesthood and the people, and the setting up of a spiritual kingdom in which all true believers were "kings and priests unto God",[4] the division would have been more stringent and the disabilities of the common people greater. Whereas, we are told again and again in effect that "in Christ Jesus there is neither bond nor free, male or female, but ye are all one in Christ Jesus".[5, 6]

Thank you, Lord, for gifted women who preach and lead. Send us more. Amen.

---

1   Romans 16:1–2.
2   Romans 16:7.
3   Acts 21:9.
4   See Revelation 1:6.
5   From a pamphlet Catherine Booth wrote on female ministry.
6   From *Catherine Booth* by Catherine Bramwell-Booth.

Do not exploit the poor... and do not crush the needy
(Proverbs 22:22 *NIV*)

Alas! Alas! Is it not too patent for intelligent contradiction that the most detestable thing in the judgment of popular Christianity is not brutality, cruelty, or injustice, but *poverty and vulgarity*? With plenty of money you can pile up your life with iniquities and yet be blamed, if blamed at all, only in the mildest terms; whereas one flagrant act of sin in a poor and illiterate person is enough to stamp him, with the majority of professing Christians, as a creature from whom they would rather keep at a distance.

Further, "the criminal classes" is another of the cant phrases of modern Christianity, which thus brands every poor lad who steals because he is hungry, but stands hat in hand before the rich man whose trade is well known to be a system of wholesale cheatery. It is inconvenient for ministers or responsible church wardens to ask how Mr Moneymaker gets the golden sovereigns or crisp notes which look so well in the collection. He may be the most "accursed sweater" who ever waxed fat on that murderous cheap needlework system, which is slowly destroying the bodies and ruining the souls of thousands of poor women, both in this and in other civilized countries; he may keep scores of employees standing wearily sixteen hours per day behind the counter, across which they dare not speak the truth, and on salaries so small that all hope of marriage or home is denied to them; or he may trade in some damning thing which robs men of all that is good in the world and all hope for the next, such as opium or intoxicating drinks; but, if you were simple enough to suppose that modern Christianity would object to him on account of any of these things – in fact, you were alluding to such as he in the "criminal classes", how respectable Christians would open their eyes and, in fact, suspect that you had recently made your escape from some lunatic asylum. So the wholesale and successful thief is glossed over and caused by all manner of respectable names by the representatives of [an illegitimate form of] Christianity.[1,2]

> Thank you, Lord, for a growing awareness within your Church of issues
> such as fair trading and decent wages. Help your people to carefully exercise
> their purchasing power on behalf of the poor and oppressed. Amen.

---

1   From *Catherine Booth* by W. T. Stead.
2   This was probably the closest Catherine Booth came to making overt political statements. She was sometimes sympathetic to socialism, but had little faith in its ability to change the hearts of people.

I DO BELIEVE; HELP ME OVERCOME MY UNBELIEF

(Mark 9:24 *NIV*)

I had been earnestly seeking all the week to know Jesus as an all-sufficient Saviour dwelling in my heart, and thus cleansing it every moment of all sin; but on Thursday and Friday I laid aside almost everything else, and spent the chief part of the day in reading and prayer, and trying to believe for it. On Thursday afternoon at teatime I was well-nigh discouraged, and felt my old visitant irritability, and the Devil told me I should never get it, and so I might as well give it up at once. However, I know him of old as a liar and the father of lies,[1] and pressed on, cast down, yet not destroyed.[2]

On Friday morning God gave me two precious messages. First, "Come unto me all ye that labour and are heavy laden, and I will give you rest."[3] Oh, how sweet it sounded to my poor, weary, sin-stricken soul! I almost dared to believe that he did give me rest from inbred sin – the rest of perfect holiness. But I staggered at the promise through unbelief, and therefore failed to enter in. The second passage consisted of those thrice-blessed words, "Of him are ye in Christ Jesus, who is made unto us wisdom, righteousness, sanctification, and redemption."[4] But again unbelief hindered me, although I felt as if getting gradually nearer. I struggled through the day until a little after six in the evening, when William joined me in prayer. We had a blessed season. While he was saying, "Lord, we open our hearts to receive thee," that word was spoken to my soul, "Behold, I stand at the door and knock: if any man hear my voice, and open unto me, I will come in, and sup with him."[5] I felt sure he had long been knocking, and oh, how I yearned to receive him as a perfect Saviour! But oh, the inveterate habit of unbelief! How wonderful that God should have borne so long with me![6]

Father, thank you that you understand those times when I struggle with faith
and unbelief. Thank you that you graciously bear with me. Amen.

1   John 8:44.
2   See 2 Corinthians 4:9.
3   Matthew 11:28, KJV.
4   See 1 Corinthians 1:30, KJV.
5   See Revelation 3:20.
6   From *Catherine Booth: A Sketch*.

APRIL 12TH

I HAVE MORE INSIGHT THAN ALL MY TEACHERS,
FOR I MEDITATE ON YOUR STATUTES

(Psalm 119:99 *NIV*)

I have not changed about the school.[1] I still think a great deal of the teaching would be useful to you, and I would like you to have it, but I fear the associations will lead you to strive after too much, and to imbibe a worldly spirit and aim. I do not think your desire to learn *sinful*, if it be subordinated and rendered helpful to your serving God; but you see, it is so difficult for us to judge for ourselves as to whether things are thus subordinated. I am sure I don't want to think one unjust or unkind thought of you. I never loved you so deeply; not when you were my baby girl, as pure and beautiful as a snowdrop; but oh, I do so want you, and all my children, to live supremely for God. I do so deeply deplore my own failure, compared with what my life might have been, that I feel as though I could die to save any of you from making a mistake. I see as I never saw before that all God wants with us, in order to fill us with the Spirit and make us flames of fire, is that we should be honest and wholehearted with himself; and I want you to begin life by being so. And yet how can I expect it if I allow you to go into associations such as prove too much for so many older and wiser people than you are? I would rather pay twice the money, and go without necessaries to pay it, in order that you might have the teaching without the danger. I want you to have some of the advantages, but I am so afraid of the spirit of such an establishment. "What hast thou to do in the way of Egypt, to drink the waters of Sihor?"[2] seems to sound in my heart. "Why shouldst thou go to the world for implements of war to use in my battle? Is it not I who give victory and strength? Do not I furbish the spear, and cause the sword to devour?"[3]

Father, thank you for teachers who provide an excellent standard of education.
Thank you for teachers whose influence is entirely positive.
Help and guide parents in their choices for schools for their children. Amen.

---

1   Catherine Booth received a generous offer from a Christian acquaintance, to send her daughters to a first-class school. Catherine visited the school, and was alarmed by the fashionable "worldly" dress of the pupils.
2   Jeremiah 2:18, KJV.
3   From *Catherine Booth The Mother of The Salvation Army, Vol. II.*

Continue to work out your salvation with fear and trembling
(Philippians 2:12 *NIV*)

Paul wrote some things which, as Peter, a fellow-Apostle, says, are "hard to be understood" and which "many wrest" (misinterpret and misapply) "as they do also other scriptures, to their own destruction"[1] and, alas! alas! to the destruction of others also. Perhaps no utterances of man have been more unfairly dealt with than those of Paul, odd paragraphs having been separated from the arguments or illustrations of which they form a part, and made to teach doctrines and dogmas which other parts of his writings show to be entirely at variance with both his spirit and design; in fact, whole systems of theology have been built on some of these isolated paragraphs, systems as repugnant to our innate perceptions of rectitude and benevolence as they are inimical to the character of God. Alas! these theories have been pressed on the minds of benevolent and thoughtful men as the true theory of Christianity, and, knowing no other, they have rejected it altogether and become infidels. Until theologians arrive at some settled consistent fundamental principle of interpretation, they can make the Bible teach anything; and while they persist that it contradicts itself, they must expect it to be held up to ridicule and contempt. We must ever bear in mind that there can be no inconsistency or contradiction in the divine mind: "God is light, and in him is no darkness at all."[2] Consequently, when speaking under the inspiration of the Spirit, the Apostles could not contradict themselves. When I was fourteen years old, I rejected all theories about God and religion which contradicted my innate perceptions of right and wrong. I said, "No; I will never believe any theory which represents that a course of procedure is good and benevolent in God which in man would be despicable and contemptible. I cannot receive it."[3]

Lord, your word can indeed sometimes be difficult to understand.
In my pilgrimage, I pray for light and wisdom as I read the Bible. Amen.

---

1   See 2 Peter 3:16, KJV.
2   1 John 1:5, KJV.
3   From *Life and Death.*

The Lord remembers us and will bless us
(Psalm 115:12 *NIV*)

William is working hard and with wonderful results. The chapel was crowded out all day on Sunday, and sixty-three cases at night, a large proportion of them men. The work up to the present surpasses that of last year. Notwithstanding all this, he is very much harassed in mind regarding his future course. Reports are continually reaching us of the heartless manner in which the preachers let the work down after we have gone, so that as far as our community is concerned, it is almost like spending his strength for naught. The cold, apathetic, money-grubbing spirit of some preachers and leading men is a constant thorn in his side. Oh, for a church of earnest, consistent, soul-saving men! But alas! alas! such is difficult to find.

My precious husband is tugging at it, full of anxiety and greatly exercised as to the success of the effort. Many things have transpired to discourage him. Nevertheless, God honours him in the conversion of souls every day. The work is rising gloriously, chapel full every night and packed on Sundays. It is worth making sacrifices to minister bliss and salvation in Jesus' name. We are trying to lose sight of man and second causes and to do what we do more exclusively unto the Lord. I realize this to be the only way to find satisfaction and peace in the prosecution of our mission. But I am not nearly such an apt scholar at it as my beloved. He can bear non-appreciation and opposition much easier than I can. Perhaps I could endure it better if it did not concern him. But I am trying to rise. May the Lord help me. It is a cause of great rejoicing to us to find such numbers who turned to the Lord when we were in Sheffield before, standing fast and adorning their profession, some of them giving promise of great usefulness. All glory to God.[1,2]

> Lord, when times of discouragement and disappointment appear, and when
> I feel let down by others, touch my heart with memories of your blessings in
> times past. Encourage those who feel downhearted today. Amen.

---

1 From letters Catherine Booth wrote to her mother in 1856, when William was employed as a revivalist preacher with the Methodist Connexion.
2 From *The Life of Catherine Booth Mother of The Salvation Army, Vol. I.*

GATHER ROUND SO THAT I CAN TELL YOU WHAT
WILL HAPPEN TO YOU IN DAYS TO COME

(Genesis 49:1 *NIV*)

They did not leave the chapel last night till a quarter-past eleven o'clock. They had a splendid prayer meeting, and took sixty names. I suppose there were 2,500 people at the service. The tea meeting last night was a first-rate one. I do wish you could have heard William's speech. I ventured there enveloped in a mountain of clothes, and I feel no worse for it, except it be *worse* to feel a little prouder of my husband, which I certainly do. We took leave of the people amid a perfect shower of tears and a hurricane of sobs, and many more are coming to take leave of us today.

As to my own feelings, I cannot describe them. My heart was ready to burst as I listened to the solemn, earnest, and really beautiful address given by my dearest William. I felt unutterable things as I looked at the past and tried to realize the present. I felt as though I had more cause to renew my covenant engagement with God than any of his children; but, oh, I realized deeply, inexpressibly the worthlessness of the offering I had to present him. Alas! I had so often renewed, but so seldom *paid*, my vows to the Lord, and yet he has so richly filled my cup with blessings, and so wonderfully given me the desire of my heart. Oh, for grace rightly to enjoy and improve my many mercies! Pray for me. I often think that God is *trying* me by prosperity and sunshine, for I am, so far as outward things go, happier than I ever was in my life. Sometimes my heart seems burdened with a sense of my own unmerited mercies, and tears of gladness stream down my cheeks. I tremble lest any coldness and want of spirituality should provoke the Lord to dash the cup from my lips, even while I am exulting in its sweetness.[1,2]

Thank you, Lord, that you often use our experiences to prepare us for things yet to be. Help me to appreciate your lessons in my life, and trust you. Amen.

1   From notes and letters Catherine Booth wrote to her mother, from Dewsbury, Yorkshire, England. William had just preached his final sermon in the Wesleyan Chapel there (1855), before moving on to preach elsewhere in Yorkshire. It is not difficult to sense something of the Lord's preparation of William and Catherine; their ministry within Methodism helping to fit them for the leadership of The Salvation Army, still to come.
2   From *Catherine Booth The Mother of The Salvation Army, Vol. I.*

I REMAIN CONFIDENT OF THIS: I WILL SEE THE GOODNESS
OF THE LORD IN THE LAND OF THE LIVING

(Psalm 27:13 *NIV*)

20 June, 1847. Sunday was a day of peace and enjoyment. I went to chapel twice. I felt it good; my heart swelled at the thought of heavenly rest… *I feel the power to leave myself and my all in the hands of God*… He knows what is best; sometimes I think he will restore me to perfect health, though I never feel led to pray for this, but rather that I may glorify him in death… but whichever way, it will all be well… I feel better in many respects for my visit. I suffer most from pain in my breast and shoulders and difficulty of breathing at times and general fever with a craving for food which I cannot satisfy.

Sunday, 11 July. Yesterday I felt so poorly that I could scarcely bear anything… I can say thy will be done. I have been reading from "Baxter's Saints' Rest"[1] the importance of living a heavenly life on earth. I am determined to try.

Sunday, 25 July. I have not written in my journal this past week, it has been one of spiritual conflict and bodily weakness. I have felt as though I could not pray at times. Such rebellious thoughts and feelings have arisen in my mind as I cannot express, and irritability of temper… This morning I went to Southwell with my dear mother and heard young Mr Thomas[2] preach a beautiful sermon and I am going tonight. Lord bless me, thou knowest I would not willingly grieve thee… and if I have given way now, forgive me through Jesus… keep me to the end, save me whether by suffering of health, life or death, only let me be fully thine.

4 October. This time last year I was very ill. I had just commenced my six months' confinement by affliction but, bless God, I am able to attend my Sunday school which increases first. O that I may be able to sow some seed to the glory of God.[3, 4]

> Lord, in sickness or in health, grant me your peace and presence.
> Draw alongside those who are ill this day, at home or in hospital.
> Bless those for whom pain or discomfort make faith difficult. Amen.

1   *The Saints' Everlasting Rest* by Richard Baxter (1650). Baxter (1615–91) was a church leader, poet, theologian, and hymn-writer.
2   Dr David Thomas, Congregationalist minister, Stockwell New Chapel, south London.
3   Excerpts from Catherine Mumford's journal shortly after she returned home from a period of convalescence in Brighton, Sussex, England.
4   From *Catherine Booth* by Catherine Bramwell-Booth.

BE THOU FAITHFUL UNTO DEATH,
AND I WILL GIVE THEE A CROWN OF LIFE

(Revelation 2:10 *KJV*)

Methinks that the inhabitants of Heaven stood still and looked over the battlements at that glorious, illustrious Sufferer, as he hung there between Heaven and earth. The Pharisees, I know, spat upon the humbled Sufferer, and wagged their heads and said, "He saved others; himself he cannot save."[1] Ah! But he was intent on saving others. That was the dignity of Almighty strength allying itself with human weakness, in order to raise it. It was the dignity of eternal wisdom shrouding itself in human ignorance, in order to enlighten it. It was the dignity of everlasting, unquenchable love, baring its bosom to suffer in the stead of its rebellious creature – man. Ah! It was incarnate God standing in the place of condemned, apostate man – the dignity of love! Love! Love! Oh, precious Saviour! Save us from maligning thy gospel and thy name by clothing it with our paltry notions of earthly dignity, and forgetting the dignity which crowned thy sacred brow as thou didst hang upon the cross that is the dignity for us. It will never suffer by any gentleman… carrying the gospel into the back slums or alleys of any town or city in which he lives. That dignity will never suffer by any employer talking lovingly to his servant maid or errand boy, and looking into his eyes with tears of sympathy and love, and trying to bring his soul to Jesus. That dignity will never suffer even though you should have to be dragged through the streets with a howling mob at your heels, like Jesus Christ, if you have gone into those streets for the souls of your fellow men and the glory of God. Though you should be tied to a stake, as were the martyrs of old, and surrounded by laughing and taunting fiends and their howling followers – that will be a dignity which shall be crowned in Heaven, crowned with everlasting glory. If I understand it, *that* is the dignity of the gospel – the dignity of love.[2]

> Father, I pray today for those who suffer persecution for your sake; those who
> are ridiculed, silenced, beaten, tortured, misrepresented or imprisoned.
> Draw very close to your suffering witnesses. Amen.

1 Matthew 27:42, KJV.
2 From *Aggressive Christianity*.

Beware of being negligent
(Ezra 4:22 *NASB*)

Suppose, by way of illustration, that you have a vine, and that this vine is endowed with reason, and will, and moral sense. You say to your vine dresser, "Now, I want that vine *trained* – made to grow in a particular way, so that it may bear the largest amount of fruit possible to it." Suppose your vine dresser goes to your vine every morning, and says to it, "Now, you must let that branch grow in this direction, and that branch grow in another; you are not to put forth too many shoots here, nor too many tendrils there; you must not waste your sap in too many leaves"; and having told it what to do and how to grow, he shuts it up and leaves it to itself. This is precisely the way many good people act towards their children. But, lo! the vine grows as it likes; nature is too strong for mere theory; words will not curb its exuberance, nor check its waywardness. Your vine dresser must do something more effectual than talking. He must nail that branch where he wishes it to grow; he must cut away what he sees to be superfluous; he must lop, and prune, and dress it, if it is to be trained for beauty and for fruitfulness. And just so, mother, if you want your child to be trained for God and righteousness, you must prune, and curb, and propel, and lead it in the way in which it should go. But some mother says, "What a deal of trouble!" Ah, that is just why many parents fail; they are afraid of trouble; but, as Mrs Stowe[1] says, "If you will not take the trouble to train Charlie when he is a little boy, he will give you a great deal more trouble when he is a big one." Many a foolish mother, to spare herself trouble, has left her children to themselves, and "a child left to himself bringeth his mother to shame"![2] Many parents *teach* their children in theory the right way, but by their negligence and indifference, *train* them in just the opposite.[3]

Lord, bless busy parents everywhere!
Soothe their stress and help them to prioritize. Amen.

1 Harriet Elisabeth Beecher Stowe (1811–96), American abolitionist and author. She came from a famous religious family and is best known for her novel *Uncle Tom's Cabin*. Her father, Lyman Beecher, was president of the Lane Theological Seminary, Ohio, USA.
2 Proverbs 29:15, KJV.
3 From *Practical Religion*.

Jesus opened a new and life-giving way

(Hebrews 10:20 *NLT*)

Another most important bearing of the work of The Salvation Army on the State, is its effects on the children! We say that "Prevention is better than cure". Then I contend that it is better to prevent a child from becoming a waif and stray than to house it and reform it after it has become one. Do you ask me, what is the great cause for so many destitute and vicious children? I answer, drunken and profligate parents! *Regenerate the parents*, and you will *save the children*! No sooner is a father saved, than his conscience, nay, his very instincts, lead him to do something for the improvement and education of his children. It was only the demon drink and its attendant iniquities that crushed in the man all the better and nobler aspirations of his nature. The Devil cast out, and the husband and father asserts himself, and the man is willing to make any sacrifices for the good of his family; hence his children are properly fed, clothed, and sent to the best school his means will allow; and in addition, they are trained at home to the best of the parent's ability, and at least loved, prayed with, and warned against the sins which used to be the plague and horror of their lives in the person of their father! Who can estimate the results of such altered conditions to tens of thousands of children?

Do I exaggerate? How can this be when it is a notorious fact that we have many thousands of reclaimed drunkards and other profligates in our ranks? In one procession the other day, and that a comparatively small one, there were counted 355 converted drunkards alone. We all know that thousands of parents means tens of thousands of children. Think of the saving to the nation from the redemption of the majority of these children from lives of drunkenness, idleness and, in many cases, crime! And think of the gain accruing from their sobriety, industry, and virtue![1]

Redeeming God, for those whose lives you have turned around, I give thanks.
For children who continue to suffer at the hands of drunken fathers, I pray.
Amen.

---

1   From *The Salvation Army in Relation to the Church and State.*

THE CHURCH SUBMITS TO CHRIST

(Ephesians 5:24 *NIV*)

There seems, nowadays, in the Church and the world, as many different views of the gospel as there are of secondary matters and of minor doctrines. One person has one notion of the gospel, another has another, until there has come to be a fearful distraction in the minds of many who are constantly listening to what is called the gospel. May God the Holy Ghost help us to look at it impartially and carefully! "Oh!" people say. "It is good news." Yes, thank God, it is good news, indeed – news without which we must all have been lost. It is the news of the free, measureless, undeserved, reconciling mercy of God, offered to me through the vicarious, infinite, glorious sacrifice of his Son, to the end that I may be saved from sin here and Hell thereafter! But this news involves a great deal. It is the news of a definite, practical end, involving conditions; for even good news to me involves certain conditions on my part, if I am to procure the good which the news brings… I am particularly anxious that you should all understand me. Supposing that a province of this empire were in rebellion against our Sovereign. Supposing that the people of that province had trampled underfoot our laws, and set up their own in opposition – and suppose the Queen, in her gracious clemency, desired not to destroy these rebels, but to save them, what would be the necessary and indispensable condition in the very nature of the case, in order for her to save them? Not merely a proclamation of pardon. That would be a glorious movement towards the result, but there would want something else; for a proclamation of pardon merely, while the rebels remain in an unchanged state, would only be giving them greater facilities for further rebellion… It is a necessity that a change of mind should be produced in the rebels themselves, for the Queen not only wants to save them from destruction, but to restore them to allegiance…

Just so with God's proclamation of salvation.[1]

> Thank you, Lord, for this illustration of beneficial submission. Thank you for such a wonderfully gracious gospel. All to Jesus I surrender – afresh, today.
> Amen.

---

1 From *Aggressive Christianity*.

FOR THIS BOY I PRAYED... SO I HAVE ALSO DEDICATED HIM TO THE LORD
(1 Samuel 1:27–28 *NASB*)

I was still very weak, and unable therefore to attend many services,[1] but those at which I was present were very blessed times. Perhaps in no town that I had yet visited was there so intense an excitement, such crowded audiences, and such large numbers seeking mercy. One striking feature of this revival consisted in the crowds of women from the silk factories,[2] who attended the meetings and came forward for salvation. It was a touching sight to watch them on their way to the chapel, with their shawls over their heads. They were especially kind to me and the baby. Sometimes they would come in troops and sing in front of my windows. Bramwell was baptized during our stay at Macclesfield, his father performing the ceremony. There were about thirty babies baptized at the same time. Not wishing the ceremony to interfere with the revival services, we had them all postponed to one day, making it the occasion for a special demonstration, and an appeal to parents to consecrate their children to the service of God. I had from the first infinite yearnings over Bramwell. I held him up to God as soon as I had strength to do so, and I remember specially desiring that he should be an advocate of holiness. In fact, we named him after the well-known holiness preacher,[3] with the earnest prayer that he might wield the sword with equal trenchancy in the same cause. I felt from the beginning that he was "a proper child". At an early age, he manifested signs of intelligence and ability. He resembled me especially in one particular, that was in taking upon himself responsibility. As he grew up I always felt that he was a sort of father to the younger children. He was very conscientious too. I remember once letting him go to a friend's house to tea when he was only three years old, telling him that he must not take more than two pieces of cake. I was not present, and the friends tried to persuade him to take more, but he would not disobey.[4]

Father of all, I pray for babies being dedicated, baptized or christened.
Bless their lives, bless their parents, and bless their families. Amen.

1   From a letter written shortly after the birth of William Bramwell Booth on 8 March 1856. His father, the Reverend William Booth, was on campaign in Macclesfield, Cheshire, England. Bramwell (as he was known) became the Army's second General.
2   Macclesfield was one of a number of silk-weaving towns in north-west England.
3   William Bramwell (1792–1818), Wesleyan preacher and evangelist. He died suddenly, possibly from asthma.
4   From *Catherine Booth The Mother of The Salvation Army, Vol. I.*

DO NOT QUENCH THE SPIRIT
(1 Thessalonians 5:19 *NIV*)

It has always been a cause of amazement to me how it is that intelligent people can fail to perceive the connection between feeling and demonstration. How utterly unphilosophical is the prevailing notion that persons can be deeply moved on religious subjects, any more than on worldly ones, without manifesting their emotions! This insane idea has done more, I doubt not, to grieve the Spirit of God[1] and discourage and extinguish vital religion than almost anything else. It has always seemed to me better to have wild fire than no fire at all. Certainly it would be more in keeping with the spirit and practice chronicled in the Bible, to allow individuals too wide an expansion of joy and sentiment, rather than to damp the light and extinguish any manifestation whatever.

The cold, formal services of the Protestant Church have done more to shut out from it the sympathy and adhesion of the masses than any other cause, or indeed than all other causes put together. The people will forgive anything better than death and formality. Had I my time to go over again, I would not only be far more indulgent toward the natural manifestation of feeling, but would do more to encourage it than I have done before. Not that I would advocate a rowdy and boisterous manner. But the attitude of many churches seems to me to be illustrated by some families, where the father is so austere, and keeps at so great a distance from his children, that they hardly dare speak or breathe in his presence. There is no natural spontaneous expression of either thought or feeling, but the whole family seem to live, move, and have their being in a constrained atmosphere of awe, whereas if you follow the same children into the nursery, or see them where they are alone with their mother and free to act out the impulses of their nature, you would hardly believe they were the same creatures.[2,3]

Lord, breathe through your Church with the living wind of your gracious Spirit.
Renew us, revive us, release us, more and more!

---

1 Ephesians 4:30.
2 Catherine Booth reflecting on ministry, 1856.
3 From *The Life of Catherine Booth Mother of The Salvation Army, Vol. I.*

THY WORD IS A LAMP UNTO MY FEET, AND A LIGHT UNTO MY PATH

(Psalm 119:105 *KJV*)

Don't imagine that the repugnant views of the character of God which have been forced upon you by professed theologians will form any excuse for your rejection of this book [the Bible] or of the divine authority of it in the great day of account. God will say, had you not the light for yourself?

You do not shut your natural eyes against the light of the sun, and permit yourself to be led about the world anywhere people choose to lead you. No; you open your eyes, and look where you are going! Why don't you open the eyes of your soul, and take in the light of the spiritual sun, that you may walk and not stumble? If you refuse to do this, you will be condemned amongst those who love darkness rather than light.[1] Don't imagine that these supposed contradictions will be an excuse for you at the judgment seat. It is not many weeks since a gentleman said to me, "While you Christians are quarrelling, there's hope for us sinners. One teaches one thing and another another, till a poor fellow doesn't know what he is to believe." Ah! That is a comfortable way to put it, down here; but when you get to the Bar of God, he will say to all such: "Thou wicked and slothful servant, why didst thou not go to my book for yourself, and be at the *trouble* to get to know my will?" We ought to study this book as a whole... surely we should take that which is plain and unmistakable as a key to unlock that which at first sight is difficult and contradictory. Is this not the principle which prevails in all rightly constituted human courts? Are not all human documents judged and disposed of according to this rule? Is it not insisted that these shall be interpreted consistently with themselves and with the general scope and design of the writer? You say, "Yes; and that is the only rational rule of interpretation."[2]

Father, thank you for your written word. I pray for your illumination
as I read and study; shield me from incorrect interpretation and
grant me holy tenacity to learn. Amen.

1   John 3:19.
2   From *Life and Death*.

I am writing to you with my own hand
(Galatians 6:11 *ESV*)

I was so very sorry last night that my letter was late. I am a mile and a half from General Post, and expected someone to come to post it, who did not, and I could not get *anyone*, so, much to my mortification, yours and Pa's and others were late... The girls[1] at Jarrow[2] are with a nice old woman who does all for them except make their beds, for 7/6[3] per week the two, has a cup of something hot for them when they go in, and is quite a mother... I am off to look at the circus, but it is such a storm, bitter cold with snow! I am obliged to have a cab... Ballington[4] writes me, place full at night, nine souls and £9 including £2 book money... I gave them a part of a service tonight in the Alexandria, and on Thursday night Bethesda... you should prepare a list of questions for lassies who are candidates... Oh, I forgot to say that I read Katie's article and I like it. With a little of the quotations taken out, it will take with a lot of our folk better than mine... Put it in and encourage the lass a bit. Have you heard of a man yet for office?

I do hope you will not throw a lot of money away in trying him just for want of courage to tell him at once that he will not do... He is a *drone* and nothing, no change of place or position, can ever make him into a bee... He ought never to have left his trade; he never would if he had thought missioning was harder work![5, 6]

Father, we see here a glimpse of how busy Catherine Booth must have been;
mother of an Army, yet mother to her own children too. Bless all busy mothers
who seek to serve you with their time and resources. Their pressures are unique!

1   Female officers stationed at different parts of the country, in whom Catherine took a motherly interest.
2   North-east England.
3   Seven shillings and six pence (roughly £16 in decimal currency).
4   Ballington Booth (1857–1940).
5   Catherine Booth travelled continuously throughout 1879, as the work of The Salvation Army expanded at an incredible rate. In that year alone, she visited fifty-nine districts. She tried to write home daily with news, counsel, and advice. This letter was written to Bramwell.
6   From *Catherine Booth* by Catherine Bramwell-Booth.

WHOEVER FINDS THEIR LIFE WILL LOSE IT, AND WHOEVER LOSES THEIR LIFE FOR MY SAKE WILL FIND IT

(Matthew 10:39 *NIV*)

Another gain to the State from Salvation Army influence, is the saving resulted from decreased workhouse and prison accommodation! In some instances whole families have been fetched out of the former, and in others, individuals forsaken by those who ought to have cared for them. Quite a considerable number of prisons have been half-emptied, and magistrates left with comparatively nothing to do. White gloves have in several towns been given to them, which have been openly attributed to the results of our work...

We believe ourselves to be carrying out the very highest principles of moral and social reform, and that we are not blind fanatics, raising a smoke without much fire. You object to the noise and *éclat* connected with our measures; but if you will look into the subject, you will see that they are indispensable, because we seek those who cannot be reached without. I deplore their condition as much as you do, but *there it is*, and if you are to reach them, you must adapt your modes of thought, expression, and action to them. It is demonstrated by sad and awful experience that they will have nothing to do with your quiet and genteel methods. Bishops, clergy, ministers, philanthropists are forced to confess themselves powerless to reach them; then common sense and charity alike say, send them such instrumentalities as they *will and can* appreciate. Stoop as low as you lawfully can to pick them up, rather than let them wax worse and worse while you are standing on your dignity. Self-preservation urges the same argument; for not only your dignity but your peace, your property, your families, your national privileges, and maybe your very lives are involved in this question of saving the masses![1]

Lord, on Calvary you gave your all for me. You stooped to save me. Thank you for laying your dignity to one side in order to reach me. What a Saviour!

1   From *The Salvation Army in Relation to the Church and State.*

I PRAY ALSO FOR THOSE WHO WILL BELIEVE IN ME THROUGH
THEIR MESSAGE, THAT ALL OF THEM MAY BE ONE
(John 17:20–21 *NIV*)

It will not be necessary to repeat the harrowing details of the conditions of the masses, but only to beg of you to bear those facts in mind in considering our [The Salvation Army's] relation to the churches. Let me add also the terrible fact, ascertained by carefully taken statistics, that prior to the commencement of our operations, 90 per cent of these masses never entered church, chapel, or mission hall! Surely everybody who believes in any kind of religion must see the awful necessity for some extraneous and irregular agency, adapted to reach this continent of dark, indifferent, infidel souls!… We are not antagonistic to the churches. Anyone would suppose we were, from the adverse criticisms we get from Christian papers. This is quite a mistake; it is not so in reality. They do give us credit for having a great deal of the charity which endures all things,[1] or else they must have expected we should have been driven into open opposition; but we do not intend to be. As the General said to the present Archbishop of Canterbury,[2] when speaking to him about The Salvation Army: "We think that we have a claim upon your sympathy, because we do not seek to justify our existence by finding fault with you." No; we do not attack either organizations or individuals. All we find fault with, is sin: but if some people in the churches find that the cap fits, we cannot help it. It is not with the Church, or the good and godly people in it, that we find fault. It is one of our most emphatic instructions to our officers: "It is not your business to go and find fault with other people. Rejoice in all the good done, by whomsoever it is done. Be glad whenever you find a good man or woman at work for God, and for the salvation of the people. Never try to find a hole in their coat, or pull them to pieces. Mind your own business, which is seeking and saving the lost."[3]

Father of all, I pray today for all those involved in ecumenical ministry;
bless them as they promote harmony and goodwill in church and community.
Amen.

---

1   From 1 Corinthians 13:7, KJV.
2   Edward White Benson (1829–96), Archbishop of Canterbury 1883 until his death. This lecture was presented on 20 March 1883.
3   From *The Salvation Army in Relation to the Church and State.*

Rightly handling the word of truth
(2 Timothy 2:15 *ESV*)

The mischief is in us. Take the illustration of the prodigal son.[1] The mischief was all in him – not in his father. The father loved him before he went away, and the father loved him afterwards. The father's benevolent heart yearned over him all the time he was away, and many a time, perchance, he went to the roof of his house to look over the expanse of the country over which the rebellious lad had gone, and wondered whether he would ever come back. The father's heart was yearning over him all the time. How was it that he could not be reinstated in the father's love and in the family privileges? Because there was needed a change of heart – a change of mind in him. If he had come back to the old homestead with the same rebellious spirit in him, the same desire to be free from the father's oversight, the same unwillingness to be put under the father's dominion and discipline, he would still have been a rebel and a prodigal. In the very nature of the case, there was the necessary change; a wise and righteous father could not pardon him; he must insist, though he loves him dearly, upon a certain change of mind before he can consistently pardon him. Just so. The laws of the mind are the same whether operated upon by either God or man. This is not laying any necessity upon God any more than he has laid upon himself. He has made us with a certain mental constitution, and therefore he must adapt the conditions and means of our salvation to that mental constitution, otherwise he would reflect upon his own wisdom in having given it to us at the first. Therefore when he purposes to save man he must save him as man – not as a beast or a machine! He must save him as man, and he must propound such a scheme as will fit and adapt itself to man's nature. Just as the father might not pardon the prodigal, irrespective of the prodigal's state of mind and heart, so neither can God pardon the sinner irrespective of the state of his mind and heart.[2]

Father, thank you for this teaching regarding the nature and theology of mercy.
Thank you that you deal with us as we are.
Bless those who teach theology and correct doctrine. Amen.

1   Luke 15.
2   From *Aggressive Christianity*.

STUDY TO SHEW THYSELF APPROVED UNTO GOD

(2 Timothy 2:15 *KJV*)

You talk, my darling girl, about Herbert[1] becoming a mighty man in God's Israel. Mightier youths than he have fallen. Besides, where did he get the principles you have such faith in? Under his mother's thumb and eye; not at a school for little boys preparing for college, and where deception and lying and infidelity are the order of the day – where the lazy or overtaxed mistress has no time to ferret out sin, and expose it and correct it, and weep over and pray with her poor little motherless charge, as you remember I used to do when any of you were at fault! The tree is known by its fruits,[2] and this deadly rage for education ruins tens of thousands. It is as rank idolatry as the worship of Baal, and God is as jealous of it, and as angry with it, and will have no more to do with it! Look at the ministry. It is an *educated* ministry!

Perhaps you say that they put it in the place of the Spirit. This fact shows the *danger there is of doing this*. It is well known in Methodism that hundreds of young men have gone into their colleges like flames of fire, *soul-winners*! But they have gone to be taught Latin and grammar, etc., and in numberless cases they come out the Devil's charred sticks! How is this? Does it not look as if there were something antagonistic between learning and godliness? Does it not prove the great danger of setting the heart on learning, and forgetting where the strength for usefulness really lies? How is it that all great soul-savers, even highly educated men, have invariably thrown aside their studies when they have given themselves up to soul-saving? I have read of numbers doing so. Finney loved the study of the law, but when he gave himself fully to God he abandoned it and began to study gospel, and gospel only![3, 4, 5]

Lord, whatever else I study, help me to keep your ways uppermost in my mind.
Amen.

---

1 Herbert Henry Howard Booth (1862–1926), the third son of William and Catherine.
2 Luke 6:44.
3 Charles Grandison Finney (1792–1875), American minister and evangelist. He studied to become an apprentice lawyer, but relinquished his studies in order to preach the gospel.
4 From *Catherine Booth The Mother of The Salvation Army, Vol. II.*
5 An extract from a letter Catherine wrote to one of her daughters, on the issue of education.

AS A MOTHER COMFORTS HER CHILD, SO WILL I COMFORT YOU
(Isaiah 66:13 *NIV*)

The secret of a great deal of the lawlessness of these times, both towards God and man is, that when children, these people were never taught to submit to the authority of their parents; and now you may convince them ever so clearly that it is their duty, and would be their happiness, to submit to God, but their unrestrained, unsubdued wills have never been accustomed to submit to anybody, and it is like beginning to break in a wild horse in old age. Well may the prophet enquire, "Can the Ethiopian change his skin, or the leopard his spots? Then may ye also do good that are *accustomed* to do evil."[1] God has laid it on parents to begin the work of bringing the will into subjection in childhood; and to help us in doing it, he has put in all children a tendency to obey. Watch any young child, and you will find that, as a rule, his instincts lead him to submit; insubordination is the exception, until this tendency has been trifled with by those who have the care of him. Now how important it is, in right training, to take advantage of this tendency to obedience, and not on any account allow it to be weakened by encouraging exceptional rebellion! In order to do this, you must begin early enough. This is where multitudes of mothers miss their mark; they begin too late. The great majority of children are ruined for the formation of character before they are five years old by the foolish indulgence of mothers.

I am sometimes asked, "What do you consider the secret of successful training?" I answer, "Beginning soon enough! Not letting Satan get the advantage of us at the start." That is the secret of success. "Well, but," mothers say, "it is so hard to chastise an infant." There is seldom need for chastisement where mothers begin early and wisely. There is a way of speaking to and handling an infant compatible with the utmost love and tenderness, which teaches it that Mother is not to be trifled with.[2]

**Lord, be with parents everywhere as they search for that elusive
skill of gentle discipline. Guide them in that difficult task!**

---

1   Jeremiah 13:23, KJV.
2   From *Practical Religion*.

IF ANYONE HAS THE WORLD'S GOODS AND SEES HIS BROTHER IN NEED, YET
CLOSES HIS HEART AGAINST HIM, HOW DOES GOD'S LOVE ABIDE IN HIM?

(1 John 3:17 *ESV*)

[Jesus] preferred talking to a thief in his last moments[1] to holding conversation with a priest, or any whitewashed Temple worshipper[2] standing around. The man who hung by his side was a great ruffian, no doubt, but then he had been trained in that way; and if we want the judgment of Jesus Christ on such a point, he would certainly give it against the pet of modern Christianity and in favour of this poor rough. The man whom Jesus Christ consigned to a hopeless perdition was he who made long prayers, and at the same time devoured widows' houses, or whose barns were filled with plenty, while Lazarus lay covered with sores at his gate.[3]

Certainly it is a shameful scandal on those Christian landlords who keep their tenants in buildings unfit for dogs; but, after all, not so much more shameful than the conduct of those who, although aroused to the frightful condition of the masses, deliberately attempt their improvement on the same principles as if they were cattle, mainly by means of buildings which pay a liberal interest. No one could possibly be more thankful than I should to see the compassion which has of late found such loud expression in words, embodied in some practical scheme for the provision of comfortable, wholesome houses for the poor, at such rental as they could comfortably pay; but to provide this, with land under our present iniquitous system, will require benevolence willing to lend, hoping for nothing gain.[4]

> Lord Jesus, you humbled yourself for my sake. You exchanged riches
> for poverty. To be like Jesus, this hope possesses me. Amen.

---

1   Luke 23:32–43.
2   Matthew 23:27.
3   Luke 16:19–31.
4   From *Catherine Booth* by W. T. Stead.

LOVE KINDNESS
(Micah 6:8 *ESV*)

Banish those who manufacture this distilled damnation; those who rob man of his reason, woman of her virtue, and children of their patrimony and bread. Cease to recognize, not only as Christians, but as men, those who feed on the weaknesses, wickedness, and sufferings of others. Hoist the flag of death over the breweries and dramshops. Christians of England, the time has come, when to remain silent on this drink question is high treason to Christ. Tell us no more of your charity to brewers and publicans. Your false charity has consigned millions to Hell. Such charity savours of the Devil. Its speech betrayed it. Arise and fight this foe; you will come off more than conqueror, for your God will fight for you.

Here is His Grace the Duke of Rackrent, and the Right Honourable Woman Seducer Fitzshameless, and the gallant Colonel Swearer, with half the aristocracy of a county, male and female, mounted on horses worth hundreds of pounds each, and which have been bred and trained at a cost of hundreds more, and what for? This "splendid field" are waiting while a poor little timid animal is let loose from confinement and permitted to fly in terror from its strange surroundings. Observe the delight of all the gentlemen and noble ladies when a whole pack of strong dogs is let loose in pursuit, and then behold the noble chase. The regiment of well-mounted cavalry and the pack of hounds all charge at full gallop after the poor frightened little creature. It will be a great disappointment if by any means it should escape or be killed within such a short time as an hour. The sport will be excellent in proportion to the time during which the poor thing's agony is prolonged, and the number of miles it is able to run in terror of its life. Brutality! I tell you that, in my judgment at any rate, you can find nothing in the vilest back slums more utterly, more deliberately, more savagely cruel than that.[1,2]

Father, show me what I can do today to build a better world right where I am;
one based upon your law of love. Give me the courage to be kind. Amen.

1   From Catherine's notes and articles on social and moral issues.
2   From *Catherine Booth* by W. T. Stead.

GIVE THANKS TO THE LORD, FOR HE IS GOOD

(Psalm 107:1 *NIV*)

God's dealings with our race are merciful and restorative, and that in the case of the very worst of men God is doing all he can for their salvation – that he in no single instance consigns to wrath before he has truly and honestly tried to save. Bless the Lord, we ought to get up and sing a song of praise before we go any further. Poor sinner, don't think there is any eternal decree barring thy way back to pardon and peace – not a bit of it. Don't think there is any subtle, mysterious influence beating thee back, while God professedly is inviting thee near. Away with such blasphemy! Thou art welcome this very hour, this moment, however far thou hast travelled on the way to ruin. God has spared thee for this very purpose – to bring thee to repentance… God is good to all men, even to those who despise his goodness and perish. "Despisest thou the riches of his goodness and forbearance and longsuffering; not knowing that the goodness of God leadeth thee *(is intended to lead thee)* to repentance?"[1] Moses, early in the world's history, asked the Lord to show him his glory. Moses was one of God's favourites, because he chose to be, because he loved and sought after God before anything else. When you forsake the riches of Egypt in all its phases, and choose rather to be a doorkeeper in the house of God than to dwell in the tents of wickedness or worldliness, you will be one of his favourites. Well, this favourite of God, when he got close to him one day, said, "I beseech thee to show me thy glory." What did the Divine Being do? Did he unveil the splendours of his person? Oh! No. Did he draw aside the curtain of his dwelling place? No. Did he summon to his side countless multitudes of created intelligences who run to do his bidding? No. Perhaps Moses expected something of this kind, for he was only a man; but God said, "I will make all my goodness to pass before thee"[2]… His goodness was his greatest glory! He is good to all.[3]

What a wonderful thought, Lord God – that your glory is your goodness!

---

1   Romans 2:4, KJV.
2   Exodus 33:18–19.
3   From *Life and Death*.

PRAISE THE LORD. GIVE THANKS TO THE LORD, FOR HE IS GOOD;
HIS LOVE ENDURES FOR EVER. WHO CAN PROCLAIM THE MIGHTY ACTS
OF THE LORD, OR FULLY DECLARE HIS PRAISE?

(Psalm 106:1–2 *NIV*)

He [God] hateth nothing that his hands hath made. He is good. And, oh! How this goodness has flown out from the very beginning! How many orders of beings and how many myriads of beings his goodness has enriched, and will enrich, to all eternity, we cannot tell. We do know that it has peopled Heaven with glorious, happy beings, and that it is trying to save and rescue from earth those who have fitted themselves to become vessels of destruction. We know that it flowed out to man at Eden, where the Father placed him in innocence and purity, and surrounded him with all possible facilities for temporal and spiritual happiness; and we know that the Fall did not even interrupt its flow, but that immediately the divine plan for man's restoration and salvation was launched, and a way made back again to the Father's heart and home!

But, sinner, do you want any proof that God is good? Granted that there is a God, and that he is infinitely powerful and holy, which your very instincts tell you he is – I say, grant me these two premises... If he had not been good, where would you have been? His holiness forcing him to hate every speck of iniquity that ever showed itself upon your soul, and his power great enough to damn you in a moment – where would you have been? But you live. Is this not proof enough that he is good? And although in an especial sense the Father and protector of his own people, he is in a very important sense the benevolent Father of all mankind. As Paul said to the philosophers of Corinth, "For we are all his offspring."[1, 2]

Thank you, Lord, for such heart-warming theology.
By your Spirit's grace, melt it over my heart, I pray. Amen.

1   See Acts 17:28, KJV.
2   From *Life and Death*.

MAY 4TH

HIS MOTHER TREASURED UP ALL THESE THINGS IN HER HEART
(Luke 2:51 *ESV*)

See that mother seated at some important piece of work which she is anxious to finish; her three little children are playing around her – one with his picture book, another with his horse and cart, and baby with her doll. It is Monday afternoon, and only yesterday she was giving those children a lesson on the importance of love and goodwill amongst themselves; that was the teaching, now comes the training. Presently Charlie gets tired of his pictures and, without asking permission, takes the horse and cart from his younger brother, whereupon there is a scream, and presently a fight. Instead of laying aside her work, restoring the rightful property, explaining to Charlie that it is unjust and unkind to take his brother's toys, and to the younger one that he should rather suffer wrong than scream and fight, she goes on with her work, telling Charlie that he is a very naughty boy, and making the very common remark that she thinks there never were such troublesome children as hers! Now, who cannot see the different effect it would have had on these children if that mother had taken the trouble to make them realize and confess their fault, and voluntarily exchange the kiss of reconciliation and brotherly affection? What if it had taken half an hour of her precious time, would not the gain be greater than that which would accrue from any other occupation, however important? Mothers, if you want your children to walk in the way they should go, you must not only teach, you must be at the trouble to train… The first and most important point is to secure obedience. Obedience to properly constituted authority is the foundation of all moral excellence, not only in childhood, but all the way through life. And the secret of a great deal of the lawlessness of these times, both towards God and man is, that when children, these people were never taught to submit to the authority of their parents; and now you may convince them ever so clearly that it is their duty, and would be their happiness, to submit to God.[1]

> Father, deliver mums (and dads) everywhere from being so preoccupied with other matters that they inadvertently miss important opportunities to exert a positive influence. Enrich their loving care with alert consistency. Amen.

1 From *Practical Religion*.

IF A LIAR AND DECEIVER COMES AND SAYS,
"I WILL PROPHESY FOR YOU PLENTY OF WINE AND BEER,"
THAT WOULD BE JUST THE PROPHET FOR THIS PEOPLE!

(Micah 2:11 *NIV*)

In America... almost every Christian minister has become an abstainer; and I venture to affirm, that the religious instinct of Christians in both countries has pronounced this action to be consistent and praiseworthy. If consistent and praiseworthy in America, would it not be equally so in England? God grant that such may soon be the case here!... Abstinence is valuable to those who are called to make such an effort, as a source of strength. No man can deny himself, constrained by divine love for the good of others, without improving his own moral nature and giving increased scope for the operation of the divine Spirit within him. "Let us not love in word, neither in tongue; but in deed and in truth. And hereby we know that we are of the truth, and shall assure our hearts before him."[1] Abstinence is valuable to the Christian labourer as a safeguard against temptation. It is well known that a large majority of those who become subjects for church discipline owe their fall directly or indirectly to drink. The man who never uses it can never fall through its influence. He is safe thus far, because he goes not into temptation. Abstinence is valuable to the labourer, because it helps to beget a conviction of his disinterestedness in the minds of those whom he seeks to benefit, which conviction is indispensable to his success. Doubtless the unwillingness of religious teachers to forego their own indulgence in the use of wine and spirits has greatly diminished their influence, and helped largely to beget that prejudice with which great numbers of the common people regard them. We are satisfied that if the gospel is to make any great advance on the masses of this country, those who seek to propagate it must abandon the use of drink.[2]

Lord God, I pray for ministers today, that you will bless them with the grace to minister well and effectively. With all the responsibilities and pressures that are theirs, help them along. Bless my own minister. Amen.

---

1 1 John 3:18–19, KJV.
2 From *Practical Religion*.

SOME PEOPLE MAY CONTRADICT OUR TEACHING, BUT THESE ARE THE WHOLESOME TEACHINGS OF THE LORD JESUS CHRIST

(1 Timothy 6:3 *NLT*)

We believe that God cares very little about our sectarian differences and divisions. The great main thing is the love of God and the service of humanity; and when we find people actuated by this motive, we love them by whatever name they are called. We do not set at nought their opinions. Friends would little imagine how carefully we have considered their suggestions. It is not very long since a minister said he had found out that "we were only playing at soldiering". These things, of course, are very painful to us, after my dear husband's thirty-five years' toil for the masses, and very much anxious thought, study, and prayer as to the best way to advance the Master's Kingdom. We have done the very best we could, and we must leave such criticisms to rectify themselves, or rather for God and time to rectify them. People think that we have adopted these plans and measures because of some personal predilection. They forget that we had to fight our way out of traditionalism and conventionalism just the same as they would have had to do if they had been laid under the same painful necessity. We were resolved on reaching the people, and therefore we have accepted the only conditions possible under the circumstances… Neither are we diverse from the churches in the great fundamental doctrines of Christianity. We have not adopted any of the new gospels of these times. We have not given up any of the fundamental doctrines of Christianity, such as the Fall, the universal Call to repentance, Justification by Faith through Jesus Christ, a life of obedience, Heaven and Hell… The main difference is in our *aggressiveness*. This is manifested in several ways. The Bishop of Durham, the learned Dr Lightfoot,[1] says: "The Salvation Army has at least recalled us to the lost ideal of the work of the Church – the universal compulsion of the souls of men."[2]

> Father, how it must grieve you when your people haggle over minor differences
> at the expense of promoting the glorious truth of Christ as Saviour. In your
> mercy, forgive us, and remind us to keep the main thing the main thing. Amen.

---

1 Bishop Joseph Barber Lightfoot (1828–89), prolific theological author and Chaplain-in-Ordinary to Queen Victoria.
2 From *The Salvation Army in Relation to the Church and State*.

I TELL YOU... THERE WILL BE MORE REJOICING IN HEAVEN
OVER ONE SINNER WHO REPENTS THAN OVER NINETY-NINE
RIGHTEOUS PEOPLE WHO DO NOT NEED TO REPENT

(Luke 15:7 *NIV*)

There is a father yonder who has a bad, rebellious, prodigal boy. He began to trample on his commandments at twelve years of age, and has despised his goodness, wasted his money, and ruined, as far as he could, his father's influence and reputation; he has gone on till he is thirty-three, and there is that father, bearing, weeping, entreating, and promising still. You say, do you want any further proof that the father is good? The very fact that that son is not finally cast off, the fact that his father will hold any communication with him, proves of a truth that he is good. How much more in the case of the great benevolent and holy God?... Some of you have been living in utter neglect of him, some of you perchance have been absolutely denying him, others have been abusing him, and yet here you are alive today, when, by a look, a volition, he could have sent you to the bottomless pit years ago! Further, I want you to note that the Apostle positively asserts that the end or purpose of this goodness is man's salvation. "Despisest thou" (language implying rebuke, blame) "his goodness and longsuffering, which is intended to lead thee to repentance?"[1] Repentance here covers the whole of salvation, as it frequently does in the New Testament. That is, it is equivalent to saying, leadeth thee to salvation. In Scriptural language, when a man truly repents, he is saved. Oh! You say, "But that cannot always be true, because I have been repenting a long time, and I am not saved." Then yours is not *true* repentance. Oh! There is nothing will be shown up at the last day more than the oceans of crocodile tears that have been shed by professed penitents! Making God out to be a liar, and throwing back the blame of people's damnation on him. Do not be deceived. Your repentance is a spurious repentance, or it would long ago have led to your salvation... God never left a truly repentant soul in the dark.[2]

Lord, for your gracious impartation of conviction, leading to repentance,
thank you. I am grateful too, for your patience, longsuffering God. Amen.

1   See Romans 2:4, KJV.
2   From *Life and Death*.

LOOK! I STAND AT THE DOOR AND KNOCK.
IF YOU HEAR MY VOICE AND OPEN THE DOOR, I WILL COME IN,
AND WE WILL SHARE A MEAL TOGETHER AS FRIENDS

(Revelation 3:20 *NLT*)

The Apostle [Paul]… asserts that God tries to lead the worst of men to repentance… The goodness of God is intended to lead; whom? Those who despise the riches of his goodness, and longsuffering, and forbearance – those, in short, who are heaping up to themselves wrath against the day of wrath.[1] Those very men God's goodness is trying to save; but they frustrate his purposes, and turn the very means he uses to save them into a means of cursing. Sinner, do you see what he has spared you for – what his longsuffering mercy desires and intends?…

Forbearance: this looks like the *withholding* attitude of divine mercy – like a father who is going to chastise his child, but his forbearance pleads, and he holds back the rod. Here is divine mercy holding back the long-deserved blow. And longsuffering seems to indicate the *waiting* attitude of divine mercy. Not only holding back the blow, but holding it back a long time – waiting, waiting if perchance the sinner will repent and turn back to him. "Behold I" (your God and Saviour) "stand at the door and knock." Wonderful! Infinite! Incomprehensible! And how long has he been knocking at some of your hearts? Any other friend you would have got up and let in years ago, but it was only Jesus, so you have kept him out, some of you till your hair is grey! Oh, what longsuffering mercy! How long he has waited! Years ago, under that godly minister whom you can never forget, you woke up to realize it. You looked at yourself. You contemplated the dark, guilty past, and you couldn't help saying –

Oh! Depth of mercy, can there be
Mercy still reserved for me?[2, 3]

God's love to me is wonderful! I humbly thank you, Father, that the resounding answer to Charles Wesley's question is "Yes!" Seventy times seven, "Yes!"

---

1   Romans 2:4–6, KJV.
2   From Charles Wesley's (1707–78) hymn, "Depth of Mercy".
3   From *Life and Death*.

YOU STRAIN YOUR WATER SO YOU WON'T ACCIDENTALLY SWALLOW A GNAT, BUT YOU SWALLOW A CAMEL!

(Matthew 23:24 *NLT*)

Oh! My dear sir, if you only knew the indifferent, besotted, semi-heathenish condition of the classes on whom we operate, you would, I am sure, deem any lawful means expedient if only they succeeded in bringing such people under the sound of the gospel.

It is a standing mystery to me that thoughtful Christian men can contemplate the existing state of the world without perceiving the desperate need for some more effective and aggressive agency on the side of God and righteousness. It is so evident that the revolutionary, murderous spirit of multitudes of people is only kept down by physical force, and infidelity and socialism are everywhere prevailing...[1]

The state of the masses in our own country is to me a cause of daily, hourly grief and apprehension. Since coming more in contact with them, I have found their condition to be so much worse than anything I had previously conceived, that I have often felt confounded, disheartened, and almost paralyzed. I have seen many hundreds of thousands of the lower classes gathered together during the last two or three years, and have often said to myself, "Is it possible these are our fellow-countrymen in this end of the nineteenth century, in this so-called Christian country?"[2, 3]

Heavenly Father, some things matter more than others! In all my dealings, please guide my priorities and remind me to invest my spiritual energy accordingly. Keep me from being a gnat-straining Christian!

1   From a letter Catherine Booth wrote in response to correspondence she had received regarding the relationship between Protestants and Roman Catholics.
2   A similar reference to Catherine Booth's anxiety over the state of the nation, expressing her priorities.
3   From *Catherine Booth* by W. T. Stead.

THY HARDNESS AND IMPENITENT HEART TREASUREST
UP UNTO THYSELF WRATH AGAINST THE DAY OF WRATH AND
REVELATION OF THE RIGHTEOUS JUDGMENT OF GOD

(Romans 2:5 *KJV*)

The minister said *Come*, and the Holy Spirit said *Come*; your own conscience said *Come*; Jesus said *Come*. But there was another preacher.

The Devil! He said, "Not now: a more convenient season." And here you are today, with added years of guilt, added years of hardness and unbelief and rebellion, and added years of wrath! "Despisest thou," O man, "the riches of his goodness?"[1] You have been despising them all this time. Mind, mind, there are bounds even to his patience. If he bears long and endures much, the stroke comes at last; and the longer it is withheld the heavier it will fall. "Wrath against the day of wrath".[2] Shall the past suffice thee, sinner? Wilt thou listen and flee from the wrath to come? The Apostle [Paul] asserts that this is the very end and purpose of God in sparing your life. Hence he says in another place, "those who fitted themselves to destruction as vessels of wrath, he endured with much longsuffering."[3] Oh! What a wonderful thought! But then, you see, God is *God* – that is the reason. You would not have borne with a fellow-creature like the degree that he has borne with you; but he is God, and there is no sounding the depths of his infinite compassion. *He knows what it will be to be lost.* I often think of that. Oh! It doesn't seem to me so wonderful, after all, that Jesus Christ should die, because he comprehended the depths of the unutterable desolation to which sinners were going. He realized the bitter cup they would have to drain, and so he took it and tried to save them from it. But mind, a sorer punishment awaits those who despise such love! And, oh! It seems as though some people were making haste and trying their best to *treasure up* wrath, as the Apostle says, as though there would not be enough, against the day of wrath.[4]

Lord, I pray today for those who have heard the loving claims of Christ upon
their lives, yet resist and procrastinate. In your mercy, answer prayer. Amen.

1   See Romans 2:4, KJV.
2   Romans 2:5, KJV.
3   See Romans 9:22, KJV.
4   From *Life and Death*.

QUENCH NOT THE SPIRIT
(1 Thessalonians 5:19, *KJV*)

If all our friends were of your spirit, it would be so different, but you can never know quite what it has been to fight the battle we have fought with conventionalism and prejudice... You see, this whole question of demonstration depends so entirely on the spirit which prompts it, that while the things of the Spirit remain to the natural man foolishness, it would be impossible to find any demonstration at all which would be agreeable to him. You see, dear friend, all men are by nature ashamed of God and his claims on their hearts... this is the crowning triumph of the Devil; not only to separate men from God, but to make them ashamed to own allegiance to him in any way offensive to the world!... The whole history of the Christian Church shows that Satan has always raised the loudest and most determined opposition towards any demonstration of real feeling in religious exercises, such as men naturally allow and practise in regard to all other subjects... This being the case, we have seen – I believe the Spirit has revealed to us – that we must set ourselves at all costs against this false shame, and allow the people to "shout with a great shout",[1] or to cry "Hosanna" in the open-air... or to have a wave offering of kerchiefs instead of palm leaves when they feel like it, and when their hearts are full of holy enthusiasm; or to have music and merrymaking when they are glad in the Father's house, whatever the elder brother may say or feel... Let us not be more careful for the ark than God is; better have the ark shaken by oxen, with the divine blessing and glory in it, than ever so steady and genteel – empty! I believe the Church has suffered as much from the interference of Uzziahs as from Judases... Our critics would have smitten David, not Uziah![2, 3, 4]

Let me be, Lord, an encourager, a smiler, a blesser. Today. Amen.

---

1   Joshua 6:5, KJV.
2   From a letter to Frank William Crossley (1839–97). He was a religious leader and gave generously to the work of The Salvation Army. His gifts amounted to well over £100,000.
3   See 2 Samuel 6.
4   From *Catherine Booth* by Catherine Bramwell-Booth.

AND WHEN HE COMES, HE WILL CONVICT THE WORLD OF ITS SIN,
AND OF GOD'S RIGHTEOUSNESS, AND OF THE COMING JUDGMENT

(John 16:8 *NLT*)

I know, by personal contact with hundreds of souls, that there is an alarming amount of misunderstanding and of what I consider false apprehension of the gospel of Christ... Hence, you have speakers saying, without anything to guard or qualify their words, "Only believe, and you shall be saved";[1] "Whosoever believeth hath everlasting life."[2] Blessed and glorious truth, *when rightly applied, and applied to the right characters,* but dangerous error, in my opinion, *when applied indiscriminately to unawakened, unrepenting, rebellious sinners.* I have met with disastrous consequences of this all over the land – so disastrous that I would not like to repeat them here. Now, I say, we should be careful to let the people understand what we mean by the gospel; I dare not do any other. I am so satisfied of the thousands of souls that are deceived at this point that, while God gives me voice to speak, I dare not but try to warn them, and show them their fatal mistake...

You say, "The man is, so to speak, dead in trespasses and sins. How can he see his own error? How can he lay down the weapons of rebellion? How can he, by himself, come back to the Father?" Granted. Hence, God, in his wisdom and love, has provided for that incapacity which man has induced by his rebellion, by the gift of his Spirit... Temporal rebels can find out by themselves the insanity and wickedness of their course. They can see where it will lead them. They can see the destructive consequences, and be sorry for the course they have taken. They can lay down their weapons of rebellion... Of course, because he has so hardened his heart that even if he *can*, he never *will* without the Holy Spirit of God. Hence, God has taken compassion on us, and sent his Spirit into the world for this purpose, to convict the world of sin.[3]

Thank you, Lord, that you not only convict, but you also enable. You don't just
leave us with an awareness of our sins, but you show us a way out too. Amen.

1   See Acts 16:31.
2   See John 3:36, KJV.
3   From *Aggressive Christianity*.

MY CONSCIENCE BEARS ME WITNESS IN THE HOLY SPIRIT
(Romans 9:1 *ESV*)

Having, by the Holy Ghost, made us realize our desperate condition, then comes the gospel to meet us just where we are, on condition that we abandon our evil ways, and do the works meet for repentance, which we are *able to do* by the power of the Holy Spirit, as well as to lay down the weapons of our rebellion and accept of Christ, put our neck under his yoke, and pledge ourselves in heart to follow him all the days of our life. These are the conditions involved, and this is the end the gospel contemplates, and there you see the gospel accomplishes its end in this case. The heart of the rebel is won back to its Lord, and the indispensable change has taken place in the *being himself.* He has come back to God. His eyes are opened to see the evil of sin, and the desperate state he is in. Tired of himself, and tired of his evil ways, as the prodigal was of the swine-yard, he arises, leaves them, and goes to the father... You will say, "If we are to abandon our evil courses, and lay down the weapons of rebellion, is that not saving ourselves?" No, dear friends; it is altogether different. You see, it is the indispensable condition of salvation... that we abandon our evil ways. Now, what does that mean? A gentleman in a letter to me said, "We cannot save ourselves from heart sins." Granted, but we can *will* to be saved from them. Then, there is a great distinction between those sins of the heart which are involuntary, and those deliberate transgressions of God's law which unregenerate men commit. God requires me to abandon all that I can, as a condition of salvation,[1] and then, when he saves he will give me power to abandon all that I could not before. The prodigal had to come away from the swine-yard, the filth, and the husks, before he got into the father's house, and sat down at the father's feast, but when he had done so, then the father said, "Come in," and he brought the best robe and put it on him, and killed the fatted calf, and put the ring of forgiveness upon his hand.[2] Hence, as the old divines used to put it, "You must wait for the Lord in the path of his ordinances,"[3] the path of obedience, as far as is possible to you.[4]

What a wonderfully gracious plan of salvation this is, Lord. Thank you. Amen.

---

1   A moot point, if we believe that salvation is by grace alone, and that our works are only ever our response to salvific grace.
2   Luke 15.
3   From Isaiah 26:8.
4   From *Aggressive Christianity.*

FOR WE DO NOT HAVE A HIGH PRIEST WHO IS UNABLE TO
FEEL SYMPATHY FOR OUR WEAKNESSES, BUT WE HAVE ONE WHO
HAS BEEN TEMPTED IN EVERY WAY, JUST AS WE ARE

(Hebrews 4:15 *NIV*)

My very dear Emma,[1] I hope you are recovering from the fit of [the] dumps into which you had fallen when you wrote me. I note all you say, and am quite willing to admit that most girls of sixteen would feel very much as you did about Katie[2] coming, my being away, etc. But then my Emma is not one of these "most girls". She has more sense, more dignity of character and, above all, more religion. She only got into the dumps, and for once felt and spoke like "one of the foolish women"! Well, that is all over now, and I doubt not she is herself again, acting as my representative, taking all manner of responsibility and interest in her brothers and sisters – tired often with them, but never tired of them – acting the daughter to her dear precious papa, the mother and sister to Ballington,[3] and the faithful, watchful friend to the whole household. I know that is her character, and I shall not receive any opinion that would contradict it, even from herself! My dear child, don't grow weary in well doing,[4] or in enduring; the reward is always greater than the sacrifice. Jesus reigns, and he will never forget the work of faith and the labour of love which nobody else sees. When a friend does a secret kindness, we say, "Ah, it was not only a great kindness, but the way in which it was done was so nice, so acceptable, that it made it double the value. There was no splash, no fuss, no telling folks and talking about sacrifice. It was all so quiet, so hidden, but so real." "Verily, verily, I say unto you, a cup of cold water shall not lose its reward."[5] Jesus feels very much as we do. Only he knows how to reward, and he won't forget! Bless his name, my dear child, and take courage.[6, 7]

Thank you, Lord, that you know our weaknesses and our cares;
that you are a God who understands. Amen.

---

1   Emma Moss Booth (1860–1903), fourth child and second daughter of Catherine and William Booth.
2   Catherine Booth-Clibborn (Katie Booth) (1858–1955), oldest daughter of the Booths. She brought The Salvation Army to France, becoming known as "*la Maréchale*".
3   Ballington Booth (1857–1940), second child of William and Catherine.
4   Galatians 6:9.
5   See Matthew 10:42, KJV.
6   From a letter Catherine wrote to her daughter Emma, while she (Catherine) was away in Leicester (1876).
7   From *Catherine Booth The Mother of The Salvation Army, Vol. II.*

I WILL BUILD MY CHURCH
(Matthew 16:18 *NIV*)

We have been teaching our own people first, and through their influence, others, that by the help and grace of God such measure of influence and power may be brought to bear upon men as may lead them to salvation. We teach them that we are to compel men to come in, that we are to seek by our own individual power and by the power of the Holy Ghost in us to persuade men, that the gospel idea of preaching is not merely laying the truth before men, for the exercise of their intellectual faculties; but that a teacher and saviour has something more to do than this – that he ought to be possessed of sufficient divine influence to thrust his message in upon the heart, to make the soul realize and feel his message. This is our great characteristic – pressing the gospel upon the attention of men. We have not only to a large extent resuscitated this *idea*, but by the power of God (we claim nothing of ourselves) we have also raised a force of men and women who are now working it out, to an extent that no people preceding us, so far as Church history shows, have ever conceived of – a people who have a more comprehensive idea of their responsibility, both as individuals and as an organization, than ever existed in the world before. There have existed exceptional men, many, thank God; but *as an organization* there is no record since the days of [the] Apostles of a body that has so compassed the divine idea, all its members being taught to make all the other objects and aims of life subservient to the one grand purpose of preaching the gospel to every creature, and striving to win every soul with whom they come into contact to its salvation. The same Spirit also that has awakened us to this continued and persistent activity, has also directed us as to the course in which it was to be directed. This same Divine Spirit has directed our attention to the moral cesspools of the country.[1]

> Lord, you have established agencies and organizations to further your work;
> bless all such groups as they work for righteousness, justice, and peace in your
> name. I pray for those close to my own heart. Amen.

---

1   From *The Salvation Army in Relation to the Church and State.*

COMMIT YOUR WORK TO THE LORD,
AND YOUR PLANS WILL BE ESTABLISHED

(Proverbs 16:3 *ESV*)

Our path embraced all the comforts and prospects of a successful ministerial career; but as by miracle (I cannot account for it in any other way) we were led into this particular description of work.[1] The General was led in the first instance, more especially, to contemplate these waste masses, this continent of souls, it seemed, without any light, life, or power, left untouched, confessedly by our bishops, clergy, ministers, and philanthropists, without any humanizing, much less to say Christianizing influences. My dear husband was led especially to contemplate these masses, and commenced in the east of London without any idea beyond that of a local work. God showed him that between the churches and the working classes, as a rule, there was a great gap; he saw that there was needed some instrumentality that would come between the two, and take hold of this lower stratum, which, in the great majority of cases, was uncared-for and unthought-of; and he set himself to do it in the east of London.[2] God so wonderfully blessed him that the work soon began to grow of its own aggressive and expansive force. Some of the greatest reprobates in London got converted in the East London Mission.[3] They came for seven, ten, and fifteen miles to those services, to look at "Bill", "Bob", or "Jack", some fighting, dog-fancying, or pigeon-flying companion, who was reported to have been saved on the previous Sunday – and some of those got caught also. They were changed, transformed, and put into their right minds; and immediately became anxious for the salvation of their fellows. Some of these came to my husband and said there were whole streets of working men in their neighbourhoods who never went to a place of worship – could they not do something for them? Could they not open little mission rooms and set to work to try and save them?[4]

Lord, you have a plan and a purpose for each of us – thank you. Please guide
those whom today are seeking your will and plan for their future. Amen.

---

1   William and Catherine were engaged in a successful ministry within Methodism. Their preaching was appreciated and a number of options might have been explored.
2   One evening in 1865, William Booth walked along Mile End Waste, east London. Outside the Blind Beggar pub, he listened to some evangelists, and was invited to speak. Returning home, he told Catherine he had "found his destiny".
3   The forerunner of The Salvation Army.
4   From *The Salvation Army in Relation to the Church and State*.

AT THAT TIME I WILL CARRY OUT AGAINST
ELI EVERYTHING I SPOKE AGAINST HIS FAMILY

(1 Samuel 3:12 *NIV*)

One would think, to hear some parents talk of their relations with their children, that they did not possess an iota of *power* over them. All they dare to do seems to be to reason, to persuade, to coax. I have frequently heard mothers using all manner of persuasion instead of exerting the authority which God has given for the safeguard and guidance of their poor children. They give their commands in such a voice as leaves it optional whether the child shall obey them or not, and this he understands very well; there is no command, no firmness, no decision, no authority, and the child knows it by its instincts just as an animal would. Men are much wiser in breaking in and training their horses than their sons… What has God given you authority for, if he did not intend you to use it – if your child can do as well without it?… You recollect the fearful punishment that came upon Eli, one of the most terrible strokes of vengeance recorded in the whole Bible.[1] What was it for? Not for using profane language before his children, not for training them in unrighteousness or immorality, for he was a good and righteous man, but because "he restrained them not" [KJV] that means he did not use his authority on the side of God and righteousness. Doubtless, this had been his failing all the way through; he had indulged his sons in their own way, until at last they set both him and his God at open defiance. Alas! This has been the case with millions since his day: having sown the wind they reaped the whirlwind. What a contrast the conduct and fate of Eli present in this respect to the conduct of Abraham! "I know him," said Jehovah, "that he will *command* his children and his household after him".[2] Not merely remonstrate, persuade, and threaten, as Eli did, but "*command*" – he will use his authority on my side; and, as a consequence, the Lord promised that they should "keep the way of the Lord, to do justice and judgment". Parents, if you fulfil your part of the covenant, never fear but that God will perform his.[3]

Once again today, Lord, I pray for parents. Give them over and above all
they will need this day, to love and guide their children. Amen.

---

1   See 1 Samuel 3 ff.
2   Genesis 18:19, KJV.
3   From *Practical Religion*.

TRUTHFUL WORDS STAND THE TEST OF TIME, BUT LIES ARE SOON EXPOSED
(Proverbs 12:19 *NLT*)

Another important point in training a child in the way he should go is to train it in the practice of truth and integrity. Human nature is said to go "astray from [the] birth, speaking lies"[1] and, doubtless, untruthfulness is one of the most easily besetting and prevalent sins of our race. To counteract this tendency, and to establish the soul in habits of truth and sincerity, must be one of the first objects of right training. In order to do this, parents should beware of palliating or excusing the tendency to falsehood in their children. In nothing have I been more amazed than in this. I have actually seen mothers smile at, and almost extol the little artifices of their children in their attempts to deceive them and to hide some childish delinquency. No wonder that such parents fail to inspire their offspring with that wholesome dread of falseness which is one of the greatest safeguards to virtue in afterlife. No mother will succeed in begetting in her child a greater antipathy towards any sin than she *feels for it herself*. Children are the quickest of all analysts, and instinctively detect in a moment all affectation of goodness. They judge not so much from what we say as how we feel. They are not influenced so much by our teaching as by our spirit and example. For instance, a mother teaches her child that he is to be truthful, and on no account to tell a lie; but what effect will such teaching have if he hears her tell one, or sees her act one, the next day? Parents teach their children to be sincere, and take occasion to point out examples of the meanness and wickedness of deception, but by their own example they very frequently train them in the grossest insincerity. Take an illustration. A person calls to see you whose society your child knows that you neither esteem nor desire, but you are all smiles and compliments, pressing her to come again, and assuring her that her visit has given you very great pleasure. What more effectual lesson could you give your wondering little one in deception and double-dealing than this?[2]

Father, how easily we justify "white lies"! Help me to be tactful and truthful.
Amen.

---

1 Psalm 58:3, ESV.
2 From *Practical Religion.*

GOD IS NOT UNJUST; HE WILL NOT FORGET YOUR WORK

(Hebrew 6:10 *NIV*)

In these early days [of The Salvation Army] we had no funds or helpers except a few voluntary working men, the richest of them not earning more than thirty shillings a week. My husband would say: "I have no funds, and I have nobody to be responsible; but if you can get anybody's kitchen or an old dancing saloon or penny gaff, I will get some of my working men to come and help you on Sundays, and you must do the rest yourselves." Thus, little missions at Poplar, Canning Town,[1] and other places were opened; and in this way the Christian Mission has grown into The Salvation Army! It grew because of the divine life that was in it. We could not help it, even if we had desired to do so. All life must grow and develop; if you cramp it – shut it in – it will die. If it is to become powerful, you must let it have room to express itself. The Salvation Army has grown so fast because it has been allowed to have free course! God has helped us to raise a gigantic spiritual force in the land, which is carrying out the idea of the "compulsion of souls", and we have, today, something like 1,200 officers of The Salvation Army, or what you would call evangelists – paid officers; and when I say paid, I only mean supported.[2] We do not reckon to *pay anybody*, not even our staff officers. We have officers on our staff who a little while ago held positions worth from £200 to £800 a year, only receiving enough to keep themselves and their families in a moderate degree of comfort, who have made all sorts of pecuniary sacrifices in order to become Salvation Army officers; and we have many others waiting, who are ready at this moment to renounce lucrative businesses and situations to come and throw themselves into this work. We had, some months ago, 20,000 voluntary public speakers unpaid, that is, men and women whom their captain could call upon at a moment's notice.[3]

Lord, your work done in your way will never lack your resources. May The Salvation Army ever be a spiritual force in the land, assured of your provision. Meet its needs for international mission and social care. Amen.

---

1 East London.
2 Salvation Army officers work full-time for the Movement.
3 From *The Salvation Army in Relation to the Church and State.*

INSTEAD, GOD CHOSE THINGS THE WORLD CONSIDERS FOOLISH
IN ORDER TO SHAME THOSE WHO THINK THEY ARE WISE

(1 Corinthians 1:27 *NLT*)

At an Exeter Hall[1] meeting not long ago, my husband had called upon what was once a poor rag-picker,[2] a woman who was rescued from drink and depravity, though a woman of good natural ability, and a woman who, when her husband was worsted in a fight, he used to hand over his opponent to her, and she could manage him. This woman got converted, and when she reached home at ten o'clock at night, and dragged her three little children out of bed, and setting them on her knees round a chair, said: "Your mother never prayed with you before, but she will do it now." After such a beginning it is not surprising she succeeded in getting them converted, and in inspiring them with the love of God and of souls, so that they have become perfect heroines in this Army. My husband called upon this woman on Exeter Hall platform, without a moment's notice, to speak, and she did so. An influential clergyman said to me afterwards in the committee room: "It is perfectly astonishing. There is not one in a hundred of us could do as well as that woman did if we were called upon at a minute's notice." Oh, yes; it is astonishing what, by the power of God in these people, they can accomplish.

We had months ago 20,000 people of that type, and now near double that number, of course not all so gifted as that one, who speak nightly, and two or three times on a Sabbath in the open-air, who have literally to fight with wild beasts, and to encounter the biggest rowdies and cut-throats in the country. They buttonhole these men, and talk to them with tears in their eyes. They often kneel down in the snow or mud and pray and plead with them, in *their way*; and it suits them much better than ours would, because it matches their nature better.[3]

Lord, you are much more interested in our availability than our ability.
I have not much to give you, Lord, but all I have is yours. Amen.

---

1   A hall on the north side of the Strand, London, England, built between 1829 and 1831 on the site of Exeter Exchange and used for a variety of meetings and events. The site is now occupied by the Strand Palace Hotel.
2   A rag-picker, or *chiffonier*, was someone who made a living by rummaging through refuse, collecting material for salvage.
3   From *The Salvation Army in Relation to the Church and State*.

IN PEACE I WILL BOTH LIE DOWN AND SLEEP
(Psalm 4:8 *ESV*)

Suppose that your son of six months old is in a fractious mood, and indisposed to take his morning nap; his nurse has put him in his cot and struggled with him till she is tired, and the child is tired too; at last you come and take the baby, after he has been rolling and tumbling about, and lay him down with a firm hand, saying with a firm voice, "Baby must lie still and go to sleep," putting your hand on him at the same time to prevent his rising in the cot or turning over after you have spoken. Now, if this child for the previous three months has been trained in this line, if this is not the beginning, he will, as a natural consequence, lie still and go to sleep; but if he has not been accustomed to this kind of handling, he will perhaps become boisterous and resist you; if so, you must *persevere*. You must on no account give up; no, not if you stop till night. If he conquers you this time he will try harder next, and it will get more and more difficult. Almost all mothers mistake here; they give up because they will not inflict on themselves the pain of a struggle, forgetting that defeat now only ensures endless battles in the future. Remember you must conquer in the first battle, whatever it may be about, or you are undone. "Ah, but what time and patience this requires!" Yes, but it is only for once or twice; and what is that compared with the time and toil of conquering further on? But you say, "It is so hard." Not half so hard as the other way; for when the child finds that mother is not to be got over, he will yield as a matter of course. I have proved it, I think, with some as strong-willed children as ever came into the world. I conquered them at six and ten months old, and seldom had to contend with any direct opposition after.[1]

> Lord of my nights, I pray for those whose sleep is disturbed
> or elusive, for whatever reason. Be with them in their sleeplessness,
> and help them with the problems that keep them awake. Amen.

---

1 From *Practical Religion*.

REPROVE, REBUKE, AND EXHORT,
WITH COMPLETE PATIENCE AND TEACHING

(2 Timothy 4:2 *ESV*)

I once stayed in the house of a lady who had a fine promising boy of about eighteen months old. He used to kick and scream violently when he found that she was going out of the house... But what did she do? Instead of facing the difficulty, and in a calm, firm, and affectionate manner curing her little son of this bad habit, she used to promise every time that she would bring him a pony that he could ride on, and the little fellow believed and believed until he got tired, and then put down his mother, in his baby-mind, as a liar. Of course, he would not have understood such a definition, but the deception would be burned into his soul never to be eradicated. A child hurts himself against the table: the mother strikes it, and says, "Oh! Naughty table! You have hurt baby," but the child soon learns that the table was not to blame, and at the same time learns to distrust his mother, who said it was. A mother invites some little friends to spend an afternoon with her children, during which games are played... Her little boy wins several of the games, and although his brother or one of his little friends says that he... cheated, she does not appear to notice it, but contents herself by saying, "Oh, you must be good children and not quarrel"; thus inflicting an unjust reflection on the child of honour and integrity, while encouraging the other in the meanest and most selfish form of sin, allowing him to rejoice over the victory won, through fraud... Can such a mother wonder if her boy turns out a thief or a gambler? Well, but you say how unpleasant it would be in such a case to go into particular investigation, spoil the enjoyment of the party, and expose your child as a cheat before them! Certainly it *would* be very unpleasant... but, to a mother who esteems the honour and integrity of her boy more than all appearances or opinions in the world, such an opportunity of correcting his fault and fortifying him against future temptation is more than the breaking up of a dozen parties.[1]

Lord, confrontation is never easy, whether that be with children, colleagues,
church friends or loved ones. Pour your grace upon any such troubled waters.
Amen.

---

1   From *Practical Religion*.

HAVING DISARMED THE POWERS AND AUTHORITIES, HE MADE A PUBLIC
SPECTACLE OF THEM, TRIUMPHING OVER THEM BY THE CROSS
(Colossians 2:15 *NIV*)

We have a new order of officers called "Sergeants", who come between the corps and the paid officers; and we hope soon to have a force of those who will systematically visit every public house in the country, and scavenge houses of worse repute still, who will make it their duty to scavenge the back alleys, and worst places of resort in the nation, irrespective of abuse or ill-usage. We are raising such people. God is doing it through our instrumentality. Is this any more than needs to be done? Nay, will anything less than this determined hand-to-hand fight with evil, serve to stem the tide of sin and demoralization which threatens our national life? What a long time the Church has been singing – I don't want to reflect on anybody – but how long has the Church been singing:

Onward, Christian soldiers,
Marching as to war,
With the cross of Jesus
Going on before?[1]

How long have we been singing:

Am I a soldier of the cross?[2]

And yet how little hand-to-hand fighting with sin and the Devil! God has, however, taught us better, and we are determined to carry the battle into the very strongest fortresses of the enemy. A further difference between us and the majority of the churches is the resuscitation of the supernatural, of the divine. *Here, I think, is our real power...* We have resuscitated this old-fashioned religion. We defy infidels to account *on natural principles* for the results we have to show.[3]

Lord, you are Lord of all; high above all powers.
May your Church live in that confidence, and exercise bold mission accordingly.
Help us not to make our God too small!

---

1   Sabine Baring-Gould (1834–1924).
2   Isaac Watts (1674–1748). (Watts wrote this hymn to match a sermon he was preaching.)
3   From *The Salvation Army in Relation to the Church and State*.

IN THE PATH OF YOUR JUDGMENTS, O LORD, WE WAIT FOR YOU

(Isaiah 26:8 *ESV*)

Can the drunkard wait for him while he abides at his cup? Can the thief wait for him while he continues in his diabolical trade? Can any man indulging in open sin find the Lord? Must he not, as the Saviour says, cut off that right hand, and pluck out that right eye? He can never cleanse his guilt, but he can cut off his hand, and when he does that, the Holy Spirit will come in and apply the blood, and do the cleansing. Therefore, you perceive, I take the gospel to be aiming not merely at saving, but restoring us. If it were merely to save me without restoring me, what would it do for me? As a moral agent, if the gospel fails to put me right, it will fail eternally to make me happy; and if you were to transplant me before the throne, and put me down in the inner circle of archangels with a sense of wrong in my heart, being morally out of harmony with the laws of God, and the moral laws of the universe, I should be as miserable as if I were in Hell, and should want to get away. I must be made right as well as treated as if I were right. I must be changed as well as justified. This is the gospel...

It was through the lips of the glorified Lord himself, after he had risen, to the great Apostle of the Gentiles, after the gospel dispensation was fully opened, that this unmistakable commission was given, "unto whom I now send thee, To open their eyes".[1] What to, their sins?... Peter opened the eyes of the murderers of our Lord, on the Day of Pentecost, "Whom ye have crucified and slain",[2] driving in the convicting truth of God until, in their agony, they cried out, "What must we do?"[3] He tore off the bandages which Satan had wrapped around them, and... [drove] them to the cross of the crucified One. "Open their eyes" – that was the first thing.[4]

Thank you, Lord, that your gospel is all-sufficient. Thank you, too,
that you love me enough to want to change me. Open my eyes, illumine me,
so that I see more of Jesus and his transforming power at work in my life. Amen.

---

1   Acts 26:17–18, KJV.
2   See Acts 5:30.
3   See Acts 2:37.
4   From *Aggressive Christianity*.

DO NOT NOW BE STIFF-NECKED AS YOUR FATHERS WERE,
BUT YIELD YOURSELVES TO THE LORD

(2 Chronicles 30:8 *ESV*)

Sinner, remember for every sin there is so much wrath. You can label it off as surely as you do the profits of your day's business. Every day's forbearance, so much more wrath. You are heaping it up, treasuring it up. It is hovering over the path you tread like some great towering black mountain. Just a puff of God's breath, or a touch of his finger, and it will come down and overwhelm you, as the waters did Pharaoh and his host.[1] You are making it higher, denser, blacker, every day you live. You know it is true. You have had a foretaste of it already. The rumblings of its hidden fires have scathed your soul, and darkened your mind, and blighted your happiness, even now while you only catch the outer foam of its angry billows! Loving mercy is holding it off, but it has done enough already to show you what it will be when it overwhelms you for ever. Will you give up despising the riches of his goodness? Will you now begin to flee from the wrath to come? The Lord help you... God's purpose is frustrated continually by impenitent sinners... This idea shocks some people's notions of the divine sovereignty. I cannot help that. Here it is as plain as ABC: "not knowing that the goodness of God leadeth thee to repentance? But after thy hardness and impenitent heart treasurest up unto thyself wrath against the day of wrath"...[2]

God's sovereignty... asserts itself in legislating how man ought to act and in punishing him for disobedience, and not of divesting him of his *freedom* in order to *prevent* disobedience.[3]

Lord, your gift of free will is one that is often abused, yet it is
evidence of your love and goodwill towards humanity. Thank you that
you love and continue to love, even when love is not returned. Amen.

---

1   Exodus 14:28.
2   Romans 2:4–5, KJV.
3   From *Life and Death.*

LET NO SIN RULE OVER ME

(Psalm 119:133 *NIV*)

Both Paul and all the inspired writers deplore again and again the fact that men frustrate the loving purposes of God, and thus bring upon themselves destruction. Did not the Jews? What did Jesus Christ mean when he wept over Jerusalem, and said, "Oh that thou hadst known in this thy day?"[1] Away with a theology that makes out to be hypocrisy! It was the heart's sincerity of the Son of God, and he meant every word he said. What more could he have done to make them or us believe that he was sincere? He wept, he groaned, and spread his hands over the rebellious people, and said, "How often would I have gathered thy children together, even as a hen gathereth her chickens under her wings, and ye would not."[2] Ye hard-hearted, stubborn, and rebellious, as Stephen said of them, "As your fathers did, so do ye; ye do always resist the Holy Ghost."[3] *That* was the secret of their destruction, and, alas! They treasured up wrath both for this world and the next, such as never fell on any other people. Alas! Men do frustrate God's purposes. We see it all around us. Now God's desire is that all men should be saved, and come to a knowledge of the truth – that those very men who despise him should be saved and come to repentance. But all these are *not* saved. Then God's purpose is frustrated in their case, is it not? Some of you confess that you are not saved. Then, my friends, the purpose of God's goodness is not answered in your case. Whose fault is it? Dare you look him in the face and charge him with the murder of your soul? Whose fault, I demand, will it be if you are lost?… You are not saved. Why? Because you are *despising the riches of his goodness*, forbearance, and longsuffering.[4] Because you are throwing back the offer of his mercy in his face, and saying, "No, no, I love my sins."[5]

> Lord, you are most willing to offer pardon and forgiveness, as well as your unique enabling power, to grant victory over sin and temptation. I pray for those who today are struggling with besetting sin. Give them success. Amen.

1 See Luke 19:42, KJV.
2 See Luke 13:34, KJV.
3 See Acts 7:51, KJV.
4 Romans 2:4, KJV.
5 From *Life and Death*.

THE ZEAL OF THE LORD ALMIGHTY WILL ACCOMPLISH THIS
(2 Kings 19:31 *NIV*)

Some people would have said to the Lord Jesus, "What a great deal you are making of human agency for, after all, Paul is but a man, and you are setting him to open the eyes of the unconverted, and turn them from darkness to light, and from the power of Satan unto God: are you not making too much of human effort?" But the Lord Jesus knew what he was about. He knew that Paul had a power in him which every really renewed child of God has – the Holy Ghost – to equip him for this work, and he says, "unto whom now I send thee, To *open their eyes*".[1] Go and awake them to their sense of their danger. Take them, metaphorically speaking, by the collar and shake them and make them realize their peril, as you would if they were asleep in a burning house! And then when you have awakened them, what are you to do? Leave them alone? No, no, for Christ's sake, no. Take hold of them by the mighty power of your moral suasion and zeal, and love, and energy, and turn them right "round from sin and Satan unto God".

Jesus Christ set Paul to do this, and Paul did it. He says, "Knowing, therefore, the terror of the Lord, we persuade men". His was no meek and mild putting of the truth, and leaving people to do as they liked. "Knowing, therefore, the terror of the Lord, we persuade men... because we thus judge, that if one died for all, then were all dead"[2] and, oh! What success the Lord gave him in his desperate enterprise. What multitudes did he persuade, and succeed in turning round from darkness to light, and from the power of Satan unto God! Turn them round! "Oh! But," you say, "if they are turned round from darkness, which represents evil, to light, which represents righteousness, are they not saved?" No, not yet. This is only the change effected in their will, which is beautifully exemplified by Paul in Romans vii – willing to keep the law, willing to obey God, willing to do his will, and follow him, yea, struggling, but yet unable.[3]

Have I lost my sense of mission? If so, Lord, seal my dedication with fresh fire.

Amen.

---

1   Acts 26:17–18, KJV.
2   2 Corinthians 5:11,14, KJV.
3   From *Aggressive Christianity*.

THOSE WHO PAY REGARD TO VAIN IDOLS FORSAKE
THEIR HOPE OF STEADFAST LOVE

(Jonah 2:8 *ESV*)

I am satisfied that this gospel-enlightened England of ours is full of people… who come crying, and praying, and longing, as they call it, after God. They come up to Jesus Christ again and again. They try to believe; they want to follow him, but they are kept back by the right hand and the right eye which the Holy Ghost has told them they must cut off and pluck out before he will receive them.[1] They will not do it, and so they are ever learning, and never able to come to a knowledge of the truth. You must renounce evil in your will, you must *will* to "obey the truth".[2] You must say, "Yes, Lord." I remember, on one occasion, in the west of England, I had been delivering a weekday morning address. We had a blessed meeting on this particular day. We began at half-past ten, and the Lord was so with us that he supplied the want of refreshment till we had it at 5.30 p.m. He made up for the want of dinner or tea. A gentleman was there, with whose appearance I was struck. He was tall, and intelligent, a man of about forty or forty-five. He knelt down without any emotion, more than deep solemnity, at the end of the communion rail. I had been talking about the reason people walked in darkness – controversy with the Holy Spirit. I said to him, "My dear sir, have you had a controversy with the Holy Spirit?" "Yes," he said. "I have had one for fifteen years. I am ashamed to say it, and it has eaten up all the joy and power of my Christian life, and I have been a useless cumberer of the ground." I did not know till afterwards that he was a deacon of the church, and had come up there in the sight of all the congregation. I said, "Well, my dear sir, you know the gospel as well as I do. It is of no use to preach faith to you until you are willing to renounce your idol."[3]

All to Jesus I surrender. Amen.

Cont/…

---

1   Matthew 5:29.
2   Galatians 5:7, KJV.
3   From *Aggressive Christianity*.

YOU WILL TREAD ON THE LION AND THE COBRA;
YOU WILL TRAMPLE THE GREAT LION AND THE SERPENT

(Psalm 91:13 *NIV*)

Cont/...

He said most emphatically, "I know it." I said, "Are you willing?" Oh, with what tenacity the human heart holds on to its idols! Though he had come up to the rail in the face of that congregation, so deeply was he under the power of the Spirit, yet he hesitated. I said, "Well, my dear sir, you must make up your mind. In your case, it is between the choice of this, whatever it may be, and Christ," and I retired under the pulpit pillars for a minute, and left him to himself and the Lord. I lifted up my heart to God for him, and then I went back, and said, "Will you renounce it?" and, lifting his eyes up to Heaven, and bringing his hand down upon the communion rail, he said, "By the grace of God, I do," and his whole frame heaved with agony, but he stepped into immediate liberty. His blessed Saviour was waiting with arms wide open. There was only this accursed thing which had stood between them, and when he trampled it under his feet, and was willing to forsake it, as a natural consequence, he sprang into the everlasting arms, and received the assurance of salvation. It was all over the town for the next fortnight. People remarked, "Did you ever see such a change come over a man as has come over Mr So-and-so; he is like a new man. He prays in the prayer meeting with such fervour. He was at the chapel doors, speaking to the unconverted, and inviting them to come back. He is visiting up and down the town – why, he's a new man!"

Had he received any fresh light? It was only the old story – only that he had put away the idol, and trampled underfoot that which was keeping the life-power of God out of his soul.[1]

Lord, your power is available – thank you. We are weak, but you are strong.
Impart your trampling power today, to those who need your help
and feel on the brink of defeat. I pray for them now. Amen.

1   From *Aggressive Christianity*.

THESE ARE THE THINGS YOU ARE TO DO: SPEAK THE TRUTH TO EACH OTHER, AND RENDER TRUE AND SOUND JUDGMENT

(Zechariah 8:16, *NIV*)

Charlie is ill, and it is needful for him to take a dose of unpleasant medicine; but he has been so badly trained that his mother knows he will not take it if she tells him it is nasty. So she resorts to stratagem, and tells him that she has got something good, and thus coaxes him to take it into his mouth, but before it is swallowed he detects the cheat, and medicine and mother's veracity are spat out together. In this way thousands of children are taught deception and untruth, and you may labour in vain in after years to make them truthful and sincere – the soil has been ruined by early abuse.

Mothers, if you want your child to be truthful and sincere you must not only *teach* it to be so, you must be so yourself, and see that your child *practises* what you teach. You must not wink at, or cover up any kind of falseness or deception in him because he is *yours*. Sin should be the more awful to you because you see it in those so dear, and those for whom you are responsible. If you have any reason to suspect your child of insincerity or falsehood, do not rest until you have bottomed the matter; never mind what trouble or pain it involves, drag it out, even though it should bring for the time exposure and disgrace. This may prove a useful chastisement, and a warning in the future. Anything is preferable to sin covered up, and consequently encouraged. Resolve that you will make your child truthful and sincere, if you can do it no other way, from very despair of being able to hide anything from you. God acts on this principle with adults: why should not we with our children? "Be sure your sin will find you out."[1, 2]

Father, honesty such as this doesn't always come easily!
Sometimes, it is more convenient to choose the easy option and compromise.
Grant me wisdom this day, to deal openly and honestly. Amen.

---

1 Numbers 32:23, KJV.
2 From *Practical Religion*.

HE WILL DIRECT HIS CHILDREN AND HIS HOUSEHOLD
AFTER HIM TO KEEP THE WAY OF THE LORD

(Genesis 18:19 *NIV*)

I know some children amongst whom it is a common remark, "It is of no use trying to hide anything from Mamma, for she is sure to find it out; so it is best to tell her at once." How much misery it would save if it were thus in every family! Mothers, take the trouble to make your children true, and God will enable you to do it. If you work *for him with* your children, he will work *with you in* them, and you shall have the joy of seeing them grow up into Christ, their living head in all things[1]... To train a child in the way it should go[2] we must not stop with those qualities and virtues which bear on man; but it must be trained in the exercise of devotion and piety towards God. Of course, none but truly Christian parents are equal to impart *this* kind of training. The Holy Ghost must needs be in the heart of the mother who undertakes to lead her child to God. The bias to evil is too strong to be turned aside by unassisted human wisdom or strength, however great. But, bless God! There is every encouragement to those parents who are truly his, to hope for success in training their children for him. And, perhaps, the first important point in such effort is, to lead our children to regard themselves as standing in a special relationship to God... There is a sense in which the children of believers are already set apart for him. Many parents seem to lose sight of this covenant relation, and bring up their children under the idea that they must needs live in sin till they come to be fifteen or sixteen years old, and then they hope God will convert them in the same marvellous and sudden manner in which drunkards and profligates are converted. Now, I am as firm a believer in conversion as anyone can be; and I also believe that the children of believers need to be converted as much as others, but I say this is not the way to teach our children to expect it.[3]

For mums and dads of children, and mums and dads of teenagers,
I pray today. For Christian parents anxious for their children to walk
with God, hear my prayers today, loving Father. Amen.

---

1   Ephesians 1:22.
2   Proverbs 22:6.
3   From *Practical Religion*.

I WILL REFRESH THE WEARY

(Jeremiah 31:25 *NIV*)

It was a wearying affair. I have not yet got over it, though considerably better than I was yesterday. William is also very poorly with his throat and head. I fear he took cold on the journey.[1] "Babs"[2] seems to have stood it the best of any of us. Bless him! He was as good as a little angel, almost all the way through. He has just accomplished the feat of saying "Papa". It is his first intelligible word. Truro is a neat, clean little town, and surrounded by very lovely scenery. The climate is much milder than that of Bristol.[3] The vegetation is much more advanced, flowers in full bloom, hedges in leaf. It reminds me somewhat of Guernsey.[4] There is just the same softness and humidity about the atmosphere.

You will be glad to hear that my precious husband had a good beginning yesterday. There was a large congregation in the morning, and at night the chapel was very full. I trust there will be a glorious move. If so, it will be worth all the toil, and I shall be amply repaid.

Bristol has been a heavy drag upon his spirits.[5] There was something mysterious about the whole thing, and he never had his usual liberty in preaching. Yet I never knew him in a better state of soul. Now here he seems full of faith and power. To God be all the glory![6]

> Father, as the varied way of life we journey, some days are better and easier
> than others. For those who aren't feeling great today, I pray renewed strength,
> especially if they have responsibilities to carry out, or if they need to travel.
> Amen.

---

1   From a letter written after an arduous, cramped coach journey undertaken during torrential rain (1857).
2   Possibly Ballington.
3   Truro and Bristol, south-west England.
4   Channel Islands.
5   William Booth had spent three weeks on campaign in Bristol, but was struggling with a cold and, unusually, saw relatively little fruit for his labours.
6   From *The Life of Catherine Booth Mother of The Salvation Army, Vol. I.*

TAKE THIS BABY AND NURSE HIM FOR ME
(Exodus 2:9 *NIV*)

To those parents who are able to keep servants, I would say, make any sacrifice to keep a really good Christian girl with your children. I have made it a rule never to have any other as a nurse, and have sometimes put up with great inexperience and incompetency, because it was associated with goodness. Better take a girl whom you have to teach how to wash a child's face, or to stitch a button on, if she is true and sincere, than have one ever so clever who will teach your children to lie and deceive...

Your children want to know how to comport themselves *now* in the little duties, trials, and enjoyments of their daily life. It is to be feared that as with adults so with children, a deal of so-called teaching is right away above their heads, dealing with abstract truths and far-off illustrations, instead of coming down to such everyday matters as obedience to parents and teachers; the learning of their lessons; their treatment of brothers, sisters, and servants; their companionships; their amusements; the spending and giving of their pocket money; their dealings with the poor; their treatment of animals – in short, everything embraced in their daily life. The great end of Christian training is to lead children to realize the fact that they belong to God, and are under a solemn obligation to do everything in a way which they think will please him. Parents cannot begin too early, nor labour too continuously, to keep this fact before the minds of their children. In the family devotion in the morning, the father or mother, or whoever conducts it, should bring the children specially before the Lord, asking him "to give them grace this day, to be obedient to those who have the care of them. To be diligent at their lessons, so that they may lay in knowledge, which shall make them *useful to their fellow-creatures*, and enable them to do something for God and souls, if he sees fit to spare them".[1]

Father, thank you for this reminder about the importance of good
company for our children, whether that be professional care or friendships.
Help parents to observe and organize such matters with care and wisdom.
Amen.

---

1   From *Practical Religion*.

WHEN I AM LIFTED UP FROM THE EARTH,
WILL DRAW ALL PEOPLE TO MYSELF

(John 12:32 *NIV*)

I will now try to give to you, as I perceive them, those modern representations of Christ which, instead of drawing all men unto him, have driven the great mass away from him, and disgusted many of the ablest minds with the whole system of existing Christianity...

Christ of this age seems to be a sort of religious myth or good angel – a being of imagination who lived in the long distance, and who does very well to preach, write, and sing about, or to make pictures about, with which to adorn people's dwellings – a kind of religious Julius Caesar, who did wonderful things ages ago, and who is somehow or other going to benefit in the future those who intellectually believe in him now; but as to helping man in his present need, guilt, bondage, or agony, they never even pretend that he does anything of the kind. This Christ makes no difference in them or their lives; they live precisely as their neighbours do, only that they profess to believe in this Christ while their neighbours do not. Now, this is not the Christ represented in the New Testament. The Christ of God was a real veritable person, who walked about, and taught, and communicated with men; who helped and saved them from their evil appetites and passions, and who promised to keep on doing so to the end of the world; who called his followers to come out from the evil and sin of the world to follow him, carrying his cross, obeying his words, and consecrating themselves to the same purposes for which he lived and died; seeking always to overcome evil with good, and to breast the swelling tide of human passion and opposition with meekness, patience, and love; promising to be in them an Almighty Divine presence, renovating and renewing the whole man, and empowering them to walk in His footsteps.[1]

Heavenly Father, in my daily striving, may this message be heard;
the message of an authentic, living Christ who changes lives. Amen.

---

1   From *Popular Christianity*.

> Who is this coming from Edom, from Bozrah, with his garments stained crimson? Who is this, robed in splendour, striding forward in the greatness of his strength? "It is I, proclaiming victory, mighty to save"
>
> (Isaiah 63:1 *NIV*)

I am afraid there are thousands who sit in our churches and chapels and hear the modern Christ descanted on, who, if asked their idea of Christ, would be utterly at a loss to give it. They have no definite conception of what his name or being means. They would not like to say whether he is in Heaven or on earth. If asked whether he had done anything for them personally, they cannot tell; the most they say is that they hope so, or that they hope he will do something someday. He is to them a mere idea. Another false but very common view of Christ in these days is that he is a sort of divine make-weight. You will hear people say, when spoken to about their souls, "Yes, I know I am very weak and sinful, but I am doing the best I can, and Jesus is my Saviour; he will make up what I lack." In these instances there is not even the recognition of the necessity of pardon, much less of the power of Christ to renew the soul in righteousness, and to fit it for the holy employments and companionships of Heaven. This Christ is simply dragged at the tail, not only of human effort but of human failure, and offered, as it were, in the arms of an impudent presumption, as a make-up in the scale of human deserts. And yet how many thousands of church and chapel-going people, it is to be feared, are deluded by supposing that this imaginary Christ will meet the needs of their souls before the judgment bar of God? To others this imaginary Christ is only a superior human being, a beautiful example – the most beautiful the world has ever seen; not divine, yet the nearest to our conception of the divine which even they think possible, but only human still. This Christ is held up as the embodiment of all that is noble, true, self-sacrificing, and holy – an example of what we are to be, but supplying no power by which to conform ourselves to the model.[1]

> Lord Jesus, you are indeed a beautiful example, yet you are so much more than that. You have a unique power to transform lives and situations.
> I pray for those in need of your transforming grace, especially those known to me personally. Reach them with power. Amen.

1   From *Popular Christianity*.

A SAVIOUR, AND A GREAT ONE

(Isaiah 19:20 *KJV*)

The people who make so much ado about the example of Christ are the furthest from following it. They say it is not intended to be followed literally. But how else can you imitate anyone? How can an example be followed figuratively? Alas! The admirers of this human Christ make it sadly manifest in their lives and experience that humanity needs not only a model, but an inspiring presence to restore its lost balance, energize its feeble faculties, and rekindle its spiritual aspirations. Conceiving only of a human model, the paralyzed soul finds no higher source of strength than its own desires and resolutions, and after the oft-repeated experiment at self-deliverance, sinks at length overwhelmed with a sense of failure and despair. It is not in man or angel, however sublime, to free the human soul from its fetters of realized guilt, or to empower it… Another modern representation of the Christ is that of a substitutionary Saviour, not in the sense of atonement merely, but in the way of obedience. This Christ is held up as embodying in himself the sum and substance of the sinner's salvation, needing only to be believed in, that is, accepted by the mind as the atoning sacrifice, and trusted in as securing for the sinner all the benefits involved in his death, without respect to any inwrought chancre in the sinner himself. This Christ is held up as a justification and protection in sin, not as a deliverer from sin. Men and women are assured that no harm can overtake them if they believe in this Christ, whatever may be the state of their hearts, or however they may, in their actions, outrage the laws of righteousness and truth. In other words, men are taught that Christ obeyed the law for them, not only as necessary to the efficacy of his atonement for their justification, but that he has placed his obedience in the stead of, or as a substitution for, the sinner's own obedience or sanctification, which in effect is like saying, "Though you may be untrue Christ is your truth; though you may be unclean, Christ is your chastity; though you may be dishonest, Christ is your honesty; though you may be insincere, Christ is your sincerity." The outcome of such a faith only produces outwardly the whited sepulchres of profession, while within are rottenness and dead men's bones.[1, 2]

Christ is all. My Christ is all in all. Amen.

---

1 Matthew 23:27.
2 From *Popular Christianity*.

The morning stars sang together and all the angels shouted for joy

(Job 38:7 *NIV*)

A gentleman once said to me, "I never did shout in my life, but today upon my word I couldn't help it." I said, "Amen, It's time, then, you began." I hope it may be the same with many of you. When the Lord comes to his Temple and fills it with his glory you won't know what to do. You must find vent somewhere, or you will be as the poor old African said he was, "ready to burst his waistcoat". We feel so about temporal things. People drop down dead with joy. People shriek with grief. People's hearts stand still with wonder at the news they have heard, perhaps from some prodigal boy. I heard of a mother not long ago, whom someone injudiciously told of the sudden return of her son, who dropped down dead, and never spoke. And when the Master comes to his Temple, that glorious blessed holy Saviour, whom you profess so to long after and to love, and who has been absent… many years, and whom you have been seeking after with strong crying and tears, do you think it will be too much to shout your song, or go on your face, or do any extravagant thing? Oh no, if there is reality, you cannot help yourself. The manifestation will be according to your nature. One will fall down and weep in quietness, and the other will get up and shout and jump. You cannot help it… When he comes, you won't be ashamed who knows it. When you really get a living Christ for your husband, you will be more proud than the bride is who has got a husband worth being proud of, and you will love to acknowledge and praise him; and the day is coming when you will crown him before all the host of Heaven.[1,2]

> Thank you, Lord, that you graciously accept worship offered in spirit and in truth; whether we jump up and down, clap, shout, or bring homage in silence, stillness, and reflective adoration. Receive my humble worship this day. Amen.

---

1   William Booth objected to outbursts of enthusiasm, shouting, dancing, and jumping while he was preaching, preferring order and decorum. He gave orders for people to stop doing such things. Having realized his order destroyed the spirit of meetings, he acknowledged his mistake. Catherine Booth defended those who gave vent to such enthusiasms. This defence was written in 1857. Subsequently, The Salvation Army sometimes held "Charismatic Meetings". There were prayer lines and people who were filled with the Holy Spirit were said to be "slain in the Spirit", which the Army called "stacking". Others were said to have "glory fits".

2   From *The Life of Catherine Booth The Mother of The Salvation Army, Vol. I.*

WE, THOUGH MANY, ARE ONE BODY IN CHRIST...
HAVING GIFTS THAT DIFFER ACCORDING TO THE GRACE GIVEN TO US,
LET US USE THEM: IF PROPHECY, IN PROPORTION TO OUR FAITH;
IF SERVICE, IN OUR SERVING; THE ONE WHO TEACHES, IN HIS TEACHING;
THE ONE WHO EXHORTS, IN HIS EXHORTATION; THE ONE WHO
CONTRIBUTES, IN GENEROSITY; THE ONE WHO LEADS, WITH ZEAL;
THE ONE WHO DOES ACTS OF MERCY, WITH CHEERFULNESS

(Romans 12:4–8 *ESV*)

You will see from William's letter what has been the subjects of our thoughts, and the cause of the anxiety we have experienced during the last few days. I have felt it far more keenly than I thought I should; in fact, it is the first real trial of my married life. Personally considered, I care nothing about it. I feel that a year's rest in one place will be a boon to us both, and especially a relief from the wearying anxiety which my dear husband has experienced of late. But as a manifestation of the spirit of a handful of ministers towards him in return for his toil – as an exhibition of the cloven foot of jealousy, and as a piece of rank injustice in allowing lying reports to be reiterated in open Conference, and this without any formal charges having been brought or any inquiry as to their truthfulness instituted, I regard as little better than an old priestly persecution over again, and am ready to forswear Conferences for ever! However, we shall see. We can afford to wait. A year's rest will be an advantage to William's mind and body. Time will do great things – the people will be able to look at and contrast the year's returns. Our friends, whom this discussion has proved to be neither few nor feeble, will spread their own report on this matter, and perhaps next Conference the trumpet will sound on the *other side*. Anyhow, if God wills him to be an evangelist, he will open up his way. I find that I love the work itself far more than I thought I did, and I am willing to risk something for it, but we shall see.[1, 2, 3]

> Father, your giftings are varied and multiple – thank you that there is room for everyone. Please guide those seeking to identify their sphere of service. Amen.

1   From a letter Catherine Booth wrote to her mother.
2   In 1857, the Booths were embroiled in a strong disagreement with the Methodist New Connexion Conference, over the future of William's ministry; whether to remain as an itinerant evangelist or to accept a more settled role as a circuit minister. A vote was taken that William Booth should accept a circuit appointment. A number of letters were exchanged, all of them frank and robust. An appointment to Halifax, Yorkshire, England, was agreed upon, and the Booths were to live in Brighouse.
3   From *The Life of Catherine Booth The Mother of The Salvation Army, Vol. I.*

God did not send his Son into the world to condemn the world
(John 3:17 NIV)

Another false idea of Christ… is that of a divine condemnation… People seem to think that they ought to spend all their lives bewailing and bemoaning their sins, and are forever crying out, "Oh, wretched man that I am";[1] "Christ have mercy on us, miserable sinners" and they go on crying this every day of their lives… They forget that the deliverer is here – that pardon is offered, and that he is ready to witness it and fill their souls with peace and joy. If Christ be only for condemnation, what are these poor souls advantaged by his coming?… The law made them realize their bondage, writhe under a sense of their sins, and set them longing after freedom and deliverance. It was their schoolmaster (or should have been) to bring them to Christ… who was to make them free; but alas! In this case, he is made a much harder schoolmaster than the law itself, for these poor souls get no deliverance, no peace, no joy, or power. They are always piping Paul's bewailing notes, in which he personified a convicted sinner, struggling under the fetters of condemnation. But they never get into his triumphant notes, where he declares, "There is now… no condemnation"[2]… The exhibition of a Christ too unsympathetic and implacable to be approached without a second intercessor, a far-off, austere judge, rather than a pitying, pardoning Saviour, has kept millions of poor souls in bondage all their lives. I must say, however, that I have more sympathy with such souls, because they are sincere, and earnest, and willing to deny themselves, in order to find the right way, than with those who thoughtlessly take refuge under any of the false representations of Christ to which we have referred… The Christ of God came not to bring condemnation but pardon, peace, and gladness to every penitent sinner on the face of the earth… The Christ of God is not a condemnatory Christ, but a pitying, pardoning Saviour, calling to his bosom the weary and heavy-laden.[3]

Thank you, Father, for such grace and mercy,
personified in Jesus. Here I am to worship. Amen.

1 Roman 7:24, KJV.
2 Romans 8:1.
3 From *Popular Christianity*.

THE SPIRIT OF THE LORD WILL COME POWERFULLY UPON YOU...
AND YOU WILL BE CHANGED INTO A DIFFERENT PERSON

(1 Samuel 10:6 *NIV*)

God's gifts are far more generously and impartially distributed than we are apt to imagine. Polish is not power; education is not intellect. We have found that out in The Salvation Army, if we had not done so before. Nevertheless, ours is not a religion of intellect, of culture, of refinement, of creeds, or of ceremony or forms. We attach very little importance to any of these in themselves. We gladly take hold of some of these, and use them as mediums through which to convey the living energy of the Spirit; but the power is in the life, not in the form. Where there is no life you can only get death. You may get it in beautiful forms, in beautiful ceremonies and symbols; but if there is no life you cannot beget life. The vital point is the life – the spirit. We have resuscitated this old-fashioned religion. We defy infidels to account on *natural principles* for the results we have to show. We do not pretend that the presenting [of] certain truths to a man's intellect, *even if he accepts those truths*, will change his moral nature. We recognize the soul as the reigning power in man, and we know that the only power that can really affect and transform the soul is the Spirit of God, therefore we do not attach much importance to people merely receiving the truth! Herein we differ very materially from most other evangelistic agencies. I receive many letters from people after reading our books, congratulating us that we do not teach the Antinomian doctrines[1] of a great deal of the evangelistic teaching of this day, that we don't preach the "only believe gospel", but that we preach repentance towards God, as well as faith in Jesus Christ, and a life of obedience to God.[2]

> Lord, your Spirit gives life, and everything else is the outworking of
> your life in our Christian experience. Help us never to look to symbols,
> rituals, and traditions for our deepest spiritual succour and
> sustenance, helpful though they can sometimes be. Amen.

---

1 A doctrine holding that under the gospel dispensation of grace, the moral law is of no use or obligation because faith alone is necessary to salvation. This was attacked by Luther and Wesley (among others) as an exaggeration and distortion of the teaching that justification is by faith alone.
2 From *The Salvation Army in Relation to the Church and State.*

FROM HOUSE TO HOUSE, THEY NEVER STOPPED TEACHING
(Acts 5:42 *NIV*)

As I began to talk to him [a man whose house Catherine Booth was visiting], with my heart full of sympathy, he gradually raised himself in his chair, and listened with a surprised and half-vacant stare. I spoke to him of his present deplorable condition, of the folly and wickedness of his course, of the interests of his wife and children, until he was fully aroused from the stupor in which I found him.

I read to him from the parable of the prodigal son,[1] while the tears ran down his face like rain. I then prayed with him as the Spirit gave me utterance,[2] and left, promising to call the next day with a pledge book,[3] which he agreed to sign.

I now felt that my work was done. Exhausted in body but happy in soul, I wended my way to the sanctuary, just in time for the conclusion of the service, and to lend a helping hand in the prayer meeting.

On the following day I visited this man again. He signed the pledge, and listened attentively to all I said. Full of hope I left him, to find another similarly lost and fallen. From that time I commenced a systematic course of house-to-house visitation, devoting two evenings per week to the work. The Lord so blessed my efforts that in a few weeks I succeeded in getting ten drunkards to abandon their soul-destroying habits, and to meet me once a week for reading the Scriptures and for prayer.[4]

> Lord, here we see a great example of practical service and organized
> evangelism. Thank you for the thoroughness of these ways.
> Bless your Church with a similar heart of systematic concern. Amen.

---

1 Luke 15.
2 Acts 2:4.
3 Popular in Methodism and with the Band of Hope, a book rather like a school register, to be signed and dated by the person pledging to abstain from alcohol.
4 From *Catherine Booth* by W. T. Stead.

DO YOU THINK YOU CAN PERSUADE ME TO BECOME A CHRISTIAN...?
(Acts 26:28 *NLT*)

The one great rule to be observed in all teaching is to make your lessons interesting. If you cannot awaken the interest of your child you had better give up, and school and inform *yourself* till you can. I have not a doubt that many an impetuous, earnest, high-spirited child is driven to hate the Bible, the sanctuary, and religious exercises in general by the cold, spiritless, insipid, canting manner in which he hears them read and performed. He knows by instinct that this is not the way people go through things in which their *hearts* are deeply concerned. He hears father and mother and friends talk in a natural, easy, interesting manner on business and family matters, and consequently he listens with interest, but the moment they begin with religion he *feels* there is no heart in it, he feels that it is because they *must*, not because they *like*. He is taught to sing "Happy, happy Sunday, the brightest of the seven" but he knows that in his home it is the dullest day of the week, and that the whole household are relieved when it is passed and they are able to be back at this world's employments and enjoyments.

Now, if you want your child to love and enjoy the Sabbath, you must make it the most *interesting* day of the week. If you want him to love and read his Bible you must so tell him its stories, and elucidate its lessons as to make it *interest* him. If you want him to love prayer you must so pray as to interest and draw out his mind and heart with your own, and teach him to go to God, as he comes to you, in his own natural voice and manner to tell him his wants and to express his joys or sorrows. The themes of religion are of all themes most interesting to children when dealt with naturally and interestingly.[1]

> Father, the stories of Jesus are the greatest stories of all time – God
> Incarnate, dead and buried, resurrected! Help me to retain a sense of infectious
> wonder and awe as a component of my worship and witness. Amen.

---

1 From *Practical Religion*.

SINCE WE LIVE BY THE SPIRIT, LET US KEEP IN STEP WITH THE SPIRIT
(Galatians 5:25 *NIV*)

I am pleased that Mr W puts such confidence in you, but do not be puffed up by it. Remember how weak you are, and ask the Lord to save you from conceit and self-sufficiency. Try to be fair and just in all your dealings with the boys; i.e. do not be hard on a boy whom you may not happen to like so well as another, but be fair, and treat all alike when left in charge. I know you will listen to these counsels because they are from your mother, and are given in love and desire to do well both for your soul and body.

We had a good service last night in one of the chapels; there was a splendid influence, and towards the close of my sermon I asked all those who would go all lengths with God to stand up, and some thirty or forty rose to their feet right in the public congregation. Pray for Sunday. I wish you could come and help me.[1]

My dear boy, walk consistently. It is the great source of strength, next to the Holy Spirit, and we must be consistent in order to *keep* the Spirit. Cast yourself afresh on the Lord for strength. Try simple trust, a moment at a time. Mind and observe all laws. Keep your own counsel. Never allow any boy to approach you with a secret which you would not like me to hear. Then you are safe.

I am in haste now, so goodbye,

From your loving, anxious mother.[2,3]

Father, in all my ways, at church, in the congregation, within my own family, help me to follow you and walk in your ways; simply trusting, every day. Amen.

---

1 Catherine Booth was on campaign in Leicester.
2 From a letter written by Catherine Booth to one of her sons, from Leicester, possibly 1876.
3 From *Catherine Booth The Mother of The Salvation Army, Vol. II.*

WE BELIEVE AND ARE SURE THAT THOU ART THAT
CHRIST, THE SON OF THE LIVING GOD

(John 6:69 *KJV*)

It is to be feared that thousands are looking to him [Christ] to save them from the consequences of sin – that is, Hell, who continue to commit sins; they utterly misunderstand the aim and work of the Christ of God. They do not see that he came not merely to bring men to Heaven, but to bring them back into harmony with his Father; they look upon the atonement as a sort of makeshift plan by which they are to enter Heaven, leaving their characters unchanged on earth. They forget that sin is a far greater evil in the divine estimation than Hell; they do not see that sin is the primal evil. If there were no sin there need be no Hell. God only proposes to save people from the consequences of sin by saving them from the sin itself; and this is the great distinguishing work of Christ – to save his people from their sins!…

Men have made up their minds that they can possess and enjoy all they can get of this world in common with their fellow men, and yet get to heaven at last. They have made up their minds that it is all nonsense about following the Christ, becoming a laughing stock to the world, which he made himself every day he lived, and setting themselves to live a holy life, which he said if they did not they were none of his; all this they have abandoned as an impossibility, and yet, not content without a religion, and finding it impossible to look into the future without a hope of some sort, they have manufactured a Christ to meet their views, and spun endless theories to match the state of their hearts. The worst of all, however, is that a great many of the teachers of Christianity have adopted these theories, and spend their whole lives in misrepresenting the Christ of the gospel.[1]

> Lord, whatever theories abound, confirm in my heart today the
> true and living presence of an authentic Christ; saving me now and
> saving me for eternity; saved from sin and saved from self. Amen.

---

1   From *Popular Christianity*.

I AM NOT COME TO CALL THE RIGHTEOUS, BUT SINNERS TO REPENTANCE
(Matthew 9:13 *KJV*)

At some services in the west of England, a gentleman largely interested in an unlawful business came every night for five weeks, and used to sit there, the picture of despair and wretchedness, till after ten o'clock. He went on in this way until his friends thought he would lose his reason. He was walking about his bedroom with his Bible open, kneeling down every now and then, struggling and wrestling to believe; but every time he thought of this ungodly business which he could not give up, despair seized him (for he thought of his money – he thought of the consequences to his family), until at last he said, "Money or no money, I will settle it." He gave it up, came out, and got saved at once… You see what a different thing this is to presenting Christ to people just as they are, where they are, doing what they like. You see what a different gospel it comes to, insisting upon a thorough renouncement and abandonment of evil as a condition of Jesus Christ receiving the sinner. This was Paul's gospel. Will you give me any other definition of it? Can you explain it any other way? Paul goes on to show us how he understood – "Whereupon, O king Agrippa, I was not disobedient unto the heavenly vision: but [showed] first unto them of Damascus, and at Jerusalem… and then to the Gentiles, that they should repent and turn to God, and do works meet for repentance."[1] Was this like saying "Only believe" without respect to any antecedent change of mind? Can anybody show me anything here in the slightest degree approximating to the Antinomian Gospel grafted on to some other of Paul's utterances? And yet surely the Apostle could not contradict himself. His writings about faith must be in harmony with this most unmistakable putting of the gospel to both Jews and Gentiles.[2] Moreover, did he tell Agrippa and Festus to believe? No, he left them trembling at it, because they were not willing to abandon their sins.[3]

> Today, Lord, I pray for all those who will be preaching your word in churches and chapels this weekend. I pray for pastors and ministers who have the responsibility of sharing the gospel. Bless them and their study. Amen.

---

1   Acts 26:19, KJV.
2   See Romans 1.
3   From *Aggressive Christianity*.

I DO BELIEVE; HELP ME OVERCOME MY UNBELIEF!

(Mark 9:24 *NIV*)

To the Philippian gaoler, who said, "Men and brethren, what must I do?" and who brought them out and began to wash their stripes, thus doing works meet for repentance at once, he said, "Believe on the Lord Jesus Christ, and thou shalt be saved".[1] Ah! My friend, you may try to get hold of Christ to your dying hour and at the last be lost, while you are holding on to your idols. If he could have saved us after the fashion we needed no Christ, we could have gone into Heaven without a Saviour; but he came to save his people from their sins, and while you are in love with your sins you may struggle and tremble as Agrippa and Felix did, and as the young ruler did, and you will meet a similar fate. You must let go your idols and be willing that Jesus should come and save you, now down among the dirt and mud of sin, but life you out of it, wash you, make you clean, and keep you clean, circumcise your hearts, and put his law in them, and then you shall know the gladness of his salvation! I have some people writing to me in this condition… This is what you have to do – let go your idols and say as the gentleman said of whom I told you, "Poverty or no poverty, business or no business, position or not position, suffering or prosperity never mind – Christ, Christ, I let all go for thee!"

Have you forsaken evil? Have you cut off the right hand? Have you plucked out the right eye?[2] I have people coming to me… groaning and sometimes worn to skeletons. They tell me they are in distress, they have got into bondage, they want the joy of the Lord and his daily fellowship, and when I ask the reason, they generally say, "Well, I don't know, but it seems to be want of faith."[3]

> Lord, have mercy on those who are stuck in sin, and can't
> seem to relinquish that which keeps them stuck. Persist with them,
> and enable their victory, Lord of the breakthrough. Amen.

---

1   Acts 16:31, KJV.
2   Matthew 5:29–30.
3   From *Aggressive Christianity*.

How shall we escape, if we neglect so great salvation[?]
(Hebrews 2:3 *KJV*)

God will not put you out of being to oblige you, and to save you from the consequences of your wilful rebellion. You exist. You must exist. At the judgment day you will exist, and you will exist for ever! God will have to do something with you; and seeing that you would not let him wash, and sanctify, and glorify you, he has no option but to leave you in your filth, to curse you, and to put you in the scavenging house of his universe with the Devil and his angels!

You say, "Stop, stop, I am not despising his goodness." Are you not? What is it to despise anything? It means treating it with contempt, neglecting it. It does not mean saying bad words about it; it does not mean blaspheming God. I should hope none of you are bad enough for that. It does not mean throwing it absolutely back and telling him in so many words that you will not have him to reign over you. Oh! No; it means treating him with contempt, and his salvation as a light thing. You are doing this, and some of you have been doing it for long rebellious years. If you had some money in a certain bank, and you heard that it was in a shaky condition, what a hurry you would be in to secure your treasure! You would not lose a moment. You would be investigating, and enquiring, and running to the bank to secure your money. You would not treat that with contempt; you would not despise the opportunity of securing it. Why? Because you deem your money an important thing. Now, if you valued the mercy and love of God for your poor soul, you would deem that an important thing, and you would not neglect it. Mind, it is written that all those who forget, or neglect God, shall be turned into Hell![1]

> Lord of eternity, grant me time today to pray specifically for those who do not want to know you. Bring to mind the names of loved ones who pay no heed to their eternal destiny. In your mercy, hear my prayers for their salvation. Amen.

1 From *Life and Death.*

DURING THE NIGHT PAUL HAD A VISION OF A
MAN OF MACEDONIA STANDING AND BEGGING HIM,
"COME OVER TO MACEDONIA AND HELP US"

(Acts 16:9 *NIV*)

Mind your soul. Do not let your thoughts be so absorbed even in study as to lead you to forget your Bible and to neglect prayer. I am sure the Lord will help you to learn and understand, if you constantly look to him and trust him. I am as certain that God gives mental light as that he gives natural light, if we only seek it from him and watch against those things which tend to darken the mind. It appears very wonderful that the Lord has opened the path for you. You little thought, when praying for him to undertake for you, that he would do so in agreeable and sufficient a manner as this! Let this encourage you to trust him more and more...

Since writing the above, your letter to Willie[1] has been forwarded to me. I am delighted to hear that you are going on so well, and that the Lord is using you amongst the boys. Nothing could rejoice me more than to hear that you are prospering in your soul; only keep right with God and everything else will go well, i.e. *for your good*, though not always as you would like. I had a good time in the theatre on Sunday night. It was packed, and hundreds, they tell me, were unable to get in. I trust the work has begun in reality, but I am so poorly that I fear I shall not be able to go on long. I thought I must have sent for a doctor yesterday. I was so prostrated I could scarcely stand. Papa came at night quite unexpectedly, and has gone on today to Stockton to interview some candidates. The man they sent here is a perfect sell: neither soul nor sense for Christian Mission work. Poor Papa, it is very trying for him. Make haste and get ready to help us.[2, 3, 4]

> Lord, I pray for preachers and evangelists who travel in the course
> of their ministry. Bless them as they make the sacrifice of being away
> from home and their loved ones, for the gospel's sake. Amen.

---

1 William Bramwell Booth.
2 From a letter Catherine Booth wrote to one of her boys, when she was in Leicester, England, possibly 1876.
3 The pattern of mission was that local people would often band together after a campaign in order to form a branch of the Christian Mission. Following the visit of a preacher/evangelist such as Catherine Booth, candidates to develop the work of the local branch would be assessed.
4 From *Catherine Booth The Mother of The Salvation Army, Vol. II.*

LET US DO GOOD TO EVERYONE, AND ESPECIALLY TO
THOSE WHO ARE OF THE HOUSEHOLD OF FAITH

(Galatians 6:10 *ESV*)

Our religion is not a religion of mere enjoyment, nor of faith only, but we recognize the power of God, transforming and keeping the soul of man… We are one in aim with the churches. Our object is the enlightenment and salvation of the people. We have sacrificed all things for this. We have given, at any rate, the best proofs that human beings can give of our sincerity, in having made everything in our lives subservient to this one object. And surely this is the aim of all good and true men. Surely there is nobody professing to be the disciple of the Lord Jesus, who would say that their time, influence, position, and wealth ought to be consumed upon themselves! Surely men only actuated by philanthropy would say, "Of course these blessings must be used for the general good, for the exaltation and blessing of those who have not been so favoured by Providence."

A Member of Parliament said, a short time ago, "If it were only for the material benefits you are conferring by the reformation of all these drunkards and blackguards, bringing them back to useful occupations and to the position of reliable citizens, you deserve well of your generation." We think so too; but then we think that this can only be permanently accomplished in one way. Here is where we differ from merely philanthropic and temporal reformers – the power of the Holy Ghost. We have had a great deal of experience, and we find that drunkard who sign the pledge, if they do not get the grace of God, soon fall back again. They want this spiritual restoration, and it is being actually accomplished on tens of thousands of them…

I think that these results ought to draw towards us the sympathy, prayer, and love of all really philanthropic, to say nothing of religious, men.[1]

Thank you, Lord, for people of charity and goodwill. Thank you too for
those in influential positions who are happy to use their influence for altruistic
means. Bless them this day, and use them for good. Amen.

---

1   From *The Salvation Army in Relation to the Church and State.*

CARE FOR THE CHURCH OF GOD
(Acts 20:28 *ESV*)

Here is the secret of the Church's failure! She is like Israel of old: She "hath multiplied her defenced cities and palaces, but she hath forgotten the God of Israel, in whom her strength is".[1] If you will read the history of the Church from the beginning, you will find it is true what I say, that just to the degree that the Church has increased in the material she has decreased in the spiritual. I do not say it ought to be so; I do not say that it is a necessity. I only give you a significant fact that it has been so.

You say: "How do you account for it?" I account for it because we poor, wretched, tiny, helpless creatures cannot get anything good in the creature, but we begin to *trust* in it. But when God teaches us that we have nothing to trust in, when he makes us realize our own nothingness and utter helplessness, and gives us hold of him with the grasp of despair, then we will begin to be of some use – and *never till then*. It is God worketh in us and by us.[2] The Apostle [Paul] labours all the way through to show and convince everybody that it was God in him and not of himself at all. Though he could have preached with enticing words of man's wisdom and, no doubt, had many a temptation to do it, as everybody has who has dipped into the flowery paths of human rhetoric and learning… he eschewed this as he would the Devil. He said – "No, this one thing I do"[3] – putting aside absolutely all else, he went on straight to the work till they cut his head off. I believe you do perceive; if you do not, take the book and examine it yourself. Be at the trouble. You will not get at the mind of the Lord without a great deal of trouble on these matters of power, spiritual union, and the like. Take the Bible with you on your knees before the Lord, and say, "Now, Lord, show me the meaning of this."[4]

> Lord, you are gracious enough to answer the prayers of your people, when we set our hearts after your will. Help me to see all that you wish me to see within the Bible, especially in regard to understanding the role of your Church. Amen.

---

1 See Hosea 8:14, KJV.
2 See Philippians 2:13.
3 See Philippians 3:13.
4 From *The Holy Ghost*.

CONSECRATE YOURSELVES TODAY TO THE LORD
(Exodus 32:29 *KJV*)

The Bible fits the human soul, and as the word exhorts us to holiness without, the Holy Spirit exhorts us to it within; and wherever you find a true child of God, you find him aspiring to this full conformity to the will and mind of Christ, whether his creed endorses it or not…

Almost the whole of the two epistles of St John have to be ignored or frittered away to meet the great mass of professing Christians of this day, as well as great portions of the word of God in other places – they are literally inapplicable to the majority of modern Christians. Everybody feels it, and the awful part of it is that instead of these Christians saying, "This is the standard, here is the glorious privilege, here is the grand truth, I do not come up to it, my experience does not match it, I have no faith to stretch myself to this measure, but I will never pull down the standard, though it damns me," they say, "Oh! It can't mean what it says" and so they begin to cut away at the very foundation of God, and take off the most glorious top stone which he has put on the Temple of grace – sanctification, holiness complete, and unreserved consecration to God. Now, I say, when you find that class of passages which refers to the lower walks of experience quoted, held up, exhibited, and enforced, as though they covered the whole realm of Christian experience, to the utter neglect and rejection of the other class, what becomes your duty as an individual wanting to know the will of God in order that you may do it? I say it becomes your duty to examine carefully this word for yourselves, and not to take this person's or the other person's opinions, but to ask God, by his Holy Spirit, to teach you… determining that whatever it costs you, though it should be friends, church associations, reputation, money, ease, comfort, all you have in this world… that this salvation is for you.[1]

> Lord, I would be your holy Temple, sacred and indwelt by your Spirit.
> Bend my will to the Bible's truths, and help me to resist any temptation to bend
> the Bible's truths to my will. Teach me the rich blessing of consecration. Amen.

1   From *Holiness*.

JUNE 21ST

WE THEN THAT ARE STRONG OUGHT TO BEAR
THE INFIRMITIES OF THE WEAK

(Romans 15:1 *KJV*)

You will be anxious to hear how I got on last night. Well, we had a splendid congregation. The chapel was very full, upstairs and down, with forms round the communion rail. I never saw it fuller on any occasion except once or twice during the revival. It was a wonderful congregation, especially considering that no bills had been printed. The Lord helped me, and I spoke for an hour with great confidence, liberty, and, I think, some power. They listened as for eternity, and a deep solemnity seemed to rest on every countenance. I am conscious that mentally and for delivery it was by far my best effort. Oh, how I yearned for more *divine influence* to make the most of that precious opportunity. Great numbers stayed to the prayer meeting. The bottom of the chapel was nearly full. Many are under conviction, but we had only three cases – I think all good ones. I kept the prayer meeting on until ten. The people did not seem to want to go. The man whom I told you about as having been brought in a month ago under "Be ye reconciled"[1] prayed last night with power…

The people are saying some very extravagant things. I hear a stray report now and then. But I think I feel as meek as ever, and more my own helplessness and dependence on divine assistance. Don't forget to pray for me. I have borne the weight of circuit[2] matters to an extent I could not have believed possible… When you come you will not only resume the command, but yourself take the reins.[3, 4, 5]

Thank you, Lord, for those who step in to help when another is unwell.
Today I ask your blessing on carers, helpers, nurses, and health visitors. Amen.

---

1 2 Corinthians 5:20, KJV.
2 Methodism is organized into circuits – geographical areas of responsibility.
3 William Booth was heavily committed to his duties with the Methodist Connexion in Gateshead, Tyneside, England. This led him to a complete breakdown in 1860, so the circuit officials asked Catherine to take on many of her husband's appointments while he received hydropathic treatment in Matlock, Derbyshire, England. Mrs Booth undertook responsibilities for "Sabbath night meetings".
4 From a letter Catherine Booth wrote to William Booth.
5 From *Catherine Booth* by Catherine Bramwell-Booth.

PREPARE YOUR MINDS FOR ACTION
(1 Peter 1:13 NASB)

The churches of this land, it is admitted, are not keeping pace by a long way with the increase of the population, much less overtaking the lapsed multitudes beyond. Then you have only to keep going on at this rate, and you see what will happen! If vice continues to aggress upon virtue, you see what is before us as a nation. You have all the elements of demoralization, disorganization, and destruction existing in your midst today. They are only waiting the development of circumstances, and then look out! I am sure of that. The conviction is burnt into my soul, and yet we cannot get the respectable and well-to-do classes to awaken to the fact. "Oh!" as somebody said the other day. "The great want of this generation is public spirit." It is so difficult to get people to wake up to what is going on outside their own four walls. They separate themselves from these tumultuous elements and refuse to see them, and think themselves secure, when all the while they are sitting on the crater of a great volcano, which will, if they don't mind, burst and blow them up! What is to be done? Oh that God would awaken all really earnest and thoughtful men to ask this question! You must face this overwhelming torrent of evil with a direct antagonistic force of good, truth, righteousness, the fear and love of God, righteous living, and vigorous effort. You may educate; but don't you know, some of you, the state of the educated classes? Is it any better than that of the uneducated? Has not the education only increased the capacity for mischief? You know it is so. You know how fast we have been going back for the last fifty years in morality. It was time somebody tried to do something; and we have tried, and God has owned and blessed our efforts.[1]

Lord, you call your Church to action. Give us holy concern
and heavenly ideas to meet the world's great need. Amen.

---

1 From *The Salvation Army in Relation to the Church and State.*

DO TWO WALK TOGETHER, UNLESS THEY HAVE AGREED...?
(Amos 3:3 ESV)

We [The Salvation Army] have never allowed any consideration of interest, or ease, or aggrandizement, or popularity to weight with us for one moment. We have been satisfied to know we have been doing the will of God. We have only waited to be satisfied in our own minds with respect to the steps we have taken, and then we have gone forward in the face of the world, and shall continue to do so. We want you [the Church] to do so. We do not say, "Do it in our way," only do it. Face the evil, and do something. Do not sit still in indifference and supineness. If you have any regard for your children, or for the future of this nation, or for the future destiny of the world, which so much hangs upon this nation, do something.

God only knows how deeply I desire that all godly men could present one common front to the foe, that we might be one in heart, one in purpose, and one in united effort. If this cannot be, let us all do our best. We intend to go on doing so, and we shall prepare the way for others. The Salvation Army is the friend of all and the enemy of none. We do not hinder, but help the churches. For whatever helps to humanize and civilize the people, we must help the churches.... As a rule, the churches have been revived and helped by our operations in most of the towns to which we have gone. It is one of the disadvantages under which we have laboured, that as our people got more refined and prosperous, many of them go off to the churches, leaving us to struggle on with the masses beneath; and these are the people who could most help us with funds. Therefore we feel we have a double claim upon the sympathy of Christians.[1]

> Lord of the Church, you prize unity and harmony amongst your people.
> The glory of the Church is that there is room for all styles of worship and
> spiritual expression. Bless all denominations in their work and witness.
> Thank you for placing me in a church where I feel I belong. Amen.

---

1 From *The Salvation Army in Relation to the Church and State.*

WHOEVER LOVES MONEY NEVER HAS ENOUGH; WHOEVER LOVES WEALTH IS NEVER SATISFIED WITH THEIR INCOME

(Ecclesiastes 5:10 *NIV*)

One would think, from the meanness and the discomfort of the ordering of many families, that money was the household god at whose shrine every consideration of comfort, health, friendship, and benevolence had been sacrificed. "What will it cost?" is the first question that meets every suggestion of improvement in any direction, and this frequently, not because money is scarce, but simply because it cannot be parted with!

Now, children soon find out the ruling principle in the family administration, and if they see it to be covetousness or avariciousness, parents may *teach* all the catalogue of Christian virtues from morning till night, but their children will grow up selfish in the very core of their souls. Like begets like the world over, and you show me a household where the spirit of covetousness reigns, and I will show you ungenerous, cunning children. "The love of money is the root of all evil"[1] is an axiom as true as it is neglected; and until parents, by their actions, show their children that they deem domestic comfort and religion, the claims of Christian hospitality, the blood and lives of their servants, the claims of the suffering and the destitute, and the crying need of the benighted multitude of more importance than the hoarding of money, they must go on reaping the reward of their covetousness in the selfish indulgence, ungrateful neglect, and open profligacy of their children. Ah, how many a parent, who has sacrificed all the higher and nobler impulses of his own and his children's natures to moneymaking, has had it scattered by thousands by wicked, selfish sons? There is an inordinate estimate of the value of money.[2]

Lord, take my silver and my gold. (It's yours anyway!) Guide me in my spending, in my desiring, and in my sharing, this day. Amen.

---

1   1 Timothy 6:10, KJV.
2   From *Practical Religion.*

HOLD ON TO WHAT IS GOOD
(1 Thessalonians 5:21 *NIV*)

Another great evil which I have seen even in families where there has in the main been much good training, is the yielding in an emergency on points of principle for the sake of expediency. Take an illustration. Here is a family who are trained in the principles of abstinence from intoxicating drinks, as all Christian families undoubtedly ought to be. These parents have wisely taught their children that strong drink is an evil and bitter thing, and that all traffic and countenance of it brings a curse; but on a certain day, a letter comes announcing that General So-and-so, or Captain Somebody is coming to pay a visit to his cousin, on his return from India. Of course there is much excitement and expectation among the junior members of the family, and a becoming anxiety on the part of the parents worthily to entertain their guest, but a difficulty presents itself. The General is not an abstainer, he has always been accustomed to his wine and spirits. "What shall we do?" says the mother. "He will think it inhospitable and mean to deny him his favourite beverage." "Well, yes," says the father. "I don't see how we can do it in *this instance*; you see, he is an old man, and would not appreciate our views or our motives. I fear we shall have to order a little wine for him. I don't like to bring it in sight of the children, but we must explain the circumstances to them, and we will hope no harm will come of it." These parents sacrifice principle to expediency, and admit the mocker to their family circle. Can they be surprised if one of their sons turns out a drunkard? "Ah!" said a broken-hearted father once to my husband. "I trained my boy in abstinence principles, but I did not keep him out of the society of those who thought there was no harm in moderate drinking, and now he is an outcast and an alien whom I cannot allow to cross my threshold – he has killed his mother, and will bring down my grey hairs with sorrow to the grave."[1,2]

> Whatever the issue, Lord, please grant me good grace to keep the same
> principles in private as I do in public. Help me against the temptation to
> compromise. Help me too, to respect points of view that are different to mine.
> Amen.

---

1   See Genesis 44:29, KJV.
2   From *Practical Religion*.

THE WORD BECAME FLESH, AND DWELT AMONG US, AND WE SAW HIS GLORY, GLORY AS OF THE ONLY BEGOTTEN FROM THE FATHER, FULL OF GRACE AND TRUTH

(John 1:9 *NASB*)

The incarnation was a mystery, looked at from a human standpoint, but no greater mystery than many other incarnations taking place all around us, and because a mystery, nonetheless a necessity. Humanity must have a deliverer able to save, and no less than an Almighty deliverer was equal to the task. Here, all merely human deliverers, all philosophers and teachers of the world, had failed, because they could only teach, they could not renew. They could set up a standard, enunciate a doctrine, but they could not remove man's inability, or endue him with power to reach it. Here even the law of God failed, and that which was ordained to life wrought death. Here was the sunken rock, the bitter maddening failure of all systems and deliverers, they failed to rectify the heart; they could not give a new life or impart another spirit... Man needed some being outside of himself, above him, and yet able to understand and pity him in his utmost guilt, misery, and helplessness – able to inspire him with a new life, to impart light, love, strength, and endurance, and to do this always and everywhere, in every hour of darkness, temptation, and danger. Humanity needed an exhibition of God, not merely to be told about him, but to see him; not merely to know that he was an Almighty Creator, able to crash him, but that he is a pitiful Father, yearning and waiting to save him. God's expedient for showing this to man was to come in the flesh. Can the wisest modern philosopher or the most benevolent philanthropist conceive a better? How otherwise could God have revealed himself to fallen man? Since the Fall, man has proved himself incapable of seeing or knowing God; he has ever been afraid of the heavenly, running away even from an angel; and when only hearing a voice and seeing the smoke which hid the divinity, he exceedingly feared and quaked... God desired that man should see him – that is, know him – and live, notwithstanding his fall; he promised a Saviour.[1]

Jesus came down to *show* me God, because words are insufficient.

---

1   From *Popular Christianity*.

When she speaks, her words are wise,
and she gives instructions with kindness

(Proverbs 31:26 *NLT*)

The first and most common objection urged against the public exercises of women, is that they are unnatural and unfeminine. Many labour under a very great but common mistake – that of confounding nature with custom. Use, or custom, makes things appear to us natural which, in reality, are very unnatural; while, on the other hand, novelty and rarity make very natural things appear strange and contrary to nature… Making allowance for the novelty of the thing, we cannot discover anything either unnatural or immodest in a Christian woman, becomingly attired, appearing on a platform or in a pulpit. By *nature* she seems fitted to grace… God has given to woman a graceful form and attitude, winning manners, persuasive speech and, above all, a finely toned emotional nature, all of which appear to us eminent *natural* qualifications for public speaking. We admit that want of mental culture, the trammels of custom, the force of prejudice, and one-sided interpretations of Scripture, have hitherto almost excluded her from this sphere; but, before such a sphere is pronounced to be unnatural, it must be proved either that woman has not the *ability* to teach or to preach, or that the possession and exercise of this ability unnaturalizes her in other respects; that so soon as she presumes to step on the platform or into the pulpit, she loses the delicacy and grace of the female character. Whereas, we have numerous instances of her retaining all that is most esteemed in her sex, and faithfully discharging the duties peculiar to her own sphere, and at the same time taking her place with many of our most useful speakers and writers. Why should woman be confined exclusively to the kitchen and the distaff, any more than man to the field and workshop?[1]

Father, keep my mind clear regarding what is custom or social preference, as opposed to Scriptural truth. Help me not to mistake one for the other. Amen.

---

1 From *Female Ministry*.

WHOEVER SAYS HE ABIDES IN HIM OUGHT TO WALK
IN THE SAME WAY IN WHICH HE WALKED

(1 John 2:6 *ESV*)

The most important question that can possibly occupy the mind of man is how much like God we can be and how near to him we can come on earth… The mystery of mysteries to me is how anyone with any measure of the Spirit of God can help looking at this blessing of holiness and saying, "Well, even if it does seem too great for attainment on earth it is very beautiful and very blessed, and I wish I could attain it"… We all should hunger and thirst after it, and feel that we shall never be satisfied till we wake up in the likeness of the Saviour. And yet, alas, we do not find it so. In many instances the very first thing professing Christians do is to resist and reject this doctrine of holiness. I heard of a leader of religion saying that for anybody to talk about being holy showed that they knew nothing of themselves and nothing of Jesus Christ. It has come to something if holiness and Jesus Christ are at the antipodes of each other. I thought he was the centre and fountain of holiness and through him holiness could be wrought in us. Large numbers of people make infirmities into sins. They insist that the requirements of the Adamic law have never been abated. We are not, they say, under the evangelical law of love, or the law of Christ, as the Apostle puts it, but still under the Adamic law, and imperfections and infirmities are as sins. I wonder such people do not think of a certain passage which must for ever explode such a theory, where the Apostle says, "Most gladly therefore will I rather glory in my infirmities, that the power of Christ may rest upon me."[1] Had these infirmities been sins we should have the outrageous anomaly of an Apostle of Jesus Christ glorying in his sins. These infirmities were only those defects of mind and body which were capable of being overcome and overruled by grace to the glory of Christ.[2]

The likeness of Christ I would wear. There is no lovelier adorning.
Come today, Spirit of Jesus, as guest of my soul. Amen.

---

1   2 Corinthians 12:9, KJV.
2   From *The Highway of our God.*

"THE VIRGIN WILL CONCEIVE AND GIVE BIRTH TO A SON, AND THEY WILL CALL HIM IMMANUEL" (WHICH MEANS "GOD WITH US")

(Matthew 1:23 *NIV*)

Those who reject his [Christ's] divinity say he is the nearest to the divine of anything we can conceive. They say he is the best of the good of our race – even infidels cannot find fault with his character; they bow down before the spotless purity, the beneficence and moral beauty of Jesus Christ. All schools grant this. Then, taking my stand here I say that this perfect being claimed to be divine, and he claimed it so unmistakably and persistently that if you take it out of his teachings, you reduce them to a jumble of inconsistencies. His divinity is the central fact around which all his doctrines and teachings revolve, so that if this be extinguished, they become like a system of astronomy without the sun – dark, conflicting, and inconsistent. Read the gospels and eliminate for yourselves all his assumptions of divinity, and then see what you can make of his teaching... These assumptions were understood and resented by the people to whom he spoke, and they surely were the best judges as to what he meant. If they had mistaken His meaning, he was bound, merely as a man of honour, to explain himself, but he never did; so when the Jews said, "Whom makest thou thyself?" or, "This man maketh himself equal with God",[1] he did not demur nor retract, but repeated, "Yet I came forth from the Father, and I go to the Father."[2] This was the one intolerable point in his teaching, which the Jews, who owned no plurality in gods, could not endure; that any other being should be one with their Jehovah was to them insufferable, and for this they ultimately crucified him. "What further need..." has said the high priest, "of witnesses? behold, now ye have heard his blasphemy"[3]... If he were so near an approach to perfection as even infidels admit, how was it that he allowed such an impression of his teachings to go abroad, if he were not divine?[4]

Jesus Christ – Immanuel. Fully God and fully man. Amen.

1   From John 10:33, KJV.
2   See John 16:28, KJV.
3   Matthew 26:65, KJV.
4   From *Popular Christianity*.

THE MASTER COMMENDED THE DISHONEST MANAGER BECAUSE HE HAD
ACTED SHREWDLY. FOR THE PEOPLE OF THIS WORLD ARE MORE SHREWD IN
DEALING WITH THEIR OWN KIND THAN ARE THE PEOPLE OF THE LIGHT

(Luke 16:8 *NIV*)

I am to speak… on the adoption and carrying out of common sense business principles in religion… Let us look for a moment at the aim, the purpose, of all business operations, and in fact, of all effort amongst men. What is the end? It is patent, of course, at first sight, that the end is gain in some form or another. Everybody labours, uses means, exercises their talents, uses their opportunities, to acquire something which they could not otherwise acquire. Nobody dreams of making labour the end, but only the means to the end. It is not enough for businessmen that an establishment is kept up, that the men are kept employed, that the books or the goods are in order, the routine of business kept going. Every such establishment has an eye to the result – the profit accruing to the owners. Profit is the end which men propose to themselves in every department of business or labour; and nobody imagines that they are going on tiling, and keeping business machinery going without reaping adequate profit as the result. Nobody quarrels with businessmen for seeking to do a large business, so that they do it legitimately. I should not. I don't mind how much business a man does, if he does it righteously and for the Kingdom of God – especially if he sends The Salvation Army a slice of the profits! Now, why should we not adopt the same principle in religion? That is, why should we not look for and labour with a view to results? We believe that we have as much right to expect success in spiritual things as men of the world have in temporal things. God has shown us that it is just as rational to expect spiritual results from the use of certain spiritual power exercised through certain measures or agents, as it is to expect a good harvest when the husbandman ploughs, harrows, and sows at the right time and in the right way.[1]

> Lord, let me be a learner; picking up ideas and suggestions
> wherever I can, for Kingdom benefit. Amen.

---

1   From *The Salvation Army in Relation to the Church and State.*

BUT REMEMBER THE LORD YOUR GOD, FOR IT IS HE WHO GIVES YOU
THE ABILITY TO PRODUCE WEALTH, AND SO CONFIRMS HIS COVENANT,
WHICH HE SWORE TO YOUR ANCESTORS, AS IT IS TODAY

(Deuteronomy 8:18 *NIV*)

The farmer could not reap a harvest without the sunshine, the shower, and the blessing of God; but he gets that *in conjunction with his own effort.* On the other hand, all the sunshine and shower and blessing in the world would not bring him a harvest if he sat at home in idleness. We believe that there are laws in the spiritual Kingdom as unerring in their operation, and as certain in their results, as any physical laws; and that if we conform ourselves to those laws, and act upon them, we may be as certain of a good harvest morally as the husbandman can be naturally. In other words, we believe *we shall reap according as we sow*; and we contend that the history and the success of The Salvation Army prove it. We cannot see why religious establishments should be kept going without reference to the results, any more than temporal establishments. We do not think that religious teachers or people should be content with maintaining an existence – with just operating upon the same number of people from year's end to year's end, without making any appreciable aggression on the territory of the enemy outside. We believe that all rational measures, all the measures which men use with respect to this world, if they are lawful and good, may be transferred by the sanctification of the motive, by the transposition of aim, to the Kingdom of God. That by transferring the Kingdom into the place of self, we may use every good and lawful measure for its extension; yea, that we are *bound to do it*... I don't want to make any reflections, but everybody knows that the Christians of this generation do not act, as a rule, on this principle; I am afraid we may safely say, in the great majority of instances, they lose the end in the means. They rest in the labour, without looking for adequate profits – that continual increase and everlasting aggression which is evidently contemplated and provided for in the gospel of our Lord Jesus Christ.[1]

Lord, in business, at home, in church matters,
help my standards to be Kingdom standards. Amen.

---

1   From *The Salvation Army in Relation to the Church and State.*

MANY ARE THE PLANS IN A PERSON'S HEART,
BUT IT IS THE LORD'S PURPOSE THAT PREVAILS
(Proverbs 19:21 *NIV*)

Another great enemy to the formation of righteous character is ambition for what is called position in society! Some parents are continually putting before their children future aggrandizement and fortune as a stimulus to industry and effort, thus holding up to their young minds this world's prosperity and applause as the great aim and object of life. To get to be more learned, more genteel, more wealthy than men of their own class, so that they may be received into higher circles of worldly society. Such parents often fail, and in the attempt to leap the chasm which bars his upward course, many a son falls headlong through the abyss of disappointed ambition, down to damnation, and many a daughter to that path, the steps of which "take hold on hell".[1] Ah, but some succeed! Yes, and what reward do the parents often get? The son and daughter, whom they toiled and struggled so hard to push up, get so high they can scarcely see the poor, neglected parents down below, and often leave them to die with a broken heart. Truly "godliness with contentment is great gain".[2]

I cannot close these remarks without lifting up my voice against the practice now so prevalent amongst respectable families, of sending children to boarding schools before their principles are formed or their characters developed. Parents are led away by the professedly religious character of schools, forgetting that, even supposing the master or governess may be all that can be desired, a school is a little *world* where all the elements of unrenewed human nature are at work with as great variety, subtlety, and power as in the great world outside. You would shrink from exposing your child to the temptation and danger of association with unconverted worldly men and women; why should you expose them to the influence of children of the *same* character, who are not unfrequently sent to these schools because they have become utterly vitiated and unmanageable at home? I... made up my mind to keep my children under *my own influence*... To this end I have rejected several very tempting offers in the way of educational advantage.[3]

Father, in all respects, help me to regard the long-term consequences of my actions and decision. Grant me clarity of thought when planning my days.

Amen.

---

1   Proverbs 5:5, KJV.
2   1 Timothy 6:6, KJV.
3   From *Practical Religion*.

In Christ all the fullness of the Deity lives in bodily form

(Colossians 2:9 *NIV*)

[Christ's] character supported his assumptions [of divinity]… Millions of the best of the human race have accepted these assumptions without being shocked by them. If he be not divine, how comes it to be that the greatest of human intellects, the sincerest of human souls, and the most aroused and anxious of human consciences, have ventured their all upon this divine word, and have seen nothing contradictory between his claims and the actual character which he sustained in the world; whereas, imagine the very holiest and best who ever trod our earth putting forth such assumptions, and how would they sound?

Suppose Moses, who had talked with God in the burning bush, or Isaiah, whose tongue was touched with the live coal from off the altar, or Daniel, the man greatly beloved, to whom the angel Gabriel was sent again and again, or the Apostle of the Gentiles, who was admitted into the third heaven,[1] or the beloved Apostle John, suppose any of these men saying, "I am from above, Ye are from beneath", "I am not of this world", "if ye believe not I am he, ye shall die in your sins", "I came forth from the Father, and am come into the world". Again, "I leave the world and go to the Father"; and in his prayer on the eve of his agony, "The glory which I had with the Father before the world was", and again, in answer to Philip's request, "Show us the Father", "Have I been so long time with you, and yet hast thou not known me…? he that hath seen me hath seen the Father"; "Believest thou not that I am in the Father, and the Father in me?"[2, 3]

> In my life, Lord Jesus, be glorified – not merely as
> a good teacher or as a moral example, but as my God. Amen.

---

1   Exodus 3; Isaiah 6:6; Daniel 9:21; 2 Corinthians 12:2.
2   See John 8:23; John 17:16; John 8:24; John 16:28; see John 17:5; John 14:9; John 14:10, (all scriptures KJV).
3   From *Popular Christianity*.

HARD WORK IS WORTHWHILE, BUT EMPTY TALK WILL MAKE YOU POOR
(Proverbs 14:23 *CEV*)

We of The Salvation Army have to some extent learnt wisdom by the failures of others; and believing that we have a right to calculate on results, we are determined to use all lawful means and to put forth all possible effort in order to secure them!

God has shown us that in order to this end, we must have definite plans of operation, reliable agencies, and plenty of hard work. Men act on these lines with respect to the affairs of this world. When they want to excavate a tunnel, make a railway, lay a telegraph cable, they don't talk about it for generations in a vague, sentimental way, but lay their plans and set to work to accomplish the thing. If any businessman were to talk and act as many Christians do, he would be set down as having a screw loose. Some of you have may had experience of what I mean, you have known a young man full of vague notions of how he is going to get rich. He is going to make a fortune. He is quite sure he can accomplish it. He looks upon that which his neighbours have been struggling for all their lives as an already accomplished fact. He sees none of the difficulties. He has grand notions of how it is to be done. A wise businessman says to him, "That is not the way. You will have to begin at the bottom of the ladder and climb slowly. You will not do it by building castles in your airy brain. You will have to set to work. You will have to concentrate your mind and form a definite idea of what you are going to do, and how you are going to do it." Thousands are just like that young man with respect to religious affairs. I often say: "Oh! God help us to be definite, help us to recognize common sense in religion, as we do in other things; for it is wonderful what a deal of vapouring and vagueness there is in religious matters."[1]

> Talk, Lord, is cheap. Remind me not to hide behind it while the time for action comes and goes. God forbid that I should merely talk, and not walk. Amen.

---

1 From *The Salvation Army in Relation to the Church and State.*

I WILL HASTEN AND NOT DELAY TO OBEY YOUR COMMANDS
(Psalm 119:60 *NIV*)

We must give up sentimentalizing. Sentimentalizing is of no more use in religion than in business, and we must set to real practical common sense scheming and downright hard work. If ever the gospel is to make headway against the rush of evil passions, worldly ambition, and devilish animosity, it must be by determined, deadly warfare, conducted with at least as much care, sagacity, and persistency as men bestow on earthly enterprises for gain or glory.

Does anyone object that this is reducing religion to mere machinery? I answer, Oh no, it is only providing a machinery through which the Spirit of Christ can operate. It is only reducing sentiment to practice. God prescribed the machinery under the old dispensation; but Jesus Christ and his Apostles left us free as air to modes and measures, that we may provide that kind of organization most suited to the necessities of the age. There is not a bit of "redtapeism" in the whole of the New Testament. God does not care about forms or modes, so that we have the living spirit in them; and all forms are but corpses when the spirit has gone out of them. Nevertheless, we must have forms and methods; and the more intelligently planned and the more widely adapted, the better they will succeed. Haphazard, fitful, unorganized, unreliable action fails everywhere, no matter how good the cause in which it is engaged. You never trust to this kind of action in business. If you want to accomplish anything, you call your heads of departments together and plan how it is to be done; you set the best man to the best post, and make him responsible for carrying out your plans. That is the only sensible and rational way to get anything done.[1]

What is it you would have me for (with) you today, Lord?
Help me to plan, guide my thinking, then strengthen my action. Amen.

---

1   From *The Salvation Army in Relation to the Church and State.*

To keep me from becoming conceited because of the
surpassing greatness of the revelations, a thorn was given me
in the flesh, a messenger of Satan to harass me,
to keep me from becoming conceited

(2 Corinthians 12:7 *ESV*)

I glory in my infirmities that in consequence of them the power of Christ shall rest upon me and lift me above them, that Christ shall make me independent of them and master of them, so that I shall glorify his strength and grace more than if I were perfect in mind and body...

The divine assurance, "My grace is sufficient for thee"[1] ought to forbid the idea of sin. Paul sought the Lord thrice to have this thorn removed.[2] If it had been sin, the Lord would have been as anxious to have it removed as his servant was. This thorn was doubtless some physical trial, as the words "in the flesh" indicate – some tribulation or sorrow through the patient endurance of which the strength of Christ could be magnified. Mark that this was a divinely permitted discipline to prevent Paul from falling into sin, and that is quite a different thing from sin itself. The Lord sent this to Paul not for the purpose of making him humble, for he was humbled before, but to keep him humble.

And does he not send something to us all? Do we not need trials and tribulations in the flesh in order to keep us humble? But is this evidence that pride is dwelling in us and reigning over us? It is an evidence just to the contrary. Holiness is being saved from sin in act, in purpose, in thought![3]

Thank you, Lord, for this challenging perspective on trial and tribulation.
I pour contempt on all my pride, and pray for faith to trust and obey. Amen.

---

1   2 Corinthians 12:9, KJV.
2   2 Corinthians 12:8.
3   From *The Highway of our God*.

He will sit as a refiner and purifier of silver;
he will purify the Levites and refine them like gold and silver
(Malachi 3:3 *NIV*)

A young lady wrote me that she had been the bond slave for four or five years of a certain besetting sin which she had struggled and wrestled and prayed to overcome. Now and then she would gain the victory, and then down she would go again. She said, "It is such a subtle thing, connected with my thoughts and imagination, so that I do not think I ever can be saved." I showed her how dishonouring this unbelief was, and that if she would trust Christ to come and reign in her heart, he could cleanse the very thoughts and imaginations. She made a little advance, but said she could not come so far as to think that Christ could purify her thoughts. She believed that he could save her from putting them into practice, but not that he could purify them. I tried to show her how Jesus, by the inspiration of his Holy Spirit, could purify the very thoughts of our hearts and, thank God, she did go another step. She said, "I rejoice with trembling for fear it should be only temporary, but I have trusted him to purify the source. I must say he has done it, and instead of thinking these thoughts I have holy thoughts. If Satan presents anything to my mind it is so repulsive to me that I cannot tell you the grief and horror with which it fills me." Later she said, "I am conscious that my thoughts are pleasing to him and he has saved me from this sin which has been the torment of my life for all these years." What I say is that anything he can do for one he can do for another.

If I am wrong here I give up the whole question. I am perfectly mistaken in the purpose and aim and command of the gospel dispensation if God does not want his people to be pure... We are told over and over again that God wants his people to be pure, and purity in their hearts is the end and purpose of the gospel of Jesus Christ. If it is not so I am utterly deceived.[1]

> Lord, your love is pure. You are pure. You long for me to be pure.
> Purifying God, ignore any reluctance I might portray, and make me like you.
> Amen.

---

1 From *The Highway of our God.*

OUR GOD AND SAVIOUR JESUS CHRIST
(2 Peter 1:1 *NIV*)

Not only does he [Jesus Christ] claim... oneness of essence with the Father, but also that omniscience which enables him not only to be with his people but to dwell in them, as shown in his answer to the question of Judas, when he asked how it was that he would manifest himself to his own people and not to the world. Jesus answered, "If a man love me, he will keep my words: and my Father will love him, and we will come unto him, and make our abode with him."[1] Think of any creatures – David, a Paul, a John, daring to claim for himself this omniscience. If this Christ were not divine, then there is no alternative; he was altogether an impostor and a deceiver. From such a conclusion, however, even infidels and blasphemers shrink, and therefore we must be allowed to hold to our faith in our divine Redeemer – our Immanuel, "God with us"[2]... Would any less than an almighty, omniscient, infinite deliverer meet the needs of your souls? If so, you must feel much better and stronger, and more able to help yourselves than I do. "Great is the mystery of godliness: God was manifest in the flesh, justified in the Spirit, seen of angels, preached unto the Gentiles, believed on in the world, received up into glory."[3] But take this mystery out of Christianity, and the whole system utterly collapses. Without a divine Christ, Christianity sinks into a mere system of philosophy, and becomes as powerless for the renovation and salvation of mankind as any of the philosophies which have preceded it. But no, our Joshua has come, our Deliverer is here... He comes now in the flesh of his true saints, just as really as he came first in the body prepared for him, and he comes for the same purpose, to renew and to save; he is knocking at the doors of your hearts even now.[4, 5]

Not a philosophy. Not a theory. Not a moral system. A person. A man. Flesh and blood. God as a human being. Jesus came down. Wonderful, wonderful love.

Amen.

---

1   John 14:23, KJV.
2   Matthew 1:23, KJV.
3   1 Timothy 3:16, KJV.
4   Revelation 3:20.
5   From *Popular Christianity*.

THE WORD OF THE CROSS IS FOLLY TO THOSE WHO ARE PERISHING, BUT TO US WHO ARE BEING SAVED IT IS THE POWER OF GOD

(1 Corinthians 1:18 *ESV*)

Men do fill up… the measure of their iniquity. They do put the last drop into the cup, and God says, "It is enough." It is not always by an outward or manifest act that the cup of rebellion is filled; it is often done in secret. Those Jews little thought they were filling it by neglecting and despising the Nazarene. You may think you are only neglecting the entreaties of a little woman, and yet before the next Sunday you may be in Hell. Every time I hear of such things, I say, "I will be clear of the blood of souls. I don't care what people say of me; I will never speak to sinners so that one man or woman in my audience can stand up and say, 'You might have warned me more faithfully, told me more plainly than you did.'" I would rather die than that should be the case.

Sinner, what will you do? Mind, Paul says, "Or treasurest up to *thyself* wrath against the day of wrath."[1] It is not God who treasures it up. It will be God's wrath against your sins; but you, and you alone, will be responsible for its coming on *you*. You need not inherit it, for another has borne it for you, if you would only accept him as your sacrifice and your Saviour. Will you deliberately reject his way of escape, and in spite of all his goodness make good your claim to his everlasting wrath? Will no mercy, no longsuffering, no past experience, no forebodings of conscience, no shadows of the pit, bring you to repentance? Will you despise any longer, or will you yield now? Will you give up? Will you go down at his feet? Will you turn away from sin and evil companions, your old associations, and come right to the foot of the cross?[2]

The cross! The old rugged cross! Where the price of my sins was paid!
At your feet, Lord Jesus, I bow adoring.
Thank you for the cross; proof of mercy, emblem of grace. Amen.

---

1   See Romans 2:5, KJV.
2   From *Life and Death.*

Whoever comes to me I will never drive away
(John 6:37 NIV)

I am afraid that sin lieth at the door, and when we come to close quarters we generally find there is some idol, some course of conduct, or some *doubtful* conduct which keeps God out of the soul, and when this is confessed and renounced, people get the presence of God and go away rejoicing in him. It is so in nearly every case. God does not arbitrarily withdraw himself from his people. He wants to dwell with them. We are his proper abode. He has promised to come and abide with his people, and if he does not, depend upon it there is something in the temple offensive towards him, something with which he will not dwell. Will you put that away, and consecrate your hearts this day unto the Lord to be his Temple, his Temple only, and leave consequences with him? He will be able to look after his own…

When you have come to this decision, then look and live; take the final leap into the arms of a crucified Saviour. With some souls who have been the subjects of the drawings of the Spirit for years, the difficulty is in the surrendering their wills. They have learned to reason with God; they have lost the little children's way; they are afraid to take the final leap, and there they stand before the cross, not conscious of anything between them and Christ. What are *you* to do? What Paul told the Philippian gaoler to do – "Believe on the Lord Jesus Christ".[1] And you say, "What is that, and how am I to believe?" Wonderful how it has got mystified! Believe what? That he just means what he says, and that when you come, he does receive – not he will tomorrow, not he did yesterday, but that he does now, this moment. When did he receive the sinners who came to him on earth? When they came to him.[2]

Welcoming Lord, my prayers today are for those who are struggling
to make that "final leap". It is not for me to judge the reasons for their hesitancy;
I simply pray for them to find the courage they desire and need.
Help them to leap into the Kingdom. Amen.

---

1   Acts 16:31, KJV.
2   From *Aggressive Christianity*.

ALL ISRAEL WAS LISTED IN THE GENEALOGIES

(1 Chronicles 9:1 *NIV*)

My dear Eva,[1] You have one of the prettiest names in the English language. I hope your character will match it, because I dislike bad matches in anything, but most of all in names and characters! I used to like my name when I was a little girl, and took pleasure in finding out all about the good "Catherines" who had lived in past generations, and I struggled and prayed to be as good as they were. I thought I should like to be clever, too, but I remember thinking how hateful a very clever, wicked person was; it seemed to me that to be *clever without being good* was just like Satan, and I would rather be ever so *foolish and good*, than ever so *clever and naughty*. I hope you have the same choice, and that you are striving and praying against everything that you know to be displeasing to God. I cannot bear the thought of my little Eva, my special Christmas-box,[2] being naughty. Oh, no, I will not think of such a thing! I believe she will be a good Christian child, and grow up a devoted woman of God; to live, not for her own pleasure or profit – not to show, and shine, and be admired – but to *do her duty* wherever the Lord may put her, and to win souls for him. I want you to help Papa in the Mission,[3] if you only grow *good* enough. I want you to help the weak and the poor, and the ignorant and the wicked, and lead them to Jesus and to Heaven. That will be something like a life that is spent for such a purpose; will it not? Now, to this end, "work while the day is bright".[4] Read, write, sum, practise, talk French,[5] learn lessons, all for this, and God will help and bless you. So prays your loving mother.[6, 7]

> Father, the Booth children had a lot to live up to! In my prayers today,
> I think of those of whom great things are expected; bless them with
> a reassurance that your love remains the same, come what may.
> Thank you, Lord, that you know us each by name. Amen.

---

1 Evangeline Cory Booth (1865–1950), a flamboyant and charismatic character who became the fourth General of The Salvation Army, from 1934 to 1939. She was the Army's first female General. Catherine Booth had recently read *Uncle Tom's Cabin* (despite her fierce warnings to converts on the dangers of reading novels!) and wanted to name her baby "Eva". William Booth objected, writing "Evelyne" on the birth certificate. Evelyne eventually adopted the name Evangeline.
2 Eva was born on Christmas Day, 1865.
3 The Christian Mission, which became The Salvation Army in 1878.
4 Probably from John 9:4.
5 As General, Evangeline Booth toured the world, but did not visit France until her seventieth year.
6 From Catherine Booth's letter to Eva, written in Stockton-on-Tees, England, November 1876.
7 From *Catherine Booth The Mother of The Salvation Army, Vol. II.*

JACOB SHALL... HAVE QUIET AND EASE
(Jeremiah 30:10 *ESV*)

I am very glad of your letter, so very glad that you are better. Do not worry about anything at present. Remember you are there to benefit your health; to get strength of nerve and brain to fight in the future some of the giant evils of which you are only just getting a fair view now.[1] You can talk to Mr – on *heart* religion. He loves God, and desires to know more of him. Talk on experimental subjects. Read those parts of the Bible which he overlooks, and show him how much is made of human responsibility and will. I long to be with you and help you. Do not fear to speak out your convictions, but try to be gentle and courteous in your manner.[2] Mrs Newenham has often said that if my visit to St John's Wood[3] had done nothing but deliver her from the doctrinal difficulties, it would not have been in vain. I spent hours meeting her difficulties and overturning her arguments. Mind you go to the Lord for yourself, and do not allow the deadly poison to infect *you*. Do not think of studying Greek. There is such able criticism of men of all creeds, who have spent their lives at it, that it is useless bestowing time and trouble on acquiring what would, after all, be but a mere smattering. Mind, however, your health is the first great consideration. Get stronger, and keep near to God, and he will make everything else right for you. Garner wrote most enthusiastically about your services at Stockton;[4] says the people were delighted, and he adds, "Bless him, there is a mighty man of God in him!" I trust so. In fact, I don't think we know yet what *one* man can do, or could do, if as well filled with the Spirit as we all might be. May the mighty God of Jacob own and use you for himself![5]

> Lord, a life of ease is not what we seek, for then we grow lazy. However, times of rest are crucial, lest we invite overload and burn out. I pray today for Salvation Army leaders, church ministers and heads of congregations, especially those who are overtired. Help them, please. Amen.

---

1   Bramwell Booth was seriously ill in 1876, and had been sent to Scotland to convalesce.
2   Catherine Booth sent Bramwell a volume of *Theological Lectures* by Charles Finney, the American theologian and evangelist. Catherine was a great admirer of Finney's theology.
3   Lucy Newenham was greatly impressed by Catherine Booth during the latter's series of meetings in St John's Wood, London, England. The two became friends and exchanged lively theological opinions.
4   Possibly, a member of the Garner family, workers in the Christian Mission in Stockton, England.
5   From *Catherine Booth The Mother of The Salvation Army, Vol. II.*

WORSHIP CHRIST AS LORD OF YOUR LIFE

(1 Peter 3:15 NLT)

Christ must be the best expounder of his own system, and he declares over and over again that his first and highest work in this world, was to glorify his Father and to reveal God to man. He further taught that there was no other way of doing this than by the revelation of, and the reception of, himself.[1]

Christianity is as much a spirit as a practice, and herein it differs from all other religions and ethical systems, inasmuch as the practice of it is impossible without the infusion of the living spirit of the author. A man must live, by Christ and in Christ, a supernatural life before he can exemplify the principles, or practise the precepts, of Christianity; they are too high for unrenewed human nature, it cannot attain unto them.

To love the brethren for Christ's sake, and because of Christ's love shed abroad in the heart, is quite different from loving the brethren for their own sakes, or even for the gratification of mere mutual generosity or benevolence.

Praise up humanitarianism as much as you like, but don't confound it with Christianity, nor suppose that it will ultimately lead its followers to Christ. This is confounding things that differ, and is fitly set forth by the old illustration of a family of prodigals doing well for themselves and each other, while united in ignoring and rejecting the authority and claims of their Father.[2, 3]

> Christ is the answer. Father, in my life, prevent me from ever regarding Jesus
> merely as someone similar to a fine humanitarian leader or moral teacher; may
> I set him apart as God incarnate and Master; Lord of my life and Lord of all.
>
> Amen.

---

1   See John 14:8–9.
2   From a letter Catherine Booth wrote to her friend W. T. (William Thomas) Stead. Stead was a newspaper editor and investigative journalist. He did not profess a Christian faith, but he was a great ally of The Salvation Army, not least in the headline-making case known as "The Armstrong Girl". He knew that Catherine regarded him as a fine humanitarian, but she disputed (and challenged) his spiritual convictions.
3   From *Catherine Booth* by W. T. Stead.

Invite the poor, the crippled, the lame, the blind
(Luke 14:13 *ESV*)

Whatever success or blessing I may attribute to the efforts and measures of The Salvation Army, I *always* presuppose a pre-existing qualification – Equipment of the Holy Ghost… We deem it a great mistake to suppose that any human learning, any human eloquence, any human qualification whatever, fits a man or woman for ministering God's word or dealing with souls. Whatever else there is or is not, there *must be the equipment of the Holy Ghost*, for without him all qualifications… are utterly powerless for the regeneration of mankind… I do not want to tell merely about The Salvation Army… but I want to make the intelligence (i.e. information) the means of enlightening you Christians, and stirring you up to more vivid responsibilities towards the degraded unchristian, uncivilized masses of this country. I want you to go to work, if not in my way, then in your way. I do not care how genteelly, how quietly, how respectably, so that *you do it*… Statistics not of our taking (I believe that of the Church of England)… ascertained… only ten out of every 100 of the working-class population ever entered your churches and chapels. Think of that, and then think if it is not time something should be *done*!…

A lady came to one meeting, and she said, "I was perfectly disgusted… the way some behaved outside was scandalous!" She seemed to reflect upon The Salvation Army as if it were our fault… Ask yourselves, do *we* create this mass of heathenism?… You have let them grow up at your very doors, under your church steeples. Here they are, essentially heathen, not caring about God… you Christians – Independents and Churchpeople – have let them grow up so, and when we try to gather them together, you turn about and slap us in the face![1,2]

> Show me today, Lord, what you would have me do to reach others
> with your love. I acknowledge my need of your Spirit's help. Amen.

---

1   Catherine Booth was responding publicly against strictures made on Salvationists by Dr Harvey Goodwin, Bishop of Carlisle, England, during a sermon he gave in Carlisle Cathedral. She organized a meeting in the Theatre Royal, Carlisle, on 29 September 1880, to outline the aims and objectives of The Salvation Army, but was anxious to avoid any impression of retaliation.
2   From *Catherine Booth* by Catherine Bramwell-Booth.

HE RESTORES MY SOUL
(Psalm 23:3 *ESV*)

You will not be able to read a page of the New Testament without seeing holiness in almost every sentence. The Holy Spirit will show it to you and if you miss it, it won't be for want of light; it will be because you are too idle to seek it. The Lord showed me this early in my Christian experience, and I resolved to seek it for myself. My innate perceptions told me God must delight in holiness, that the gospel scheme was not merely a scheme for atonement, but a scheme for *restoration*, and I knew that the chief difficulty in my way was in my *heart*, therefore I felt it must be God's plan to restore my heart, for that is the spring and inspiration of my moral being; and I searched the word of God carefully and besought him to show me, saying, "If thou hast provided this salvation, if there never was another person entered into it on earth, I will try, and I will follow if thou wilt lead." If you will come to that, God will reveal it to you.

This is just the condition you must come to. "The whole Bible," as a gentleman said to me the other day, "beams with light now." Of course it does, *because you have got hold of the key*. You know it is easy to unlock a difficult lock when you have got the key, and the man who gets hold of this central truth of Christianity gets hold of the key and, of course, he can unlock all its mysteries and walk in and out...

I suppose that persons have selected or coined names to express this blessing which would be most compatible with their theological views, seeing that this experience has been recognized and professed by Christians of almost every shade of opinion, and they have adopted that mode of expression which has best coincided with their different views, but this makes no difference.[1]

Lord, whatever names are given to describe an encounter with Jesus, I thank you today that you are a God who holds the keys of atonement, restoration, and wholeness; all your actions beautifully framed in love and mercy. Amen.

1 From *Holiness*.

HE WILL BAPTISE YOU WITH THE HOLY SPIRIT
(Mark 1:8 *NIV*)

You say, "Can we have this power equally with the early disciples?"[1] I say, reasoning by analogy, assuming that what God has done in the past he will continue to do in the future, is it not likely that he will give it to us because we equally need it? We poor things, in our day, as they did in theirs, we equally need it... *because the character of the agents is the same.*

We are very much like them, and they were very much like us. Thank God. It has often encouraged me. If they had been men of gigantic intellects and extraordinary education, training and position; if they had possessed all human equipment and qualifications, we might have looked back through the ages in despair, and said, "I can never be such as they were."

Look what they were, naturally, apart from this gift of power. The Holy Ghost has taken care to give them their true characters. They were men of like passions, weaknesses, tendencies, liability to fall, with ourselves – just such poor, frail, weak, easily tripped-up creatures and, in many instances, unbelieving and disobedient, before Pentecost. Now, I say this is encouraging for us all.

You may remember what Jesus said to Mary – "Go and tell my disciples and Peter."[2] Mary, perhaps, would have left Peter out after his shameful denial of the Lord; for fear of this, Jesus said, "Go and tell my disciples and Peter."[3]

> What lovely grace! Peter the despairing denier was not excluded.
> On the contrary, he was singled out for inclusion! Give me a heart that
> ever seeks to include and embrace, in imitation of Christ. Amen.

---

1   See Acts 1:8.
2   See Mark 16:7.
3   From *The Holy Ghost.*

ELIJAH WENT BEFORE THE PEOPLE AND SAID,
"HOW LONG WILL YOU WAVER BETWEEN TWO OPINIONS? IF THE
LORD IS GOD, FOLLOW HIM; BUT IF BAAL IS GOD, FOLLOW HIM."

(1 Kings 18:21 *NIV*)

Ahab was one of the worst kings that ever sat on the throne of Israel.[1] He was the son and the grandson of idolatrous kings; and for fear he would not be able to carry out his wicked intentions sufficiently by himself, he married a heathenish and idolatrous woman, and by her help he managed to spread the apostasy almost over the entire nation of Israel. We do not wonder we read in 2 Kings xviii, 33, that they feared the Lord and *served* their own gods, for these were poor heathen colonists from Assyria. But Israel was a nation professedly worshipping Jehovah. And although no doubt Ahab and his wife intended utterly to subvert the worship of the true God, and to put that of Baal in its place; they could not, they dare not aim to do all this at once, and so they supplemented the worship of God by the worship of Baal. They built a house for Baal, planted a grove, and established his worship alongside the worship of the God of Israel, and they succeeded in inducing the majority of the nation to follow them.

Alas! Alas! This is generally the case when those in high places give their influence on the wrong side and against God. What an awful reckoning-day is coming for wicked kings and rulers, in fact for all people in places of influence and authority who use it against God! It will be bad enough for a man to have to answer for the damnation of his own soul; but oh! What will it be to have to answer for the damnation of thousands of others? You who are influencing others – your wives, your children, your husbands, your friends, your servants, those who live in the same house with you – there is a reckoning-day coming, and an awful reckoning-day it will be.[2]

Lord of nations, today I pray for those who have power and influence in
national and international ways; monarchs and rulers, presidents and prime
ministers. Father, grant them wisdom to match their responsibilities. Amen.

---

1   See 1 Kings.
2   From *Life and Death.*

> "LORD, IF IT'S YOU," PETER REPLIED, "TELL ME TO COME TO YOU
> ON THE WATER." "COME," HE SAID. THEN PETER GOT DOWN OUT OF
> THE BOAT, WALKED ON THE WATER AND CAME TOWARDS JESUS
>
> (Matthew 14:28–29 *NIV*)

If you are to be saved by faith, you must exercise faith before you will be saved. If it is by faith you are to be saved, you must believe first, and be saved afterwards, if it is only the next second. "But," you say, "I do not feel it." No, but you will feel it when *you have got it*. You must believe it before you get it, on the testimony of his word – "I will in no wise cast you out"…[1]

Now I come, Lord, I come. I have put away my idols; I have put away everything that consciously stood between me and thee. I will to serve thee, I will to follow thee, I will to put my neck *under thy yoke for ever*,[2] asking no more questions, but being willing for thee to lead me whithersover thou wilt. Now, Lord, I come – thou dost receive.

Leap off the poor old stranded wreck of your own effort, or your own righteousness, or your own sinfulness, or your own unworthiness, or anything else of your own, into the glorious lifeboat. It is on the top of the wave this afternoon – another step, and you will be in – one bound, and you will feel the loving arms of the Saviour around you. Faith is trust. Trust. He will do for you what he promised. *Believe that God does now accept you wholly for the sake of the sacrifice of his blessed Son*; that he justifies you freely from all things from which you could not be justified by the law. You stand a condemned, guilty, Hell-bound criminal, and nothing but his free, sovereign mercy can save you. Throw yourself upon this, and the moment you do so in real faith you will be saved.[3]

> There's mercy still for me! Thank you, Lord, that goodness and
> mercy shall indeed follow me all the days of my life. My prayers today
> are for those who need to take that step of faith; help them to do so.
> I name them before you today in prayer – those known to me. Amen.

---

1   John 6:37, KJV.
2   See Matthew 11:30.
3   From *Aggressive Christianity*.

A WOMAN... CAME BEHIND HIM,
AND TOUCHED THE HEM OF HIS GARMENT
(Matthew 9:20 *KJV*)

Perhaps you will say, as a curate of the Church of England, writing to me... said, "I refuse to be saved by logic." So did I, and I struggled for six weeks because I refused to be saved by logic – because I *would* have a living, personal Christ. I admire your decision, my brother... but let this logic help you; nevertheless, Jesus Christ has promised, if I come, that he will receive me – then, I do come, and he does receive me, for he cannot lie. Let that help you. Faith is not logic, but logic may help faith.

Oh! How I should rejoice if some of you were to launch into the arms of Jesus this moment. It often happens that while I am speaking souls *do* get into the ark of God's mercy, and come, or write to tell me afterwards that the Spirit has come, and he is crying "Abba Father,"[1] and now they know they have passed from death unto life. They don't want logic then. It is a matter of demonstration with them. When you have come up to the place where saving faith is possible to you, you have no more to do, no more to suffer, no more to pay. By simple trust we are saved. This is the way every saint on earth was saved. This is the way every saint in glory was saved. This is the way we are kept saved, too, by living, daily, obedient faith. The Lord help you just now. Put away the ungodly companion. Give up the unlawful business, or the worldly conformity. Put away whatever has stood between you and Jesus. Trample it underfoot and press through the crowd of difficulties as the woman did, and go right up and touch him with this touch of faith, and you shall live and know that you are healed. Then this gospel will be good news indeed to you, and Jesus will be the author of salvation,[2] because you obey him![3]

> Lord, again, this day, my prayers are for those who are just that one "touch"
> away from Christ and his salvation. Maybe they feel unworthy, or afraid,
> or unconvinced. Lord of the breakthrough, meet them, I pray. Amen.

---

1 Galatians 4:6, KJV.
2 Hebrews 12:2.
3 From *Aggressive Christianity.*

WHAT HE OPENS NO ONE CAN SHUT,
AND WHAT HE SHUTS NO ONE CAN OPEN
(Revelation 3:7 NIV)

William received a letter from the President yesterday, objecting to the present arrangement, and after a day's deep anxiety and fervent prayer we decided on our knees to send in our resignation. Accordingly it is, I expect, in the President's hands this morning. We both attended the tea-meeting last night. William made a thrilling speech. It told well on the people. At the close of it he announced the step he had taken, which evidently produced a great impression on the audience. Much to our surprise, Mr Clifton, one of the ministers who occupied the chair, instead of getting up to defend the Connexion, said that, while he deeply regretted the step Mr Booth had taken, nevertheless he could not but honour him for acting out of his conviction. He believed that never had a man done so much with a single eye to God's glory who had suffered for his action. He had no doubt that God would give him the desire of his heart and accompany his labours with success. This was very cheering under the circumstances. The people were most affectionate at parting, and sang with us all up the road on the way home. I believe they were much pleased with both my services... We had a blessed time. I enjoyed great liberty, and although it poured with rain, which made a great noise on the canvas, I managed with some effort to make myself heard to the end of the tent in which the services were being held. The people listened well, and nearly all stayed for the prayer meeting, when we had nine cases, two of them old men. One of them I should think was seventy. He wept like a child, and cried, "What a merciful God he has been to spare me so long in my rebellion!" All glory to Jesus![1, 2, 3]

Faithful God, there are sometimes tough decisions to make.
These can stir up all sorts of emotions; fear, failure, anxiety and even depression.
I pray you will draw alongside those who need to make such decisions today;
especially those who need to switch jobs or face unemployment.

1   From a letter Catherine Booth wrote to her parents in 1861.
2   William Booth had been at the centre of a growing dispute with the Methodist Connexion over the style and nature of his ministry. Strong opinions were exchanged in correspondence, as William reached the conclusion of an inevitable break with Methodism in a formal sense of regular employment.
3   From *The Life of Catherine Booth The Mother of The Salvation Army, Vol. I.*

The people... will come from a northern land
(Jeremiah 3:18 *NIV*)

We came here on Thursday afternoon for the Easter Anniversary meetings. I preached on Good Friday to a full chapel, William on Sunday morning, and I again in the afternoon to a chapel packed, aisles and pulpit stairs, while many turned away unable to get in. This morning William returned to Gateshead to attend our tea-meeting at Bethesda.[1] I am staying here to preach again tonight, and shall return all well tomorrow. There were many under conviction last evening, whom I hope to see converted tonight. The Lord has been very graciously present with me hitherto, and has given me great influence and liberty; I am in my element in the work, and only regret that I did not commence it years ago. Oh, to live for souls! It is a dark, sinful world and a comparatively dead and useless Church. May God pour out his Spirit! There is a nice society here, considering it is a new one – a beautiful chapel, seats about 750. They say there were nearly 1,000 in it yesterday afternoon...

You will be surprised to find I am still here, but so it is. I told you I had to stay on Monday evening. Well, the Lord came down amongst the people so gloriously that I dare not leave, so the friends telegraphed to William and I remained... I preached again on the Wednesday and Friday evenings, and also gave two addresses on holiness, and the Lord was very gracious with me. *Above* 100 names were taken during the week... Oh, it would have rejoiced your hearts to have heard one after another bless God for bringing your feeble and unworthy child to Hartlepool![2, 3, 4]

Thank you, Lord, for unexpected blessings, such as this one in Hartlepool.
Help your Church to be flexible when you choose to change our plans. Amen.

1   An important part of the life of the early Methodist Church was the Tea Meeting. Tea Meetings were held on a variety of occasions including Shrove Tuesday, Christmas Day and even New Year's Day. The church would provide a social gathering to try to bring people away from alcoholic drink.
2   From letters written by Catherine to her parents, Easter 1861.
3   Gateshead and Hartlepool, north-east England. Hartlepool in particular made a strongly positive impression upon Mrs Booth, as she witnessed the hand of the Lord at work in a northern working-class fishing port, hence her reluctance to leave.
4   From *The Short Life of Catherine Booth The Mother of The Salvation Army*.

WE DO NOT WANT YOU TO BE UNINFORMED, BRETHREN,
ABOUT THOSE WHO ARE ASLEEP, SO THAT YOU WILL NOT GRIEVE
AS DO THE REST WHO HAVE NO HOPE. FOR IF WE BELIEVE THAT
JESUS DIED AND ROSE AGAIN, EVEN SO GOD WILL BRING WITH
HIM THOSE WHO HAVE FALLEN ASLEEP IN JESUS

(1 Thessalonians 4:13–14 *NASB*)

It is highly probable that this is the way in which demons personate departed human friends, both amongst the saved and the lost, for we can never believe that lost souls are allowed to cross the impassable gulf which is fixed between them and the living, at the call of any less a power than that which fixed that gulf;[1] much less can we believe that the saved who are already with Christ in Paradise are subject to be ordered about by either men or demons. The fact that such great numbers have been led to believe in and seek unto familiar spirits is to me only a sign that the world, having forsaken God and turned a deaf ear to the voice of the Eternal Spirit, whose office is to enlighten, reprove, and renew the human soul, and finding itself unable to do without a spirit, has turned to demons![2]

My dear children and friends – My place is empty, but my heart is with you. You are my joy and my crown. Your battles, sufferings, and victories have been the chief interest of my life these past twenty-five years. They are so still. Go forward. Live holy lives. Be true to the Army. God is your strength. Love and seek the lost; bring them to the blood. Make the people good; inspire them with the Spirit of Jesus Christ. Love one another; help your comrades in dark hours. I am dying under the Army flag; it is yours to live and fight under. God is my salvation and refuge in the storm. I send you my love and blessing.[3, 4]

Lord Jesus, you are Lord of life and death. Other refuge have I none.
My soul is safe in Christ – hallelujah! It is enough that Jesus died for me. Amen.

---

1   Luke 16:26.
2   From Catherine Booth's response to a correspondent who wrote to her asking her views on spiritualism.
3   From a greeting to Salvationists Catherine Booth wrote from her deathbed, shortly before her promotion to Glory on 4 October 1890, aged sixty-one.
4   From *Catherine Booth* by W. T. Stead.

CHENANIAH, LEADER OF THE LEVITES IN MUSIC,
SHOULD DIRECT THE MUSIC, FOR HE UNDERSTOOD IT

(1 Chronicles 15:22 *ESV*)

Are we born to the heritage of fools? Are we forced to keep holding back on the chariot car of progress? Must we always be in the background? Can we not learn wisdom from the children of this world; and if the glorious gospel *is* what we all profess to believe it, can we not put forth more thought, and more effort, and more care, to bring it to bear upon men? Will Christians never rise up to emulate the *wisdom* of this world, and act on common sense business principles in pushing the gospel on the attention of mankind? If we find that the masses will not look at a bill with sermons on it – as they won't, because sermons on religion is the last thing they want to hear about – why should we not attract their attention by some novel or startling announcement, so that the terms be innocent? What does it signify that they are strange and unconventional? Look at the sagacity of worldly men in advertising; think of the size and cost of their bills. Why do they go to such expense and trouble? Because they know that in the rush and drive of this age, little unostentatious notices will not be looked at. Why should we be content with such for our Master's business? If we find their processions and music will draw the people together better than any other means to listen to our message, why should we not use them? Who so worthy of a banner as our King? And to whom does all the music of earth and Heaven belong, if not to him? I contend that the Devil has no right to a single note; and we will have it all away from him yet. We find that music not only draws the people, but it begets friendly feeling and secures attention from the very lowest and worst. We have numbers in our ranks today who were enticed out of the public house by our music and processions.[1]

What a lovely challenge, Lord! To look at the successful strategies
of "the world" and claim them for the Kingdom! Why should the Devil
have all the best tunes? Give your people holy boldness and Spirit-led
initiative – we should never be the poor relations. Amen.

1   From *The Salvation Army in Relation to the Church and State.*

HE HAS... SET ETERNITY IN THE HUMAN HEART

(Ecclesiastes 3:11 *NIV*)

The subject is "A mock salvation in comparison with Christ's salvation"... With respect to salvation... there will be no difference of opinion as to the need of our race for a salvation of some sort. This must be too patent to need argument, that our world is disordered, disjointed, morally diseased, and that it needs some sort of regenerating, rectifying process, if society is not to be disorganized by its own corruptions, or sunk for ever in the hell of its iniquities. Every man knows this to his own hurt. All men have a personal consciousness of being wrong, whether they believe in a divine revelation or not; nay, whether they believe in God or not.

I do not think I have spoken to more than half a dozen people in my life – and I have spoken, I suppose, to some thousands of different classes – who have maintained that they were right. Even infidels, when you face them with the question, "Are you right? Are you living according to the dictates of your judgment and conscience?" dare not say that they are. The universal cry of our poor humanity is, "O wretched man that I am",[1] whether it be looking for any divine deliverance or not. Men everywhere know that they are not living according to their own conceptions of right, and therefore they have a sense of self-condemnation; and this asserts itself in spite of their arguments and excuses. It is of no avail to the soul tormented with a sense of guilt to say, "The woman tempted me" or "I was under the pressure of great fear, or shame, or dread"; this is no real palliation.[2]

> Lord, your grace is such that the spark of divine life and light continues to burn even though it might be ignored for years. I pray today for those who sense that gracious nudge, yet suppress it. Turn that spark into a flame. Amen.

1   Romans 7:24, KJV.
2   From *Popular Christianity*.

BE AS SHREWD AS SNAKES AND AS INNOCENT AS DOVES
(Matthew 10:16 *NIV*)

Not only do all men feel this sense of wrong in themselves, but they expect wrong in others.

Even parents anticipate and provide for it in their children. Every parent knows that there is a tendency in his children to go astray from the very first moment of accountability. He knows that there is in his child a tendency to speak lies as soon as it can speak at all, that there is a tendency to perverse tempers and wicked passions. Hence, wise parents universally recognize, whether they make any pretensions to Christianity or not, the necessity of family government and careful training in order to check, counteract, or eradicate, as the case may be, these tendencies to evil; and thus they acknowledge the necessity for a certain kind of salvation in their children, and they recognize also this fact, that if they do not attempt to work out this salvation in their children, the children will bring them to wreck and ruin. A child left to itself brings its mother to shame; we know that sadly too well.[1]

There is the same recognition of the need of a salvation amongst men of the world. Every intelligent businessman goes on the assumption that he has to encounter wrong in the hearts and conduct of his neighbours; in fact, the world takes it as a sign of intelligence that a businessman goes on this assumption, and would call him a fool if he did not. He knows that he is beset on all hands by those who will overreach, cheat, and ruin him for anything that they can, if they can promote their own interests by doing so. Hence the necessity for a kind of legal salvation, in the form of agreements and bonds, between man and man.[2]

Lord, help me today to be wise and astute.
Give me a mind that is fair and alert, but not cynical. Amen.

---

1   See Proverbs 29:15.
2   From *Popular Christianity*.

I DISCIPLINE MY BODY AND KEEP IT UNDER CONTROL, LEST AFTER
PREACHING TO OTHERS I MYSELF SHOULD BE DISQUALIFIED

(1 Corinthians 9:27 *ESV*)

Abstinence [from alcohol] is valuable to those who are called to make such effort... as a source of strength. No man can deny himself, constrained by divine love for the good of others, without improving his own moral nature and giving increased scope for the operation of the divine Spirit within him... Abstinence is valuable to the Christian labourer as a safeguard against temptation. It is well known that a large majority of those who become subjects for church discipline owe their fall directly or indirectly to drink. The man who never uses it can never fall through its influence. He is safe thus far, because he goes not into temptation... Abstinence is valuable to the labourer, because it helps to beget a conviction of his disinterestedness in the minds of those whom he seeks to benefit, which conviction is indispensable to his success. Doubtless the unwillingness of religious teachers to forego their own indulgence in the use of wine and spirits has greatly diminished their influence, and helped largely to beget that prejudice with which great numbers of the common people regard them. We are satisfied that if the gospel is to make any great advance on the masses of this country, those who seek to propagate it must abandon the use of drink. As Dr Guthrie[1] remarks, in his preface to *[The] Scriptural Claims of Teetotalism*,[2] "I am astonished that so many ministers of the gospel and Christian people can turn aside from the fight as they do. When I laboured among the lower, and, indeed, lowest classes of society in this city, I was met at every corner by the demon of drink. I found it utterly useless to attempt to evangelise the heathen and raise the lapsed masses without the aid of total abstinence. With all my trust in the promises of God, and blessings of the Holy Spirit, I felt that I must be able to say to the people not 'Forward,' but 'Follow.' This first induced me to become an abstainer; and I am convinced that it is the duty of every man, who would do his utmost for the glory of God and the good of his fellow-creatures, to discountenance by his example the use of intoxicating stimulants."[3]

Lord, be with those who need extra strength this day. Help them. Amen.

---

1   Dr Thomas Guthrie (1803–73); preacher, writer and social reformer with great influence in the areas of education, social care and temperance.
2   By Reverend Dr Christopher Newman Hall (1816–1902); English nonconformist and social activist; an advocate of temperance.
3   From *Practical Religion*.

The Lord bless you and keep you
(Numbers 6:24 NIV)

Sanctification must be the will of man. If it is not my will, the divine will can never be accomplished in me. I must will to be sanctified, as God is willing that I should be sanctified. James, in his epistle, says, "Draw nigh to God, and he will draw nigh to you. Cleanse your hands, ye sinners; and purify your hearts, ye double minded."[1] This was said to people who had been professing to believe, but had gone back under the dominion of their fleshly appetites. There are two or three other texts which seem to sum up the whole matter as, for instance, "[Jesus Christ]... gave himself for us (that is, for us Christians, the whole Church of God) that he might redeem us from all iniquity, and purify unto himself a peculiar people, zealous of good works."[2] Then 1 Timothy 1:5 shows God's purpose and aim in the whole method of redemption: "Now the end of the commandment is charity out of a pure heart, and of a good conscience, and of faith unfeigned" [KJV] – cleansed and kept clean, for if it had been clean and had become dirty again it would be not a good, but a bad conscience. And again, in 1 John 3:3, "Every man that hath this hope in him purifieth himself, even as he is pure" [KJV]. These are summing-up texts and there are numbers of others to show that the whole purpose of redemption is to restore us to purity; not only to purge us from the past, but to keep us purged to serve the living God. This shall be by the application of the blood of Christ to the conscience, and by the power of the Holy Ghost keeping us in a state of purity and obedience to righteousness. If God through Christ cannot do this for me, what is my advantage at all by his coming?[3]

As I pray today, Lord, I thank you that you are not only a
saving God, but a keeping God too. Keep me this day. Amen.

---

1   James 4:8, KJV.
2   Titus 2:14, KJV.
3   From *The Highway of our God*.

GOD CARED FOR YOU ALL ALONG THE WAY AS YOU
TRAVELED THROUGH THE WILDERNESS

(Deuteronomy 1:31 *NLT*)

Affliction occupies a large place in the economy of salvation for, though suffering is the result of sin, God transmutes it into one of the richest blessings to his own people. From whatever secondary causes the afflictions of the righteous may arise, whether from the sins of their forefathers, the cruelty of their enemies, their own mistakes, or the mistakes of their friends, or the malice of Satan, their blessed privilege is to realize that God permits and overrules all, and that in every sorrow he has a gracious end. Happy the Christian who, though he cannot see this "end" at present, is able to trust in the goodness which chastens, and cleave to the hand that smites... There is a sense in which trial reveals us to God; makes manifest to him what is in our heart. Perhaps someone may object, and say, "No, no; we need nothing to make manifest to God what we are. He understands us perfectly. He knows what is in man, and needs not anything to tell him." True; yet he said to Abraham, "Now I know that thou fearest God, seeing thou hast not withheld thy son, thine only son from me."[1] And Moses said to the Israelites, "And thou shalt remember all the way which the LORD thy God led thee these forty years in the wilderness, to humble thee, and to prove thee, to know what was in thine heart, whether thou wouldest keep his commandments, or no."[2] Now God knew that Abraham feared him, and he also knew how far Israel would keep his commandments, but he did not know as a matter of actual fact until the fact transpired... In your various afflictions, the Lord is leading you about in the wilderness to prove you, and to see (to make manifest to himself) what is in your heart, and whether you will keep his commandments or not. Remember also that in nothing is love made so manifest as in willing, cheerful suffering for the sake of its object.[3]

For those who are suffering, Lord, and for those whose lives are something
of a wilderness experience at present, I pray your encouragement. Amen.

---

1   Genesis 22:12, KJV.
2   Deuteronomy 8:4, KJV.
3   From *The Highway of our God.*

IT IS BETTER NOT TO EAT MEAT OR DRINK WINE OR TO DO ANYTHING ELSE THAT WILL CAUSE YOUR BROTHER OR SISTER TO FALL

(Romans 14:21 *NIV*)

The motives, arguments, and persuasions of the gospel are addressed to the reason, conscience, and feelings of men and, of course, presuppose a sane condition of mind. Everybody knows that it is useless to present these to a man when intoxicated; therefore, in the case of thousands who live in a perpetual state of intoxication, the only chance of salvation is to rescue them from the influence of drink. Drunkenness is a physical as well as moral disease, and if we would remove it, we must proceed on the same principle as we do with the insane; we must restore the reason before we can sanctify the heart. Some of our Christian friends object to this, and say, "Then it is the gospel *and* total abstinence." We say emphatically, "Yes, just in the same sense as in the case of a lunatic or a man raving in a fever; it is the gospel *and* the physician." If any of our friends doubt whether so many are thus perpetually under the influence of drink, let them pay us a visit in the east of London; and, alas! we can point them to multitudes of besotted, benighted beings, who are never sufficiently sober to be able intelligently to comprehend the truth, even if they could be got to listen to it. Their mental faculties are so benumbed with the imbruting drink, that a vacant stare is often the only response to the first attempt at arousing and reclaiming them… Thanks be to God, many of this class have been reclaimed and transformed in connection with our mission work; but I am not acquainted with a single instance in which the drink has not been entirely abandoned. In our last year's report, "The Masses Reached",[1] Mr Booth has selected 100 instances, out of hundreds of a similar character, of the power of the gospel to save the vilest and worst of sinners, and at least eighty of these were drunkards of the most terrible description… It would be difficult to believe that man could fall so low, unless one had indisputable proof.[2]

I would hate my life to be any kind of stumbling block to
someone seeking faith. So help me, God, only ever to be a stepping stone.
Amen.

---

1   1873.
2   From *Practical Religion*.

PETER STOOD AND WARMED HIMSELF. THEREFORE THEY SAID TO HIM, "YOU ARE NOT ALSO ONE OF HIS DISCIPLES, ARE YOU?" HE DENIED IT AND SAID, "I AM NOT!" ONE OF THE SERVANTS OF THE HIGH PRIEST, A RELATIVE OF HIM WHOSE EAR PETER CUT OFF, SAID, "DID I NOT SEE YOU IN THE GARDEN WITH HIM?" PETER THEN DENIED AGAIN

(John 18: 25–27 NKJV)

The Holy Ghost is equal to the emergency. He can cure you. He can baptize you with his power. You may have denied him, if not as Peter did, yet practically as bad. It makes no difference to God whether you have been a little bad or very bad; whether you have denied him once or thrice, or whether you have denied him with oaths and curses. If you will only come and comply with the conditions, he will look on you, heal you, and baptize you with his power. Did they not all forsake him and flee, except for a few poor faithful women? All the world forsook him and fled in the hour of his extremity. "Ah!" you say. "Well, I have done the same myself. I would not watch with him one hour. I have betrayed him before my friends and acquaintances in the world, where I have brought into circumstances that tested my fidelity. My courage has failed, and I have failed to witness for him." Yes, I know and agree with you that it was base ingratitude. You were a traitor, indeed, but still, if you will come back, "Peter", and repent, and do your first works, he will receive you – baptize you with power. Oh! What they [the disciples] were before Pentecost, and what they were after. Poor Peter, who could not stand the questionings of a servant maid, who could not dare to have it said that he was one of the despised [Nazarenes], what a valiant soldier he afterwards became for the Lord Jesus Christ, and how tradition says he was crucified for his Master at last. Anyway, we know he was a faithful and valiant soldier to the end of his journey. Now, this baptism will transform you as it did them; it will make you all prophets and prophetesses, according to your measure.[1]

> I pray today, faithful God, for those who feel unable to return to your embrace because they have let you down at some time or other. By your Spirit, bring to their minds the heart-warming story of your gracious dealings with Peter.
> Amen.

---

1 From *The Holy Ghost.*

THE LORD SUSTAINS THEM ON THEIR SICK-BED
(Psalm 41:3 *NIV*)

I want to define the blessing [of holiness] as we believe it and as I believe God will show it to those who really and honestly want to understand or rather experience it, because it [is] one of those mysteries of divine love and grace that you will never understand until you experience...

Only the other day a gentleman wrote to me... and another was conversing with me, which made it appear how very far both had mistaken the teaching of the word of God on this matter...

It is not freedom from infirmity either in mind or body. How anyone can come to imagine such a thing in our present physically fallen and depraved condition I cannot think. It was not necessary for the accomplishment of his redeeming purpose that we should be made perfect again, in the way of our apprehension, memory or capacity. This was not necessary for our redemption, or he would have provided for it; but he left us still physically imperfect. He can save us from sin in our present crippled state of body and mind, and it magnifies his grace the more. If people choose to call infirmity sin, the controversy comes simply to a definition of terms. If a lapse of memory, a mistake in judgment, a surprise or aberration of feeling is sin, I do not contend that we are saved from these, but I do not gather from the law of Christ that any such things are accounted sins, neither do I believe the common sense of a little child would so account them. I leave everybody, however, to form their own conclusion, only that when we speak of entire sanctification or holiness, we do *not* mean that a man is saved from simple infirmity.[1]

Be close to those who suffer in mind or body, Lord Jesus.
I pray for anyone I know who is ill, mentally or physically. May their
needs and your great fullness meet as I lift their names in prayer. Amen.

---

1   From *Holiness*.

I KEEP MY EYES ALWAYS ON THE LORD.
WITH HIM AT MY RIGHT HAND, I WILL NOT BE SHAKEN

(Psalm 16:8 *NIV*)

Think of the state of the people, and then say whether any [redtapeism], or conventianlism, or fastidiousness ought to be allowed to bar our way to their ears and their hearts. I often think how the higher classes will curse their fastidiousness when their mansions are burning about their ears! How they will wish then that they had helped The Salvation Army! I can honestly say that I have suffered more from the obtuseness and inertness of professedly Christian men as to the pressing needs of the people, than from all the slander, persecution, toil, and anxiety that this movement has brought upon me; and yet only God knows how great these have been. But I can bear all this easier than the maudlin half-and-half view of the situation which leads these men to say, "Why attempt so much?" "You are going too fast." "What will this grow to?" I say, I don't care what it grows to, so that it grows in holiness and devotion as it grows in size; and as to the future, God must look after that. I don't see that much has been done for the great mass of the people by the catering of past generations for the future! I think some of the huge forms and cumbrous organizations handed down to us only hamper good and true men! Our work is, "To serve our generation according to the will of God",[1] and leave him to look after the next! And so to our going too fast; what can they mean when there are millions in our own land yet in positive heathenism? If God has shown us a way of reaching them (which all admit now), how can we go too fast in carrying it out? Why should enterprise be shut out of religion any more than of business? A man's idea in business is, not to get through with as little as he can do; but to do all he can.[2]

Lord of encouragement, I pray for anyone who is feeling discouraged today.
I pray for those who have been on the receiving end of criticism.
Remind me to be an encourager. Amen.

---

1 See Acts 13:36.
2 From *The Salvation Army in Relation to the Church and State*.

REMEMBER THE LORD YOUR GOD, FOR IT IS HE WHO GIVES YOU THE
ABILITY TO PRODUCE WEALTH, AND SO CONFIRMS HIS COVENANT

(Deuteronomy 8:18 *NIV*)

If anybody were to say to an enterprising man, "You are getting on very nicely, making a comfortable living; if I were you, I would let well alone, I would not open branch establishments or enlarge my connection, but rest and be thankful", would he not answer, "My dear fellow, I have a lot of capital lying idle, do you suppose I am going to keep it so? No, no, I am going to do all the business I can lawfully, and make as much money as is possible to me." And nobody would blame him; even high-standing Christians would not condemn him. And yet, because we import this spirit of enterprise into the propagation of the Kingdom of God, these very Christians are down upon us, charging us with being ambitious, extravagant, and I don't know what else. We believe that if there is anything worth being energetic and enthusiastic about, it is salvation. We believe the same power which has within a few years reached and regenerated thousands of the very worst classes of our population can regenerate millions more, if we can only get near enough to them to make them feel its force. Then, who has any right to accuse us of personal ambition or senseless fanaticism because we are trying to do it? I turn round on our accusers and say, Where is *your* zeal for the Lord, that you will not put forth as much effort or display as much enterprise in pushing the Kingdom of God as you do in pushing your own business, or as the men of the world do in promoting their schemes for their own gain or glory? The Salvation Army owes its success, next to the Spirit of God, to this spirit of enterprise. People say it is the spirit of the leader runs through the whole Army; well, be it so. It is God's order that like begets like; and there is sense in which the spirit of the man, as well as the Spirit of God, infuses itself into the spiritual progeny. Thank God![1]

Lord, may those who succeed in business remember your blessing. Likewise,
for any "success" you give to your Church, may we always give you the glory.
Amen.

---

1   From *The Salvation Army in Relation to the Church and State.*

NO ONE CAN SERVE TWO MASTERS...
YOU CANNOT SERVE BOTH GOD AND MONEY
(Matthew 6:24 *NIV*)

Oh, Christians! by your peace of conscience on a dying bed; by the eternal destinies of your children; by your concern for the glory of your God; by your care for never-dying souls; by the love you owe your Saviour, I beseech you banish the drink. Banish it from your tables, banish it from your houses, and oh! for Christ's sake, banish it from his house. Put no longer the sacrifice of Christ and of devils on the same altar! Banish also those who manufacture this "distilled damnation" from your communion, aye, from your society. Have no fellowship with those who get rich by robbing man of his reason, woman of her virtue, and children of their patrimony and their bread. Cease to recognize, not only as Christians, but as men, those who fatten on the weakness, wickedness, and suffering of their fellow men. Hoist the flag of death over their breweries, distilleries, and dramshops, warning the unwary that death and damnation lurk behind their finely decorated bars, and run like the lurid fires of perdition through their brightly polished taps!... The time has come when to trim on this drink question is the highest treason to the cause of Christ, and the grossest inhumanity to suffering, perishing millions. Tell me no more of charity towards brewers, distillers, and publicans. Your false charity to these has already consigned millions to an untimely Hell! Tell us not of a charity that takes sides with the Pharisees who devour widows' houses, and leaves the poor victims of avarice and power to groan, and suffer, and die. Tell us not of the charity that would have welded the shackles on three millions of slaves in America yonder, rather than have disturbed the comfort and impoverished the wealth of a few rich planters. Such charity savoureth of the old serpent, its speech betrayeth it. Such was not the charity of Jesus. His charity went out after the suffering multitudes, while it consigned those who gloated on their wrongs and sorrows to their own place, notwithstanding that they garnished the tombs of the prophets and paid tithes of mint, anise, and cummin![1]

Lord of justice, give me the courage and presence of mind to
repel any dealings that might cause others to struggle. Amen.

---

1   From *Practical Religion*.

DELIVER US FROM EVIL
(Matthew 6:13 *ESV*)

O Christians! look on the multitudes who are led as sheep to the shambles by this great destroyer [alcoholic drink].

Look on thousands, yea, tens of thousands, of your fellow-countrymen, husbands and fathers, robbed at once of their earnings, their manhood, their reason, and turned loose on their hapless wives and children, worse, more unreasonable, tyrannical and savage, than the wild beasts of the forest. Look upon thousands of poor suffering women called wives, who have to endure all a drunkard's tyranny and fury, while working for the children's bread, and struggling vainly to keep a home where they may lay their heads. Look on multitudes of our youth, lured from their homes, inspired with contempt of parental counsel, drawn into immoral societies, dragged down from comparative innocence and virtue to idleness, debauchery, and crime!

Look on hosts of helpless, neglected children, ten times more to be pitied than those whom the heathen mother casts into the Ganges or the Nile; look on their half-starved, half-clad bodies, their untaught, benighted minds and souls, and then say how long this modern juggernaut shall roll down your streets unchallenged – this chief of Satan's empire sway his spectre over this vaunted Christian land! Arise, Christians, arise, and fight this foe! You, and you alone, are able, for your God will fight for you! Oh, come up to his help against this might champion of Hell, and he wilt empower you to lay him low, and take all his armour wherein he trusted.[1]

> These are strong words about strong drink! I reach out in prayer
> for those whose lives are blighted by the "juggernaut" of alcoholism.
> Hear my prayers for their deliverance, and for their loved ones. Amen.

1 From *Practical Religion.*

THEY SOLD PROPERTY AND POSSESSIONS TO GIVE TO ANYONE WHO HAD NEED

(Acts 2:45 *NIV*)

Our officers… are already, as a rule, truly *spiritual and devoted men and women*. Every address they hear at the Training Homes,[1] every illustration and story, is used to show them that they will reap exactly as they sow.[2] They are told that it is useless to expect God to own and bless them if they are idle or negligent, if they don't attend to the open-air work and do their visitation, hold up and pray with people; in short, if they are not good soldiers of Christ, warring a good warfare, and enduring all needful hardness thereto. They are taught, on the other hand, that while they are faithful and true, fully consecrated to God, they need fear nothing in earth or Hell, but may boldly march into the strongholds of the enemy, always being sure that he is with them, even to the ends of the earth! If God raises up men and women and so fills them with his love that they cheerfully leave all and embrace lives of toil and self-sacrifice, in order to save these millions who are yet without God and without hope, can we possibly be too fast in opening their way to reach them? Would to God that we could put down two red-hot salvation officers amidst every 1,000 of these neglected masses, the world over; we should see the dawn of a brighter day! Then, why should we not aim at it, and why should you not help us to do it? Are you sure that the fortunes you are hoarding for your children will ever come into their possession? What if these neglected multitudes should rise up and assert themselves, what will become of your houses and land then?… The same enterprise which actuates businessmen with respect to their *buildings* should be incorporated into religion. What care and sagacity is exercised as to the situation and suitability of business premises? What contrivance to economize space, and do the largest amount of work in the smallest room. This is thought to be wise and prudent, and so it is.[3, 4]

Lord, this is all relative. I may not have a fortune to share or a building
to donate, but I pray for a generous heart, nonetheless. Amen.

---

1   School for officer training.
2   Galatians 6:7.
3   A typically forthright challenge from Catherine Booth to wealthy property owners and churchgoers whose support she thought should have been forthcoming. She was keen to utilize church buildings she felt were underused through lack of enthusiasm for the gospel.
4   From *The Salvation Army in Relation to the Church and State.*

GIVE TO THE ONE WHO ASKS YOU, AND DO NOT TURN AWAY
FROM THE ONE WHO WANTS TO BORROW FROM YOU

(Matthew 5:42 *NIV*)

Think of the numbers of great religious buildings all over the land shut up in sepulchral darkness five days per week, and many of them six, a vestry or schoolroom being sufficient to accommodate all who think it worthwhile publicly to worship God, or to seek the salvation of men, once a week! Buildings which cost from one to thirty thousand pounds each! Who would ever suppose that these buildings represented a religion which demands that the service of God shall be the first great business of life, and the drawing of the people to him the next, every day of every week, all the days of our lives? Here again the children of this world show the superiority of their wisdom to promote their ends, by opening the theatres, dancing halls, tap-rooms, and gin palaces every day, and making them attractive by night by flaring gas, music, and other attractions. We believe that God's buildings ought to be open every night, and every innocent means used to draw the people into them. Thank God, we *can* get the people; as a rule, we have large congregations on week nights, and crowds shut out on Sunday nights. Why should we not appropriate every place we can get hold of to soul-saving purposes? At any rate, we are determined on doing so, and this is the reason for our loan scheme, which has been so criticized in certain quarters...[1] Our plan hitherto has been to borrow seven or eight hundred from a building society, paying 6 or 7 per cent, and make up the deficiency from the Parent Fund. Now we know this is perfectly safe, because the corps will be abundantly able to pay back in rent, not only the interest, but the loan itself; and when the loan is paid off, we borrow on this building again and buy another. Now, what is there wrong in that? Are there not mortgages on half the chapel property in the land?[2]

Lord, grant me wisdom so that I may give or lend wisely;
with my head as well as my heart. Grant me divine discretion. Amen.

---

1   The Salvation Army was investigating the possibility of borrowing funds from supporters and well-wishers, as opposed to lending institutions. Catherine Booth appealed to wealthy Christians to view their lending as a means of serving God.
2   From *The Salvation Army in Relation to the Church and State.*

WHOEVER DOES THE WILL OF GOD LIVES FOR EVER
(1 John 2:17 NIV)

The spirit of… [worldly] amusements is manifestly adverse to the dignity, gravity, and usefulness of the Christian character. What are its effects? Lightness, foolish jesting, a false estimate of creature delights, obtuseness to spiritual things, and frequently uproarious merriment and godless mirth.

We put it to any Christian who has ever allowed himself to take part in such amusements whether these are not their inevitable and bitter fruits, and whether he has not found their spirit to be utterly antagonistic to the spirit of Christ? We have heard many backsliders in heart attribute their declension to mingling in such scenes of folly and frivolity, and we never met with one whom we had reason to believe had been renewed in the spirit of his mind who could say he could enter into them without condemnation. Doubtless there are thousands of professing Christians who live in perpetual strife with their consciences and with the Holy Spirit on this subject; and verily they have their reward. Trying to hold Christ in one hand and the world in the other, they lose both. They have no joy in their godless amusements, neither have they any joy in the Lord. All is darkness, condemnation, and death. "Ye adulterers and adulteresses, know ye not that the friendship of the world is enmity with God?"[1] The testimony of the word is too explicit, and the voice of the Spirit too clear, for any child of God to err for want of light if he will but listen to his divine counsellor. But, alas! too many seek to silence his voice by vain and worldly reasoning, lowering the standard which he has given them *because somebody else does so*. They do not hear him saying, "What is that to thee? follow thou me."[2] "Love not the world, neither the things of the world. If any man love the world, the love of the Father is not in him."[3, 4]

Lord, even in a world of shifting values, where Victorian standards
might be seen differently today, there are standards that remain. Give me grace
to follow humbly, without ever condemning the choices of others. Amen.

1   James 4:4, KJV.
2   John 21:22, KJV.
3   1 John 2:15, KJV.
4   From *Practical Religion*.

THE LORD TAKES PLEASURE IN HIS PEOPLE

(Psalm 149:4 *ESV*)

Not only is the testimony of the word and of the Spirit against... [worldly] amusements, but the testimony and example of the most devoted and intelligent Christians of all ages have been against them. The following are a few extracts bearing on the subject:

"There is no earthly pleasure which has not the inseparable attendance of grief – and that following it as closely as Jacob came after Esau.[1] Yea, worldly delight is but a shadow; and when we catch after it, all that we grasp is substantial sorrow in its room. The honey should not be very delightful, when the sting is so near." *Alleine.*[2]

"If there be any sorceress upon earth it is Pleasure; which so enchanteth the minds of men, and worketh the disturbance of our peace with such secret delight, that foolish men think this want of *tranquillity* happiness. She turneth man into swine with such sweet charms, that they would not change their brutish nature for their former reason." *Bishop Hall.*[3]

"Consider, this is not the season that should be for pleasure! The apostle James lays it as a great charge upon many in his time, that they lived in pleasure on earth.[4] This is the time to do the great business for which we were born." *Ambrose.*[5, 6]

Father, the last thing I want is to be a Christian killjoy.
Nevertheless, for you, all the pleasures of sin, I resign. Help my
joys and delights to be holy and wholesome – and fun! Amen.

---

1 Genesis 25:26.
2 Joseph Alleine (1634–68), English author.
3 Bishop Joseph Hall (1574–1656), English bishop and devotional writer.
4 James 5:5.
5 Bishop Ambrose (Aurelius Ambrosius) (337–397), Bishop of Milan.
6 From *Practical Religion.*

AND NOW ABIDETH FAITH, HOPE, CHARITY, THESE THREE;
BUT THE GREATEST OF THESE IS CHARITY
(1 Corinthians 13:13 *KJV*)

It must be a precious thing to be greater than *faith*, and greater than *hope* – it must, indeed, be precious! – and, just in proportion as things are valuable and precious amongst men, so much trouble and risk will human speculators take to counterfeit them. I suppose that [in] no department of roguery in this roguish world has there been more time and ingenuity expended than in making money, especially bank notes. Just as wicked men have tried to imitate the most valuable of human productions for their own profit, so the Devil has been trying to counterfeit God's most precious things from the beginning, and to produce something so like them that mankind at large should not see the difference and, perhaps, in no direction has he been so successful as in producing a *spurious charity*.

I almost think he has got it to perfection in these days. I don't think he can very well improve on the present copy. This charity – this love – is God's most precious treasure; it is dearer to his heart than all the vast domains of his universe – dearer than all the glorious beings he has created. So much so, that when some of the highest spirits amongst the angelic bands violated this love, he hurled them from the highest Heaven to the nethermost Hell! Why? Not because he did not value those wonderful beings, but because he valued this *love more*. Because he saw that it was more important to the well-being of his universe to maintain the harmony of love in Heaven than to save those spirits [that have] allowed selfishness to interfere with it. So our Lord says, "I beheld Satan as lightning fall from Heaven."[1, 2]

Lord, your rule is love. Heaven is a place of perfect, untainted love.
Thank you, Lord, that Jesus died to remove my sin, so that when I die,
I may live with you in Heaven. There was no other good enough. Amen.

1   Luke 10:18.
2   From *Godliness*.

SOW TO YOURSELVES IN RIGHTEOUSNESS, REAP IN MERCY;
BREAK UP YOUR FALLOW GROUND: FOR IT IS TIME TO SEEK THE LORD,
TILL HE COME AND RAIN RIGHTEOUSNESS UPON YOU

(Hosea 10:12 *KJV*)

Let us look... at this precious, beautiful charity... What is it? It is divine. It must be shed abroad in the heart by the Holy Ghost.[1] In vain do we look for this heavenly plant among the unrenewed children of men – it grows not on the corrupt soil of human nature; it springs only where the ploughshare of true repentance has broken up the fallow ground of the heart, and where faith in a crucified Saviour has purified it, and where the blessed Holy Spirit has taken permanent possession. It is the love *of* God, not only love *to* God, but *like* God, *from* God, and fixed on the same objects and ends which he loves. It is a divine implantation by the Holy Ghost. Perhaps some of you are saying, "Then it is useless for me to try to cultivate it, because I have not got it." Exactly! You may cut and prune and water forever, but you can never cultivate that which is not planted. Your first work is to get this love shed abroad in your heart. It is one of the delusions of this age that human nature only wants pruning, improving, developing, and it will come out right. No, no! Every plant which my Heavenly Father hath not planted shall be rooted up. If you want this divine love, you must break up the fallow ground of your hearts, and invite the Heavenly Husbandman to come and sow it – shed it abroad in your soul... I want you to note that this love is a divine principle, in contradistinction to the mere love of instinct. All men have love as an instinct; mere natural love towards those whom they like, or who do well for them. "If ye love them which love you, what reward have ye? do not even [the] publicans the same?"[2] Wicked men love one another for mere natural affinity, as the tiger loves its cubs.[3]

> Love must rule me, love must have me. Lord, let your work in my
> heart be one of love, producing love and expressing love. Amen.

---

1   See Romans 5:5.
2   Matthew 5:46, KJV.
3   From *Godliness.*

OUR STRUGGLE IS NOT AGAINST FLESH AND BLOOD,
BUT AGAINST THE RULERS, AGAINST THE AUTHORITIES,
AGAINST THE POWERS OF THIS DARK WORLD AND AGAINST THE
SPIRITUAL FORCES OF EVIL IN THE HEAVENLY REALMS

(Ephesians 6:12 *NIV*)

Religious prejudice is perhaps the most inveterate of all, and is most difficult to overcome. This has been the most formidable enemy to the work of The Salvation Army. Nevertheless, it is wonderful, in the short time of our history, to how great an extent prejudice *has* been broken down. It is perfectly astonishing the impression which this movement has made upon public opinion during the time it has existed, in comparison with the great revival movements of the past. There is nothing in Church history to compare with it. Of course the facilities for travel and spreading information are much greater than in bygone times. This work is now drawing towards it and improving in its favour thousands of the most honest-hearted and devoted people in the world; and we don't care about the opinions of any others. These are drawing near to see and judge for themselves; and this spirit of enquiry, we hope, will go on increasing until we shall see prejudice break down on every side. I can quite understand the feelings of conventionally trained religious people when our measures first burst upon them, and I think we have had a great deal of patience for many years with objectors; but I do think, when people get the light and come and profess to be convinced, it is too bad for them to turn round upon us with old objections which we have answered 150 times. However, we must persevere with our measures as long as there is the necessity for them. It is astonishing, considering how much we ought to be known by this time, what a great deal of prejudice we have had to contend with, personally. Of course Satan knows that everything depends on our being believed to be sincere, consecrated, disinterested people, and therefore he has done his utmost to start all manner of doubts, suspicions, and misrepresentations concerning us; and certainly he has found plenty of agents, mostly, alas! in the shape of professing Christians, ready to help in this evil work.[1]

Father, may I only ever encourage your people, of whatever denomination.
If I am tempted to criticize, help me to remember who is pulling the strings,
and of that great spiritual warfare raging in the background. Amen.

---

1 From *The Salvation Army in Relation to the Church and State.*

WHO THEN WILL CONDEMN US? NO ONE – FOR CHRIST JESUS DIED
FOR US AND WAS RAISED TO LIFE FOR US, AND HE IS SITTING IN THE
PLACE OF HONOR AT GOD'S RIGHT HAND, PLEADING FOR US

(Romans 8:35 *NLT*)

[The Salvation Army's] antecedent history, our motives, our aims, our measures, and our teaching have been assailed in turn; but so far, thanks be unto God, he has stood by us, and convinced thousands of the honest-hearted of our integrity and disinterestedness, confounding those who would not be convinced, and turning their weapons of slander and abuse back upon themselves. The divine promise has been literally fulfilled in our experience; the more we have been evil spoken of and persecuted, the more has the Spirit of glory and of God rested upon us, and everywhere, even in the thickest of the fight, God has given us the ear of the people, accompanying our testimony with the outpouring of his blessed Spirit, working signs and wonders equal to anything recorded in the Acts of the Apostles. Notwithstanding all this, however, there is still much misunderstanding and prejudice abroad. I believe that many still think that my husband is an ambitious, designing man, who wants virtually to be another Pope, get a great deal of power, and be at the head of a great, worldwide movement. I do not wonder at persons with such notions hating him. I am sure I should, if I knew him to be actuated by any such motives; and no considerations should induce me to countenance or help him. But I am as sure of his integrity and singleness of eye in all his movements as I am of my own, and therefore I have no doubt about the Lord leading and inspiring him.[1]

Lord, you are a faithful God, and you vindicate your people,
whatever misrepresentations abound. Thank you for William Booth,
whose spirit remained strong even in the face of prejudice, misunderstanding
and lies. Grant me that same singlemindedness today, I pray. Amen.

---

1   From *The Salvation Army in Relation to the Church and State*.

IT IS BETTER TO TAKE REFUGE IN THE LORD THAN TO TRUST IN HUMANS
(Psalm 118:8 *NIV*)

Have the topics of our glorious Christianity become so stale and uninteresting? Have the themes of gospel enterprise and individual effort lost all their inspiration? Have the songs of Zion lost their enchanting and inspiriting influence? Has the voice of social prayer become quite silent? Has every spark of real enthusiasm in religion gone out, that when Christians want to find interest and enjoyment, they must seek it in themes and things peculiarly belonging to the god of this world, and his votaries?

Has it come to pass that Christians have so little confidence in the God of the Bible, and the religion of Jesus, that they must seek an alliance between Christ and the world in order to *interest* their children and save them from open profligacy and vice? If so, how does this reflect on themselves? What sort of training does it imply? Have they trained their sons and daughters so truly in the *spirit* of the world, under the garb of a religious profession, that nothing but the most sensuous amusements of worldlings (who make any pretence to morality) will satisfy them? Has it come to pass that the children of Christians must dress like harlots – dance, sing songs, read novels, attend concerts, where worldly and even comic songs are sung, evoking uproarious laughter and unseemly jests? And all this for their *amusement*, their parents, and even ministers, looking on: and striving by the most blind and wicked perversion of the word of God, to justify their worldliness and salve their consciences? Alas, it has come to this! "Oh that my head were waters, and mine eyes a fountain of tears, that I might weep day and night for the slain of the daughter of my people."[1, 2]

Lord, how easy it is to imagine that the old gospel is insufficient or irrelevant!
How easily that thought creeps in! Help me to rest on gospel truths for this day
and age, knowing that they hold their power. Amen.

1   Jeremiah 9:1, KJV.
2   From *Practical Religion*.

WALK IN ALL HIS WAYS
(Deuteronomy 10:12 *ESV*)

"What am I to do?" is the still recurring cry of some timid Christian mother or father. "Must I keep my children out of society altogether?" Yes, verily, if you cannot find any truly Christian society for them. Humble yourself deeply before God for having trained your children with worldly tastes and associations, and set yourself, as far as possible, to remedy the evil.

Get more *spirituality, more real life*, and you will find your religion astonishingly more *interesting* both to yourself and to your children. "Well, but my children must have companions." Oh no, there is no *must* in the case; better live without them than have such as lead them *away from God*, and into friendship with the world. If you have not yet learnt this, I fear you have never realized your responsibility to God for your children's souls. Do you regard your children as *your own or the Lord's*? If your own, you will train them on worldly principles; but if the Lord's, you will surely train them for him, that they may serve their generation *according* to his will. You have nothing to do with consequences; it is yours to obey. God will take care of his own.

Act on your convictions of duty. If you stand alone in your family – your circle – your church – never mind; act for yourself, as you must give account for yourself. Perhaps, if you make a beginning, somebody else will follow. Somebody must begin – somebody must make a stand, *why not you*? You say, "I am so uninfluential – so weak – and the cross will be so heavy." All the more blessing in carrying it; and he who chooses the weak things will bless your testimony, and use it for his glory. Only "honour God, and he will honour you."[1,2]

> Father, my prayer this day is for Christian parents whose
> children have little or no interest in matters of faith.
> May your grace sustain them, and reach their loved ones. Amen.

---

1 See 1 Samuel 2:30.
2 From *Practical Religion*.

IF I GIVE ALL I POSSESS TO THE POOR AND GIVE OVER MY BODY TO
HARDSHIP THAT I MAY BOAST, BUT DO NOT HAVE LOVE, I GAIN NOTHING

(1 Corinthians 13:3 *NIV*)

Spurious charity is selfish – it is never exercised but to gratify some selfish principle in human nature. Thousands of motives inspire it – too many to enumerate…

A man might give his goods to feed the poor, and his body to be burned, and yet [be] destitute of true charity. Now, what an anomaly. But we have wonderful illustrations that such a thing is possible… A man may do this to support and carry out a favourite system of intellectual belief of which he has become enamoured, just as men become absorbed in politics, or in what they consider the good of their nation, so that they will even go to the cannon's mouth[1] to promote it. Further, a man may do it in order to merit eternal life. Paul did this when he went about to establish his own righteousness. He tells us afterwards that self was the mainspring of all his zeal. It was all his own exaltation; there was no divine love; he was an utterly unrenewed, Christless, and selfish man, at the very time he was doing this… Or, it may be… to gratify a naturally generous disposition. I used to say to a generous friend of mine, when he was talking in a confidential way about his giving, and the delight it gave him, attributing it to divine grace – I used to put my hand on his, and say, "Hold! My friend; I am not sure it is all grace. You like giving better than other people do receiving. Look out that you do not lose your reward through not taking the trouble to see what you give to; don't give your money to every scheme that comes across you. Remember that you are answerable to God for your wealth, and that God will demand of you how you have bestowed your goods."[2]

Thank you for this insight, Lord.
Would you please, today, be the Master of my motives. Amen.

---

1 Shakespeare's *The Seven Ages of Man* ("All the world's a stage"). A metaphor; to place oneself in the mouth of a gun cannon was to voluntarily risk danger or even death for the sake one's beliefs or convictions.
2 From *Godliness*.

AHAB SON OF OMRI DID MORE EVIL IN THE SIGHT OF THE LORD THAN ALL
WHO WERE BEFORE HIM... HE MARRIED JEZEBEL THE DAUGHTER OF KING
ETHBAAL OF THE SIDONIANS. THEN HE WORSHIPED AND BOWED TO BAAL

(1 Kings 16:30-31 *NET*)

This king and queen [Ahab and Jezebel] succeeded in instituting... heathen religion in
Israel; they set up this idol Baal alongside the Temple of the God of Israel, and induced
nearly the whole nation to bow down to it. They had got idolatry, as they thought,
firmly established, and were eating and drinking and making merry over the conquest,
when down drops Elijah on the scene,[1] as though he had fallen from Heaven. This
man, dressed in goat's hair, with a leather girdle about him, a true, courageous prophet
of the Lord of Hosts, faces Ahab as none but one sent of God dare, and he says, "As
the LORD liveth" – mark the allusion, your Baal is a dead God – "there shall be neither
dew nor rain in Israel these years"[2]... and then he disappeared as suddenly as he had
appeared. The Lord had provided a hiding place for his servant. He sends him to the
brook Cherith, there to be fed by a miracle,[3] while he comes out of his place to chastise
this idolatrous, backsliding, rebellious people. Perhaps the Lord wished to spare Elijah
the scenes he would have had to witness, or he foresaw that this grim tyrant would be
everlastingly harassing him and trying to slay him. Whichever way it was, God hid
him; but when the famine began to make its appearance, then they began to search for
Elijah. I wonder what Ahab wanted with Elijah. His guilty conscience told him that
that man had the key of the clouds, that that man was nearly associated with this dread
calamity, and so he sends out his messengers to find him – as Obadiah tells Elijah,
"There is no nation or kingdom, wither my lord hath not sent to seek thee".[4, 5]

Father, my prayers today are for your people who are persecuted for
their faith; those who stand for righteousness in the face of harassment
and threats of torture. Be with them as you were with Elijah. Amen.

---

1 1 Kings 18.
2 See 1 Kings 17:1, KJV.
3 1 Kings 17:6.
4 1 Kings 18:10, KJV.
5 From *Life and Death*.

IT IS GOD'S WILL THAT YOU SHOULD BE SANCTIFIED
(1 Thessalonians 4:3 *NIV*)

Saying "yes" to temptation is sin – not temptation itself. You may be tried to the very extremity, but if you will hang on to the power of God he will save you to the uttermost of your needs. There is no necessity to sin. "I write unto you, little children, and you, fathers and young men, that ye *sin not.*"[1] There is no necessity if you do but yield yourselves up unto God and not to the Devil – "unto whom ye yield yourselves servants to obey, his servants ye are, whether of sin unto death or of righteousness unto God,"[2] so that you may be severely tempted and yet not sin...

Sanctification... does not imply final attainment. You must discriminate between purity and maturity. You may have the most perfect baby but he is not a man yet. He has to grow and develop and increase; but people really and truly do not begin to grow in grace until they are sanctified. It is more frequently a falling down and a getting up again than an ever-onward progress in grace and salvation. Hence, if you really want to grow in grace, if you want to rise to the possibilities of your nature in the salvation of God, you must be delivered from sin, for sin undoes you, knocks you down into the mud, as it were, and you have to be, as the apostle says, "Always laying the foundation for repentance from dead works."[3] How can such people grow? Instead of growing on, and on, and on, until they attain the stature of the perfect man in Christ Jesus, they stop short in perpetual babyhood... We believe it [sanctification] to be deliverance from sin – full conformity of heart, and mind, and will, to the law and mind of God... his Spirit in us causing us to walk in his statutes and ordinances blamelessly, an inward transformation into the very likeness of Christ.[4]

Thank you, Lord, that sanctification is not merely an outdated instruction or a dusty doctrine, but a life-changing gift. Sanctify me afresh, I pray. Amen.

1   See 1 John 2:1, KJV.
2   See Romans 6:16, KJV.
3   See Hebrews 6:1, KJV.
4   From *Holiness*.

Be strong in the Lord

(Ephesians 6:10 *NIV*)

The great thing to be done by... God is to subdue the naturally evil, wicked, and rebellious heart of man. Now God alone is able to do that. That is a superhuman work. You may enlighten a man's intellect, civilize his manners, reform his habits, make him a respectable, honest, industrious member of society, without the power of God, but you cannot transform his soul.

That is too much for any human reformer. This is the prerogative of the Holy Ghost, and I have not a shadow of a doubt that the eternal day will reveal other kinds of work to be wood, hay, stubble. All the sham conversions, all the persons whose lives and opinions have been changed by anything short of this power will be wood, hay, stubble.[1] It is the prerogative of the Spirit of God.

Therefore, we want this Spirit to do this work. What! You set yourself to enlighten a darkened human soul, to convince a hardened rebellious sinner, to convert a rebel in arms against God, with an inveterate hatred in the very core of his soul against God and all about God. You set yourself to bring down that – to transform that evil, wicked heart, to subdue that soul to submission and obedience! – you try it, try it without the Spirit of God. Oh! No, you want that Spirit. You want the same measure of that Spirit, just the same, which Paul had.[2]

> The arm of flesh will fail me, Lord. I have no spiritual power except that which you provide. Deliver me from the temptation of thinking I can serve you without your Spirit's daily infilling. Help me not to run on empty. Amen.

1 1 Corinthians 3:12–13, KJV.
2 From *The Holy Ghost*.

MY MESSAGE AND MY PREACHING WERE NOT WITH WISE AND PERSUASIVE
WORDS, BUT WITH A DEMONSTRATION OF THE SPIRIT'S POWER

(1 Corinthians 2:4 *NIV*)

No person who followed us [The Salvation Army] carefully can imagine for a moment that we would hold, or teach, any adaptation of the gospel itself… We deemed this so above all adaptation – so above any change, that we would not be responsible for transposing its order, much less altering its matter; that we would not take a dot off one of the "i's," so sacredly intact do we believe the gospel of Christ in its matter ought to be kept. We believe also that the Okdek[1] of God ought to be strictly maintained; that it is as rational and true in philosophy as it is in divinity; and that the way the Spirit operates upon the minds of men is just the same as ever. This we clearly and most carefully pointed out, so that what we have to say now you will please bear in mind, has nothing to do with the gospel message itself. We have tried to show our idea (or what we believe to be the Holy Spirit's idea) of a pure gospel…

We start with the lying clearly before us as a fundamental truth in every page of the New Testament, that forms and ceremonies, whatsoever they may be, are nothing except as they embody and represent real spiritual life, and truth and action – *action*!… It was the great sin – the crowning condemnation of the Jews – that they had frittered away the spirituality and practical bearing of the divine law, clinging on to those forms and ceremonies which were instituted only to embody and symbolize it. Would to God they had let go the form when they let go the spirit. Jesus Christ wishes they had. He tells them it would have been far better. He told them they were children of the Devil,[2] notwithstanding their holding on to their relationship to Abraham and all the spiritual forms and ceremonies of their ritual.[3]

Lord, ceremonies have beautiful form, but that beauty is enhanced and
magnified by the presence of your Spirit within. Likewise, life itself. Amen.

---

1   The life path number of Okdek is 1. The destiny number 1 is one of the most important figures within numerology, because it symbolizes the origin of life; the symbol of a new beginning considered to be the number of God.
2   See John 8:44.
3   From *Aggressive Christianity*.

After a long time, in the third year, the word of
the Lord came to Elijah: "Go and present yourself to Ahab,
and I will send rain on the land." So Elijah went to present
himself to Ahab. Now the famine was severe

(1 Kings 18:1–2 *NIV*)

The man whom God hides, the Devil will never find, until God gives him permission, and then he will not be able to touch a hair of his head. How safe are they who are in the keeping of Elijah's God! How independent they are of men's opinions and threatenings! The famine spreads desolation all over the land, until there is great scarcity of food for men and beast, and the king sends Obadiah to find out the little rivulets that might be left, or the springs that are not dried up, so as if possible to find a little green stuff for the cattle; and Obadiah proceeds on his way, Elijah meets him, and says, "Go, tell thy lord, Behold, Elijah is here."[1] And Obadiah replies, "Thou sayest, Go, tell thy lord, Behold, Elijah is here. And it shall come to pass, as soon as I am gone from thee, that the Spirit of the Lord shall carry thee whither I know not; and so when I come and tell Ahab, and he cannot find thee, he shall slay me." But Elijah gives him the assurance he needed. "As the Lord of hosts liveth, before whom I stand, I will surely show myself unto him today." Here is courage – the true courage of one whom God has sent. "I am not afraid of thy master; I am not afraid of his dungeons or his blocks. I am going to show myself to him." He says, moreover, "Go and tell him Elijah is here" – not that Elijah is coming, but here – "if he wants me, he can come and find me. I shall not run away for fear of him"; and so Obadiah goes and tells Ahab. What was it that drove Ahab to meet Elijah? It might be that he was impelled by hope; it might be that he was driven by fear; but he had to go and meet him. The famine had brought things to a climax. He must meet with this man of God. He must try either to wrench this power from him by threatening, or he must persuade and entreat him.[2]

I pray today for those who need courage to stand their ground;
believers in countries where furious opposition to the gospel is commonplace.
Place your angels around the persecuted Church, Father. Amen.

---

1   See 1 Kings 18:8 and following.
2   From *Life and Death*.

"THIS IS THE COVENANT I WILL MAKE"... DECLARES THE LORD.
"I WILL PUT MY LAW IN THEIR MINDS AND WRITE IT ON THEIR HEARTS.
I WILL BE THEIR GOD, AND THEY WILL BE MY PEOPLE"

(Jeremiah 31:33 *NIV*)

It is so much easier for an unregenerate man to be circumcised or to be baptized, as the case may be, to partake of the Lord's Supper, to keep outwardly the Sabbath Day, to abstain from acts of immorality and open sin, and to be decently and morally religious – all this he can understand and do for himself, and it looks to him so much easier, and so it is, in the first instance, than bringing his evil, unregenerate heart to God for him to circumcise it, and write his law in it, as he promised to do under the new covenant.

Now, that is what God wants every man to do. He wants to bring this *heart to him*, and let *him renew it*. He says, "I will circumcise your hearts to keep my law."[1] But, no! The unregenerate man rests in the outward form. He will not be at the trouble to sacrifice his idols, and cry mightily unto God. He will not seek until he attains the fulfilment of these promises; so he sits down and rests in the form. Alas! Alas! How many thousands in this so-called Christian land of ours today are just there. They have got the form; they are like the Jews – they are Pharisees with a Christian creed instead of a Jewish, the same in character, only different in name. That is all the difference, hanging on to the creed of Jesus Christ, while they know nothing of its spirit, the form without the power; and they deny their professed Lord every day... My friend, my friend, if you never find it out until you come to die, you will find it out then, but it may be too late. May God, the Holy Spirit, help you to find it out this day, and bring that unrenewed, unrepentant, evil heart of yours to the cross; bring it to God, and wait, and weep, if need be, and struggle, and knock, and cry, as he tells you, until he does renew it and write his law in it; then the outward form will be the expression of inward grace.[2]

Lord, let any work you do in my life be real. Amen.

1   See Deuteronomy 30:6.
2   From *Aggressive Christianity*.

WHY DO YOU CALL ME, "LORD, LORD," AND DO NOT DO WHAT I SAY?
(Luke 6:46 *NIV*)

This tendency to rest in form is just as great as ever and, instead of putting away their idols, and bringing their conscience to be cleansed and kept clean by the precious blood, prayerfully and carefully walking before God, striving in all things to please him, people get an outside form, but live just like the world around them, calling Jesus, "Lord, Lord," but not doing the things that he says. Now, I say that a pure gospel requires that we bring our evil hearts to God to be renewed, and that we resolutely put away our idols, and that we wait on him by the cross until he renews our motives, tempers, tendencies, feelings, and dispositions, and makes us new creatures in Christ Jesus. Instead of doing this, people go on being circumcised or baptized, and they call themselves "Israel"; whereas, of the spiritual Israel they are utterly ignorant. They are like the children of Hagar (as Paul says),[1] and not the children of the promise...

There is such a tendency to rest in form, so in the Church collectively, hence this tendency to a formal religion. Just as it was with the Jews – their Temple service and the paraphernalia of Judaism – was all in all to them, and they thought that Jesus Christ was the most awfully severe and uncharitable person who ever appeared on the face of the earth, because he told them the truth. And the same class of character presents the same attitude now. We shall see when we get to the judgment seat of Christ which is the true charity – that which covers up bad things, or that which tears off the bandages, and shows people their hypocrisy, and, as we have just read, reveals to them the secrets of their hearts.[2]

> When you are offering life with a capital "L", Lord, why would I want a counterfeit? Send a new touch of power today, I pray. Keep it real! Amen.

---

1   Galatians 4:25.
2   From *Aggressive Christianity*.

MAKE EVERY EFFORT TO... BE HOLY
(Hebrews 12:14 *NIV*)

Holiness is attainable because it is expressly emphatically and repeatedly commanded. Jesus Christ, whose teachings were all, or nearly all, prospective, concludes one of his addresses on the Mount with saying, "Be ye therefore perfect, even as your Father... in heaven is perfect."[1] What does he mean? It must at least mean, that in our measure and according to our capacity we are perfectly to fulfil the law of benevolence as God does with his capacity.

But some people think to get out of the difficulty by saying that the context shows that our Lord here refers to forgiving and loving our enemies. I say you don't get out of the difficulty that way, for if a man can in his heart forgive his enemies and pray for them that despitefully use him, he is a sanctified man, and I defy any other man to do it. This is the highest test of sanctification. Then again the first great commandment was never abrogated, and never will be. "Thou shalt love the Lord thy God with all thy mind, and soul, and strength." And the second is like unto it, "Thy neighbour as thyself" – the Scribe, in answer to whose question this was spoken was better instructed than many modern Christians, for he replied, "Well, Master, thou hast said the truth." And Jesus answered, "Thou art not far from the kingdom of God."[2] Jesus saw that the man was sincere, and ready to receive the truth without quibbling.

The first and greatest commandment remains in force today as much as it ever was, and must continue in force throughout eternity. It must ever remain the duty of the creature to love the Creator with all his heart, and the duty of the creature to love his fellow as himself.[3]

Lord, my prayers today are with those who are "not far from the Kingdom" –
people who try to live good lives, people whose hearts are kind and forgiving,
yet pay little attention to the claims of Christ. Bless them. Amen.

1 Matthew 5:48, KJV.
2 See Mark 12:30–34, KJV.
3 From *Holiness*.

THE SPIRIT OF THE LORD IS ON ME, BECAUSE HE HAS
ANOINTED ME TO PROCLAIM GOOD NEWS TO THE POOR
(Luke 4:18 *NIV*)

He [General William Booth] left a happy and prosperous ministerial career (this is well known to thousands), gave up all that is commonly regarded as valuable in life, came out with any human encouragement or guarantees, and subsequently gave himself to labour amongst the neglected masses with no thought beyond that of a local work in the east of London, as is abundantly evident from our early records.[1] We gave up home, income, every friend we had in the world, save my parents, with four little children under five years old, to trust only in God, as truly as Abraham did when he left his native land.[2] We had no more idea than anybody... of what God was going to do with us; but we both had the inward conviction (against which I had struggled for four years) that he wanted to use us to the masses in a way in which we could not be used in our denomination. After travelling for three years as an evangelist, during which time he saw many thousands united with the various charges with which he laboured, my husband was led as by miracles to the east of London. After a severe struggle with myself, I was led, I believe by the Holy Spirit, to sympathize with him in his yearnings over the East End poor, and consented for him to begin to work amongst them, though God only knows what it cost me in many particulars. I often think how little our criticizers know of what we have gone through in establishing this movement. Its early history is fortunately so far recorded as to present a triumphant contradiction to all sane minds of the absurd insinuations to which I have alluded. During the first ten years we were groping our way out of the conventionalism in which we had been trained, and often most reluctantly following the pillar of cloud by which God was leading us. We tried committees, conferences, and all sorts of governments, showing how far we were (until God revealed it to us) from the grand military idea which is now proving such a wonderful power in organizing the converts for aggressive effort.[3]

Bless those, Lord, who are today seeking their vocation. Amen.

---

1   The Booths had the option of a settled ministry in Methodism. They felt led to reject this in favour of mission in London's East End, notorious for its deprivation and poverty.
2   Genesis 12:1.
3   From *The Salvation Army in Relation to the Church and State*.

THE ACCUSER OF OUR BROTHERS AND SISTERS
(Revelation 12:10 *NIV*)

I ask any sane person, does this [the progress of The Salvation Army] look like the path of a man inspired by ambition and a love of power? Does it not rather look marvellously like God's way of making a new departure? – beginning with one man, as in the case of Luther, George Fox, and Wesley, inspiring him and leading him by a way he knew not, but using him to bring about a great spiritual revolution? I think so, and I believe in my inmost soul that my husband has been as truly raised up and led of God for this work as any of these were for theirs… I wish some of our detractors could have been behind the door this morning, when my precious daughter should have started for Paris.[1] Through an accumulation of disappointment and perplexity, some of it occasioned by the most cruel treatment of those who owe us nothing but gratitude and love, she broke down, and was utterly unable to go. If you could have seen the agony of nature that we all endured, you might comprehend that it is not so easy a thing after all to send your child to a foreign land, to bear the responsibility and anxiety and toil of propagating a real spiritual work amongst infidels and socialists, with all the malice and spleen of the Pharisees arrayed against you! Oh, what a comfort in such hours to be able to look up into that face that was marred more than any man's, and say, "Lord, thou knowest all things; thou knowest I do this for thee"[2] … I say, that when all this prejudice shall be removed, and when the honest and true come really to know us and what we are trying to do, I leave you to judge whether all the slanders of earth and Hell will be able to keep back the flow of sympathy which will set in upon us from all parts of the world.[3, 4]

Lord, for those facing criticism, prejudice, and rejection today,
for the gospel's sake, I pray your blessing and encouragement. Amen.

---

1   Catherine Booth-Clibborn (Katie Booth) (1858–1955), oldest daughter of William and Catherine. She took The Salvation Army to France.
2   See John 21:17, KJV.
3   Catherine Booth was angered and dismayed by criticisms levelled at her and her family by people suspicious of their motives. A lot of gossip was centred upon William Booth's supposed selfish and egotistical ambition to promote himself as a great church leader.
4   From *The Salvation Army in Relation to the Church and State*.

RETURN, THOU BACKSLIDING ISRAEL, SAITH THE LORD; AND I WILL NOT CAUSE MINE ANGER TO FALL UPON YOU: FOR I AM MERCIFUL, SAITH THE LORD, AND I WILL NOT KEEP ANGER FOR EVER

(Jeremiah 3:12 *KJV*)

Your conscience was once tender as the apple of the eye; you eschewed evil, and kept as far from its very appearance as you could. You had no fellowship with the godless multitudes who crucified your Lord, and trampled underfoot his blessed laws. You kept as far aloof from the world as you might, weeping over its sins, and looking down with pity on its hollow amusements. What is your present attitude in this matter? Are you still separate from sinners, following the Lamb wheresoever he goeth?... You were once full of zeal for the glory of your divine deliverer, and the salvation of those for whom he died. You could then reprove sin, and weep over and expostulate with sinners. You could deny yourself almost your necessary sleep and food, in order to promote the interests of your Redeemer's Kingdom. Where is now your zeal for the Lord of Hosts? Can you deny self, sacrifice your ease, honour, reputation, or wealth, for his glory, as you once did? Remember! Compare your present state with your former one. Let conscience speak, let facts speak, and honestly admit the truth; and if you are condemned, write yourself down – backslider in heart. You say, "I do not like the conclusion." Perhaps not; but if it be true, honesty will be the best policy here, as in everything else. Look the fact in the face, and try to realize its desperate meaning. I fear too many Christians have far too light an estimate of heart-unfaithfulness. I have sometimes heard them speak of five or ten years' half-heartedness as a very light thing, slurring it over, as it were, with a very thin and superficial sort of confession; but our Lord does not so regard it; he looks upon it as a very serious matter, a very heinous sin, a most God-dishonouring experience.[1]

These are hard words, Lord. Yet, your mercy is great.
I pray today for those known to me who have drifted away from faith.
Draw them back to yourself with forgiveness and grace. Amen.

---

1   From *Practical Religion*.

IF YOU HAVE BEEN MERCIFUL,
GOD WILL BE MERCIFUL WHEN HE JUDGES YOU

(James 2:13 *NLT*)

Ask for the realizing light of the Holy Spirit to reveal to you your backslidings, and to set your secret sins in the light of his countenance. Ask him to help you to remember by quickening your spiritual perceptions, and opening your eyes, to see the monstrous ingratitude and cruel infidelity of which you have been guilty. Instead of refusing to remember, because of the mental suffering involved in the process, methinks we should rejoice to suffer. Seeing that we have wounded our Lord in the house of his friends, we ought to be willing to weep our lives away at the remembrance of our sin, and if we could, to shed tears of blood, as an evidence of our penitence. To have been unfaithful to his saving grace; to have been untrue to his dying love; to have withheld from him that which he purchased with his heart's blood, demands a deeper grief, a more bitter repentance, than that of our unconverted state. May the Lord help those of you who are convicted of this sin to remember; until the fallow ground of your heart is broken up,[1] and your souls cry, "O remember not against us former iniquities: let thy tender mercies speedily prevent us: for we are brought very low. Help us, O God of our salvation… and deliver us, and purge away our sins, for thy name's sake."[2] The next step is repentance. Now, true repentance implies humiliation, confession, and renunciation.[3]

God of grace and God of mercy, draw alongside those who
want to repent, but struggle to. Look with pity, I pray. Amen.

---

1   Hosea 10:12.
2   Psalm 79:8–9, KJV.
3   From *Practical Religion*.

LORD, TEACH US TO PRAY

(Luke 11:1 *NIV*)

There is no experience, perhaps, more common in these days than this, nothing more constantly said to me by professing Christians: "Well, I have prayed a long time for certain things, but I don't seem to get any answers to my prayers." I often wonder such people don't give up praying altogether. I think I should if I never got answers... This is a very God-dishonouring experience, and there must be something wrong somewhere when this is the case. There must be something wrong either with the supplicants or the Giver. Oh! I feel often what a deeply God-dishonouring thing it is when Christians meet, as they frequently do, up and down the country, to pray for a revival, to pray for a specific thing in their churches and in their families, and it never comes. Some years ago, when the wave of revival was sweeping over Ireland and America, you know the churches in this country held united prayer meetings to pray that it might come to England; but it did not come, and the infidels wagged their heads, and wrote in their newspapers: "See, the Christians' God is either deaf or gone a-hunting, for they have had prayer meetings all over the land for a revival, and it has not come." Oh! How my cheeks burned with shame as I thought of it; how I mourned over it! I knew it was not because our God was asleep[1] – not because his arm was shortened[2] – not because his bowels of compassion did not yearn over sinners[3] – not because he could not have poured out his Spirit and given us the same glorious times of refreshing they had in other places. That was not the reason. There was only one reason, and that was, that his people asked amiss. They did not understand the conditions of prevailing prayer. They did not fulfil them.[4]

> Lord, teach me how to love you. Teach me how to pray.
> Teach me how to serve you better every day. Amen.

---

1   Psalm 121:4.
2   Isaiah 59:1.
3   See 1 John 3:17.
4   From *Godliness*.

BLESSED ARE THOSE WHO HAVE LEARNED TO ACCLAIM YOU,
WHO WALK IN THE LIGHT OF YOUR PRESENCE, LORD

(Psalm 89:15 *NIV*)

Young converts, never drop out of living union with Jesus. Keep in it – hold it fast – walk in it, and you will get answers to your prayers every day. You will be as sure of it as if you saw God doing what you ask, and heard him speaking to you. You will be able to say, "I know that thou hearest me always."[1] Bless his name! Those who abide in him can say that in their measure…

What does it mean to walk in obedience? Well it does *not* mean, searching this New Testament to find out how little of God's grace will get you into Heaven! It does not mean, running round to see what this person says and the other person says about such and such a text, in order that you may escape from the real, practical meaning of the text! Such people are hypocrites at heart, whoever they are; or at least, insincere. They don't want to know God's will; they would much rather not know it. They want to get away from the plain, practical, common sense meaning of the text, and then they say, "It doesn't mean exactly what it says," and "It should be interpreted so-and-so" and they stroke themselves down, and try to make themselves feel comfortable when they are traitors at heart…

Walking in the light is like walking in the sun – not running behind a pillar there, and a tree yonder, to get away from the light. It is coming right out, and saying, "Now, Lord Jesus, I want to know thy will. Lord, pour thy light upon me. I am prepared to follow it, even though it is to the block and to the stake."[2]

Lord, I want my prayers to be answered. I know you are a God
who wants to answer prayer. Therefore, search me and try me so that
there may be no obstruction in this channel of grace. Amen.

---

1   See John 11:42, KJV.
2   From *Godliness.*

Work hard and serve the Lord enthusiastically
(Romans 12:11 *NLT*)

Hayle,[1] we found, was but a small struggling place with a port, at which some little coasting trade was carried on, and a large foundry employing six or seven hundred men. The chapel was a barn-like affair, holding perhaps 600 people. The number we crowded into it night after night was quite a different matter. The Cornish system of packing a congregation was certainly somewhat singular. The first comers occupied the seats, and then another row of people would stand in front of them. The aisles would next be filled, beginning at the pulpit stairs, till the whole place was literally gorged. Then the windowsills would be besieged, and through the open windows another crowd outside would listen to the echoes of the songs and to such stray sentences as might reach their ears.

The plan laid down for our labours, which was more or less followed throughout our Cornish campaign, was that Mr Booth should preach on Sunday morning and evening, and on the first four evenings of the week, while I took the Sunday afternoon and Friday night meetings, frequently speaking on the afternoon of several weekdays as well. In addition to these regular services, we often held noonday meetings, visited the sick, and conducted other accessory gatherings. The Saturdays were devoted to rest and to preparation for the Sabbath.

Our first meetings at Hayle were held on Sunday, 11 August. I must confess we had looked forward to them with considerable anxiety, so much appeared to depend upon their success. In the morning there was a good congregation. My dearest preached, and although he did not experience much liberty, nevertheless the people were evidently interested and impressed.[2, 3]

> Lord, for busy preachers and pastoral visitors, I pray extra strength today.
> Keep them from exhaustion and burnout. Keep their work fresh. Amen.

---

1   Cornwall, England.
2   The Booths had accepted an invitation to lead an evangelistic campaign in Cornwall, on behalf of the Methodist New Connexion there, in 1861.
3   From *Catherine Booth* by Catherine Bramwell-Booth

THE LORD OPENED HER HEART TO RESPOND

(Acts 16:14 *NIV*)

On our way home from the chapel, a gentleman said that he hoped I should in the afternoon service give them something of a cheering character, as what they had heard in the morning had completely capsized them. To this our hostess added, as we sat at the dinner table, "Before you came, my husband and I had a very good opinion of ourselves; but now we see that we are nothing – absolutely nothing, and worse than nothing."

In the afternoon the place was jammed, and the Lord gave me great liberty. At night there was another crowd, and a powerful impression was made. Indeed, I have always reckoned that God in an especial manner put his seal upon the services of that day, giving us, as it were, a new divine commission for our subsequent life-work, though we little dreamed at the time how much was involved in it.

There was, however, no immediate break… The people listened with the utmost earnestness, and assented to the truth, but they would not respond to our invitations to come forward to the communion rail. The next night the result was much the same. In spite of the strongest appeals, not a single person would come forward. Knowing that there were many present who were deeply convinced of their sin, the invitation was repeated again and again, without eliciting the slightest response, when suddenly the silence was broken by the loud cries of a woman, who left her seat, pushed her way through the crowd, fell upon her knees at the penitent form, and thus became the first-fruits of what proved to be a glorious harvest of souls.[1,2,3]

> Father, I pray today for anyone who has recently responded to your call
> on their heart. Bless new converts. Protect them. Feed them. Amen.

1   A further report from the Cornish Campaign, 1861.
2   The idea of people making their way forward in response to a sermon or an appeal is commonplace in Salvation Army meetings today, where people are invited to kneel at the mercy seat and ask for prayer.
3   From *Catherine Booth* by Catherine Bramwell-Booth.

For to me, to live is Christ and to die is gain
(Philippians 1:21 *NIV*)

"Those poor Indians," she continued… "I was going to sleep. No, I was not, for I was wide awake. But I was lying here the other night, and such a funny thing happened. I was lying here, and the gas shone on that brass knob" (pointing towards it), "and there came up the most perfect African face. Two eyes. I shall never forget it to all eternity. It looked like a woman's face, and there was a white bandage around the top of her head, like they do have, and her eyes seemed to come out to me. I had just been thinking of Heaven, and how I should enjoy it, when that woman's face seemed to say to me, 'Won't you help us, won't you help us?' And I said, 'Oh, yes, Lord, I will go anywhere to help poor struggling people – struggling, many of them, after God, better than I have done.' I would go on an errand to Hell if the Lord would give me the assurance that the Devil should not keep me there."

Never think of me as in the grave. I shall not be there anyway. I tell Emma[1] there may be a lot of people there [in Heaven]. I believe there will be the same differences in people there that there are here, and those who like to sit in a corner, playing a harp all day, they will let them, perhaps; but the people who will prod about and look after things and help the good, they will let them. I don't believe there are so many of them that one can be spared. I shall go about, you may depend. I have in this world, and I shall in the next. I shall know what you are doing. I shall know all about it.[2, 3]

Thank you, Lord of eternity, for the promise of Heaven.
This side of eternity, it is a mystery, yet I know my soul is safe in your hands.
When we all get to Heaven, what a day of rejoicing that will be! Amen.

---

1 Emma Moss Booth (1860–1903).
2 Some of Catherine Booth's thoughts in her dying days, as she speculated on the life to come.
3 From *Catherine Booth* by W. T. Stead.

Many people had gathered and were praying
(Acts 12:12 NIV)

They are most impatient for us to go to St Ives,[1] but we think of staying here another week. The work gets better and better. The whole place is roused. On Sunday night the Wesleyan superintendent sent one of the circuit stewards, offering the loan of their chapel for Sunday and Wednesday evenings.

We accepted it, and accordingly William preached last night in the Wesleyan chapel, crammed to suffocation, and I in the New Connexion, well-filled, even though I was not announced.

We had a glorious prayer meeting in both chapels, about thirty cases in the Wesleyan and twenty with us, some of them the most precious ones I ever witnessed. I could fill sheets with the account of one gentleman which would thrill you with interest, and make you shout the praises of God.

There was much new material last night at the Wesleyan chapel. Hundreds went away convicted. If the Wesleyans would open their two chapels and invite us to labour in them, there is no telling what the work would rise to. We are both very much exhausted this morning, especially myself. I shall not do so much again. The prayer meeting was very heavy. I was drenched in perspiration. But it is wonderful how God brings me through.[2, 3]

> Lord, how wonderful it is to read of prayer meetings in
> support of preaching campaigns! Please keep me faithful in prayer
> for those who preach, so that I may play my part in winning souls.
> How wonderful it is to talk with God in prayer! Amen.

---

1   Cornwall, England.
2   From a letter Catherine Booth wrote to her parents on 2 September 1861, during the Cornish Campaign.
3   From *Catherine Booth* by Catherine Bramwell-Booth.

I TELL YOU THE TRUTH; IT IS EXPEDIENT FOR YOU THAT I GO AWAY:
FOR IF I GO NOT AWAY, THE COMFORTER WILL NOT COME UNTO YOU;
BUT IF I DEPART, I WILL SEND HIM UNTO YOU

(John 16:7 KJV)

What is our work? To go and subjugate the world to Jesus; everybody we can reach, everybody we can influence, and bring them to the feet of Jesus, and make them realize that he is their lawful King and lawgiver; that the Devil is a usurper, and that they are to come and serve Christ all the days of their lives. Dare any of us think of it without this equipment of power [the Holy Spirit's indwelling]?

Talk about "Can we have it?" We are of no use without it. What can we do without it? This is the reason of the effeteness of so much professed Christianity; there is no Holy Ghost in it! It is all rotten. It is like a very pretty corpse – you cannot say there is this wanting, or the other wanting, it is a perfect form, but *dead*. It is like a good galvanic battery. It is all right – perfect in all its parts – but when you touch it there is no effect – there is no fire or shock. What is the matter? It only wants the fire – the power.

Oh! Friends we want the power that we may be able to go and stretch ourselves upon the dead in trespasses and sins, and breathe into him the breath of spiritual life.[1] We want to be able to go and touch his eyes that he may see, and speak to the dead and deaf with the voice of God and make them hear. This is what we want – power. If we equally need it, *is it likely that God will withhold it?*... Our Saviour distinctly told us that he bought it for us – that it was more expedient that his people should have it than that he should remain with them. It is promised to all believers to the end of time.[2]

I am weak, but you are strong. Grant me whatever power I will need for today.

Amen.

---

1   See 1 Kings 17.
2   From *The Holy Ghost*.

I CHOSE YOU AND APPOINTED YOU
SO THAT YOU MIGHT GO AND BEAR FRUIT
(John 15:16 *NIV*)

Let me remind you – and it make my own soul almost reel when I think of it – that God holds us all responsible.

He holds you responsible for all the good you might do if you had it [the infilling of the Holy Spirit]. Do not deceive yourself. He will have the *five* talents with their increase. He will not have an excuse for *one*, and you dare not to go up to the throne and say, "Thou wast a hard Master, reaping where thou dost not sow, and gathering where thou hadst not strewn. Thou biddest me to save souls when thou knewest I had not the power." What will he say to you? "Wicked and slothful servant, out of thine own mouth will I judge thee. You know where you could have got the power. You knew the conditions. You might have had it. Where are the souls you might have saved? Where are the children that I would have given you? Where is the fruit?"

Oh! Friends, these are solemn and awful realities. If I did not believe them I would not stand here. Oh! What you might do! Who can tell?

Who would ever have thought twenty years ago when I first raised my voice, a feeble trembling woman, one of the most timid and bashful the Lord ever saved, [that] hundreds of precious souls would be given me? I only refer to myself because I know my own case better than that of another; but let me ask you – supposing I had held back and been disobedient to the heavenly vision, what would God have said to me for the loss of all this fruit?[1]

Send a new touch power on my soul, Lord.
Send it now, Lord. I pray for a fruitful faith! Amen.

---

1   From *The Holy Ghost.*

**In all things God works for the good of those who love him,
who have been called according to his purpose**

(Romans 8:28 *NIV*)

It has been publicly stated at several diocesan councils here and there… by bishops, leading clergy, ministers, and leading laymen, that the effect of The Salvation Army on the churches has been to stir them up to greater devotion, love, and zeal for the salvation of men. This is notorious the world over. The testimony of these men, summed up, is that the Army has taught them many valuable lessons. Amongst others, "The universal compulsion of souls", "Aggressive Christianity" – having coined the very term – "The employment of women", "The utilization of the laity" etc. And although each of these witnesses has his difficulties and objections, which it would be *too wonderful* if he had not, from an ecclesiastical standpoint, yet all agree in holding up the love and devotion and zeal of our soldiers for universal admiration and imitation!

Surely, then, so far, the effect of the movement on the churches has been good and healthy. We know for a positive fact that many churches and organizations have gained large accessions of members through our work, and that their old members have been quickened and stirred up. Surely this is a good effect; and yet the poor Salvation Army has received evil for good at the hand of many an Alexander[1] and Demetrius,[2] and has met with more of the spirit of the vulture than of the dove. Alas that it should be so! However, it won't do for people who are set to lead a revolution to be thin-skinned; therefore we go on, knowing that out of all this God will work his own gracious design. One pastor went back to Paris… saying, "The worship of The Salvation Army is destined to become the worship of the future!" And at any rate, it is already working marvellous changes.[3]

> Lord, my prayers today are for the churches in my area.
> As I think of them, I pray your blessing on their ministers,
> leaders, and members. Bless my own church too. Amen.

---

1   2 Timothy 4:14, NIV.
2   Acts 19:24.
3   From *The Salvation Army in Relation to the Church and State.*

As iron sharpens iron, so one person sharpens another
(Proverbs 27:17 *NIV*)

We have now between four and five hundred women officers; and the great majority of them are successful soul-winners, in many cases whole populations feeling their influence. Think of the effect of this on the public opinion of the churches and of the country! Here are agents for evangelizing the masses at home and the heathen abroad – simple, earnest, devoted, successful, and *inexpensive!*

Yes, thank God, we are teaching the churches that others can be used for the salvation of men. The multitudes have too long been left to these. As a clergyman said to me the other day, "There are 35,000 souls in my parish, what can one do?" What indeed! Set the carpenters and washer-women on to them, saved and filled with the Spirit! We are teaching the value of organizing these rough forces of the Lord's army, and sending them ahead as sappers and miners to prepare the way of the Lord; and we will go on teaching them, though they do abuse us between the lessons.

The Salvation Army has also taught some who are apt to learn the value of all night of prayer, penitent forms, holiness meetings, and open-air marches, etc., etc. Thank God, we don't want to get all the blessings; we want The Salvation Army to be like Samson's foxes, going through the churches with a fire-brand, setting every true Christian on fire.[1] God is my witness; I should rejoice in such a result. If they will only get people saved, I don't care very much what sort of creed or forms or ceremonies they adopt. As the General says, "If we make the man, the man will clothe himself. Get the man right, and he will get himself a house to live in; he will betake himself to the organization which best suits him."[2]

Lord, grant me that generous heart, whereby anything I may know
about reaching others for the Kingdom, I may always be willing to share.
Let that spirit prevail throughout all denominations, for Jesus' sake. Amen.

---

1   Judges 15:4–5.
2   From *The Salvation Army in Relation to the Church and State.*

THEY GOT NOT THE LAND IN POSSESSION BY THEIR OWN SWORD,
NEITHER DID THEIR OWN ARM SAVE THEM: BUT THY RIGHT HAND,
AND THINE ARM, AND THE LIGHT OF THY COUNTENANCE

(Psalm 44:3 *KJV*)

It makes my heart ache – I was going to say boil – with righteous indignation, in jealousy for God's honour, to think that he should be so traduced and blasphemed by those who profess to love him – who try to make out that they get wrong for want of light.

Nothing of the kind. Here is plenty of light; but you must say, "Yes, Lord, I am willing to have it, even if it condemns me. If it condemns my heart, my head, Lord, pour it on me. If it condemns my life, pour it on me. If it condemns those companions, those indulgences, pour it on me: I will give them up. If it condemns my business, pour it on me: I will abandon such business, and sooner die in the workhouse than continue in it. If it condemns my family relations, I will come out from them, and follow thee."

The Lord will always answer such a soul as that. He will put his finger down on this sore spot and the other, and he will tell you what to do, and you will be as sure of it as if you heard his audible voice.

What does it mean to walk in the light? Obey his voice. Don't stop to confer with flesh and blood but, as Paul did, get up, and set off to commence the career which your Master commands. Paul did not stop to confer with flesh and blood. He did not stop to reckon what it would cost him. *That* is walking in the light – obeying – not standing, quibbling with the Lord about it; not saying, "Oh! But," – but *doing* it.[1]

Lord, keep me in your light; walking in the light of God, living in
the light of God, working in the light of God, moving in the light of God. Amen.

1   From *Godliness.*

When you ask, you do not receive, because you ask with wrong motives

(James 4:3 *NIV*)

When you have made the sacrifice, when you have entered upon the road, the joy, the light, the power, and the glory are worth a hundred times as much. Did any man that ever for the pearl of great price feel that he had given too much for it, even if he had given all that he had? Never!

Martyrs and confessors have gloried in the possession of it while they have writhed on the rack and in the flames, and you never heard one solitary testimony that any man or woman of God ever thought that they had paid too highly for it. Never!…

Thousands of Christians pray and never get answers. They are selfish in their prayers; they are earthly; they ask amiss, that they may consume it upon their earthly desires, affections, and propensities. Mothers tell me that they have prayed for their children for years, and not got one of them converted. I say, "More the pity; more the shame on you."

Why? Because they prayed merely selfish, instinctive prayers, because they were *their* children, or because they wanted them to be religious; but they don't want them to be righteous over much; they don't want them to be given up to God as to cut off the vanities and fooleries of this world, and to give themselves up wholly to Christ – that is too much; but just religion enough to make them a comfort to themselves. How would *you* answer such prayers *if you were God*? Hundreds and thousands of prayers are put up every day that go no deeper and no higher than that, if the motives were analyzed – and the Holy Ghost *does analyse*.[1]

Lord, this seems like a hard word. Nevertheless, please analyze my heart, my motives, and my prayer life. In my life, Lord, be glorified. Amen.

---

1 From *Godliness*.

HER CHILDREN ARISE AND CALL HER BLESSED;
HER HUSBAND ALSO, AND HE PRAISES HER

(Proverbs 31:28–29 *NIV*)

I am afraid many wives pray for their husbands [but] they are not troubled that their husbands are living in disobedience to God, squandering their times, talents, and money, and robbing the Kingdom of Jesus Christ of what they might be doing for it; the agonizing consideration is that, if religious, they would spend so much more time at home; that they are wasting the money, instead of laying it up for the children; and that, if they were religious, all this would be right.

Now, I say, God will never answer that wife's prayer for her husband!

You must think of what your husband could be for God – what he could do for God's Kingdom – how Jesus Christ has shed his blood for him – how dishonouring a life of sin is to God; and you must dwell on this until your heart is ready to break, and you will soon get your husband converted, if you act wisely along with your prayers.

God hates selfishness – selfishness is the Devil, the very embodiment of him. You must get out of self; you must look at your child always as God's, as having a precious soul redeemed with the precious blood of Jesus, and having talents and capacities to *glorify him* and spread his Kingdom; and you must ground your prayers on that, and say, "I would rather lay them in the grave, a thousand times – rather they were poor and despised – than they should grow up to dishonour thee." Then you will get your prayers answered![1]

> Lord, I pray today for Christian wives and mums. Bless them. They are
> privileged people who carry special responsibilities. Thank you for them. Amen.

---

1   From *Godliness*.

DON'T LET ANYONE LOOK DOWN ON YOU BECAUSE YOU ARE YOUNG, BUT SET AN EXAMPLE FOR THE BELIEVERS

(1 Timothy 4:12 *NIV*)

It is a marvellous thing, if we are wrong, that wherever we go the testimony of Christians who receive our teaching is, that they are quickened and blessed, and begin to live a new life. That is a curious effect of wrong teaching, is it not? Yet that is the universal testimony. Multitudes of Christians have abandoned the use of strong drink, who had taken it all their previous lives; others, the use of tobacco and similar indulgences. Perhaps someone may answer, "But you cannot prove the use of tobacco to be sinful." That depends on a man's light; but it must be a higher degree of devotion for a man to abandon it for the good of others, than to smoke for his own indulgence.

Numbers of women have given up fashionable dressing, and now dress as simple Christian women ought. I say then, if, with so imperfect an organization, having had everything to learn, and so much to contend against, the Army has produced such a wonderful effect on the churches, what may we not hope for with a more perfect system and an ever-increasing force? We have more than doubled our speed since Christmas, having taken out 260 officers since then, nearly all of whom are working [in] prosperous corps in different parts of the country. A very important item to be borne in mind in calculating the future of the Army, is the youth of its officers. They are mostly under twenty-five years of age – young men and women full of fire and energy, numbers of them having sacrificed home, or friends, or situations, or offers of marriage, or something which constituted their earthly life! Think of the absorption and heroism such people are capable of, and what they are likely to become with three or four years' experience.[1]

> Lord, you entrusted the early work of The Salvation Army to young officers. Today I pray for young leaders; inexperienced but committed to your cause. Bless them as I think of them. Amen.

---

1   From *The Salvation Army in Relation to the Church and State.*

SELECT CAPABLE MEN FROM ALL THE PEOPLE – MEN WHO FEAR GOD,
TRUSTWORTHY MEN WHO HATE DISHONEST GAIN – AND APPOINT THEM AS
OFFICIALS OVER THOUSANDS, HUNDREDS, FIFTIES AND TENS

(Exodus 18:21 *NIV*)

We got a letter the other day from Major Simmonds (formerly Clapham), of the Training Home, whom, some of you will remember, we sent to the Cape about two months ago. She says: "You would hardly know me. I am nothing but skin and bone. I have been sick every day of the whole voyage." Poor little thing! She was not very stout before. She goes on to say: "I am so thankful to be over it, and once more on dry land, and able to write you. And now for the war; we have begun already."

No moaning or groaning, no wishing herself home again; but "Now for the war!" This is the spirit of our officers as a rule. You can see at a glance that we have only to go on multiplying such people sufficiently to be able to put a sufficient number of them down among the forces of the enemy, and we can once more turn the world upside down! You say, "It will never be accomplished." How do you know? Don't tell me that the dispensation of the Spirit is going to end in this ignominious fashion. I don't believe it. I believe that the fullness of the Gentiles has to come in, and the remnant of Israel too. My son was speaking the other day with one of the sons of Abraham; and he was perfectly delighted when he found out that we believed in the Old Testament as well as the New, that we had not abolished the moral law, and that we do not believe that Jesus Christ ever intended to abolish it, but brought us power to keep and love it. He was amazed to hear that we believed that God still loved Israel, and was longing to restore them and to unite all real saints, whether Jews or Gentiles, in one grand spiritual Israel, under one king, even the Son of David.[1, 2]

> Heavenly Father, I pray specifically for Salvation Army officers today.
> Bless those men and women who seek to uphold your name
> and reach out in practical mercy. Amen.

---

1 The Booths believed that The Salvation Army had been raised up by God to usher in the Second Coming of Jesus Christ. They viewed their revival efforts in such a light.
2 From *The Salvation Army in Relation to the Church and State.*

PEOPLE WILL COME FROM ALL OVER THE WORLD
(Luke 13:29 *NLT*)

Another future effect of The Salvation Army, will be the opening of the prison doors to them that are bound. How do I know? Because we are inspiring hope in the hopeless all over the world! Christians who have given up hope, in despair of being able to do anything for their fellow men, are inspired afresh by our work. This was beautifully expressed by a French writer who visited our hall in Paris one night. He said, "The aspect of the work that struck me was most was, that it was reassuring." He said, "I had been hearing of the state of the Church, and I had been looking with despair of anybody being able to do anything for these people; but here I found a handful of men and women who were *acting out their belief*, and who believed *in success*, and at least I was [reassured]." Yes; and if you knew the numbers of letters we receive from all parts of the world, you would see this too. We had a letter only the other day from a gentleman in Persia, in which he tells us how he had been hearing and reading about The Salvation Army; and he says: "I am so impressed that it is this that we want here, and I am so sure you will come, that I have got thirty young men, teaching them to read, and getting them ready for you to make officers of." It is the same with Russia. A Russian count, a man of great experience in Christian work, said to me: "You might go for a thousand miles in Russia, and not find a cottage or a place without a Bible, and you might go the same distance and not find *one living Christian*. It is The Salvation Army we want." Yes; and, we doubt not, God will raise us up officers one day who will go to Russia.[1,2]

> International God, today I pray for your work overseas, in lands other than my own. Bless the spread of the gospel and those who work abroad. Help them if they are homesick, or if they struggle to adjust to different cultures. Amen.

---

1   The Salvation Army commenced operation in Russia in 1917, with the opening of seven corps, two children's homes and two slum stations in St Petersburg. Reinforcements were sent from Sweden. As a consequence of the revolution, the Army had to withdraw the reinforcements 1918. Forty officers from Russia and Finland continued the work. In 1923, the Russian Communist Party declared that The Salvation Army must leave the country. The work there officially recommenced in 1991.

2   From *The Salvation Army in Relation to the Church and State*.

If we confess our sins, he is faithful and just and will forgive us
(1 John 1:9 *NIV*)

A dear man of God, who... during the early years of his Christian career, had been a man of extraordinary devotedness, zeal, and self-sacrifice, but gradually and almost imperceptibly... had fallen from his first love. Though still abounding in good works, and looked up to by all as a pattern of piety, he had lost the power which once characterized him. The Lord showed him from whence he had fallen in a very simple and effective manner, by bringing him into close contact with a man filled with the Spirit... thus, by the law of contrast, flashing on him the conviction that he had lost his first love. The backslider in heart began to "remember". He said to himself, "I was once like that man... but I am not like him now. Oh, my God, I am a backslider in heart." The discovery almost overwhelmed him. He realized its bitterness, and agonized over its consequences, until his distress reached a climax, and kneeling down he prayed in an agony, telling the Lord that if he would restore him to his first love, he would confess his heart-backsliding to his brethren... I need not say that the Lord heard and answered. This was all he wanted of his servant, in order to his pouring in the oil and wine of his love and consolation... The next day there was an official meeting, in which he had to take part. At the appointed time some dozen of the leading men assembled. After the business was gone through, he asked to be allowed to make a few remarks; and then, with the simplicity of a little child, like an honest-hearted man as he was, he related the experience of the last few days. He confessed to his brethren his heart-backsliding, told them how the Lord had convinced him of it, and how graciously he had restored him to his first love. The brethren present were melted into tears; they sobbed and cried like children.[1]

Forgiving Father, your conviction is our cure.

---

1   From *Practical Religion*.

IF MY PEOPLE, WHO ARE CALLED BY MY NAME, WILL HUMBLE
THEMSELVES AND PRAY AND SEEK MY FACE AND TURN FROM THEIR
WICKED WAYS, THEN I WILL HEAR FROM HEAVEN, AND I WILL
FORGIVE THEIR SIN AND WILL HEAL THEIR LAND

(2 Chronicles 7:14 *NIV*)

Oh, what a deal of praying there is for revivals, and for spiritual visitations, which is sheer hypocrisy. The Church *might have* a revival as wide and deep and powerful as she asks, if she would only comply with the conditions on which God can grant it – if she would remember her unfaithfulness, honestly confess and forsake her sins, and bring into God's storehouse the tithes of which she is so flagrantly robbing him;[1] but it is easier to utter vain repetitions and leave the responsibility of the damnation of souls upon God, than for Christians to humble themselves, confess before the world their fallen and powerless condition, and pay their vows unto the Lord. The Lord only wants a wholehearted faithful people, and the walls of many a Jericho would fall,[2] and a nation be born in a day. Oh, may the Lord send upon his backsliding Israel the spirit of conviction and of mourning! May he open her eyes to see from whence she has fallen, and enable her to repent, to come down into the dust, and cry "Unclean, unclean!" until her iniquity is purged, her backslidings healed, and her lips touched with living fire from off his pure and holy altar[3]... Repentance not only implies humiliation and confession, but renunciation, sometimes the hardest of all. "Put away the evil of your doings"[4] is an indispensable condition of restoration to the favour and peace of God. Christ Jesus came to save his people from their sins, not in them, and those who will not be saved from their sins prove beyond a question that they are none of his.[5]

Lord of the Church, send revival to my land. In your mercy,
may your will be done on earth, as it is in Heaven. Amen.

1   Malachi 3.
2   Joshua 6:20.
3   Isaiah 6:7.
4   Isaiah 1:16, KJV.
5   From *Practical Religion*.

Hope does not put us to shame

(Romans 5:5 *NIV*)

Not only has the Army resuscitated hope in despairing Christians, but also among the poor, the lost, and the forlorn everywhere.

This beautiful story reached us the other day: In a bad house, a wretched place somewhere, where the poor inmates were never allowed to go out of doors, but at certain times and under certain surveillance, there was a certain window with gratings where those poor girls could get a look at our soldiers as they passed; and one of them, who is since converted, says: "We used to rush to those gratings, and press our faces against them, and watch until we could see the last cap of the last soldier pass out of sight. We felt somehow or other that *they* were our hope, and were to be our deliverers."

Oh, yes! The very thieves and harlots everywhere, though they persecute us, armed with the saying of ministers and professors against us, yet in their souls they respect us; and The Salvation Army officer is the man they send for when they are dying... We have resuscitated hope in them, thank God for that! I was hearing some of my daughter's stories... of poor lost ones, both men and women, who came to pour out their hearts' histories to her; trodden down, hidden away, nobody caring anything about them, lost to hope. But when they found one with a heart of sympathy and love, they could go and pour out these stories. They looked, and longed for, the healing balm, the oil of consolation. They said: "Can I be saved? Do you think there is hope for such as I am?"

Oh, yes; you poor Magdalenes[1] and legion-possessed men,[2] there is hope.[3]

Lord, I pray for those who have lost hope;
those who feel hopeless today. Bless them with hope. Amen.

---

1   See Luke 8:2.
2   Luke 8:30.
3   From *The Salvation Army in Relation to Church and State.*

YOUR SORROW LED YOU TO REPENTANCE

(2 Corinthians 7:9 *NIV*)

The gentleman in whose house I was staying said to me, one morning, on our return from the chapel, "Do you know what I have done? I have 'thrown my pipe and cigars and tobacco-box on to the dunghill' and I have made up my mind to smoke no more."

He then said that he had waged a controversy with his conscience and with the Spirit of God for fifteen years about this paltry gratification, living in a state of perpetual condemnation, and sacrificing the power and usefulness which he had once realized for the sake of this idol.

Immediately on putting away the indulgence, peace was restored to his soul, and he began to labour for the Lord as in days gone by. I could give numbers of similar illustrations... to show you that it matters not whether the controverted practice involves the loss of hundreds of pounds, or only of a pipe of tobacco. It is not the greatness or smallness of the matter in itself, but the principle of obedience which is involved in the controversy. While there is a vestige of insubordination to the requirements of conscience and of God, there can be no peace. On this point thousands of professing Christians are mistaken. They allow themselves in things which they feel to be unlawful, and then strive and pray to obtain a sense of acceptance through Christ. They want the Spirit to witness with their spirits that their ways please God, while they know that their ways are such as cannot please him: therefore, they want the Spirit to witness to a lie, which is impossible. No! my backsliding friend, there is but one way back to peace and joy and usefulness, and that is your Lord's own way – repentance.[1]

Gracious Holy Spirit, you persist with us because you love us.
I pray for anyone today who is struggling with a sin they want to
relinquish; those who are addicted. Draw alongside them. Amen.

1   From *Practical Religion*.

YOU WILL ALWAYS HARVEST WHAT YOU PLANT
(Galatians 6:7 *NLT*)

It would be in vain for the husbandman to scatter his seed over the unbroken ground or on preoccupied soil. You must plough and harrow and put your seed in carefully, and in proper proportion, and at the right time, and then you must water and weed and wait for the harvest. And just so in divine things. Oh! We shall find out, by-and-by, that the laws of the spiritual Kingdom are quite as certain and unerring in their operation as the laws of the natural kingdom and, perhaps, a great deal more so; but, through the blindness and obtuseness and unbelief of our hearts, we could not, or would not, find them out. People get up and fluster about, and expect to be able to work for God without any thought or care or trouble. For the learning of earthly professions they will give years of labour and thought, but in work for God they do not seem to think it worthwhile to take the trouble to think and ponder, to plan and experiment, to try means, to pray and wrestle with God for wisdom. Oh! No; they will not be at the trouble. Then they fail, grow discouraged, and give up. Now, my friends, this is not the way to begin to work for God. Begin as soon as you like – begin at once – but begin in the right way. Begin by praying much for him to show you how, and to equip you for the work, and begin in a humble, submissive, teachable spirit. Study the New Testament with special reference to this, and you will be surprised how every page of it will give you increased light. You will see that God holds you absolutely responsible for every iota of capacity and influence he has given you, that he expects you to improve every moment of your time, every faculty of your being, every particle of your influence, and every penny of your money for him. When once you get this light, it will be a marvellous guide in all the other particulars.[1]

> The laws and requirements of your Kingdom, Lord, are often very
> straightforward and simple! Grant me a straightforward and simple faith,
> using the brain you have supplied me with to work out matters of salvation.
> Amen.

---

1   From *Godliness*.

Couldn't you watch with me even one hour?

(Matthew 26:40 *NLT*)

I shall never forget the shock that came over me once in a large gathering of Christian people, when a gentleman, who occupied a somewhat prominent position, was giving out a hymn which contained a verse something about spending one hour in watching with Jesus. He stopped in the middle of this hymn, and said words to this effect: "I am afraid we are verily guilty here. I do not know that I dare say I ever watched one consecutive hour with Jesus in my life." I shall never forget it. My cheeks burned with shame. I said, "Oh! My God, if these are the leaders, we need not wonder at the people." A man occupying such a position to dare to say it! The Lord have mercy on him. No wonder the Lord's work is done in such a bungling way! I say those who want to be successful in winning souls require to watch not only days but nights. They want much of the Holy Ghost, for it is true still, "This kind can come forth by nothing, but by prayer and fasting."[1] We have grown wiser than our Lord nowadays; but, I tell you, it is the same old-fashioned way, and if you want to pour out living waters upon souls, either publicly or privately, you will have to drink largely at the fountain yourself, and have them very ready to let out! If you have not, your talk will be as sounding brass or tinkling cymbal.[2] Oh! it makes my soul weep tears of blood to think of the misdirected effort that will be put forth this very Christian Sabbath. Plenty of labour, but how little comes of it! All because it is cramped, and ruined, and misdirected, for want of thought and prayer, and a single eye for the salvation of souls. May God rouse us up to this, and make us willing to think, and labour, and learn, and wrestle, and sacrifice in order that we may do it.[3]

Sweet hour of prayer, that calls me from a world of care.[4]

1   Mark 9:29, KJV.
2   1 Corinthians 13:1, KJV.
3   From *Godliness*.
4   *The Song Book of The Salvation Army* (1986).

A truthful witness saves lives
(Proverbs 14:25 *NIV*)

[One] qualification for successful labour is power to get the truth home to the heart. Not to deliver it! I wish the word had never been coined in connection with Christian work. "Deliver" it, indeed – that is not in the Bible! No, no; not deliver it; but drive it home – send it in – make it felt. That is your work; not merely to say it – not quietly and gently to put it before the people. Here is just the difference between a self-consuming, soul-burdened Holy Ghost, successful ministry, and a careless, happy-go-lucky, easy sort of thing, that just rolls it out like a lesson, and goes home, holding itself in no way responsible for the consequences. Here is all the difference, either in public or individual labour. God has made you responsible, not for delivering the truth, but for getting it in – getting it home, fixing it in the conscience as a red-hot iron, as a bolt, straight from his throne; and he has placed at your disposal the power to do it, and if you do not do it, blood will be on your skirts![1] Oh! This genteel way of putting the truth! How God hates it. "If you please, dear friends, will you listen? If you please, will you be converted? Will you come to Jesus? Or shall we read just this, that, and the other?" – no more like apostolic preaching than darkness is like light. God says, "Go and do it: compel them to come in.[2] That is your work. I have nothing to do with the measures by which you do it, providing they are lawful. Use just the same diligence, earnestness, and determination that you would if you were resolutely set on any human project, and always be sure that I will be with you to the end of the world.[3] Never doubt my presence when you are set on my business. I will be with you, and I will give you success."[4]

> Whatever means and methods are employed, Lord, empower
> your people to witness well. Grant us that desire to influence others
> for Christ, whatever our personal style or temperament. Amen.

1 See Jeremiah 2:34, KJV.
2 See Luke 14:23.
3 See Matthew 28:20.
4 From *Godliness*.

What is mankind that you are mindful of them, human beings that you care for them? You have made them a little lower than the angels and crowned them with glory and honour

(Psalm 8:4–5 *NIV*)

Man is a wonderful being; and this is not surprising when we remember that he was made originally in the image of God,[1] mentally as well as spiritually. Although fallen, eclipsed, dwarfed, yet the outline of man make his faculties, capacities, possibilities remain the same. Some theologians, in their desire to exalt God, very much debase and underestimate man; whereas the best way to glorify the Creator is to give him full credit for the excellency of his workmanship. God made man a wonderful being… Man is the sovereign of himself; no being, no power can coerce his will. He can resist all the moral forces of the universe; and it is this power which constitutes his greatness and his danger. There it is, an undeniable fact. He can resist all the persuasions and entreaties of his fellow man either to good or evil. He can resist all the power of the Devil. The demoniac, the possessed with a legion,[2] could not be kept back from Jesus when he willed to go to him; and we are exhorted to resist the Devil, implying, of course, that we have power to do so. Man can also resist God, and absolutely refuse to obey and serve his Maker, as did Pharaoh, Nebuchadnezzar, and the Jews. Stephen charges it on the Jews, as the climax of their wickedness, that they had persistently resisted the strivings of the Spirit of God. "As your fathers did, so did ye; ye do always resist the Holy Ghost."[3] God created man with this power, and he will not invade or ignore it. He saw it best on the whole to make man free, even though he would abuse his freedom, rather than to make him a slave, being bound to a certain result by the law of cause and effect, as the sun and stars or the animals, and consequently having no power of virtue himself, nor of bringing any moral glory to his Maker. God retains his power over man as a Sovereign, not by coercing his will, but by rewarding or punishing him according to the use he makes of his freedom.[4]

Thank you, Creator God, for the mysterious gift of free will – something of a risk on your part, but still a lovely gift. Help me to enjoy it with you. Amen.

1   Genesis 1:27.
2   Mark 5:1–20.
3   See Acts 7:51, KJV.
4   From *Life and Death*.

Wash the evil from your heart and be saved
(Jeremiah 4:14 *NIV*)

Earthly government... does not put a subject in irons in order to prevent him from committing crime, thus destroying his freedom, and taking the responsibility of his action on itself; but it reigns over him in his freedom by punishing him when the crime is committed. Thus God reigns over man as a free agent, and thus only; and there is no text in the Bible, interpreted consistently with itself and with correlative passages, which represents God as reigning in any other way – other that is, than as a moral Governor. Hence, when he wants to influence man in any given course, he condescends to reason with him, and to offer to his consideration motives and consequences, in order to induce him to choose as he desires. God does not take him by the collar, metaphorically speaking, and drive him in a given course, with his will or without it, in the same way as he drives the sun and stars along. This would be a reflection on his own wisdom in having made him a free agent at first. God is always consistent with himself, and therefore he conforms all his treatment of man to the freedom of his nature; hence he persuades and strives with man by his Holy Spirit. We want to note... the object or purpose for which the Spirit strives with man.[1] Of course, the very idea of strife between two parties supposes that they are at variance; there could be no strife if they were agreed. In this case it proves that man is in a state of alienation and opposition to God, and consequently in a state of condemnation and death. Now, God wants to win man back from this lost condition to one of submission and salvation. This is his first great aim and purpose. This is what he wants with every unsaved man and woman... that you should get down and submit to him.[2]

> Lord, you are courteous and gracious in allowing us to make our
> own decisions, even though it must sometimes grieve you when we go
> our own way. Please hold fast to those who are tempted today. Amen.

1 Genesis 6:3.
2 From *Life and Death*.

He holds success in store for the upright,
he is a shield to those whose way of life is blameless

(Proverbs 2:7 *NIV*)

Every intelligent businessman goes on the assumption that he has to encounter wrong in the hearts and conduct of his neighbours; in fact, the world takes it as a sign of intelligence that a businessman goes on this assumption... He knows that he is beset on all hands by those who will overreach, cheat, and ruin him for anything that they can, if they can promote their own interests by so doing. Hence the necessity for a kind of legal salvation, in the form of agreements and bonds, between man and man. I hear a good deal about this in connection with our negotiations for buildings, which we are carrying on every day. When proprietors and agents have made certain offers or promises, the General says, "Have you got it in black and white?" and if the answer is "No," then he says, "What is the use of it?" Alas! We know only too well that it is of no use; and I am sorry to say that this is as true of many professing Christians as of worldly men... A man's word is nothing in the great majority of instances. Hence the necessity for lawyers, magistrates, and judges; and even these have to be tied down by law, and watched and supervised, lest even the judges should turn traitors to justice and, for the sake of bribes or party considerations, sell the interests of those whom they ought to protect.... How often do politicians in different lands represent their countries as being, in some particular verging on ruin, and needing a "salvation"? What is this but a great public confession, made by those best capable of judging, that whole nations are misled?... We have it from the highest public authority that nation after nation goes astray on questions vitally affecting their highest good; and it is commonly asserted that they are deliberately led astray by men who care only for their own interests, and so contrive to delude their fellow men wholesale.[1]

> Lord, in business, in politics and in leadership; I pray for those who
> carry responsibility. May they deal honestly, with your help. Amen.

---

1   From *Popular Christianity*.

I WILL GIVE YOU A NEW HEART
(Ezekiel 36:26 *NIV*)

What kind of a salvation does God our Maker, who knows what he meant us to be at the first, and who knows perfectly what we have become through sin, what kind of a salvation does he propose for humanity?

I answer. He proposes a salvation that deals with and removes the cause of all this wrong and woe. Our Saviour, in Matthew xv. 19, goes to the root of the evil when he says: "For out of the heart proceed evil thoughts, murders, adulteries, fornications, thefts, false witness, blasphemies". [KJV] And the apostle also, in Galatians [5:19–21, KJV]: "Now the works of the flesh are manifest, which are these; Adultery, fornication, uncleanness, lasciviousness, Idolatry, witchcraft, hatred, variance, emulations, wrath, strife, seditions, heresies, Envyings, murders, drunkenness, revellings, and such like: of the which I tell you before, as I have also told you in time past, that they which do such things shall not inherit the kingdom of God."

Whether you believe in the revelation or not, you will agree with the fact that these are the works coming everywhere from the evil heart of man; there is no getting away from that. Then I say that God proposes to deal with and remove the cause – the wrong state of the heart. If all men's hearts could be set right today, we should need no more temporal, legal, or political salvations; no more lawyers, police, magistrates, or judges; for a salvation that renews the heart would render all these unnecessary. God's plan of salvation in dealing with the internal malady embraces all its external consequences. It is evident, then, that any salvation which does not deal with this leprosy of evil in the heart is a mockery.[1]

> Thank you, Father God, for a full salvation, complete and thorough.
> This is your unique gift; something the world cannot offer. Amen.

---

1   From *Popular Religion*.

The law of the Lord is perfect, refreshing the soul

(Psalm 19:7 *NIV*)

Peace is the universal want of man. Everywhere and always the race is in a state of unrest, seeking rest and finding none. Consequently, men adopt many counterfeits, and try to satisfy the aching void of their souls with the opiates of Satan. Peace is not a state of mere quietness or insensibility. Alas! Many are in this state of torpor, and when you ask them about their souls they say, "Oh, yes! I have a hope; I have a measure of peace. I hope I am right." But when you try to shake them up, and find out whether they have any thorough foundation for their peace, they don't want to be disturbed. But peace is not insensibility to existing differences between the soul and God, for in such a condition there are all the elements of awful and eternal warfare. There only needs a change of circumstances in order to land the soul into conflict, distress and desolation. We do not mean that sort of peace. True peace, divine peace – the only peace that will do to die with – arises out of a settlement of our differences and a cessation of hostilities towards God, and reconciliation with God, bringing assurance and quietness in view of the past, the present and the future. By false methods Satan lulls the souls of sinners and backsliders into a false peace. For one thing, he gets them to make a false estimate of the character and deserts of sin. When God's Spirit wakes them up, puts before them the heinousness and enormity of their sins, Satan comes and helps them to reason and search for excuses... Multitudes do that now! People want to make out that they are dying for want of light. I say no. They are not dying for want of light; they are dying for want of honesty.[1]

Grant me, Lord, grace and wisdom to discern the motives of my own heart.
Let it be your voice I listen to; not Satan's, and not my own. Amen.

---

1   From *The Highway of our God.*

IF YOU DO WHAT IS RIGHT, WILL YOU NOT BE ACCEPTED?
BUT IF YOU DO NOT DO WHAT IS RIGHT, SIN IS CROUCHING AT YOUR
DOOR; IT DESIRES TO HAVE YOU, BUT YOU MUST RULE OVER IT

(Genesis 4:7 *NIV*)

[The] spirit of finding excuses is most hateful in the sight of God. In the Old Testament he is continually reproving this spirit and threatening the backslidden people with chastisement because of it; whereas he tells them that if they would confess and forsake their sins they should be forgiven. In Revelation 2:5 it says: "Remember therefore from whence thou art fallen, and repent, and do the first works; or else I will come unto thee quickly, and will remove thy candlestick out of his place, except thou repent." Do you see that the everlasting principle on which alone God can pardon sin, laid down in the last utterances of the New Testament as well as all through the Old, is repenting and forsaking of sin, and not excusing and covering it up?... Whose works are you doing? Do not let Satan deceive you if you are living in sin, no matter what church you are a member of, no matter how long you have been a professor of the faith. By excusing yourselves you can get quietness perhaps, but peace never! Would that every soul that is quiet in sin were awakened as the gaoler at Philippi was, by an earthquake if necessary.[1] People in that condition say they have peace, but all the elements of everlasting warfare are ready to break out in their bosoms at any moment. Do not confound quietness with peace. Another method by which people get false peace is that of stifling their fears and convictions. You may succeed in stifling your convictions for a while; perhaps a long while, but when death comes it will open the floodgates of Hell. Oh, the deathbeds of people who have been burying their iniquities in their bosoms, instead of confessing and forsaking them and being saved! Some would get off their beds and hang themselves if by so doing they could get out of their misery. There is only one way to deal with sin; and that is to be out with it, to forsake it, and to have it washed away.[2]

If on my soul, one trace of sin remains, wash me, Lord. Amen.

---

1   Acts 16:25–40.
2   From *The Highway of our God*.

WE PREACH CHRIST
(1 Corinthians 1:23 *NIV*)

The divine testimony concerning Christ must be received and believed; but this is not to be the ultimate object of faith, but only the medium through which the soul's trust is to be transferred to the living person testified of. Here arises another fatal error of this day, through which, I fear, numbers never realize any other God than the Bible, or any other Saviour than a powerless, intellectual belief in the letter of it. They believe the truth about Christ, about his life and death, his sacrifice and intercession; they believe, as enquirers often tell me they do, that Jesus died for them and that he intercedes for them; but they do not believe that his sacrifice actually satisfies the Father for their sins, or that his intercession so far prevails with God for them that he does now actually pardon and receive them because of it. If they believe this of course their anxiety would immediately cease, and they would begin to sing the new song of praise and thanksgiving. The mind is too often occupied with the theory of divine truth instead of the living person whom the truth sets forth. Now, it seems clear to me that the divine testimony concerning Christ may be believed, and frequently is believed, without their existing a particle of saving trust in him as a personal Saviour. Here is the secret of so many apparently believing and devout people living in systematic disobedience to God. Their minds are convinced of the truth, and their emotions are frequently stirred by it; but they have no life, no spiritual power in them by which to resist temptation or live above the world, because their faith does not embrace a living Saviour able to save them to the uttermost, but only the truth about him. Take an illustration. Suppose you are sick almost unto death. A friend brings you a testimony concerning some wonderful physician who has cured many such cases... You may receive the record of your friend concerning the skill and success of this physician's treatment, and you may fully believe it, and yet there may be some reason why you shrink from putting yourself into his hands and trusting him with your life. You may believe all that is said about him, and yet fail so to trust in his person as to give yourself up fully into his power.[1]

Father, thank you for Jesus. In Christ alone my hope is found. Amen.

---

1   From *Practical Religion*.

He predestined us for adoption to sonship through Jesus Christ
(Ephesians 1:5 *NIV*)

The Scriptural idea of saving faith is that of the absolute committal of the whole being over to the faithfulness and power of Jesus, and not merely a belief, however firm, of the records of certain facts concerning him. I may believe that he is the Saviour – that he died for me – that he intercedes for me – that he has promised to save me, as thousands do; and yet I may have no trust in him as now doing all this for me, and consequently draw no sap, no spiritual virtue, from him. Saving faith consists in a firm trust in the person of Jesus, and committal of the soul to him by an unwavering act of confidence in him for all that the Bible presents him to be, as the Redeemer and Saviour of men: "For I know whom I have believed, and am persuaded that he is able to keep that which I have committed unto him against that day" (2 Tim. 1:12 [KJV]). And as soon as this trust is exercised, the testimony of the Spirit is given to adoption, and the soul knows that it has passed from death unto life. Of course this trust is exercised through the testimony of God to his Son, but the Son is the object of trust, and not the testimony merely. This is most important to bear in mind in our efforts to lead souls into saving faith. And now it becomes a question of deepest interest – how best to lead true penitent sinners to exercise this trust. The first thing generally to be done is to present Jesus as willing to meet the realized desperateness of the sinner's case, as every true penitent thinks himself the chief of sinners,[1] and his own a peculiarly bad case. We should try to show him that the question of salvation does not hinge on the greatness or smallness of a sinner's guilt, but on the fact of his accepting Jesus as a sufficient atonement for it. We should try to show him how almost all the instances of conversion recorded in the Bible were great sinners, and how Jesus came to seek that which was absolutely lost.[2]

> Lord, I pray for anyone who today thinks themselves too bad to be forgiven.
> Have mercy and show them the depths of your forgiveness. Amen.

---

1   1 Timothy 1:15.
2   From *Practical Religion*.

Let love be your highest goal!
(1 Corinthians 14:1 *NLT*)

Love is the very spirit and essence of the Law.

The Law is to me the highest expression of what I ought to be, in my relations to my Creator and in my relations to my fellow-creatures.

Now, can what ought to be ever be abrogated? Does it stand to sense? Can the rightness of things ever be altered? Can God ever make two and two five, and can God make evil good and good evil?

He can make an evil person good, by saving him from the evil and making him good; but God cannot make evil itself good, and good evil, and he never professes to do it.

Oh, this confounding of things! How it does ruin and befog poor souls; how can it ever be less the duty of the creature to love and serve the Creator, than it was when he first came pure and spotless from his hand? How can it ever be less my duty to love my neighbour as myself, than it was at the beginning, or how can I satisfy my conscience with less than loving all men with a pure, benevolent love such as God bears to them, in my measure and according to my capacity? The same standard remains, and the difference between God's scheme of salvation and the scheme of salvation so widely preached now, is that man's scheme proposes to get me into Heaven without fulfilling this Law, while God's scheme proposes to give me power to fulfil it. Alas! I am afraid many will not find out which is the right one, man's or God's, till they get to the judgment seat and find it out too late![1]

> Lord of love, may your law of love fill my heart, that by your grace
> I may love the unlovable and maybe lead some to Christ. Amen.

1 From *Aggressive Christianity*.

THE GENERAL OF THE KING'S ARMY
(1 Chronicles 27:34 *KJV*)

We are so confident of the divine leading in the past, that we feel able to abandon the future guidance of the Army to it also. They say, "Well, but what about this one-man government?" I reply that no other is possible with an Army; and it seems to me that we are just as safe with one man at the helm as with twenty, and far more likely to get the ship into port. Nearly all the folly that has been talked on this point is exploded by one *consideration*, namely, that this General assumes no jurisdiction over the conscience, whatever people may say to the contrary.

Nobody is bound either to join the Army or to stay in after they have joined, nobody is unchristianized or anathematized merely for leaving it. Many who have left it are now happily working for God in other spheres, procured or rendered possible to them by our recommendation…

We consider that the moral tone of any organization is the only real guarantee for purity of government; and while the spirit of the Army remains what it is, it would not be possible for an untrue or double-minded man to retain the position of General for forty-eight hours!

People little know the tremendous moral strain involved in such a work. An untrue man would sooner be in Hell than be the General of The Salvation Army. Then add to this, that there is not, and never can be, any pecuniary temptation to such a man and, for a long time to come at any rate, plenty of public abuse, and you will see how senseless are many of the fears expressed.[1, 2]

Lord, today I pray for the General of The Salvation Army. Amen.

---

1   The Salvation Army was facing regular public ridicule for its methodology. General William Booth in particular was frequently lampooned and mocked. He was publicly accused of ulterior motives.
2   From *The Salvation Army in Relation to the Church and State.*

DAVID HAD SERVED GOD'S PURPOSE IN HIS OWN GENERATION
(Acts 13:36 *NIV*)

Supposing the moral tone, that is the *spirit*, of the movement [The Salvation Army] should degenerate, and it should become worldly and lifeless? I reply, it is so constituted, and so *depends* upon its spirit, having little intellect and no learning to depend upon, that it would simply go out, and need no governing at all! And the sooner the better, when it has *ceased* to live. We don't want to create a form capable of holding together when the spirit has departed; we would rather it were buried, as all corpses should be. We only want it to serve God's purpose, and so, you see, we shall be satisfied either way. We honestly tried committees and conferences, and they failed; and we know perfectly well that if we were to admit, say, half a dozen men into our cabinet today, there would be an end of our aggressiveness tomorrow. You see, God has trained us by a very peculiar discipline for this work; he had delivered us to a great extent from the trammels of conventionalism, and used us to make this movement out of the untaught masses. Where could we find a leader so well adapted as the man who has, under God, made it? Let us go on serving our generation, leaving God to look after the next. At any rate, the present generation, so far as the masses are concerned, are not much benefited by the legislation of the churches of bygone generations; and you know there are many very good men who contend that some of our most carefully constructed forms are only a burden and hindrance to true and live men. We do not intend to allow this movement to settle down into a sect, if prayer and faith or prudence and foresight can prevent it. We desire that it should continue an ever-aggressive force, going to the regions beyond while there are any sinners left unsaved. And if we might choose its future or, rather, *the* future which we would like it to bring in, it should be one of universal peace and goodwill to men, and all the praise, honour, and thanksgiving unto God![1]

> Lord of time, may your Church serve each passing generation in ways
> that are creatively relevant. Save us from an irrelevant Church! Amen.

---

1   From *The Salvation Army in Relation to the Church and State.*

JESUS SAID TO HER, "YOUR SINS ARE FORGIVEN"
(Luke 7:48 *NIV*)

When we have succeeded in leading the soul to apprehend the sufficiency of the atonement to cover, and the willingness of Jesus to pardon the past, unbelief will generally fasten on the future, and the enquirer will say, "Ah! but if I were forgiven, I should fall again into sin." Now is the time to bring the soul face to face with a personal, living Saviour. We must present Christ's ability to save to the uttermost – of the soul's need and circumstances – all them who come unto God by him. We must get the soul's eye fixed on Jesus, not only as a sacrifice but as a Saviour, a Deliverer, an Almighty Friend, who has promised to dwell and abide with the believer, delivering him out of the hands of all his enemies. We should not give up till, by the help of the Spirit, we can lead the soul to expect in Jesus the supply of all its needs. When this is accomplished, we should lead the soul on to claim this Saviour now. When arrived at this point, I have sometimes found it very helpful to ask, "Well, now, when did Jesus pardon and receive the penitents who came to him in the days of his flesh?" Waiting for an answer, thus compelling the mind's attention to the point, the enquirer will generally say, "I suppose when they came to him." I reply, "Of course that was the only time to receive them – when they came, not an hour before or an hour after, but at the moment they came, and it is the same now. He receives returning sinners when they come. Now, you come, confessing and forsaking all your sins, and willing to follow him wherever he may lead you. Does he receive you? He said he would in no wise cast you out if you came.[1] Does he cast you out?" The penitent will generally say, "No, I trust not." Then what does he? He must either take you in or cast you out just now, because you come just now. Which is it?[2]

Thank you, Lord Jesus, for instant forgiveness and
lasting support; forgiven, saved and kept, by your grace. Amen.

---

1   See John 6:37, KJV.
2   From *Practical Religion*.

IT IS BY GRACE YOU HAVE BEEN SAVED, THROUGH FAITH

(Ephesians 2:8 *NIV*)

In some cases it requires no little sympathy, tact, and firmness to meet the wiles of unbelief and the stratagems of Satan even in dealing with very sincere and truly submissive souls.[1] Fear of being deceived is generally one of the greatest difficulties. In such cases it is well to explain to the penitent that there is no ground for this fear, seeing that this way of salvation is of God's own appointing, and that, although it seems an easy way to be saved, after living so long in sin and rebellion – the ease of it is all on the sinner's side, and not on the side of the Saviour – we should explain at what a terrible cost of sacrifice and suffering to the Son of God this simple, easy way was opened, and how ungrateful it is to put it away, as if it were too good to be true, because God has made it so simple. It is well to encourage the enquirer to trust by reminding him that every truly saved soul on earth, and every redeemed spirit in Heaven, was saved in this way – by simple faith alone. It is often very helpful to get the penitent to use the language of faith with his lips, even before his heart can fully go with it. I have seen many a one rise into faith, while repeating after me the text, rendered in the first person, "He was wounded for my transgressions,"[2] &c.; or, "Thou hast said, him that cometh to thee thou wilt in no wise cast out. Lord, I come; thou dost not cast me out";[3] "Thou takest me in" or, "'Tis done – the great transaction done; I am my Lord's, and he is mine";[4] or, "I can believe – I do believe – that Jesus saves me now,"[5] repeating such passages or stanzas over and over again till the heart follows the tongue and the venture is made.[6]

Father, I pray for those who offer counsel to those seeking faith; may their
words be wise and strong, imparting truth. Bless those sacred moments. Amen.

1   The Salvation Army invites people to kneel at the mercy seat, there to receive spiritual counsel and
    prayer.
2   See Isaiah 53:5, KJV.
3   See John 6:37, KJV.
4   From Philip Doddridge's (1702–51) hymn, "O Happy Day".
5   From the hymn "We're Kneeling at the Mercy Seat", by "E.O.E." Published 1921.
6   From *Practical Religion*.

I TRY TO FIND COMMON GROUND WITH EVERYONE,
DOING EVERYTHING I CAN TO SAVE SOME

(1 Corinthians 9:22 *NLT*)

Does it signify by what novel and extraordinary methods we get hold of the drunkards, wife-beaters, cut-throats, burglars, and murderers, so that we *do* get them?... Vast masses of the people living in positive heathenism and crime, unreached and uninfluenced by any civilizing and saving agencies; is it not wiser to go down to them by such means as they can appreciate, than to let them seethe and rot in their degradation? We believe, nay, we *know*, that a real living gospel is still the power of God to the salvation of such people, for time and eternity. The Salvation Army has thousands of people in its ranks who have been picked up from the lowest depths of social and moral degradation, now good fathers and mothers, good husbands and wives, and good citizens.

Having positive demonstrations of such results, why should we be accused of ambition or fanaticism because we are burning with anxiety to press the gospel on the attention of all men? *Why should it be kept in the background?* If indeed it *can* reclaim and regenerate mankind, and if it *does* restore peace and goodwill amongst men, why should we not use every available means to thrust it on them? Why should we not try to inspire every saved one, high or low, with an *all*-inspiring passion to preach it to every creature? Why should we not cry aloud in the "highways and hedges",[1] to the sin-stricken, fallen, and evil-possessed multitudes, "Come unto me, all ye that labour and are heavy laden, and I will give you rest"?[2] Why should we not secure every building possible to us where the people can be got to listen, and where they can be dealt with more closely about their souls?[3, 4]

Thank you, Lord, for those whose heart is for the lost; for those
who exemplify "church without walls". Bless their creativity and courage. Amen.

---

1   Luke 14:23, KJV.
2   Matthew 11:28, KJV.
3   The Salvation Army rented or bought music halls and theatres in which to hold gospel meetings, realizing the people they were anxious to reach would probably never venture into churches or chapels.
4   From *The Salvation Army in Relation to the Church and State*.

SUFFERING PRODUCES PERSEVERANCE; PERSEVERANCE, CHARACTER; AND CHARACTER, HOPE

(Romans 5:3–4 *NIV*)

Trial also reveals us to ourselves.

Although we do not agree with the adage that untried grace is no grace at all, yet unquestionably much fancied grace has proved itself, in the hour of trial, to be but as the early cloud and the morning dew. Many who have received the word with joy and for a while have believed, in time of temptation have fallen away.

Many professing Christians, if they could have had predicted to them the effect of adversity upon the heart and life, would have said with Hazael, "Is thy servant a dog, that he should do this…?"[1] Yet, when the true test of character was applied, he fell. When he had eaten and was full then his heart rebelled, or when he was chastened by the Lord he became weary and said, "Verily I have cleansed my heart in vain, and washed my hands in innocency."[2]

For the Christian, there is no surer test of the state of his heart than the way in which he receives affliction. Often, when all has appeared prosperous and peaceful, and the child of God has been congratulating himself on spiritual growth and increased power over inward corruption, some fiery trial has overtaken him which, instead of being met with perfect submission and cheerful acquiescence, has produced sudden confusion, dismay, and perhaps rebellion, revealing to him that his heart was far from that state of divine conformity which he had hoped and supposed.[3]

Lord, for those facing trial today, of whatever kind, I pray your comfort.
Strengthen the weak and support the struggling. Amen.

---

1 2 Kings 8:13, KJV.
2 Psalm 73:13, KJV.
3 From *The Highway of our God*.

OCTOBER 5TH

LET YOUR LIGHT SHINE BEFORE OTHERS, THAT THEY MAY SEE YOUR
GOOD DEEDS AND GLORIFY YOUR FATHER IN HEAVEN

(Matthew 5:16 *NIV*)

Benevolence has come somewhat into fashion of late. It has become the correct thing to do the slums, since the Prince of Wales did them;[1] and this general idea of caring in some way or degree for the poor and wretched has extended itself even into the region of creeds, so that we have now many schemes for the salvation of mankind without a real Saviour.

Do not misunderstand me. I have no objection – nay, I rejoice in any real good being done for anybody, much more for the poor and suffering – I have no objection that a large society of intelligent Christians should take up so noble an object as that of caring for stray dogs, providing it does not interfere with caring for stray babies! I desire not to find fault with what is good, but to point out the evil which, to my mind, so largely diminishes the satisfaction one would otherwise feel in much benevolent effort being put forth around us... The most precious stone given instead of bread[2] is useless to a starving man. Surely nobody ever cared for poor suffering humanity so much as Jesus Christ. He gladly put forth his mighty power for the healing and feeding of the body, and he laid it down most distinctly that all who were true to him must love the poor and give up their all for them in the same practical way in which he did; but all this real brotherhood did not prevent his keeping the great truths of salvation ever to the front.[3]

> Lord, what a great temptation it is for your Church merely to dispense
> food and clothing to those in need, without also sharing the gospel. Amen.

---

1 The Prince of Wales (Edward VII) visited slums in the East End of London, inspecting conditions in Hoxton and Shoreditch. He did so incognito, with a friend, much to the displeasure of the Royal Family, who only heard about his visits much later. This led to some public controversy and speculation about the Prince's supposed socialist views.
2 See Matthew 7:9.
3 From *Popular Christianity*.

WERE NOT OUR HEARTS BURNING WITHIN US...?
(Luke 24:32 NIV)

Why does God like people to be hot in his service? For the same reasons that we like people to be hot in ours. We have no confidence in half-and-half, fast-and-loose friends; milk-warm adherents who in times of danger wait to see which way the wind blows before they commit themselves to our views or interests – servants who will serve us, while at the same time they can serve themselves, but the moment our interests and theirs appear to clash will leave us to our fate.

We like thorough, wholehearted, all-length friends and servants, and to such only do we confide our secrets, or trust our important enterprises. We may use the half-hearted as far as they serve our purpose, but we have no confidence in them – no heart-fellowship with them, no joy over them: we would rather they were hot or cold out-and-out friends or foes.

Read in your own heart and mind, in this respect, a transcript of his, and see the reason why he says, "I would thou wert cold or hot."[1] I want you to note... characteristics of hot saints so that you may know whether you belong to the number. To be hot implies the possession of... Light – hot saints have such a halo round about them that they reveal – make manifest – sins in others. They do this, by contrast. "What fellowship... hath light with darkness?"[2] The light of God flashed from a hot saint on the dark consciences of sinners makes them feel their sin, misery, and danger, and if they will receive it, leads to their conversion. It "opens their eyes", and if they will follow it, leads them to Jesus.[3]

Lord, my prayers today are with those whose fire burns dim. Encourage them,
I pray; turn their spark to a flame and help them to overcome any obstacles.
Amen.

---

1   Revelation 3:15, KJV.
2   See 2 Corinthians 6:14, KJV.
3   From *Practical Religion*.

THE SPIRITUAL DID NOT COME FIRST, BUT THE NATURAL, AND AFTER THAT THE SPIRITUAL

(1 Corinthians 15:46 *NIV*)

[The Apostle] Paul says: "Knowing therefore the terror of the Lord, we persuade men".[1] Oh! what a beautiful insight this gives us into his ministry. Why do you persuade men, Paul? "Because I know the terror of the Lord that is coming on, and because we thus judge that, if One died for all, then were all dead. Therefore, I persuade men." He did not give up when he had put it before them. He carried them on his heart, and he says, "That by the space of three years I ceased not to warn every one night and day with tears."[2] He wept it in, as well as drove it in with his logic, and his eloquence, and with the power of the Holy Ghost in him. Make it go in – make your words felt; don't talk to them in the sickly, languid way that makes no impression – make them know it.

If you have not enough of the Holy Ghost for this, go to your closet till you have, and then come and drive the word home to their conscience as a two-edged sword,[3] dividing asunder soul and spirit... You have not only to get it home but, in order to do this, give it them simply and naturally. If I were asked to put into one word what I consider to be the greatest obstacle to the success of divine truth, even when uttered by sincere and real people, I should say, stiffness. It seems as if people, the moment they come to religion, assume a different tone, a different look, and manner – in short, become unnatural. People sometimes come to me, and say, "Oh! I would give the world to be natural, but I have got into this way of talking to people. It seems as though I cannot be natural. Can you help me?" I say, "Yes, I can help you, by this advice. Determine, by the help of God, that you will break the neck of this bondage."[4]

Holy Spirit, so live in me that the language of the Kingdom becomes my natural tongue, flowing with the rhythms of grace in an easy manner. Amen.

1   See 2 Corinthians 5:11–21, KJV.
2   Acts 20:31, KJV.
3   See Hebrews 4:12.
4   From *Godliness*.

WE ARE MORE THAN CONQUERORS
(Romans 8:37 *NIV*)

When the General asked me if I could manage to send you a few lines in connection with the week of Self-Denial[1]... it occurred to me that if the Lord were to ask me to deny myself of almost all I possess, how easy it would be in comparison with what he requires from me just now. For I am now realizing, as never before, how much harder it is to suffer than to serve. Nevertheless, my soul bows in submission to my Heavenly Father, and my heart says, "Not my will, but thine, be done."[2]

I need not say how happy I should have been to have taken part with you in the public demonstrations and private sacrifices... but as I am all but confined to my room by suffering I can only again assure you by letter that my heart is with you as much as ever, and how strongly I feel that were it the Lord's good pleasure to restore me to health, I would gladly spend every moment added to my life in helping you to extend the Kingdom of God, and to save the souls of men...

Above all else, keep your own hearts right with God. Be real Salvationists in motive, in purpose, and in action; and, while you have health and strength, push the war with all your might. Heed not the temptations which will come to you from the world, the flesh, and the Devil, which will urge you to follow after your own ease and comfort, and to live more or less to please yourselves. Regard not opposition, persecution, or misrepresentations. Fear not what man can do to you. Through tribulations and afflictions, and difficulties and deaths, you shall be brought off more than conquerors... I shall meet you in the Heavenly City, where pain and parting shall be no more.[3, 4]

Two things, Lord: I pray to be useful while I am kept alive, and I pray to
face death with faith; a productive life, and a peaceful end, please. Amen.

1   A period within the Salvation Army calendar (not necessarily a week), when special focus is given to raising funds for social work and/or missionary work. It is expected that Salvationists give of their time to help with collecting, and give of their money by way of a separate donation.
2   Luke 22:42, KJV.
3   One of Catherine Booth's last letters to Salvationists, as she lay close to death.
4   From *Catherine Booth The Mother of The Salvation Army, Vol. II.*

October 9th

AS FOR THOSE WHO PERSIST IN SIN, REBUKE THEM
(1 Timothy 5:20 *ESV*)

Hot saints will "rebuke their neighbour, and not suffer sin upon him".[1] They are full of zeal for the glory of God, and jealousy for his honour; it breaks their hearts because men keep not his law. They know that they have the light of life, and they feel that they must hold it up over the wrongdoing, deception, and hypocrisy of their fellow men in order to "open their eyes, and to turn them from darkness to light".[2]

You never hear them apologizing for sin, or calling it by smooth names; they feel towards sin, in their measure, as God feels towards it. It is the abominable thing which they hate, and therefore they cannot in any case allow it, pander to it, or excuse it. Most saints will mercilessly turn the blazing lamp of God's truth on the conscience of a sinner with reproof as pungent, pointed, and personal, as Nathan gave to David,[3] Jehu to Jehoshaphat,[4] or Jesus to the Jews...

Heat cleanses, purges away dross, destroys noxious vapours. So the burning fire of the Holy Ghost purifies the soul which is filled, permeated with it; hence, hot saints are pure. They purify themselves, as he is pure. Their garments are white, they keep themselves "unspotted from the world".[5] They improve the moral atmosphere wherever they go. Their very presence reproves and holds in check the unfruitful works of darkness, and sinners' feet, as Peter felt when he said, "Depart from me; for I am a sinful man, O Lord."[6, 7]

> Father, in all my dealings, give me grace and mercy. Let me be a gentle example, aware of my own frailty and my ongoing need of you. Amen.

---

1   See Leviticus 19:17, KJV.
2   Acts 26:18.
3   2 Samuel 12.
4   2 Chronicles 19.
5   James 1:27, KJV.
6   Luke 5:8, KJV.
7   From *Practical Religion*.

THE SEVENTY-TWO RETURNED WITH JOY, SAYING,
"LORD, EVEN THE DEMONS ARE SUBJECT TO US IN YOUR NAME!"

(Luke 10:17 *ESV*)

Hot saints are mighty. The Spirit is not given by measure unto them. They may not be very intellectual or learned, but their heat makes more impression on the hearts of sinners, and stirs more opposition from Hell than all the intellect and learning of a whole generation of lukewarm professors. The fishermen of Galilee produced more impression on the world in a few years than all the learning of the Jews had done in centuries, because they were hot in the love and service of God.

Hot saints are more than a match for their enemies. Satan himself is afraid of them. "Paul I know,"[1] said he; yea, and he knows and fears all such. Wicked men cannot stand before them; the power of their testimony cuts them to the heart, and makes them either cry out, "What must we do to be saved?"[2] or, "Away with him! away with him."[3] Hot people are not only able to work, but to suffer. They can endure hardness, suffer reproach, contend with principalities and powers, fight with wild beasts, hail persecution and death! To be hot ensures opposition… from Pharisees. They look with contempt on hot people, call them fanatics, extreme people, troublers of Israel, disturbers of the peace of the Church, occasions of reproach to the respectable and reasonable part of the Church. The Pharisees were the bitterest enemies of him who said, "The zeal of thine house hath eaten me up."[4] And they are still the bitterest enemies of those who are filled with his Spirit. It matters not that they have now a Christian creed instead of a Jewish; the spirit is the same, and will not tolerate "God… manifest in the flesh".[5, 6]

My prayers today are with church leaders who face opposition from within their own congregations as they try to move things forward. I pray too for those who would oppose; those who prefer cold to warmth. Amen.

---

1   Acts 19:15, KJV.
2   See Acts 16:30, KJV.
3   See John 19:15, KJV.
4   Psalm 69:9, KJV.
5   1 Timothy 3:16, KJV.
6   From *Practical Religion*.

A CURSE ON ANYONE WHO IS LAX IN DOING THE LORD'S WORK!
(Jeremiah 48:10 *NIV*)

It is commonly said that if you get hold of the affections of a man or a woman, you get hold of him or her. So you do. This is the touchstone, and there is nothing in which I have been so grieved and disappointed as in the manifest want of quickness, livingness in the affections of God's people for him. Oh! how I have seen this come out. The coldness, the unsympathetic character of a great many people's religion, and yet people whom one would not like to unchristianize.

I cannot explain it by any better term than want of quickness. I have often been struck with the difference when you touch individuals on some point that affects them personally, and on those which relate to the Kingdom of God, and have been tempted to say with the Apostle, "All men seek their own, and not the things that are Jesus Christ's."[1] Alas! I fear it is very largely so. You talk with a lady about the salvation of her children's souls, the souls of her neighbours, and her servants, or about the cause of God in general, and she will talk "good" with you, so to speak, and you will feel, "Yes, it is all very well," but it doesn't seem to come up from the depths. It seems to come from the throat, so to speak; a sort of superficial, surface kind of thing. But, if a child is dangerously ill, how quick the mother's sympathies, how ready to listen, how willing to do anything that you suggest to help the child. If the business is in danger, if a man has got into difficulties and you can suggest any plan by which he may get out of them, how quickly his attention is aroused. His interest doesn't flag, because the subject touches him to the quick. It is his concern, and just so in many other things. God forbid I should judge all Christians. No, no, no! – there are blessed exceptions.[2]

So many things compete for my enthusiasm, Lord!
Hobbies and interests stake their claim. Give me a heart that enthuses
about my faith, I pray. Make me a "blessed exception"! Amen.

---

1   See Philippians 2:21, KJV.
2   From *Aggressive Christianity*.

WHEREVER YOUR TREASURE IS,
THERE THE DESIRES OF YOUR HEART WILL ALSO BE

(Matthew 6:21 *NLT*)

I shall never forget reading, when only fourteen years of age, a sentiment of a precious and valiant soldier of the Lord Jesus, who is now in glory. Speaking of putting a test, he said that people might easily find out whether they loved God or themselves best: Suppose you were in business in a little village, and were doing pretty well, and everything was going smoothly with you; but there was nothing for you to do there for the Kingdom of God, no particular way in which you could serve or glorify God; and, suppose there was another little village hard by, where there was nothing whatever doing for the Kingdom, and you felt it laid upon your soul to go there in order that you might preach to unconverted people and raise a church, and do something for souls. Ah! but you have got a nice business and you don't know whether you would prosper or not in the other village. Now you may know whether you are serving God or yourself first, by this test.

If you are seeking God, you will be ready to go to that strange village and trust him with the consequences; but, if you are serving yourself, you will stop where you are.

The Lord has helped me to apply that many a time to many things besides business, and to keep the Kingdom of God as I made up my mind it should be first always – not in time merely, but in degree – all the way through. If I love him best, I shall feel for him deepest, and shall act for him first.[1]

Thank you for this fascinating little test, Lord! Help those who are
faced with any such decisions today; where to live, and what to do regarding
their livelihood and family responsibilities. Guide them by your gracious
Spirit towards making the right decisions. Give them peace. Amen.

1   From *Aggressive Christianity*.

JESUS SAID, "TRULY I SAY TO YOU, THERE IS NO ONE WHO HAS LEFT
HOUSE OR BROTHERS OR SISTERS OR MOTHER OR FATHER OR CHILDREN
OR FARMS, FOR MY SAKE AND FOR THE GOSPEL'S SAKE, BUT THAT HE WILL
RECEIVE A HUNDRED TIMES AS MUCH NOW IN THE PRESENT AGE, HOUSES
AND BROTHERS AND SISTERS AND MOTHERS AND CHILDREN AND FARMS,
ALONG WITH PERSECUTIONS; AND IN THE AGE TO COME, ETERNAL LIFE

(Mark 10:29–30 *NASB*)

If I love him [God] best, I shall feel for him more deeply than for my husband or children, near and precious as they are and dearer than my own life a thousand times; but he will be dearer still and his interests; and if, as Jesus Christ says, his interests require me to sacrifice these precious and beloved ones of my soul, then I shall sacrifice them; for the philosophical reason that I love him better than I love them and, therefore, I shall lay them on his altar, to promote his glory. If I understand it, this is the fruit of the Spirit in the affections – God first. I am afraid, in a great many instances, it is husband first, wife first, children first and, I am afraid, in some cases, business first, and then God may take what there is left and be thankful for that! Now, if you are in this condition you need not expect joy, peace, power. You will never get it if you do. God will have to make you over again before you can get it, and to alter the conditions of his salvation. Oh! but if you will lay it all on his altar, that is quite another thing. As I said to a lady, a little time ago, "The Lord can take your husband, if you refuse to give him to him"; and I am afraid God's people often compel him to take their darlings, because they make them idols; whereas, if they had laid them on his altar, they might have had them back, as Abraham received back Isaac.[1] I said to a gentleman, "Mind that God does not burn down your barns, wreck your ships, and take away your riches. God loves your soul enough to do it, if you let these things prevent that wholehearted consecration which he requires." We are in his hands.[2]

> Lord, this seems a harsh word. Help me to gladly and willingly lay my all on
> your altar; not out of fear of retribution if I don't, but because I trust you.
> Amen.

---

1 Genesis 22:1–19.
2 From *Aggressive Christianity*.

OCTOBER 14ᵀᴴ

A SPIRIT OF FIRE

(Isaiah 4:4 *NIV*)

Friends, settle this as a truth, that you will never make any other soul realize the verities of eternal things any further than you realize them yourself. You will beget in the soul of your hearer exactly the degree of realization which the Spirit of God gives to you, and no more; therefore, if you are in a dreamy, cozy, half-asleep condition, you will only beget the same kind of realization in the souls who hear you. You must be wide awake, quick, alive, feeling deeply in sympathy with the truth you utter, or it will produce no result. Here is the reason why we have such a host of stillborn, sinewless, rickety, powerless spiritual children. They are born of half-dead parents, a sort of sentimental religion, which does not take hold of the soul, which has no depth of earth, no grasp, no power in it, and the result is a sickly crop of sentimental converts. Oh! the Lord give us a real, robust, living, hardy Christianity, full of zeal and faith, which shall bring into the Kingdom of God lively, well-developed children, full of life and energy, instead of these poor, sentimental ghosts that are hopping around us.

Oh! friends, we want this vivid realization ourselves. If we have it we shall beget it in others. Oh! get hold of God. Ask him to baptize you with his Spirit until "the zeal of his house eats you up".[1] This Spirit will burn his way through all obstacles of flesh and blood, of forms, proprieties, and respectabilities of death and rottenness of all descriptions! He will burn his way through.[2]

Brightly burning fire divine, satisfy my soul. Amen.

1   See Psalm 69:9; John 2:17, KJV.
2   From *Aggressive Christianity*.

SET THE EMPTY POT ON THE COALS TILL IT BECOMES HOT
(Ezekiel 24:11 *NIV*)

Oh! what a laughing stock to Hell is a light, frivolous, easy, lukewarm professor. Oh! what a shame and puzzle to the angels in Heaven, and what a supreme disgust to God. "I would thou wert cold or hot. So then because thou art lukewarm, and neither cold nor hot, I will spue thee out of my mouth."[1]

Oh! what will that be? Talk about shame! Think of that! Shame! Some of you feel it going into the streets for God. You feel it when a few people see you kneel down… [to pray]! Think of being spewed out of the mouth of God before an assembled universe. What will that be? God helping me, I will avoid that. I will sooner hang with Jesus on the cross, between two thieves,[2] than I will bear that shame…

Some of you say, in your letters, that you will have this wholeheartedness. You say that you have given up all, and that you are consecrating yourself to a life of labour. Now, be hot. I know you will burn the fingers of the Pharisees. Never mind that. I know you will fire their consciences like Samson's foxes did the corn.[3] Never mind that. Be hot. God likes hot saints. Be determined that you will be hot. They will call you a fool: they did Paul. They will call you a fanatic, and say, "This fellow is a troubler of Israel";[4] but you must reply, "It is not I, but ye and your father's house, in that ye have forsaken the commandments of the LORD."[5] Turn the charge upon them. Hot people are never a trouble to hot people. The hotter we are the nearer we get, and the more we love one another. It is the cold people that are troubled by the hot ones. The Lord help you to be hot.[6]

Lord, may the warmth of my heart be as attractive to others as a burning fire is to a cold person; offering warmth, light and protection. Amen.

---

1 Revelation 3:16, KJV.
2 Matthew 27:38.
3 Judges 15:4–5.
4 See 1 Kings 18:17.
5 See 1 Kings 18:18, KJV.
6 From *Godliness*.

FEAR OF MAN WILL PROVE TO BE A SNARE,
BUT WHOEVER TRUSTS IN THE LORD IS KEPT SAFE

(Proverbs 29:25 *NIV*)

There must be no holding back. "Cursed be he that holdeth back his sword from blood."[1]

That curse is resting on Christendom today. Oh! they will thrust the sword a little way in, but they will not go into the core. They dare not draw blood – the soldiers of this age – for their lives. They dare not touch a man to the quick, because, alas! they are looking to themselves, and thinking of what people will say of them, instead of thinking of what God will say of them. You must not be afraid of blood if you are to be a true warrior of Jesus Christ.

You must not be afraid to say, if need be, "O generation of vipers, who hath warned you to flee from the wrath to come?"[2] You must not be afraid to say, if need be, "You have made my Father's house a den of thieves",[3] if you save some of them by doing it. Oh! this accursed sycophancy; I was going to say, this accursed fear to brave the censure of the world – this accursed making good evil and evil good, as if God were altogether such an one as ourselves. Don't you think he sees through the vile sham? Oh! my friends, if we don't mend in this respect, he will come in judgment before long, and we shall find out then the difference between the precious and the vile, if we do not find out before. If you want to be a successful worker, you must make up your minds to begin with that you will be crucified.[4]

> Lord, my thoughts and prayers turn towards Christians who live
> in daily fear of the sword or the gun; for whom witnessing might mean
> punishment or execution. Embolden them, I pray. By the same token,
> give me the courage to make the most of the freedoms I enjoy. Amen.

---

1   Jeremiah 48:10, KJV.
2   Matthew 3:7, KJV.
3   See Matthew 21:13, KJV.
4   From *Godliness*.

WHATEVER WERE GAINS TO ME I NOW CONSIDER
LOSS FOR THE SAKE OF CHRIST

(Philippians 3:7 *NIV*)

A gentleman said to me at the railway station the other day, "You were right in what you said last night." I asked in what respect. He answered, "In saying that the Lord has to inflict the heaviest chastisement in order to bring sinners to himself. I know it," he said, "it has been so in my case." I asked, "Has it answered the purpose?" "No," said he, shaking his head. "Then," I said, "look out; you are not bad enough yet. God will strip you of every blessing and every comfort you possess, rather than let you go to Hell in this state." "Oh," said he. "I have not much left; the Lord took away from me three years ago a loving, precious wife, the idol of my soul; then a little while ago I lost £30,000, and I have had other troubles since. In fact, he has been knocking me about in my circumstances for years." I said, "Yes, because he loves you too well to let you go to Hell without trying to save you. And if you will not let him do it without stripping you naked as the prodigal, you must expect this chastisement, till, like him, you are willing to leave the far country and return to your Father." But, I repeat, happy the sinner whose sorrows and sufferings lead to repentance! The first step in the right direction was reflection; this young man began to think! At length he lost sight of everything but his own destitution and the plenty of his father's home; then he said to himself, "How many hired servants of my father's have bread enough and to spare, and I perish with hunger!" What bitter reflections must have filled his mind! Can you not imagine that you see him sitting on a stone, amid the husks and filth of the swine-yard, ruminating on his past life, thinking of his folly and wickedness, and wondering whether, if he were to go back, his father would receive him?[1] Happily these reflections led him to resolution.[2]

Transforming God, you love us too much to leave us as we are.

---

1   Luke 15, KJV.
2   From *Life and Death*.

HE SET FREE ALL WHO HAVE LIVED THEIR LIVES
AS SLAVES TO THE FEAR OF DYING

(Hebrews 2:15 *NLT*)

Go ask that poor emaciated prodigal, dying of the rottenness implanted in his bones by a career of intemperance and vice, ask him what constitutes his severest suffering, his direct misery? He will not tell you of the prostration, the fever, and anguish of his body, but of the remorse, the agony, and apprehension of his soul. He cries, "Oh, never mind my body; it is my soul, my poor soul!" If anybody here has ever stood by the side of such a bed, have you not read in the more than mortal agony of such a face the words, "Be not deceived; God is not mocked?"[1] There are some cases in which it seems as though God lifted the curtain of mortality before the soul passed out of time, so that those around may see as far as possible the future heritage of woe consequent on a life of sin. Alas! We in The Salvation Army get many awful illustrations of this... One of our officers was fetched late one night to visit a young man said to be dying. In relating the story he says: "I shall never forget the scene; I could not get it out of my mind for many days and nights. When I entered the attic, I found the relic of a fine young fellow of about twenty-eight or thirty years of age, with beautiful black eyes almost standing out of his head, his hands clenched in agony, and he crying out in awful tones, 'Curse them! curse them! Where are they? They have helped me to this, and now they have left me to die alone!'" He referred to his evil companions. Our officer drew near, and tried to calm and comfort him by inspiring hope of mercy and pardon, but he could produce no effect; the young man's rage and vengeance at the realization of his desperate state, and of the villainy of those who had lured him on to it, could not be restrained, but continued to vent itself in wild denunciations and curses, until the one friend he had with him was obliged to retire and leave him to die with our officer only in the room.[2]

Gracious Holy Spirit, rush to be alongside those who are afraid of death.
As they linger on the brink of eternity, show them the Saviour. Equip those who
minister to the dying with words of salvation, even at the eleventh hour. Amen.

1   Galatians 6:7, KJV.
2   From *Life and Death*.

Teach me good judgment

(Psalm 119:66 *NLT*)

"Judge not, that ye be not judged"[1] is one of the favourite texts of popular Christianity, which is interpreted to mean that we are on no account to form an opinion of the rightness or wrongness of anybody's conduct.

Under the specious guise of charity, faith, and unbelief, obedience to God and disobedience, sin, and holiness, are to be confounded in one indiscriminate hodgepodge, and their actors and abettors treated exactly alike, making no separation between the precious and the vile.

This spurious charity is pushed to such an extent that even the man who has pledged himself to preach certain doctrines, and who is actually employed as the agent of a Church for so doing, is not to be condemned if his "riper judgment" should lead him to renounce those doctrines; while at the same time he holds fast the salary and position with which he was entrusted in view of his original engagement. On the same principle we are asked to allow that people who never go to a place of worship or bow their knees in prayer may be as good and faithful servants of God as any others. We are told that perhaps they are carrying out "the divine will in a spirit of true devotion to duty", that working is praying, and that a man's belief bounds his responsibility, and so forth. "We are all aiming at the same thing" is a favourite way of expressing this popular Christianity, which just suits the ideas of drunkards, adulterers, and liars, as well as of shallow professors. To declare positively that people are sinners, condemned already, and on their way to Hell, is accounted as "uncharitable judging", "really dreadful", and no one, we are told, can possibly be justified in coming to such a conclusion.[2]

Lord, you alone can judge a person's heart. Nevertheless, help me not
to abdicate my responsibilities. May I do so lovingly and humbly. Amen.

1   Matthew 7:1, KJV.
2   From *Popular Christianity*.

Remember the Sabbath day by keeping it holy
(Exodus 20:8 *NIV*)

"Desecrating the Sabbath" is another virtuous-sounding phrase, which is accepted as the expression of a very reverential religion… But what is desecrating the Sabbath? Well, it is not dressing up in fabulously costly clothes (sometimes unpaid for) as near in fabric, style, and fashion as can be to those worn in the very vilest services of sin. It is not to lie in bed consuming the early hours of the day, and then to flaunt in this array to one short service, as an exhibition of self and respectability, spending the remainder of the "sacred day" in an easy chair with the last new book. This is Sabbath-keeping, even though to carry it out comfortably, servants may have to work over an elaborate dinner, or the turning out of a luxuriant equipage. Then what is "desecrating"? Well, go and spend next Sunday evening in Mr Easy's mansion, and he will show you. You will not have an unpleasant time, that is, if your notions agree with his. He will give you a splendid meal, and then you will be allowed to lounge on one of his soft couches, while your host tells you spicy stories about the popular ministers of his denomination, or his daughter will play to you some "sacred" music on the piano or the harp. Fire and lamplight will gleam softly, and thick curtains shut out the night, about which someone will occasionally remark that it is "awful weather". Presently a harsh, discordant sound is heard, like shouting and singing with some brass instrumental music all mixed up; and if you looked out you would see a little handful of men and women, wet and mud-stained, nearly exhausted in the struggle with rain and storm, and the half-rough, half-good-natured crowd, who have been allured out of yonder alley, and are now going, swearing, pushing, rolling along, in a fashion of their own, to a little room, or a low music hall, where these tambourine players and the rest do congregate. Your host will jump up with an annoyed air, and exclaim with great emphasis, "Desecrating the Sabbath, that is what I call it!" and he will go on to expound his views until you understand that it is a Sabbath-breaking for those poor folks to have made a noise in the street, even though they were only… praising God with a loud voice, and confessing him before all men.[1]

> Lord, when I read the Bible, help me to sense the deeper meanings
> of what is written, not simply the literal word on the page. Amen.

---

1 From *Popular Christianity*.

AND THEY WHICH HEARD IT, BEING CONVICTED
BY THEIR OWN CONSCIENCE, WENT OUT ONE BY ONE

(John 8:9 *KJV*)

Perhaps there is no complaint more frequently on the lips of those who mourn over leanness of soul than this: "My faith is so weak: I want more faith"; and doubtless a weak faith is the secret of a great deal of the barrenness and misery of many Christians; but it never seems to occur to them to ask why their faith is weak; why they find themselves powerless to appropriate the promises of God.

"Yes," said a dying backslider to a man of God who was trying to comfort him by quoting the promises, "yes, I believe they are true, but somehow they won't stick!" The fault was in the state of his own heart. He could not appropriate the promises, because he knew that he was not the character to whom they were made.

Now it seems to me that a great deal of failure in faith is simply the result of a defiled conscience, and if those who find themselves weak and sickly in spiritual life would turn their attention to the condition of their consciences, they would soon discover the reason for all their failure. The fact is, we have a great deal of so-called Christianity in these days which dispenses with conscience altogether. We sometimes meet with persons who tell us that they are not under the law, but under grace, and therefore they are not condemned, do what they will. Now the question is, does the gospel contemplate such a state? Does it propose to depose or abjure conscience, or to purify and restore it to sovereign control?... Conscience is that faculty of the soul which pronounces on the character of our actions (Rom. ii. 15).[1]

Thank you, Lord, for this spiritual insight.
This is helpful. Help me to use it as a devotional tool. Amen.

---

1   From *Practical Religion*.

DAVID WAS CONSCIENCE-STRICKEN

(1 Samuel 24:5 *NIV*)

Conscience is an independent witness standing as it were between God and man; it is in man, but for God, and it cannot be bribed or silenced. Someone has called it "God's Spirit in man's soul". Another, "God's vicegerent in the soul of man"; and certainly it is the most wonderful part of man. All other of our faculties can be subdued by our will; but this cannot; it stands erect, taking sides against ourselves whenever we transgress its fiat: something in us bearing witness against us when we offend its integrity. Now, it is a question of vital importance to our spiritual life whether the gospel is intended to deliver us from this reigning power of conscience, and make us independent of its verdict; or whether it is intended to purify and enlighten conscience, and to endow us with power to live in obedience to its voice. Let us examine a few passages on this point. First, let us see what is done with conscience in regeneration. Heb. 9:14: "How much more shall the blood of Christ, who through the eternal Spirit offered himself without spot to God, purge your conscience from dead works to serve the living God?" [KJV] See also Heb. 10:22. Second, let us see the office which conscience sustains in regenerate men. 1 Tim. 1:19: "Holding faith, and a good conscience; which some having put away concerning faith have made shipwreck" [KJV]. Romans 9:1: "I say the truth in Christ, I lie not, my conscience also bearing me witness in the Holy Ghost" [KJV]. See 1 Tim. 3:9 and Acts 23:1. We have also set forth the consequences of allowing conscience to become defiled. 1 Tim. 4:2: "Speaking lies in hypocrisy; having their conscience seared with a hot iron" [KJV]. Also Titus 1:15. There are many other texts quite as much to the point, but these are abundantly sufficient to show that Paul had no idea of a wild, lawless faith, which ignored the tribunal of conscience.[1]

> This is good theology, Lord. I pray for those who teach the Scriptures;
> college principals, lecturers and Bible teachers.
> Bless their ministry of education as they equip your people. Amen.

1   From *Practical Religion*.

DECLARE... HIS MARVELLOUS DEEDS AMONG ALL PEOPLES
(Psalm 96:3 *NIV*)

Our churches have fallen into such grievous mistakes with reference to the propagation of the gospel in our own times. We have stood to our stereotyped forms, refusing to come down from the routine of our forefathers, although this routine has ceased to be attractive to the people, nay, in many instances, the very thing that drives them away.

The most thoughtful writers on education tell us that the first essential in a teacher of youth is to be able to interest his pupils. True. This is equally true of the people – if you would benefit and bless them, you must interest them. You must clothe the truth in such garb, and convey it by such mediums, as will arouse their attention and interest their minds. In short, we must come down to them. Whatever has caused it, it is a fact that the masses of the people have come to associate ideas of stiffness, formality, and uninteresting routine with our church and chapel worship, and if we are to be co-workers with God for them, we must move out of our jog-trot paces and become all things to them in order to win them.[1] If they will not come inside our consecrated buildings, we must get at them in unconsecrated ones, or out under the canopy of heaven. And has not Jesus by his blood consecrated every spot of earth to soul-saving purposes? If they will not listen to our college-trained and polished divines, we must send them men of their own stamp, whose habits of thought and modes of expression are familiar and congenial to them, and who, washed and filled with the Holy Ghost, are as well adapted to preach to them as were the fishermen of Galilee to the men of their generation.[2]

> Lord, your message is for all; the educated, the uneducated,
> the rich and the poor, the cultured and the uncouth.
> What a lovely truth this is, that none need be denied! Amen.

---

[1] 1 Corinthians 9:19–23.
[2] From *Practical Religion*.

PETER WAS SITTING OUTSIDE IN THE COURTYARD, AND A
SERVANT-GIRL CAME TO HIM. "YOU ALSO WERE WITH JESUS
OF GALILEE," SHE SAID. BUT HE DENIED IT BEFORE THEM ALL.
"I DON'T KNOW WHAT YOU'RE TALKING ABOUT," HE SAID

(Matthew 26:69–70 *NIV*)

The experience of Peter shows you how utterly different a man is before he gets a Pentecostal baptism and after he gets it. The man who could not stand the questionings of a servant-maid before he got this power, dared to be crucified after he got it.[1] I may just say that here is the great cause of the decline of so many who begin well. Oh! there is no more common lament on the lips of really spiritual teachers everywhere than this, that so many begin well. "Ye did run well," we might truly say of thousands in this land today, "Ye did run well." They begin in the Spirit, and then, as the Apostle says, "They go on to be made perfect by the flesh."[2] How is this? Because, you see, the Spirit puts before every soul this walk of full consecration and wholehearted devotedness to God and, instead of being obedient to the heavenly vision, the soul shrinks back and says, "That is too much – that is too close – that is too great a sacrifice," and they decline and, instead of giving up a profession and going back into the world (there would be ten times more hope of them if they did that), they cling on to the profession and kindle a fire of their own, and walk in the sparks they have kindled. But he says he is against them, and they "shall lie down in sorrow".[3] Oh! there is a deal of this. People must have a God and a religion. They will have one, and when they shrink from the true one, and will not follow the divine counsel, then they make one for themselves, and a great many of them go to sleep and never wake again. They go out of the world comfortably under the influence of narcotics, and they never wake. They die deceived; or, if they do awake, we know what sort of an awakening it is, and what sort of deathbed theirs is.[4]

Lord, have mercy on any who drift away from faith.
Rekindle the glow. Keep me faithful in prayer on their behalf. Amen.

---

1 Peter's crucifixion is not recorded in Scripture, but John 21:18–19 suggests he would die a martyr's death. It is traditionally believed Peter asked to be crucified upside down because he didn't feel worthy of a crucifixion that was the same as Jesus'.
2 See Galatians 3:3, KJV.
3 Isaiah 50:11, KJV.
4 From *Aggressive Christianity*.

MY HEART IS STIRRED BY A NOBLE THEME AS I RECITE MY VERSES
FOR THE KING; MY TONGUE IS THE PEN OF A SKILLFUL WRITER

(Psalm 45:1 *NIV*)

We think a wonderful indication of the future [of The Salvation Army] is the growth of public interest in us; for we cannot utter a word now of any moment but it goes round the world. That too is testimony, and we rejoice in it, for I contend that it is something to get a notice about The Salvation Army into *The Times* and into *The Daily News*.[1] It makes every publican, and every Member of Parliament, and every lord and lady, from the Queen on the throne downwards, read it. They cannot for the life of them help noticing it, and they cannot prevent the ideas which the word "salvation" brings up in their minds. It is the most beautiful word on earth, the most beautiful word in Heaven – salvation. "Here you are again!" says a Member of Parliament to his wife. "Salvation again" and he throws the paper to her. "What does this mean?" I contend that only raising the question may do a man good, and set him thinking. I contend that the fact that the public leading journals of this land have to report the progress, and proceedings, and persecutions, and sufferings of The Salvation Army, makes every man and woman in England begin to realize in some dim sort of way that they themselves have something to do with salvation after all, that they have got a soul, and that they will want to be saved one day! It is a wonderful achievement, to get something about God, and religion, and eternity into our public prints, where they have so long been shut out! And I must say that the secular press has done us a great deal more justice than the religious. All honour to them! I am bound to say, that in common honesty I hope the religious press will learn better by-and-by. If they don't, they will be the sufferers, and not The Salvation Army.[2]

Lord, I pray for those who earn their living by writing; journalists, authors
and reporters. Bless their work with integrity and any worthwhile campaigns
they undertake, with strength. I pray especially for areas of the world where
the freedom of the press is suffocated and protests are crushed. Amen.

1   A national newspaper founded in 1846 by Charles Dickens. *The News* often carried reports of humanitarian work and political campaigns. Editorial policy was overtly sympathetic to workers' rights.
2   From *The Salvation Army in Relation to the Church and State*.

This is God's Army
(Genesis 32:2 *WEB*)

We have changed the name of the Mission[1] into "The Salvation Army",[2] and truly it is fast assuming the force and spirit of an Army of the living God. I see no bounds to our extension; if God will own and use such simple men and women (we have over thirty women in the Field)[3] as we are sending out now, we can compass the whole country in a very short time.

And it is truly wonderful what is being done by the instrumentality of quite young girls. I could not have believed it if I had not seen it. Truly, out of the mouths of babes and sucklings he has ordained strength, because of the enemy; and the enemy feels it.[4]

In one small town where we have two girls labouring, a man, quite an outsider, told another that if they went on for much longer all the publics[5] would have to be shut up, for he went to every one in the town the other night, and he only found four men in them all! The whole population, he said, had gone to the "Hallelujah Lasses"![6] Oh, for more of the fire! Pray for our officers.[7]

Lord God, bless The Salvation Army!
Bless its General, bless its officers, bless its members. Amen.

---

1 The Christian Mission.
2 In posters and bills, the Christian Mission advertised itself as a "Hallelujah Army". In 1877, William Booth was preparing his Christmas appeal and discussing the nature of the Christian Mission with his son Bramwell Booth, and George Scott Railton (later to become Commissioner Railton). Subsequent to this discussion, William Booth struck out the words "Volunteer Army" from a circular and wrote "Salvation Army" in its place. Initially, all correspondence bore the heading, "The Christian Mission, or The Salvation Army".
3 Officers not stationed in headquarters are known as Field Officers.
4 See Psalm 8:2, KJV.
5 Public houses.
6 A nickname for young female officers who were dispatched to carry out "pub raids".
7 From *Catherine Booth The Mother of The Salvation Army, Vol. II.*

Behold, I do not know how to speak
(Jeremiah 1:6 *ESV*)

Thanks for your hints for my meeting.[1] If I get on well, and find I really possess any ability for public speaking, I don't intend to finish with juveniles. If there is any reasonable hope of success, I shall try at something higher... I went to hear a popular female lecturer, and felt much encouraged to make an attempt. If I could do so, I should be able to fit in with William's effort on his evangelistic tours nicely. I only wish I had begun years ago. Had I been fortunate enough to have been brought up amongst the Primitives,[2] I believe I should have been preaching now.[3] You laugh! But I believe it. The cares of a family and the bothers of a house now preclude any kind of labour that requires much study; but I don't think lecturing on temperance would need much.[4]

I addressed the Band of Hope[5]... and got on far better than I expected. Indeed, I felt quite at home on the platform, far more so than I do in the kitchen! There were a few adults present, and they seemed quite as much interested and pleased as the children. One of them... is the most intelligent gentleman in our congregation. I got abundantly complimented, and had the most pleasing evidence of the gratification and delight of the children... But I must not be too sanguine. Perhaps I may lose my confidence next time. I am so anxious to succeed for the cause's sake. I hope my dear father will not forget his promise by sending me some hints.[6, 7]

> Bless those, Lord, who are called to any ministry of public speaking,
> especially those who are nervous or inexperienced. Amen.

1   Catherine Booth was writing to her father, who had lapsed into a period of drinking before becoming teetotal again.
2   Primitive Methodism was a movement in English Methodism from about 1810 until about 1932.
3   It is likely that Catherine would have been given more opportunities for public speaking within the Primitive movement.
4   From a letter Catherine Booth wrote to her father in 1857.
5   A temperance organization for working-class children. Members pledged abstinence from alcohol and met weekly for lectures. The Junior Band of Hope also existed.
6   From a letter written in 1857 (possibly to William).
7   From *Catherine Booth The Mother of The Salvation Army, Vol. I.*

AVOID FOOLISH CONTROVERSIES,
GENEALOGIES, DISSENSIONS, AND QUARRELS

(Titus 3:9 ESV)

A few words about the so-called secret book... There has been endless confusion as to which book has been thus designated.[1] Please note that we have two small books – one entitled *Orders and Regulations*, the other *Doctrine and Disciplines*, and these are the only books of this character ever published. The five other parts referred to in "Orders" have not been written. Secondly, please note that the book referred to in Mr Charlesworth's letter[2] in *The Times* was *not* the *Orders and Regulations*, as his own words prove. After giving his own monstrous assertions as to our teachings, for which there is not a word of justification in either book, he says: "I challenge you to make that book public – *not* the book to which you refer when these Orders are spoken of, which is only the general orders and regulations for the members of the Army, but the book given to your trained initiated officers for their guidance and instruction, with an express direction not to show it." This book is the *Doctrine and Discipline* which, by the way, you can get for sixpence anywhere. I repeat, we have only these two books. Therefore, seeing that, as Mr Charlesworth says, he does not mean the *Orders and Regulations*, given to the whole Army, he must mean *Doctrine and Discipline*.[3]

Lord, whatever the rights and wrongs of this particular issue, it is always sad when your people fall out, especially publicly. Bless us with wisdom and grace if and when we need to disagree, remembering that the world is watching. Amen.

---

1   Speculation had arisen that officer-cadets were being taught from a secret book. Consequently, a public edition was put on sale, in 1883, with sections relative to discipline later omitted. The Reverend Charles Bullock, a prolific author, wrote *A Reply to the "Secret Book" of The Salvation Army (The Doctrine and Discipline of The Salvation Army)*.

2   The Reverend Samuel Charlesworth, whose daughter, Maud Ballington Booth (née Charlesworth) went on to marry into the Booth family, was concerned by his daughter's closeness to William and Catherine. He felt she had adopted them as her "emotional parents" and wrote to *The Times* expressing some of his concerns about the Army's ways. His letter was published on 21 February 1883.

3   From *The Salvation Army in Relation to the Church and State*.

Them that were slain for... the testimony which they held

(Revelation 6:9 *KJV*)

As the greatest manifestation of God to the world was by suffering, so the most influential revelation of his people to the world has been by suffering. They are seen to the best advantage in the furnace. The blood of martyrs has ever been the seed of the Church. The patience, meekness, firmness, and happiness of God's people in circumstances of suffering, persecution, and death, have paved the way for the gospel in almost all lands and all ages. A baptism of blood has prepared the hard and sterile soil of humanity for the good seed of the kingdom, and made it doubly fruitful. The exhibition of the meek and loving spirit of Christianity under suffering has doubtless won thousands of hearts to its Divine Author, and tamed and awed many a savage persecutor, besides Saul of Tarsus.[1] When men see their fellow men enduring with patience and meekness, what they know would fill themselves with hatred, anger, and revenge, they naturally conclude that there must be a different spirit in them. When they see Christians suffering the loss of all things, and cheerfully resigning themselves to bonds, imprisonment, and death, they cannot help feeling that they have sources of strength and springs of consolation all unknown to themselves. Patient suffering, cheerful acquiescence in affliction and anguish, mental or physical, is the most convincing proof of the divine in man which it is possible for humanity to give. "Truly this was the Son of God"[2] said those who stood by the cross when they saw how he suffered. And how many who have been thoroughly sceptical as to the professions of their converted kindred, and have most bitterly persecuted them, and withstood every argument and entreaty advanced in health and activity, have yielded almost without a word before the patience and peace with which the billows of suffering and death have been braved, nay, welcomed! Such evidence is too mighty, such proof too positive to be resisted, even by persecutors and blasphemers.[3]

I pray today for those who are persecuted because of their Christian witness.
Give them extra grace so that their persecutors may be influenced for Christ.
Amen.

---

1   Acts 9.
2   Matthew 27:54, KJV.
3   From *Practical Religion*.

IF YOU SUFFER AS A CHRISTIAN, DO NOT BE ASHAMED,
BUT PRAISE GOD THAT YOU BEAR THAT NAME

(1 Peter 4:16 *NIV*)

Abraham might have written a book and preached all his life long, as doubtless he did, but the whole, ten times told, would not have convinced his family, his contemporaries and posterity, of the depth and fervency of his love to God, as did that holy calm surrender of the best beloved of his soul to the requirements of God. Job might have been the upright, benevolent, righteous man he was,[1] but probably we should never have heard of him but for his wonderful submission, patience, and faith, under suffering. It is this which lifts him up as an example and a teacher to all succeeding generations. It was when sitting on the dunghill, apparently forsaken of God and man, and suffering the direst physical agony which Satan could inflict, that Job attained his greatest victory and made that wonderful exhibition of trust in God which has been the comfort and admiration of God's people from that day to this.[2] It was in the fiery furnace that Shadrach, Meshach, and Abednego won such glory to the God of Israel, that even a heathen king proclaimed his majesty and dominion, and commanded his subjects to worship him who could deliver after this manner.[3] It was in the furnace of persecution that Stephen, Peter, James, John and Paul proved the divinity of their characters and the genuineness of their faith. Without suffering the world could never have known the strength of their faith, the fervency of their love, or the purity of their lives. Their trials made them "spectacles unto the world, to angels and to men"[4] and won for their Master the ears and hearts of thousands.[5]

I would that others may see the hallmarks of Jesus in me.
What others perceive, they might believe. Amen.

---

1   Job 1:8.
2   Job 13:15.
3   Daniel 3.
4   See 1 Corinthians 4:9, KJV.
5   From *Practical Religion*.

October 31st

Am I my brother's keeper?
(Genesis 4:9 *NIV*)

Friends, study your New Testament on this question, and you will be alarmed to find to what an awful extent you are your brother's keeper – to what an awful and alarming extent God holds you responsible for the salvation of those around you. I want to glance... at our call to work for God...

We are called by the Word... by the underlying principle running through it all, and laying upon us the obligation to save men. In fact, the world is cast upon us: we are the only people who can save the unconverted. Oh! I wish I could get this thought thoroughly into your minds.

It has been, perhaps, one of the most potent, with respect to any little service I have rendered in the vineyard, the thought that Jesus Christ has nobody else to represent him here but us Christians – his real people: nobody else to work for him. These poor people of the world, who are in darkness and ignorance, have nobody else to show them the way of mercy.

If we do not go to them with loving earnestness and determination to rescue them from the grasp of the great enemy; if we do not, by the power of the Holy Ghost, bind the strong man and take his goods,[1] who is to do it? God has devolved it upon us. I say this is an alarming and awful consideration.[2]

> What a privilege you have entrusted to your people, Father!
> In my own way, I dedicate myself to you for service. May your Spirit work
> through me today, as he sees fit. Make me a channel of your grace. Amen.

---

1   Mark 3:27.
2   From *Aggressive Christianity*.

AND THE SPIRIT SAID...

(Acts 8:29 *ESV*)

The very first aspiration... of a newly born soul is after some other soul.

The very first utterance, after the first burst of praise to God for deliverance from the bondage of sin and death, is a prayer gasped to the throne for some other soul still in darkness.

And is not this the legitimate fruit of the Spirit? Is not this what we should expect?... Oh! yes, some of you could not go to sleep until you had written to a distant relative, and poured out your soul in anxious longings for his salvation; you could not take your necessary food until you had spoken or written to somebody in whose soul you were deeply interested.

The Spirit began at once to urge you to seek for souls; and so it is frequently the last cry of the Spirit in the believer's soul before it leaves the body. You have sat beside many a dying saint, and what has been the last prayer? Has it been anything about self, money, family, circumstances? Oh! those things are now all left behind, and the last expressed anxiety has been for some prodigal soul outside the Kingdom of God. When the light of eternity comes streaming upon the soul, and its eyes get wide open to the value of souls, it neither hears nor sees anything else! It goes out of time into eternity, praying as the Redeemer did, for the souls it is leaving behind. This is the first and last utterance of the Spirit in the believer's soul on earth; and oh! if Christians were only true to the promptings of this blessed Spirit, it would be the prevailing impulse, the first desire and effort all the way through life.[1]

> Take my voice and let me speak, always, only, for my King.
> Lord, the last thing I want to be is someone who bores people away from the Kingdom. May your Spirit keep my witness fresh and interesting.[2] Amen.

---

1 From *Aggressive Christianity*.
2 See Frances R. Havergal (1836–79), "Take My Life and Let it Be"; my paraphrase.

REJOICE IN THE LORD ALWAYS. I WILL SAY IT AGAIN: REJOICE!

(Philippians 4:4 *NIV*)

I was thinking, as I was sitting here… We have had some enthusiasm; and why not? Why should we be enthusiastic in everything but religion? Can you give me any reason for that? If there is any subject calculated to move our souls to their very centres, and to call out the enthusiasm of our nature, surely it is religion, if it be the real thing. Why should we not be enthusiastic? I have never seen a good reason yet.

Why should we not shout and sing the praises of our King, as we expect to do it in glory? Why should not a man cry out, and groan, and be in anguish of soul, as the Psalmist says, as if he were crying out of the belly of Hell when he is convinced of sin, and realizes his danger, and is expecting, unless God have mercy, to be damned? Why should he not roar for the disquietude of his spirit as much as David did? Is there anything unphilosophical in it? Is there anything contrary to the laws of mind in it? Is there anything that you would not allow under any great pressure of calamity, or realization of danger, or grief? Why should we not have this demonstration in soul matters? They had it under the old dispensation. We read again and again that when the people came together after a time of relapse, and backsliding, and infidelity, when God sent some flaming, burning prophet amongst them, and they were gathered on the sides of Carmel or elsewhere that, on some occasions, the weeping and, on other occasions, the rejoicing was so great that they made the very ground tremble, and almost rent the heavens with the sound of their crying and rejoicing.[1]

> Catherine Booth is right, Lord – if I can be enthusiastic about things of
> this earth, which are here today and gone tomorrow, how much more should
> I rejoice over my salvation? Implant in me a happy spirit, full of praise. Amen.

1   From *Godliness.*

IT IS A DREADFUL THING TO FALL INTO THE HANDS OF THE LIVING GOD
(Hebrews 10:31 *NIV*)

Christ, in bearing our punishment, though his body suffered in a violent and painful death, suffered chiefly in his soul. He said to his disciples, "My soul is exceedingly sorrowful, even unto death",[1] hours before he suffered any bodily anguish; and we are told he was in an agony, and sweat great drops of blood which ran down to the ground.[2] Now what was it that thus wrought upon the spotless soul of Jesus? It was the weight of his Father's wrath against sin. He was standing for us, in our stead, suffering in his soul the infliction of the justice of God against sin. It was this which drank up his Spirit, and made him utter that exceeding loud and bitter cry. Now, if the wrath of God were so terrible to the Son of God himself as to put him in such an agony, what will it be to the undone sinner in the great day of wrath? Well might our Saviour say, "Fear not them which kill the body... but rather fear him which is able to destroy both soul and body in hell."[3] Neither angel nor devil can affright or torment the soul but by God's permission. He is Lord of the soul of man; he created it, and he alone has power over it. Well might the Psalmist say, "Who knoweth the power of thine anger?"[4] No creature can conjecture the weight of God's wrath on the soul. Whatever comes direct from God is most stupendous, whether in the way of mercy or judgment. His love and mercy are infinite and unsearchable, and so is his wrath. The weight of his little finger is heavier than the loins of man. God sometimes in this life lets in his wrath into the soul, filling it with terror and dismay, so that it becomes intolerable. Thus it was with Judas. The wrath of God filled his conscience with such terror that he could not bear it but hanged himself to be rid of the burden, forgetting that he was rushing into greater terror still.[5, 6]

> Cruel nails that pierced the hands of Jesus, pierced the heart of
> God the Father too. Lord, my prayers today have to be for my unsaved friends,
> relatives and loved ones. Have mercy. Hear me as I pray for them. Amen.

1   Matthew 26:38, KJV.
2   Luke 22:44.
3   Matthew 10:28, KJV.
4   Psalm 90:11, KJV.
5   Matthew 27:1–10.
6   From *Life and Death*.

NOVEMBER 4TH

YOU SHALL HAVE NO OTHER GODS BEFORE ME
(Exodus 20:3 *NIV*)

Every human being has a deity. In fact, we are so made that we must have a God. Even the man who says there is no God, worships a god notwithstanding, and that god is, "to whom he yields himself a servant to obey".[1] Now God claims to be the deity of the soul of every human being; but Satan has supplanted God, and he has done it in many ways. He has assumed many different forms in order to suit different classes and conditions of men. For one class of persons he finds one idol, for another class another. But the principle here laid down is, that whatever the outward form may be, that which usurps in a man's affections, life, and action, the place of God, becomes his deity. He need not outwardly label it idol, or bow his knees and worship it. The supremacy which he gives to it in his affections and life is the point. What an awful thought that in this so-called Christian England, tens of thousands of people are as truly worshipping idols as are any of the inhabitants of Africa or China… Professing Christians speak about giving up the vanities of the world, and coming out from the world, when, alas! We need not go outside the four walls of their own dwellings to find their god. I am afraid there are quite as many people who go wrong with these inside idols as with the outside ones. The first that strikes us as the most universal god of so-called religious society in this day is the god of fashion. Now, what is fashion? What does the term mean? It means the world's way of having things, and the world's way of doing things. When we look abroad on the great majority of men and women around us, we see that they are utterly godless, selfish, and untrue, and yet the majority always fixes the fashion. It is not the few true, real, God-fearing, earnest men and women who want to serve God and help humanity who fix the fashion; it is always the majority. Consequently, you see fashion is always diametrically opposed to God's way of having things, and God's way of doing things. Therefore, the votaries of fashion cannot possibly be the servants of God.[2]

> My idols might not be carved of wood or stone, Lord, but if they become my
> focus, whatever they are, then grant me the grace of perspective, please. Amen.

1   See Romans 6:16, KJV.
2   From *Popular Christianity*.

November 5ᵀᴴ

> "You are a king, then!" said Pilate. Jesus answered,
> "You say that I am a king. In fact, the reason I was born
> and came into the world is to testify to the truth.
> Everyone on the side of truth listens to me"
>
> (John 18:37 NIV)

Christ's soldiers must be imbued with the spirit of the war.

Love to the King and concern for his interests must be the master passion of the soul. Without this, all outward effort, even that which springs from a sense of duty, will fail.

The hardship and suffering involved in spiritual warfare are too great for any motive but that of love. It is said that one of the soldiers of Napoleon, when being operated upon for the extraction of a bullet, exclaimed, "Cut a little deeper and you will find my general's name" – it was engraven on his heart. So must the image and glory of Christ be engraven on the heart of every faithful soldier of Christ. It must be the all-subduing passion of his life to bring the reign of Jesus Christ over the hearts and souls of men.

A little child who has this spirit will subjugate others to his King, while the most talented and learned and active, without it, will accomplish comparatively little. If the hearts of the Christians of this generation were inspired with this spirit, and set on winning the world for God, we should soon see nations shaken to their centre, and millions of souls translated into the Kingdom. Soldiers of Christ must be abandoned to the war. They must be thoroughly committed to God's side; there can be no neutrals in this warfare. When the soldier enlists and takes the queen's shilling, he ceases to be his own property, becoming the property of his country, going where he is sent, standing at any post to which he is assigned.[1]

Not my own; Saviour, I belong to you.

---

1   From *The Highway of our God.*

LET US CONSIDER HOW WE MAY SPUR ONE ANOTHER ON TOWARDS LOVE AND GOOD DEEDS

(Hebrews 10:24 *NIV*)

A gentleman, in advanced life, said: "When I was a young man, and in my first love, the zeal of the Lord's house so consumed me that I used to neglect my daily business, and could scarcely sleep at night; but, alas, that was many years ago." "Was it not better with you then than now?" I asked; and the tears came welling up into his eyes. Oh, yes! the Lord says of him, "I remember thee, the kindness of thy youth, the love of thine espousals, when thou wentest after me in the wilderness, in a land that was not sown. Israel was holiness unto the LORD, and the firstfruits of his increase".[1]

And, Alas! There are many such today. They have it all to do over again; they have to repent and do their first-works;[2] they have to come back and get forgiven, and washed, and saved, if they are to go into the Kingdom on high, all for want of systematically and resolutely obeying the urgings of the Holy Spirit towards their fellow men…

You want this spirit – the spirit that yearns over the souls of your fellow men; to weep over them as you look at them in their sin, and folly and misery; the spirit that cannot be satisfied with your own enjoyments or with feeling that you are safe, or even that your children are safe; but that yearns over every living soul while there is one left unsaved, and can never rest satisfied until it is brought into the Kingdom.[3]

Redeeming God, you specialize in embracing penitents. You are the
God of second chances. I pray for anyone I know who is like the gentleman
in this story. Tell me if you would like me to make contact in some way. Amen.

---

1   Jeremiah 2:2–3, KJV.
2   Revelation 2:4–5.
3   *Aggressive Christianity.*

I LOVE THOSE WHO LOVE ME, AND THOSE WHO SEEK ME FIND ME

(Proverbs 8:17 *NIV*)

Nothing wounds me more, after being at meetings for dealing with souls, where I have tried to speak in a most pointed and thorough way to make everybody know what I meant, to find, when I go to the dinner or supper table, that people have not known a bit, or, if they have, won't accept it.

Oh! this is the secret – they will not come down from their pride and high-mightiness. But God will not be revealed to such souls, though they cry and pray themselves to skeletons, and go mourning all their days. They will not fulfil the condition, "Be not conformed to this world";[1] they will not forego their conformity even to the extent of a dinner party. A great many that I know will not forego their conformity to the shape of their head-dress. They won't forego their conformity to the extent of giving up visiting and receiving visits from ungodly, worldly, hollow, and superficial people. They will not forego their conformity to the tune of having their domestic arrangements upset – no, not if the salvation of their children, and servants, and friends depends upon it.

The *sine quâ non* is their own comfort, and then take what you can get, on God's side. "We must have this, and we must have the other; and then, if the Lord Jesus Christ will come in at the tail end and sanctify it all, we shall be very much obliged to him; but we cannot forego these things." Oh! friends, friends, I tell you, this will never do.[2]

Lord, imagine Catherine Booth coming to dinner! I just pray that
my life at home may match my life at church; my interests,
my conversation, and my priorities. Grant me that grace. Amen.

1 Romans 12:2, KJV.
2 From *Godliness*.

The Lord is a jealous and avenging God; the Lord takes vengeance and is filled with wrath

(Nahum 1:2 *NIV*)

Ah, if sinners or saints, or poets or philosophers, could only find any satisfactory evidence that this wrath [of God] would ever come to an end, what a jubilee there would be amongst the wicked both on earth and in Hell!

But, sinner, remember that the same words are used to describe the duration of the misery of the wicked which are used to set forth the duration of the blessedness of the righteous – yea, and the duration of the existence of God himself. He who was the embodiment of truth and love, who came to seek and to save us, and not to mock us by false representations of future woe, declares that "it is better... to enter into life halt or maimed, rather than having two hands or two feet to be cast into everlasting fire".[1] And in another place he calls it "the fire that never shall be quenched".[2] And in speaking of the wicked in the last Great Day, he says, "And these shall go away into everlasting punishment".[3]

Others may choose for themselves, but God forbid that you or I should make the fearful experiment of finding out the meaning of these awful words.

Oh, my unsaved hearers, will you not be persuaded to flee from the wrath? Mercy still holds out; Jesus still shows his wounds and pleads his blood. Will you ground your arms, and take refuge under his cross? Will you come and drink of the water of life freely; or will you persevere in your rebellion and go on to drain the "cup of the wine of the fierceness of his wrath"?[4, 5]

Lord, in your anger, please remember mercy. Amen.

---

1   Matthew 18:8, KJV.
2   Mark 9:45, KJV.
3   Matthew 25:46, KJV.
4   Revelation 16:19, KJV.
5   From *Life and Death*.

A time to be silent and a time to speak
(Ecclesiastes 3:7 *NIV*)

With respect to this little book [*Doctrine and Discipline*], I want you to note… that it is a catechism prepared specially for our cadets, of the simplest and most understandable nature, setting forth our doctrines… It was never a secret book in the sense *our enemies insinuate*; but we, knowing that some of our views would differ from those of many other Christians, did not wish to be brought into collision by making this book public, and so at first it was confined mainly to our officers; but for some time now it has been sold at all our stations.[1] Now I contend that, seeing we *have* views, and seeing that no religious organization can exist and operate without some human rendering of the word of God, we had as much right to inculcate our views as any other teachers; and especially seeing that God had used us to make a new people from amongst those who never had either any religion or religious views before. There is not a sentence in the text of *Doctrine and Discipline* of which we see any reason to be ashamed, and we fearlessly commit it to time and to posterity for their verdict. I want you to note further, that notwithstanding Mr Charlesworth's express declaration that he did *not* refer to *Orders and Regulations*[2] our enemies have dexterously mixed up this book with the other, and tried to make this appear to be the secret book, so-called; and this they persist in doing, although they know perfectly well that *Orders and Regulations* have been commented on in many of the public journals for five years gone by, advertised in *The War Cry*,[3] and sold at all our stations![4]

Help me, Lord, to be someone who is willing to consider both
sides of an argument, and to broker agreements that are harmonious.
Where there is discord, let me bring your peace. Amen.

---

1   A document entitled *The Doctrines and Discipline of The Salvation Army* was prepared for use at the Training Homes for Salvation Army officers in 1881. It was not published for wider use, but there was criticism that cadets were being taught from a secret book. In response to criticism, a public edition was published for sale in 1883. The sections relating to discipline were later omitted and covered separately in the *Articles of War* and *Orders and Regulations*.
2   See October 28th.
3   The Salvation Army's weekly evangelical newspaper.
4   From *The Salvation Army in Relation to the Church and State*.

NOVEMBER 10TH

**THE LORD GOD MADE GARMENTS OF SKIN FOR
ADAM AND HIS WIFE AND CLOTHED THEM**

(Genesis 3:21 *NIV*)

Fashion prescribes the form of dress for almost the whole world. Doctors may talk, and advise, and warn against high heels, tight waists, and insufficient clothing, and all the monstrous and ridiculous appendages to dress which fashion from time to time prescribes. But it is fashion! That is enough. Never mind if tight-lacing does squeeze my lungs and prevent me getting the necessary amount of air, thus inducing premature disease and death; it is the fashion, and I must do it. Never mind if the high-heeled shoes produce deformity of the spine and all manner of other injuries; it is the fashion, and I must have them. I must dress myself in the most ridiculous costumes which Parisian milliners can contrive, it is the fashion; if the dress is too light, or does not half cover my body, never mind; I shall wear it because it is the fashion. So, in the furnishing of people's houses, in a great many instances, it is the same. I have been in many houses where it seems to me that almost all utility and necessary comfort for health and work is lost sight of. It is almost all show, so that you are afraid to use a table for fear you will injure it. Oh, the money and time that are squandered, and the perpetual strife that goes on to keep up this show because everybody else does it. In their very companionships fashion has decided what should be the ground and the rule of selection, and so fashionable people have only the companions that society has settled they are to have. They do not look, as you would suppose rational beings would, for congenial society in the way of congeniality of thought, and feeling, and intelligence, that which gives vivacity and interest to communion with one another. Oh, no! If a person ever so attractive and clever, and competent to interest, or instruct, or please them, happens to be a grade lower in the social scale, fashion says, "That person is not in your circle, he is out of your sphere; you cannot associate with such a person."[1]

Father, I pray today for anyone who is consumed by materialism, finding themselves enslaved to the false promises of fashion. Please help them. Amen.

---

1   From *Popular Christianity.*

For God does speak – now one way, now another

(Job 33:14 *NIV*)

I remember reading, somewhere, the story of a nobleman who was (I think) a backslider. He was stopping at some country inn, and he went up into a room in which, over the mantelpiece, there was a very good picture of the crucifixion by a good old master, and under it was written, "I suffered this for thee – what hast thou done for me?"[1] This question went home. It struck deep. He thought – Yes, what indeed? He went out into the stables to his horses, to try to get rid of the uncomfortable impression, but he could not forget it. A soft, pathetic voice seemed to follow him, "I suffered this for thee, what hast thou done for me!" At last it broke him down, and he went to his knees. He said: "True, Lord, I have never done anything for thee, but now I give myself and my all to thee, to be used up in thy service."

And have you never heard that voice in your soul, as you have been kneeling at the cross? Did you ever gaze upon that illustrious sufferer, and hear his voice, as you looked back into the paltry past? What hast thou done for me?...

Now, friends, I want to know what this is to come to – what is to be the end of it? "What are you going to do, brother? What are you going to do?" And sister, too. Is it going to die out in sentiment? Is it going to evaporate in sighs and wishings, and end in "I cannot"? God forbid! What are you do?[2]

What a lovely story, Lord! A painting of your crucifixion imparting
a message of conviction and embrace! Never allow me to underestimate
the ways in which you speak to people, so great is your love. Amen.

---

1   From Frances Ridley Havergal's (1836–79) first hymn "I Gave My Life for Thee", written after seeing Sternberg's painting *Ecce Homo* in Düsseldorf, Germany.
2   From *Aggressive Christianity*.

Serve one another humbly in love

(Galatians 5:13 *NIV*)

What have you been doing for him last week?

Ask yourselves.

You say, "Well, I have read my Bible more." Very good, so far as it goes. What have you read it for? "Well," you say, "to get to know the Lord's will, and to get instruction and comfort." Aye, exactly, but that is all for yourself, you see. "I have prayed a great deal." Very good. I wish everybody would pray. The Apostles say all men everywhere ought to pray.[1] What for? "I have been asking the Lord for great things." Very good, praise the Lord; but those are for yourself, mainly.

If you have been led out in agonizing supplication for souls, thank God for it, and go on, as the Apostle says, "watching thereunto with all perseverance",[2] "praying in the Holy Ghost";[3] but if it has been merely praying to get all you can for yourself, what profit is that to the Lord? But you say, "I am bringing up my family." Exactly; so are the worldly people around you, but what for? For God or for yourself?

Oh! Let us look at these things, friends. I am afraid a great deal of the religion is a mere transition of the selfishness of the human heart from the world to religion. I am afraid a great deal of the religion of this day ends in getting all you can and doing as little as you can – like some of your servants. You know the sort, who will do no more than they are forced – just get through, because they are hired. There is a great deal of that kind of service in these days, both towards man and towards God. Now, friends, what have you been doing for him?[4]

> Lord Jesus, may my service for you spring from my love for you.
> The more I reflect upon your love, the more I want to do. Amen.

1   1 Timothy 2:8.
2   Ephesians 6:18, KJV.
3   Jude 20, KJV.
4   From *Aggressive Christianity*.

A FARMER WENT OUT TO SOW HIS SEED. AS HE WAS
SCATTERING THE SEED, SOME FELL ALONG THE PATH, AND THE BIRDS
CAME AND ATE IT UP. SOME FELL ON ROCKY PLACES, WHERE IT DID
NOT HAVE MUCH SOIL. IT SPRANG UP QUICKLY, BECAUSE THE SOIL WAS
SHALLOW. BUT WHEN THE SUN CAME UP, THE PLANTS WERE SCORCHED,
AND THEY WITHERED BECAUSE THEY HAD NO ROOT. OTHER SEED FELL
AMONG THORNS, WHICH GREW UP AND CHOKED THE PLANTS. STILL
OTHER SEED FELL ON GOOD SOIL, WHERE IT PRODUCED A CROP – A
HUNDRED, SIXTY OR THIRTY TIMES WHAT WAS SOWN

(Matthew 13:3–8 *NIV*)

Have you ever thought of those awful words in the parable of the sower? "And the cares of this world, and the deceitfulness of riches, and the lusts of other things entering in, choke the word, and it becometh unfruitful"[1] – not abominable things, not immoral things, not shameful things, but the desire of other things. And, in another text: "who mind earthly things."[2] They attach more importance to worldly things and other things than they do to the things of his Kingdom. They practically make these things first, though they sing about his Kingdom and profess to make him first: they make the earthly things first and, therefore, they will not have their earthly things upset for his things; and do you suppose he is cheated? Do you suppose he is deceived? Do you think it likely that the great God of Heaven, who has millions of angels and archangels to worship him, is going to pour his glory on such people, and reveal himself to them, and use them? Not likely! "I will be first in your love," he says. You women here, if you knew that you were not the first and only one in the affections of your husband, what would you say? And you husbands, would you dwell with a wife if you knew you were not the only one in her affections, but that they were divided between you and someone else? "Not likely!" you would say. "I am not going to lavish my affections, and my society, and my gifts, and everything I possess on one whose heart is divided with another. If she will have her heart divided, then she must go to that other." Now you know God is a jealous God,[3] and he knows who do mock him, and he knows who will not sacrifice this conformity to the world that they may walk with him in white.[4]

Christ has the right to rule my life.

---

1   Mark 4:19, KJV.
2   Philippians 3:19, KJV.
3   Exodus 34:14.
4   From *Godliness*.

Because of their unbelief,
he couldn't do any miracles among them
(Mark 6:5 *NLT*)

My heart ached at what a lady told me this morning... She said, "A friend of mine remarked, 'You don't mean to say that you are going to call 4,000 people together to cry for the Holy Ghost?'" She said, "Yes, I do." "Well, it makes me frightened. What if anything should happen; if something should be done?"

Would to God something would happen; would to God something might be done that should frighten somebody. But oh! What did that reveal?

Depths of infidelity and unbelief; and yet people wonder that infidelity is increasing. Is it any wonder that infidels are laughing us to scorn? Is it any wonder that at Christian Evidence Societies[1] men get up and say that the Christian system has become effete? No wonder, when that is the state of heart of the Lord's people. People meet together, and pray, and talk and sing *Whiter than Snow*,[2] and they don't believe it any more than do the heathen. They pray for the Holy Ghost, and do not so much as believe there is a Holy Ghost. They ask God to do something, when they never knew him to do anything, and don't expect he ever will. The world is dying because of this unreality, and being damned by it... God help us to make some real people. You believe, some of you, that nothing is going to happen. You don't believe that God is going to do anything – so he won't in your experience. If you had lived at Nazareth, do you think Jesus Christ would have done anything for you? He would not.[3]

Father, I pray for anyone who is today struggling with unbelief;
wanting to believe, but tempted not to. Persuade them of your reliability. Amen.

1 The Christian Evidence Society is a Christian apologetics organization founded in 1870. At its peak, in 1883, it had over 400 members.
2 Possibly, James Nicholson's (1828–76) hymn. Nicholson's hymns often included a sense of his longing to be made holy. This was a theme of his hymnology.
3 From *Godliness*.

IN MY NAME THEY WILL DRIVE OUT DEMONS
(Mark 16:17 *NIV*)

I was so touched… by hearing a story from Paris, told by a young woman who has returned, and was telling me about my precious child.[1]

The story was this: A woman came, one morning, and asked for the lady. They tried to put her off, and asked, "Will not someone else do?" "No," said the woman. "I do want to see the lady herself." They said, "You can't see her today – she is too ill!" "Then," she said, "when can I see her?" They appointed a time the next afternoon, and then this poor woman came, and she told this story: "I did hear, six years ago, that there was somebody could take the Devil out. Now, see, I have got a devil in, and he do make me wicked and miserable, and I do want him taken out, and I've been running about these six years to find somebody who could pull him out. I've been to lots of priests, but they could not pull him out, because they had a devil in them; and, you see, when there's a devil in me and a devil in them, we got to fighting, and they could not pull him out." What a comment on, "Jesus I know, and Paul I know; but who are ye?"[2]

Of course, nobody can put a devil out who has a devil in them. The poor old woman's sense told her this. "And," she continued, "a gentleman told me that this lady who has come here is able to pull him out, and I have come to her to do it, for I do want him pulled out." Oh, yes! I thought that is what poor humanity wants all the world over. They want people who can cast the Devil out – people who have in them Holy Ghost power to do it. Oh! Will you be such an one?[3]

> Lord, if darkness cannot overcome light, and if evil cannot
> overcome love, then I pray for a fresh infilling of your Spirit, that your
> light and love in my life may overcome any malevolent forces I encounter.
> Have mercy on those who are in the grip of demonic powers. Amen.

1 Catherine Booth-Clibborn (Katie Booth).
2 Acts 19:15, KJV.
3 From *Godliness*.

As for God, his way is perfect
(Psalm 18:30 *NIV*)

I am told that I have a practical mind, and I am glad I have. I hope I shall keep it to the end. I believe that any other kind of mind will be found to have been a snare, when we get before the throne of God; because Jesus Christ is going to be intensely practical in that day. He is not going to say "Inasmuch as ye thought it" or "Inasmuch as ye felt it" or "Inasmuch as ye intended it" or "Inasmuch as ye promised it" – but he is going to say, "Inasmuch as ye did it."[1] I want to be among the doers, and I want you to be among the doers. Now, dear friends, are you prepared to receive this life of absolute, practical bearing of the shame and the losses, the suffering and the crucifixion, involved in following the Christ? Are you willing to be cast out by fathers and mothers, brothers and sisters, fathers-in-law and mothers-in-law, aunts and cousins, from circles and society, and to be boycotted by those round about you, in order that you may thus follow Christ in the regeneration of the Spirit? Are you prepared to accept it? Do we all accept it? Have you accepted God's version of the life of a saint, or are you seeking all round for excuses to make it a little easier? If the latter, then that fly in the pot will make all your ointment to stink, that flaw in the foundation will topple over any edifice of your resolutions and determinations, your promises, or prayers, or faith; and you will be no better... What we have to come to is to accept God's will for our lives; but in many cases people won't do this. They won't accept the hardship which following Jesus Christ involves; they like ease and comfort; but to follow Jesus Christ in the way he lays down involves a great deal of hard work. It involves the continual use of all our faculties, not allowing any of them to lie by to rust, not using any of them, either mental or physical, merely for our own gratification.[2]

> Nevertheless, Lord, not my will, but yours. If that prayer is a struggle for someone I know today, please help them to progress towards obedience. Amen.

1   See Matthew 25:40, KJV.
2   From *Life and Death.*

ENLARGE THE PLACE OF YOUR TENT,
STRETCH YOUR TENT CURTAINS WIDE, DO NOT HOLD BACK;
LENGTHEN YOUR CORDS, STRENGTHEN YOUR STAKES

(Isaiah 54:2 *NIV*)

In July 1865, William Booth, deeply impressed with the awful indifference prevailing amongst the masses in the east of London, determined to devote himself to some special effort for their salvation. He believed that there had been an atonement made, sufficient for every sinner, and that by true repentance and faith in the Lord Jesus Christ, the very worst might enter upon a new life. He did not think that there was the slightest hope of permanently improving the condition of any of the prodigals, whom he saw abounding around him, other than by leading them to see the cause of all their misery in their neglect of God, and so persuading them to turn to him with full purpose of heart. Trusting in the same Holy Ghost, who had for many years been blessing his labours as a minister, he went out into the streets, and was very soon able to rejoice over many rescued from their evil ways, and ready to serve God with all their might. Having laid a good foundation by requiring, not merely an assent of the mind to a statement of certain truths, but a thorough submission of heart to abandon and separate from all evil, and to serve the new Master with all diligence, he soon had around him a number of earnest labourers willing to devote their leisure hours, their strength, and any money they could spare from their scanty earnings, to the service of the truth. These were plain men and women, and they spoke out plainly and fearlessly to all with whom they came in contact, not only in the open-air and indoor meetings, but in their workshops, at home, and wherever they could meet with their fellows. And the consequence was that the little band steadily grew and spread from point to point, until it had, at the end of 1883, 528 corps or stations, and 245 field outposts, with 103 corps abroad.[1]

Lord of the Church, I pray for repeat miracles of growth;
that many may come in your name. I pray for the church I attend. Amen.

1   From *Life and Death*.

IF ANYONE IS IN CHRIST, THE NEW CREATION HAS COME:
THE OLD HAS GONE, THE NEW IS HERE!

(2 Corinthians 5:17 *NIV*)

Amongst the tens of thousands now marching in the ranks of The Salvation Army, are multitudes of the most wonderful trophies of saving grace – men and women who, having run into sin with all possible greediness, and having forgotten God altogether, were attracted by some of the peculiar outward appearances of the Army to its meetings, and there aroused to deep concern about their souls, and led to cry for deliverance to the only Saviour. The extreme diligence shown in impressing the truth on the attention of the people at all the meetings of the Army, has often led to an accusation of attempting to substitute excitement for a deep heart work; but surely our sowing is best judged by our reaping, and something more than excitement is necessary to produce a force of men and women who deny themselves all personal comfort and ease and, separating themselves from all their old friends, come out in all weathers, night after night, to do their utmost for the rescue of others, whom they see to be perishing around them. It is, indeed, an intense and constant realization of the great spiritual truths to which these addresses refer that causes such earnest action on the part of almost all those who are engaged in the work of the Army. Brought, time after time, face to face with thousands who are, they believe, halting within sight of the open gate of mercy, and also within a step of the wrath to come, our officers and soldiers press the people at every meeting to yield themselves without further delay to the Saviour; so that it is no fiction to use the phraseology of the battlefield with regard to our services. Each meeting is a real fight with the powers of darkness; and, thank God, the fight generally becomes a victory![1]

Thank you, Lord, for new converts. I pray for them. Supply all they will need. Keep an eye on them. Shield them. Strengthen them. Give us more of them! No doubt, Satan will organize some opposition or hostility. Bind his work. Amen.

---

1   From *Life and Death*.

A PECULIAR PEOPLE

(1 Peter 2:9 *KJV*)

It is quite true that the vast majority of the men and women who have daily opportunity to speak at our meetings are ignorant of the language of Scripture and, indeed, of all religious phraseology to a very great extent; but they are thoroughly pervaded with those great truths which, as we have shown, are so all-important; and speaking, not in the set phraseology of any school, but as the Spirit gives them utterance in the natural language of everyday life, they so warn and touch the common people, that thousands of them are, week after week, led to the Saviour's feet. The reality of the work thus done has been super-abundantly tested in seasons of trial. It must be a true and not a false faith which can enable rough men, who have been accustomed to drink and swear and fight, and delicate women to go through storms of abuse and even to endure all sorts of violence without retaliation. Amongst the more than 1,500 officers who have given up their lives to the work, there are very few who have not, at one time or another, known what it is to enjoy true peace amidst the most stormy scenes of opposition out of doors. There is no doubt that a great deal of animosity aroused against the Army has been caused by its constant plain speaking as to judgment as well as mercy; but we prefer any sort of war of this kind – no matter what it may cost us – before the false peace, which is to be got by compromise with the world, or by allowing the guilty to perish unwarned. The use by the Army of brass bands, flags, uniforms, startling announcements, and a number of other peculiar means of attracting the people, are all attributable to the knowledge that the multitudes are perishing, and that all ordinary means have utterly failed to arouse them to a sense of their danger.[1]

There is a lovely sense of confident abandon in these words, Lord.
They speak of people willing to give their all for the salvation of the masses.
Have we come a long way from those days? Is that a good thing?

1   From *Life and Death*.

WERE YOU EXPECTING TO SEE A MAN DRESSED IN EXPENSIVE CLOTHES?
(Matthew 11:8 *NLT*)

Do you envy the fate of the devotees of fashion? Will you worship this god any longer? Thank God, he emancipated me twenty-five years ago, and I have been free ever since. If you are not yet emancipated, get emancipated...

Do not consider fashion when you are settling how you ought to order your household, but plan for the highest good of your children and those around you, and for your greatest usefulness in the world. Never mind fashion.

In this day when chaplains of prisons and reformatories tell us that gaudy, flashy dressing leads as many young girls to destruction as drink, it behoves every true woman to settle before God in her closet what kind of dress she ought to wear, and to resolve to wear it in spite of fashion. If all professedly Christian ladies would do this, what a salvation this one reform alone would work in the world. You young people... resolve that you will be original natural human beings, as God would have you; resolve that you won't be squeezed into this mould, or into that, to please anybody – that you will be an independent man or woman, educated and refined by intercourse with God; but be yourself, and do not aim to be anybody else.

Set fashion at nought. If people would do this, what different households they would have! What different children! What different friends! What different results they would produce in the world, and how differently they would feel when they were dying! Oh, what wasted lives! What beautiful forms, and beautiful minds, and beautiful intellects are prostrated and ruined at the shrine of the god of fashion! May God deliver us from this idol![1]

> Maybe, Lord, this isn't so much about actual clothes or fabrics,
> as about attitude. Clothe my attitude with Christ-likeness, I pray. Amen.

---

1 From *Popular Christianity*.

His talk is smooth as butter, yet war is in his heart
(Psalm 55:21 *NIV*)

Our critics state that this book [*Orders and Regulations*] teaches dissimulation. I challenge them to prove it from the text itself. The dissimulation is imported from their own suspicious brains and hearts. If this were true, how is it that they have been so long in finding it out? For this book has been in the hands of the editors of many religious journals for years, and read and *recommended* by some of the highest dignitaries of the Church… It is wonderful that anybody can be persuaded to believe that we intend to teach men to deceive, and at the same time *sell the book with these instructions to all comers for 2d.*[1] It is *too* ridiculous, and yet it seems that nothing is too ridiculous to get up a chase against The Salvation Army.

I will just refer to… paragraphs of this book which have been taken greatest exception to… "But the only information we can rely on is that which you get by the use of your own eyes. An officer on this duty has no business with bashfulness or propriety. He should never wait to know whether he might go here or there. If a theatre door be open, walk in and inspect every part of the building until somebody objects. The remark that you want to see the manager, and that you are a perfect stranger groping your way, will generally satisfy everybody, and will prevent officials from treating you with disrespect. You can afford any quantity of apologies after you have got the information you wanted. But if you go in an humble, timid way, people will take advantage of you continually."[2]

> Lord, help me to only ever contend for the truth. Teach me to choose
> my battles carefully so that my energies are not wasted. Amen.

Cont/…

---

1   From denarius. Equivalent to roughly 1p in today's currency.
2   From *The Salvation Army in Relation to the Church and State.*

BE AS SHREWD AS SNAKES AND AS INNOCENT AS DOVES
(Matthew 10:16 *NIV*)

Cont /…

It has to be assumed, in order to import duplicity here, that the officer is *not* a stranger, and that he does *not* want to see the manager; whereas he *is* a stranger, and his visit to the town would be useless unless he did *see the manager*. We all know that theatres are public buildings; and if anybody wants to hire one, of course they need first to see it, and it would be useless for a man to go in [a] frightened timid way. As one of our friends said, "This is only what we do in business every day"; nobody thinks of pinning his heart on his sleeve when engaged for his own interests, why should we in the Lord's? The next passage is as follows:

"Ministers will, for politeness and decency sake, assure you that they take the deepest interest in your blessed work – which perhaps they do, provided it keeps at a distance from them. But if, thrown off your guard by this, you inform them of your plans, they may either mislead you by advising against the buildings where you would best succeed, or even may go so far as to persuade people to refuse the use of the places you most need."

Our critics say this teaches suspicion and disrespect to ministers and Christians. I reply, we are heartily sorry that such instruction should be a *necessity*; but I throw back the blame of it on to those who have made it one! I could give some illustrations… In Glasgow, our people were negotiating for a church which was to be let, when a leading man in evangelistic work went and offered £20 per year more, in order to keep us out! In another case we tried for a chapel which nobody else could fill, and were refused, the parties preferring to keep it empty rather than let us fill it with the perishing masses![1]

Lord, guide those who negotiate and deal in matters of church property
and finance. Bless what can sometimes be an unsung ministry. Amen.

1   From *The Salvation Army in Relation to the Church and State.*

SATAN HAS ASKED TO SIFT ALL OF YOU AS WHEAT
(Luke 22:31 *NIV*)

Get on with all your might, but don't do more than you can. Send a few texts to me that you want sermons on, and I will suggest some divisions, not in the form you need use them, but so that you can adapt them. I should have said, just at first sight, on that text you name:

I. Satan desires to have all men, but specially the Lord's servants. II. *Why* he desires them – 1st. Because he hates God, and desires to circumvent his purposes in men. (Here is a capital field.) III. *How* he tries to destroy them. By "sifting" them. This means by searching, fierce temptation. Thus he tried to conquer their great Captain... (Refer to the temptation in the wilderness.)[1] He knew that if Jesus would only yield, as Adam had done, then all would be lost. He knew that on *his obedience* depended his power to redeem us, so he pressed him hard – he "sifted" him. Thus he tempts us. He knows that on our obedience hangs all, etc. IV. This subject shows the tremendous importance of *watching*. Watch, etc. Resist, etc. 1st. Because Satan never tires or sleeps, always desiring to have us. 2nd. Because he is very wise and clever, and knows how to set a trap for our feet. Remark on his subtlety with Eve, with Jesus, etc. 3rd. Because he is very powerful. He is the god of evil, legions, etc. 4th. Because, alas! he so often succeeds. Get out at backsliders, and on the numbers who have fallen from God, etc.[2, 3]

Lord, I pray for all those who are finding their way as preachers.
Bless their study. Bless their efforts. Use them for the spread of the gospel.
Likewise, I pray for those who are being "sifted" today;
whose faith is being sorely tried. Help them. Amen.

1 Matthew 4:1–11.
2 From an outline of an address Mrs Booth sent to one of her sons in 1877 or 1878. It is not clear which son received this advice, but the Booth children were encouraged to preach.
3 From *Catherine Booth The Mother of The Salvation Army, Vol. II.*

SET YOUR MINDS ON THINGS ABOVE, NOT ON EARTHLY THINGS
(Colossians 3:2 *NIV*)

I hope, my dear boy, that, whatever sense of obligation or gratitude you have towards me, you will try to return it by resolutely resisting all temptation to evil, and by fitting yourself to your utmost to be useful to your fellow men. I ask from you, as I asked from God, no other reward. If I know my own heart, I would rather that you should work for the salvation of souls, making bad hearts good, and miserable homes happy, and preparing joy and gladness for men at the judgment bar, if you only get bread and cheese all your life, than that you should fill any other capacity with £10,000 per year. I believe in *eternal* distinction. "They that turn many to righteousness shall shine as the stars for ever and ever."[1] Not that I would have you do it for the reward, but for the pure love of him who died for you and them; still, it is not wrong to "have respect to the recompense of the reward",[2] and now that almost everybody is pulling and striving for the world's rewards and prizes, it is meet that the real children of the great King should sometimes think of *their* reward. Paul did this, though it was the love of Christ alone which constrained him to labour. "There is laid up for me a crown of righteousness, which the Lord, the righteous judge, shall give me at that day".[3] Happy they who whose ambition aims not below the skies; they will never be disappointed!

I hope you are getting on in your studies, and not allowing them to draw you from God. There is no illuminator like the Holy Ghost. He is promised on purpose to lead us into all truth, consequently to guard us from error.[4] Seek his light on all you read, and his help in all you do, and your progress will be real and rapid.[5, 6]

Thank you, Lord, for praying mothers who take an interest in the
spiritual welfare of their children. Answer their prayers. Amen.

---

1 See Daniel 12:3 KJV.
2 See Hebrews 11:26, KJV.
3 2 Timothy 4:8, KJV.
4 John 16:13.
5 Mrs Booth, writing to one of her sons on the subject of Christian ministry, 1877–78.
6 From *Catherine Booth The Mother of The Salvation Army, Vol. II.*

BOYS AND GIRLS PLAYING

(Zechariah 8:5 *NIV*)

At my meeting last Sunday we had the chapel packed, while hundreds went away unable to get in. I enjoyed fair liberty, and have heard since that the people were very much pleased, and I trust profited. I have held morning meetings through the week. They have been well attended and much blessed. This morning there was a very gracious influence. I am to speak again next Sunday afternoon…

Bless the Lord, oh my soul! How wonderful is his mercy and how marvellous are his works![1]

With all these things to do, together with morning meetings one day, children's meetings another, and the services at night, you will see we have enough on hand. I was never so busy in my life. I have to help Mary[2] with the children, in dressing them and undressing them to go out twice a day, and in washing them and putting them to bed at night. Willie[3] goes with me to the children's meetings and likes them very much. He sadly wants to write to you, but I have not had time to superintend him, and it is such lovely weather that they are out most of the time. They go off directly after breakfast and stop till eleven o'clock on the sands, and then again from two till five. They each have a spade with which they dig tunnels, mountains, brooks, etc. They never had such fun in their lives before. You would be delighted to see them running away from the waves, and then back again to their rivers, which the retreating wave has filled with water![4, 5]

Father, this letter serves as a lovely reminder of the importance of work, rest and play. Speak to those, Lord, whose hearts have forgotten play. Amen.

---

1 See Psalm 103.
2 Marian Booth (1864–1937), third daughter of William and Catherine. Also known as Marie or Mary.
3 William Bramwell (1856–1929).
4 Catherine Booth writing to her mother, Mrs Mumford, from the 1861 Cornish Campaign. This extract was written from St Ives, a small Cornish town.
5 From *Catherine Booth* by F. de L. Booth-Tucker.

Have a good reputation with outsiders
(1 Timothy 3:7 *NIV*)

I remember feeling condemned, when quite a child, not more than eight years old, at having to wear a lace tippet[1] such as was fashionable in those days. From a worldly point of view it would have been considered, no doubt, very neat and consistent. But on several occasions I had good crying fits over it. Not only did I instinctively feel it to be immodest, because people could see through it, but I thought it was not such as a Christian child should wear. As I advanced in my religious experience, I became more and more convinced that my appearance ought to be such as to show everybody with whom I came into contact that I belonged to Christ. Had the church to which I belonged worn a uniform, I should joyfully have adopted it.[2] I always felt it was *mean* to be ashamed of Christ in the street or among his enemies. And it was only in conformity to the opinions of those whom I regarded as my superiors in wisdom and grace that I conformed to the world as much as I did in the matter of dress. People have asked me, sometimes, whether we cannot be separate from the world in our *hearts* without being different in our dress. My reply has been, "What is the use to the world of a testimony for Christ up in your bedroom? The very *essence* of witnessing for God before the world is that we should not be like it." The *people* quite recognize this, whether *Christians* do or not. Hence their contempt for those who talk to them about religion while dressed as fashionably as themselves. They may listen out of politeness, but they will say in their hearts, and often, when our backs are turned, with their lips, "'Physician, heal thyself'![3] Why does she come and talk to me about giving up the world when she has not done so herself; at any rate, as far as dress is concerned?"[4, 5]

As in all things, Lord, consistency is often the key.
Help my witness to be consistent. Amen.

---

1   A shoulder covering; something like a delicate scarf or small cape.
2   Written while Catherine was involved in Methodist ministry, but hinting quite delightfully at a future that was as yet unknown to her, when her subsequent involvement with The Salvation Army would require the wearing of uniform almost every day.
3   Luke 4:23, KJV.
4   Catherine Booth was reflecting on the importance of a mother's influence in all things.
5   From *Catherine Booth The Mother of The Salvation Army, Vol. I.*

Behold, we are your bone and flesh
(2 Samuel 5:1 *ESV*)

My dearest Willie, I promised to write you a letter all to yourself, and so the first thing I do this morning shall be to write it… I do hope you are praying to the Lord every day to help you, and are trying to do as Grandmama and Mary tell you. If you are, I know this letter will find you happy and joyous, because when little children are *good* they are always *happy*. But I never knew a naughty child to be happy in my life, and I daresay Grandmama never did. Just ask her if she ever did. I often wish you were here with us. It is a beautiful place; such nice fields and lanes, where you could run about and play and romp and sing and shout, without troubling anybody, and such nice places to fly kites without trees about to catch them… Try every day to do exactly as you are bid and then you will get to do it quickly and easily… I fear you begin to think it is a long time before Papa comes to fetch you… You see, my dear boy, your Papa and I came down here to do the Lord's work, and although we have worked very hard we have not got it all done yet… so our dear little ones have to wait a long time. But, oh, what a good thing it is that you have a kind Grandma to take care of you and find you a home! The Lord does not let you want for any good thing. He sends you plenty of food to eat and nice clean clothes to put on, and a nice bed to sleep in, just the same as though you were with me. Do you ever think about this and thank him for all his kindness? I hope you do, and that you try to please him by being a very good boy… When you get here, Papa and I will take you with us to the cliffs and show you the great and beautiful sea.[1, 2]

> Lord, the "calling" to be the child of a minister is sometimes
> an unwanted blessing! I pray for children who are separated from their
> parents because of their parents' ministry. Bless all such families. Amen.

---

1   Written from Cornwall, where the Booths engaged in independent evangelistic work after leaving the Methodist New Connexion.
2   From *Catherine Booth* by Catherine Bramwell-Booth.

You will keep in perfect peace those whose minds are steadfast, because they trust in you

(Isaiah 26:3 *NIV*)

That word was spoken to my soul: "Behold, I stand at the door and knock. If any man hear my voice, and open unto me, I will come in and sup with him."[1] I felt sure he had long been knocking and, oh, how I yearned to receive him as a perfect Saviour! But, oh, the inveterate habit of unbelief! How wonderful that God should have borne so long with me!...

William said, "Don't you lay all on the altar?" I replied, "I am sure I do!" Then he said, "And isn't the altar holy?" I replied in the language of the Holy Ghost, "The altar is most holy, and whatsoever toucheth it is holy."[2] Then said he, "Are you not holy?" I replied with my heart full of emotion and with some faith, "Oh, I think I am." Immediately the word was given me to confirm my faith, "Now ye are clean through the word which I have spoken unto you."[3] And I took hold – true, with a trembling hand, and not unmolested by the tempter, but I held fast the beginning of my confidence, and it grew stronger; and from that moment I have dared to reckon myself dead indeed unto sin, and alive unto God through Jesus Christ, my Lord. I did not feel much rapturous joy, but perfect peace, the sweet rest which Jesus promised to the heavy-laden. I have understood the Apostle's meaning when he says, "We who believe do enter into rest."[4] This is just descriptive of my state at present. Not that I am not tempted, but I am allowed to know the Devil when he approaches me, and I look to my Deliverer, Jesus, and he still gives me rest.[5, 6]

> Lord, you once mentioned a peace that is unique to you; that the world cannot offer. I claim that peace today for those who are troubled, worried, or anxious.
> Amen.

1   See Revelation 3:20, KJV.
2   See Exodus 29:37, KJV.
3   John 15:3, KJV.
4   See Hebrews 4:3, KJV.
5   From *Catherine Booth The Mother of The Salvation Army, Vol. I*.
6   From a letter Catherine Booth wrote to her mother, possibly 1861.

THE KING'S HEART IS IN THE HAND OF THE LORD, AS THE RIVERS OF WATER: HE TURNETH IT WHITHERSOEVER HE WILL

(Proverbs 21:1 *KJV*)

Knowing how ill I have been, you will be surprised to hear of my Sunday effort. Well, I certainly did transgress as to time, and have had to pay the price since. But I am not much the worse for it now, and I hope many will be better for it to all eternity. It was a glorious congregation. I never saw a more imposing sight. I had liberty, and it was a very solemn and, I trust, a profitable time. Mr Hobson,[1] although I did not know it till afterwards, was present, his second preacher opening the service for me. The presence of the latter did not embarrass me the least. I am wonderfully delivered from all fear, after I once get my mouth open.

When I came down from the platform, Mr Hobson received me most kindly, took my hand in both of his like a father, and told me he should often be coming to see us now. Does it not seem wonderful how the rough places are made smooth and the crooked places straight before us? This is the chairman who sent word to Hayle,[2] in answer to the enquiries of the Superintendent there as to whether I might go into their chapel at the wish of their people, that it was contrary to their rules and usages!

Well, the Lord rules and overrules both men and rules, and I trust this is of his doing. At any rate, it enables my dear husband to get *at* the people, which was partially impossible in the small chapels, besides almost killing him with the heat and crush. You see, the Wesleyans have nearly all the large chapels.[3, 4]

Lord, our plans must sometimes make you smile!
Yet, you guide our lives with a gracious, patient touch. Your love steers well!
I pray today for those whose plans seem to have gone astray. Amen.

---

1   President of the Penzance Methodist Circuit. Penzance is a port town in Cornwall.
2   A small town and cargo port in Cornwall.
3   Catherine Booth reflecting on the Cornish Campaign of 1862.
4   From *Catherine Booth* by F. de L. Booth-Tucker.

May you experience the love of Christ, though it is too great to understand fully

(Ephesians 3:19 *NLT*)

I believe John to be one of the best of men, but he holds Plymouth Brethren[1] views for all that, on some points. His theology does not hang together. He has been a good deal at Mr – 's, and got many of his practical views from him, but they do not fit well with his former ones.

However, I believe he is right at heart. It is only in judgment he errs. It may be that he holds "Jesus only" in a right sense; but I object to the phrase as unscriptural and new-fangled, representing a highly dangerous theology.[2] It is a perversion of Scripture, being a phrase out of the middle of a narrative, not intended to teach what is tacked on to it. With this exception it does not occur in the New Testament.[3]

In all that concerns us and our salvation, the Father and the Spirit are equal with the Son in love, labour, and honour.[4] He came on purpose to reveal us to the Father, and he and the Father are one; how then can it be "Jesus only"? We must stick to the form of sound words, for there is more in it than appears on the surface. "Glory be to the Father, and to the Son, and to the Holy Ghost"[5] was the theology of our forefathers, and I am suspicious of all attempts to mend it.[6,7]

> The Trinity is a beautiful mystery. You, God, are a beautiful mystery. Help me to be satisfied with a love which I may accept and embrace, but not comprehend.
>
> Amen.

---

1   A conservative, low church, nonconformist, evangelical Christian movement originating in the 1820s.
2   Non-Trinitarian theology.
3   Possibly a reference to 1 Timothy 2:5 or Matthew 17:8.
4   The third doctrine of The Salvation Army states: "We believe that there are three persons in the Godhead – the Father, the Son and the Holy Ghost, undivided in essence and co-equal in power and glory."
5   Traditional Trinitarian theology.
6   From a letter to a friend discussing Plymouth Brethrenism.
7   From *Catherine Booth The Mother of The Salvation Army, Vol. II.*

I APPEAL TO YOU, BROTHERS AND SISTERS, IN THE NAME OF OUR LORD
JESUS CHRIST, THAT ALL OF YOU AGREE WITH ONE ANOTHER IN WHAT YOU
SAY AND THAT THERE BE NO DIVISIONS AMONG YOU, BUT THAT YOU BE
PERFECTLY UNITED IN MIND AND THOUGHT

(1 Corinthians 1:10 *NIV*)

They [some objectors to Catherine Booth's theological teaching] say, "Oh, you must not set up human reason", which means, "you must not exercise *common sense*". I heard one of them say that common sense was the greatest evil of the day! It seems to me that common sense is the great desideratum. Another told me that the Bible was not a logical book! I always thought it the highest standard of logic, and reason too, if only we could comprehend it. "God is light, and in him there is no darkness at all."[1] Therefore, he cannot contradict himself. Contradiction must involve error; God cannot err; therefore, he cannot contradict himself. When we come into the light of eternity, or the full light of God, we shall see that there is not a single inconsistent statement in the whole Bible, rightly rendered... Let us beware of wrong doctrine, come through whomsoever it may. Holy men make sad mistakes. "Well, but," say some, "is not a person who holds wrong views with a right heart better than a person with right views with a wrong heart?" Yes, but not so far as his personal state before God is concerned, but *not in his influence on man*. This was the argument put forth some time ago in favour of ministers holding public fellowship with those who believe in auricular confession and other Popish errors; specious, but false. A man may be sincere in lashing his back and consigning his daughter to a nunnery, and may himself have the love of God; but I must not on that account receive or lightly esteem his errors, because of their fearful consequences on others. My charity must extend to those likely to be deceived and ruined by his doctrines as well as him. So of all false doctrine. We must try the spirits, for "if the foundations be destroyed, what shall the righteous do?"[2, 3]

Lord, we, your people, disagree on any number of points! At least, as we
engage in dialogue, let us do so lovingly, learning from one another. Amen.

1   See 1 John 1:5, KJV.
2   See Psalm 11:3, KJV.
3   From *Catherine Booth The Mother of The Salvation Army, Vol. II.*

THESE ARE THE ONES I LOOK ON WITH FAVOUR: THOSE WHO ARE HUMBLE AND CONTRITE IN SPIRIT, AND WHO TREMBLE AT MY WORD

(Isaiah 66:2 *NIV*)

The world is dying. Do you believe it? You are called by the wants of the world. Begin nearest home if you like, by all means; I have little faith in those people's ministrations who go abroad after others, while their own are perishing at their firesides. Begin at home, but do not end there. "Oh! yes," people say, "begin at home", but they end there; you never hear of them anywhere else, and it comes to very little what they do at home, after all. God has ordained that the two shall go together.[1] Get them saved by all means, but get somebody else saved as well. Set yourself to work for God. Go to him to ask him how to do it. Go to him for the equipment of power and then begin. Never mind how you tremble. I dare say your trembling will do more good than if you were ever so brave. Never mind the tears. I wish Christians would weep the gospel into people; it would often go deeper than it does. Never mind if you do stammer. They will believe you when it comes from the heart. They will say, "He talked to me quite natural," as a man said, some time ago – wondering that he should be talked to about religion in a natural way; but mind, no mock feeling, for they will detect it in a minute. Go to the closet until you get filled with the Spirit,[2] and then go and let it out upon them… Look them in the face and take hold of them lovingly by the hand and say, "My friend, you are dying, you are going to everlasting death. If nobody has ever told you till now – I have come to tell you. My friend, you have a precious soul. Is it saved?" They can understand that![3]

> Take my trembling hand, Lord, and my trembling voice, and if you can use
> me to lead some to Christ, then please do. It has to be your work. Amen.

---

1   Luke 10:1.
2   Matthew 6:6.
3   From *Aggressive Christianity*.

JESUS TOLD THEM, "YOU ARE GOING TO HAVE THE LIGHT
JUST A LITTLE WHILE LONGER. WALK WHILE YOU HAVE THE LIGHT,
BEFORE DARKNESS OVERTAKES YOU"

(John 12:35 *NIV*)

Supposing I had held back and been disobedient to the heavenly vision, what would God have said to me for the loss of all this fruit? Thank God much of it is gathered in Heaven. People have sent me word from their dying beds, that they blessed God they had ever heard my voice, saying they should wait for me on the other side, prepared to lead me to the throne... They would never have become *my* crown of rejoicing in the day of the Lord.

Oh, who can tell what God can do by any man or woman, however timid, however faint, if only fully given up to him. He holds you responsible, my sister – you, who wrote me about your difficulties and temptations in testifying of Jesus – he holds you responsible. What are you going to do? Ask yourself. It is coming. You believe it. You say you do. Unless you are a confirmed hypocrite, you do – that you are going to stand before the throne of his glory. You believe you are going to stand before him by-and-by, when you shall receive according to the things you have done in your body.

The world is dying – souls are being damned at an awful rate every day. Men are running to destruction. Torrents of iniquity are rolling down our streets and through our world. God is almost tired of the cry of our sins and iniquities going up into his ears. What are you going to do, brother? What are you going to do? Will you set to work?[1]

While the light lingers, Lord...

---

[1] From *The Holy Ghost.*

December 4th

I WILL SURELY BLESS YOU AND MAKE YOUR DESCENDANTS AS NUMEROUS
AS THE STARS IN THE SKY AND AS THE SAND ON THE SEASHORE
(Genesis 22:17 *NIV*)

We had a letter... about a gentleman who had been re-converted in the services of The Salvation Army, telling us he had relinquished an income of £800 a year, in order to keep a conscience void of offence – this is the result of the power of the Holy Ghost. I heard of another gentleman invited to a party. After dinner the card table was got out, as usual, and when the cards were all spread and everybody was ready to begin, the gentleman jumped up and pushed it away, and said, "I have done with this for ever."

The lady who told me said, "He was down on his knees before we had time to turn around, and was praying for us and all the house. Oh!" she added, "You should have seen them."

Yes, of course, every man felt like the people round the Saviour. Every man's own conscience condemned him. "They went off home, without any more card-playing, or dancing, or wine-drinking that night."

Come out from amongst the ungodly. Testify against them. Reprove them, entreat them with your tears; but be determined to deliver your soul of their blood. God will give you the power, and he holds you responsible for doing this... you have received the light. Will you do it? If you will, we shall meet again, and rejoice with joy unspeakable. If you do, we shall praise God for ever... There shall be children and grandchildren and great-grandchildren from you spiritually, if you will only be faithful.[1]

I like the idea of being a spiritual grandparent, Lord!

---

1   From *The Holy Ghost.*

FOR THE LAW, SINCE IT HAS ONLY A SHADOW OF THE
GOOD THINGS TO COME AND NOT THE VERY FORM OF THINGS,
CAN NEVER, BY THE SAME SACRIFICES WHICH THEY OFFER
CONTINUALLY YEAR BY YEAR, MAKE PERFECT THOSE WHO DRAW NEAR.
OTHERWISE, WOULD THEY NOT HAVE CEASED TO BE OFFERED,
BECAUSE THE WORSHIPPERS, HAVING ONCE BEEN CLEANSED, WOULD NO
LONGER HAVE HAD CONSCIOUSNESS OF SINS? BUT IN THOSE SACRIFICES
THERE IS A REMINDER OF SINS YEAR BY YEAR. FOR IT IS IMPOSSIBLE
FOR THE BLOOD OF BULLS AND GOATS TO TAKE AWAY SINS

(Hebrews 10:1–4 *NASB*)

He [Christ] has undertaken the mediatorial work to bring us back to God. Yes, but the mediatorial work was twofold; it was Godward, and it was manward. Christ, as it were, put one hand on the justice of God, and the other on the sinfulness of man, and he undertook to satisfy the one by removing the other. He made atonement, glorious, full, complete, wanting nothing to be added to it – a perfect everlasting sacrifice for our sins, but it was restorative as well as atoning. The manward aspect of the atonement was to bring us back to complete and eternal harmony with God. He never contemplated leaving our hearts a cage of unclean birds – leaving rampant in us the essence of sin, the very sin of the Devil himself – rebellion against God. Impossible! He came to restore as well as to atone; to bring us back to our lost integrity and purity, and this was what made the atonement necessary. Hence, "The Son of Man was manifested, that he might destroy the works of the devil."[1] "If," says Paul, "the blood of bulls and goats sanctifieth to the purifying of the flesh: How much more shall the blood of Christ, who through his eternal Spirit offered himself without spot to God, purge your conscience from dead works to serve the living God?"[2] How much more? Who can answer that, and who dare limit it? Again "Christ loved the church – composed, of course, of individuals – and gave himself for it; That he might sanctify and cleanse it – and present it to himself a glorious church – or body of believers – not having spot, or wrinkle, or any such thing; but that it should be holy and without blemish."[3, 4]

Lord, you are indeed the God of "how much more"!

1   See 1 John 3:8, KJV.
2   From Hebrews 9, KJV.
3   See Ephesians 5:25–27, KJV.
4   From *Holiness*.

ELIJAH CAME UNTO ALL THE PEOPLE, AND SAID,
HOW LONG HALT YE BETWEEN TWO OPINIONS? IF THE LORD
BE GOD, FOLLOW HIM: BUT IF BAAL, THEN FOLLOW HIM

(1 Kings 18:21 *KJV*)

You are called on to decide between the claims of God as established and put forth in the death of his Son, and the service of the world, the flesh, and the Devil, which is your Baal. And as Elijah came and demanded of these people to whom he had previously ministered and whose prophet he was, so I come and demand in the name of the Lord God of Elijah from you who have received my messages... whom the Spirit of God has made to look at them and ponder them – *I demand a settlement of this controversy.*

Now, "How long halt ye?"

Mind, I am not speaking figuratively – God forbid. If I did not believe that I have as truly brought God's message... as Elijah did to the Jews, I should never have stood here. I fear – nay, I expect – that the salvation of some souls depends on the way they decide with respect to the message... Oh, may God the Spirit help you to decide the right way!...

I want you to note... that there is a sense in which we never *halt* – never stand still. In fact, there is a sense in which nothing stands still. But this is specially true of the world of mind and spirit. Once launched into being, sinner, you never stand still. You must increase, grow bigger in the capacity and enjoyment of good, or in the capacity for and realization of evil for ever and ever. It is a beautiful thought to the righteous that, once launched on the wave of everlasting progress, we shall stand still no more, but go on growing, and growing, and growing... in our capacity for holiness and bliss for ever.[1]

Lord, today my prayers are with the halters and waverers; the undecided.
In your mercy, prompt them to choose to grow in righteousness. Amen.

1   From *Life and Death.*

WHEN YOU COME TOGETHER, EACH OF YOU HAS A HYMN, OR A WORD
OF INSTRUCTION, A REVELATION, A TONGUE OR AN INTERPRETATION.
EVERYTHING MUST BE DONE SO THAT THE CHURCH MAY BE BUILT UP

(1 Corinthians 14:26 *NIV*)

People contend that we must have quiet, proper, decorous services.[1] Where is your authority for this? Not here. I defy any man to show it. I have a great deal more authority in [the Bible] for such a lively, gushing, spontaneous, and what you call disorderly service, as the Army services sometimes are, in [the] 14th of Corinthians,[2] than you can find for yours.

The best insight we get into the internal working of a religious service in Apostolic times is in this chapter, and I ask you – is it anything like the ordinary services of today? Can the utmost stretch of ingenuity make it into anything like them?

But that, even, is not complete. We cannot get the order of a single service from the New Testament, nor can we get the form of a single Church government. Hence, one denomination think theirs is the best form, and another theirs; so that Christendom has been divided into so many camps ever since; but this very quarrelling shows the impossibility of getting from the New Testament the routine, the order, and the fashion of mere modes. They cannot get it, because it is not there!!

The form, modes, and measures are not laid down as in Old Testament dispensation. There is nothing of this stereotyped routinism in the New Testament.[3]

Lord of the Church, I pray for those who have the sometimes unenviable
task of leading worship in churches, and planning services! The struggle to
choose hymns and styles to please everyone is not always productive! Amen.

1　Salvation Army services (meetings) attracted criticism from other denominations, who regarded them as rowdy, undignified, and improper.
2　1 Corinthians.
3　From *Aggressive Christianity*.

December 8th

Follow the way of love and eagerly desire gifts of the Spirit
(1 Corinthians 14:1 *NIV*)

I said to a gentleman, who came to me with this and that difficulty about our [The Salvation Army's] modes and measures. "I will meet your difficulties by bringing them face to face with the bare principles of the New Testament. If I cannot substantiate and defend them by that, I will give them up for ever. I am not wedded to any forms and measures. To many of them I have been driven by the necessities of the case. God has driven me to them as at the point of the bayonet, as well as led me by pillar of cloud, and when I have brought my reluctance and all my own conventional notions, in which I was brought up like other people, face to face with the naked bare principles of the New Testament, I have not found anything to stand upon! I find things here far more extravagant and extreme than anything we [Salvationists] do – looked at carefully."

Here is the principle laid down that you are to adapt your measures to the necessity of the people to whom you minister; you are to take the gospel to them in such modes and habitudes of thought and expression and circumstances as will gain for it from them a hearing. You are to speak in other tongues – go and preach it to them in such a way as they will look at it and listen to it! Oh! In that lesson we read what beautiful scope and freedom from all set forms and formula there was. What freedom for the gushing freshness, enthusiasm, and love of those new converts! What scope for the different manifestations of the same Spirit! Everything was not cut and dried. Everything was not prearranged. It was left to the operation of the Spirit, and the argument that this has been abused is no argument against it, for then you might argue against every privilege.[1]

> Lord, I am challenged and encouraged by Catherine Booth's solid
> confidence in the New Testament! Should I need to read it differently, then
> refresh my eyes, I pray. Show me glimpses of that original fire. Amen.

---

1   From *Aggressive Christianity*.

THE PEOPLE OF ISRAEL WERE CELEBRATING BEFORE THE LORD,
SINGING SONGS AND PLAYING ALL KINDS OF MUSICAL INSTRUMENTS

(2 Samuel 6:5 NLT)

I did not expect to see your faces any more. It is very kind of you to come and play to me. I only wish I were stronger, that I might say more of what is in my heart; but I rejoice in one or two points expressed in your letter very much; in one especially: and that is, that you see the importance of keeping your music *spiritual*, and of using it only for the one great end.

We had a great deal of argument regarding the first introduction of bands into the Army, and a great many fears. I had always considered music as belonging to God. Perhaps some of you have heard me say in public that there will not be a note of music in Hell; that it will all be in Heaven, and that God ought to have it all here. But, unfortunately, God has not his rights here, and the Church has strangely lost sight of the value of music as a religious agency.

I think God has used the Army to resuscitate and awaken that agency, and while the bandsmen[1] of The Salvation Army realize it to be as much their service to blow an instrument as it is to sing or to pray or to speak, and while they do one in the same spirit as they would do the other, I am persuaded it will become an ever-increasing power amongst us. But the moment you, or any other bandsmen, begin to glory in the excellency of your music alone, apart from spiritual results, you will begin at once to lose your power. It is the same with everything else – meetings, testifying, singing, marching, or praying. It is a combination of the human and the divine. And when you separate the human from the divine it ceases to have any power over souls. Don't forget that.[2, 3]

Lord, may Christian music-making only ever be to your glory; a means to
an end, that is, as music that glorifies you and brings many to the cross. Amen.

---

1   Salvation Army bands originally admitted only men.
2   On 30 January 1889, a Salvation Army band visited Catherine Booth as she lay dying. The bandmaster, a converted drunkard, handed Mrs Booth a letter in which he told her of his determination to serve God by playing his instrument.
3   From *Catherine Booth The Mother of The Salvation Army, Vol. II.*

The effectual fervent prayer of a righteous man availeth much
(James 5:16 *KJV*)

I wish you could have seen my congregation yesterday – 1,300 – about 300 of them Lancashire roughs, and they *are* rough. That sort will throw a little woman down the steps and kick her with their clogs![1] Awful! Hundreds are unable to get in – almost a riot at the doors, and no police allowed to come inside; and though one was promised outside he did not come. Oh, the blindness of our rulers![2]...

The man where I stayed said as we went home, "I am fairly astonished at the behaviour of the roughs, seeing that most of them had been Sunday scholars." So much for teaching *the letter without the spirit!*[3]

This is the hardest county we have touched yet. As I looked upon their hard and careworn faces I thought I discovered the reason. Set to work at the cotton mills as soon as they can well walk, and often kept at it fourteen hours a day by wicked, inhuman parents and employers![4] Poor things! God will judge them according to their *disadvantages*. Oh, if they only realized what a new life we would bring to them, and what joy and hopes to illumine their sunless horizon! But, alas! as of old, "they know not what they do".[5] Pray, dear, for Lancashire. Your prayers now shall avail much.[6, 7]

> For those trapped in the awful routine of hard labour, Lord, and for those
> who cruelly and selfishly inflict long hours and low wages, I pray today. Amen.

1 Strong, cheap footwear commonly worn by industrial workers who couldn't afford leather shoes. Clogs were made of wood.
2 Police protection for Salvationists was often half-hearted or only nominal, even in the face of violent opposition.
3 From 2 Corinthians 3:6.
4 Lancashire was famous for its profusion of cotton mills. Children were legally employed in the mills from the age of seven.
5 Luke 23:34, KJV.
6 From a letter written from Over Darwen, Lancashire, possibly 1879. Lancashire is a county in the north-west of England. It was at the heart of the English industrial revolution.
7 From *Catherine Booth The Mother of The Salvation Army, Vol. II.*

RELIGION THAT GOD OUR FATHER ACCEPTS AS PURE AND FAULTLESS IS
THIS: TO LOOK AFTER ORPHANS AND WIDOWS IN THEIR DISTRESS

(James 1:27 *NIV*)

I have said many times what I here deliberately repeat: that if I were dying, and leaving a family of helpless children, I would leave it as my last request that they might be divided – one here, and another there – amongst any poor but really godly families who would receive them, rather than they should be got into the most highly trumpeted orphanage with which I am acquainted; for I should infinitely prefer that their bodies should lack necessary food and attention, rather than that their poor little hearts and souls should be crushed and famished for want of love, both human and divine.[1]

Children brought up without love are like plants brought up without the sun. How blessed a way would it be of serving God and your generation, by taking some such children yourselves and bringing them up with all the love and care with which you bring up your own, or would have done so had God granted you the privilege![2]

It will be a happy day for England when Christian ladies transfer their sympathies from poodles and terriers to destitute and starving children![3, 4]

It is hard to deny, Father, that orphaned children occupy a special
place in your heart. I pray for children who are adopted or who are cared
for in children's homes. Warm their lives with your father-love.
Bless those who reach out with the ministry of adoption. Amen.

1   In Victorian times, children were regarded as orphans if their mother had died, even if their father were still alive. It is estimated that around 11 per cent of children had lost their mothers before the age of ten, largely due to appalling conditions of hygiene and sanitation. Children whose mothers were deceased were often abandoned by their families as financial liabilities. The fortunate ones were rescued by orphanages, where life was exceedingly grim, but nevertheless preferable to homelessness.
2   Catherine Booth was an outspoken advocate of the Christian's duty to adopt orphaned children.
3   Though an animal lover herself, Catherine Booth sometimes expressed her fury at the way in which domestic pets were fed and cared for better than children, regarding this as offensive and immoral.
4   From *Catherine Booth The Mother of The Salvation Army, Vol. I.*

December 12th

They shall walk and not faint
(Isaiah 40:31 *ESV*)

A false love shrinks from opposition. It cannot bear persecution. Here is one unfailing characteristic of it: *it is always on the winning side* – that is, apparently, down here; not what *will* be, ultimately, the winning side. When Truth sits enthroned, with a crown on her head, this false love is most vociferous in her support and devotion; but when her garments trail in the dust, and her followers are few, feeble, and poor, then Jesus Christ may look after himself. I sometimes think, respecting this hue and cry about the glory of God and the sanctity of religion, I would like to see some of these saints put into the common hall with Jesus again, amongst a band of ribald, mocking soldiers. I would like to see, then, their zeal for the glory of God, when it touched their own glory. They are wonderfully zealous when their glory and his glory go together; but when the mob is at his heels, crying, "Away with him! Crucify him!"[1] then he may look after his own glory, and they will take care of theirs.

True love sticks to the Lord Jesus in the mud, when he is fainting under his cross, as well as when the people are cutting down the boughs and crying, "Hosanna!"[2] I fear many people make the Lord Jesus a stalking horse on which to secure their ends. God grant us not to be of that number, for, if we are, he will topple us from the very gates of Heaven to the nethermost Hell. This false love cannot go to the dungeon – you never find it at the stake. How many would go to the dungeon? How many would stand by the truth with hooting, howling mobs at our heels, such as followed him on the way to the cross – such as stood round his cross and spat at him?[3, 4]

Lord, for the courage of martyrs, I praise you. For those who follow Jesus through prison and persecution, I pray your help. For myself, I ask the grace of faithfulness, that I may reflect their shining, mud-stained example. Amen.

1   See John 19:15, KJV.
2   John 12:13.
3   Matthew 26:67.
4   From *Catherine Booth* by F. de L. Booth-Tucker.

I PRAY THAT YOU MAY ENJOY GOOD HEALTH
(3 John 1:2 *NIV*)

I sent by this post a pamphlet on vaccination. Do read it, if only for the exhibition it gives of the prejudice of the "profession". It seems as though all advance in the right treatment of disease has to be, in the first instance, largely in spite of doctors, instead of their leading the way. As it was in the beginning it is now, in many respects. I should sooner pawn my watch to pay the fines, and my bed too, for the matter of that, than have any more children vaccinated. The monstrous system is as surely doomed as blood-letting was. This is one of the boons we shall get by waiting and enlightening. Who knows how much some of us have suffered through life owing to the "immortal Jenner"? "Let us fall into the hands of God, and not of man."[1,2]

There is nothing worse in this pamphlet than several cases I have come across personally. But these were the direct effects. It is the indirect I dread most. The latent seeds of all manner of diseases are doubtless sown in thousands of healthy children. It has only been the stupid treatment which has made smallpox so fatal. Mrs Smedley (of the Hydropathic Institute)[3] says in her last manual, that they have nursed numbers of cases, and never lost one. M was one of the worst cases. She was very delicate, had never been vaccinated, and was in her seventh year, which is supposed to be the most fatal time. Yet she recovered, and has been much better in her general health since. I do hope you will succeed in converting the parents.[4,5]

Father of health, guide those whose speciality is research,
especially when they study in the face of criticism or misunderstanding. Amen.

1   Vaccination is regarded as a major achievement in the field of public health, yet opposition was and is common. Critics opposed the smallpox vaccine in England and the United States in the 19th century, resulting in the formation of anti-vaccination leagues. Dr Edward Jenner (1749–1823) showed that he could protect a child from smallpox if he infected him or her with lymph from a cowpox blister. Jenner's ideas attracted criticism and sanitary, religious, scientific, and political objections. To add insult to injury, Jenner was the son of a clergyman!
2   From 2 Samuel 24:14.
3   Caroline Anne Smedley, author of the *Ladies' Manual of Practical Hydropathy*. Catherine Booth was a proponent of hydropathic and spa treatments.
4   From a letter to Catherine Booth's friend, Mrs Billups. Mr and Mrs Billups, of Cardiff, Wales, were staunch friends of the Booths, supporting them through many trials and experiences. Catherine and Mrs Billups in particular established a lasting friendship.
5   From *Catherine Booth* by F. de L. Booth-Tucker.

Abide in me, and I in you
(John 15:4 *ESV*)

I said to a lady once, who was seeking… deliverance and who was struggling and wrestling, as I kneeled by her side, "Wait a minute. Suppose Jesus Christ were here in his flesh, as he once was. Suppose he was to come to your side now, and put his hand upon you and say, 'Hush! I know your desire; I see your heart; I know what you are longing after. You are longing to be delivered from everything that grieves me, upon which my poor eyes cannot look with allowance. You are wanting to be brought into full conformity with my will, and that is what I have come to do now. I have come to live with you. I am taking up my abode under this roof, and I will never leave your side. I will be with you by day and I will be with you by night. I will sit at the dinner table and at the tea table with you, and walk out with you, and go to bed with you. Don't be troubled. I will never leave you and forsake you.'[1] Do you think if he were to come and say that, you would be able to trust him?" "Oh! Yes." "You would not be afraid?" "Oh! No."

"Now, what would it be that would save you? Would it be the bodily presence of Jesus, which they laid in the sepulchre and which was as dead and helpless as any other clay when the spirit had gone out of it? *No.* It would be his spiritual presence, would it not? And his spiritual eyes seeing you, and his spiritual tongue speaking to you?" "Yes." "Well, then, this is just the presence that he has promised to be with every one of his people, and now he is here and able to do this, and will abide with you and enable you to abide in him if you will just trust him. Now, just trust him."[2]

Thank you, patient Lord, that you wait for us if we find it hard to trust,
even though that must surely grieve you. You are a God of patience.

---

1   See Hebrews 13:5.
2   From *Aggressive Christianity*.

GREAT ASSURANCE IN THEIR FAITH IN CHRIST JESUS
(1 Timothy 3:13 *NIV*)

Some people think we do not make enough of Christ. We make *all* of Christ; only it is a living Christ instead of a dead one. It is Christ in us as well as for us. We believe in Christ for us, and we should not have been here at all but for Christ for us up there for ever and ever, and no one will hasten to throw the crown at his feet readier than I shall; but we believe in order to do it we must have him in us. Christ in us as well as for us, and those whom he is not *in* he will not be *for*. If he dwell not in you, ye are reprobates. But Christ in us – an ever-loving, ever-present, Almighty Saviour, is just able to do what the angels said he should do, that for which he was called Jesus, to save his people from their sins.[1]

Then how does he do this? Wherein does he supersede the Law? Wherein does Christ do for me and is made to me what the Law could not do? We have seen what the Law could do and just how far it could go. Now we see it fails just at the vital point of power. Now, how does Christ become this power to me? How is he made unto me – not for me – up in Heaven (he is there, too), but how is he made unto me down here – wisdom, righteousness, sanctification, and redemption? How does he deliver the people from their sins? How does he save us from the power of sin?… . May the Holy Ghost teach us! He does this by… giving us *assurance of salvation*. He saves and then he makes us conscious of the fact, which the Law could not do… it could not give us assurance… I mean the personal realization of my acceptance in Christ; my acceptance by the Father; my present acceptance – I mean the inward assurance which men and women find for themselves, which they know as a matter of consciousness.[2]

> I am so grateful for that blessed assurance, which enables me to believe
> that Jesus is mine. Bless any who seek that assurance today, I pray.

---

1   Matthew 1:21.
2   From *Aggressive Christianity*.

THE FRUIT OF THE WOMB IS A REWARD

(Psalm 127:3 *NASB*)

I hope if I have not both sense and grace to train mine [her children] so that they shall not be a nuisance to everybody near them, that God will in mercy take them to Heaven in infancy, but I trust I shall have and I am learning a few useful lessons from *observation*.

Children brought up without love are like plants brought up without the sun.

Happiness is the condition of health.

Food should be ample to satisfy appetite, to consist chiefly of fresh vegetables, fruit, milk, eggs and cereals, no gormandizing on rich food.[1]

Fresh air day and night.

Clothes should be comfortable and warm enough in winter.

In sickness no strong drugs. Keep warm; little food but plenty to drink. Simple hydropathic applications.[2]

Punishment. Never threaten a child unless you intend to carry it out; never do so in anger; never in a state of irritation; never by exciting a child's fears.

Be careful to provide occupation. A child should never be made to look silly. *Occupation* should be considered an essential of happiness.

Courtesy and consideration for others, including all dumb creatures, must be instilled from the child's earliest years.[3, 4]

Not only in the home, Father, but in the Church too,
may children be loved. Bless those children who belong to the
church I attend, or who are linked in one way or another. Amen.

---

1 Catherine Booth had particular objections to the pampering and indulgence of the children of wealthy parents. She regarded this as detrimental not only to their physical health, but to their moral nature also.
2 Catherine Booth's interest in hydropathic applications is fascinating, given that this was in the days of purgings, blisterings and blood-letting.
3 From some of Catherine Booth's notes on raising children.
4 From *Catherine Booth* by Catherine Bramwell-Booth.

WHEN SANBALLAT THE HORONITE AND TOBIAH THE AMMONITE
OFFICIAL HEARD ABOUT IT, IT WAS VERY DISPLEASING TO THEM THAT
SOMEONE HAD COME TO SEEK THE WELFARE OF THE SONS OF ISRAEL

(Nehemiah 2:10 *NASB*)

We [The Salvation Army] have again and again been treated without any regard to the first principles of *honour*, to say nothing of religion, compelling us to practise the sagacity of the serpent, and sometimes to "write on the ground" when we had the power to speak; but we deny that any *sinful duplicity* [in the production of *Orders and Regulations*] was taught or intended. The next paragraph is as follows: "The C.O. must always remember that everything done should be impressive, especially at the commencement of an attack like this. A large company of soldiers will itself be impressive, no matter how the men conduct themselves. They can shout and laugh and display the most perfect freedom. But two or three will not be able to produce a deep impression without far more careful conduct. They must either make a very great show of energetic zeal, or else profound solemnity and intense conviction." "Now," say our critics, "here is dissimulation! Officers and men are to appear grave or joyous as best suits their purpose; but whatever appearance they bear is to be *put on* for the occasion." No, no; nothing is to be put on, but only to be let out. This direction is given to people whom we know to be possessed of both classes of feelings, as the disciples who praised God with a loud voice on their way with Jesus from the Mount of Olives, but who a little while afterwards were overwhelmed with consternation and grief. We simply say to these inexperienced people, "If you are in sufficient force to make a demonstration, you need not restrain yourselves, but let out your joyful feelings in the most natural way; but if, on the other hand, you are almost alone, it will not be expedient to manifest your feelings of joy so freely, because they will not be so appropriate."[1, 2]

Father, it seems that whenever your people rouse themselves,
then "Sanballats" and "Tobiahs" appear on the scene to criticize and snipe!
Please be with those who are coming under fire today. Amen.

---

1   The controversy regarding criticism of Salvation Army methods continued to rumble along, with Catherine Booth feeling the need to defend its ways.
2   From *The Salvation Army in Relation to The Church and State*.

"He himself bore our sins" in his body on the cross,
so that we might die to sins and live for righteousness

(1 Peter 2:24 *NIV*)

There is one stopping-place... and only one. His [God's] infinite love could not let you go down to everlasting damnation without giving you a chance, and so he reared the cross, and stretched on it that broken, bleeding victim, and *there* is the stopping-place for every poor sinner...

God calls you from *Calvary*, and says, "Man, stop! Halt in your downward course!" And from the broken, bleeding body of his Son he cries aloud to you, "Turn ye, turn ye; for why will ye die? Come unto me and live."

There is, then, *one* stopping-place; but if you get finally past that, there is no more stopping for you for ever. The very law of your being will force you on and force you down. There will never come a time when you can turn round and say, "Well, now, I think I'm bad enough. I think I have gone far enough in the practice of iniquity and rebellion against God. I think I shall turn round now and stop" – *never*, you will have to go on growing in the capacity for evil, till you become a very devil! You can never stop any more.

Is it not true? Does not your conscience tell you it is true? Does not the Spirit of God thunder in your ears – "Amen"? You *know* it is true – no more stopping![1]

> Father of mercy, thank you for the "stopping-place" called Calvary,
> where sin meets its end and where love is magnified in its place. Lord,
> make that "stopping-place" real to me as I survey the cross. Amen.

---

1 From *Life and Death.*

ALL OF US HAVE BECOME LIKE ONE WHO IS UNCLEAN, AND ALL OUR RIGHTEOUS ACTS ARE LIKE FILTHY RAGS

(Isaiah 64:6 *NIV*)

I often hear people talking about the righteousness of the saints as "filthy rags". They confound things that differ. When Paul said his own righteousness was as filthy rags, he was referring to his Pharisaical righteousness, before his conversion; not the righteousness of God, which is wrought in the soul by faith.[1] People might see the folly of this interpretation by just transposing all the passages that refer to it, and seeing how ridiculous it sounds: "And there was given unto them white robes",[2] "filthy rags". "Blessed are the dead which die in the Lord, for their 'filthy rags' do follow them." And, "Who are these arrayed in filthy rags?" If you are a saint, your righteousness is not filthy rags. Your righteousness is the most precious and valuable thing in the universe in the sight of God, and something that he will glory in for ever and ever!

I fear thousands of people are expecting to enter Heaven who are not pure, and do not want to be pure. Friends, do not deceive yourselves, you will never enter Heaven without holiness. "Nothing that defileth or is unclean can in any wise enter therein."[3] Thank God untrue and impure people will be shut out there. We have had enough of them here, with their hypocrisy, cheating, lying, slandering, and evil deeds. All the liars, and slanderers, and sorcerers, and whoremongers and unbelievers will be left outside. We can't keep them out of our houses down here, but he will keep them out of that city for ever. All will be clean and white, washed inside and out, who walk the golden streets of the New Jerusalem![4] Won't it be beautiful? Haste, happy day, when we shall get there![5]

Lord, I worship you. Thank you for that divine exchange whereby my filthy rags are taken away and replaced with royal robes I don't deserve. Grace! Amen.

1   Romans 10:5–18.
2   See Revelation 6:11.
3   See Revelation 21:27, KJV.
4   Revelation 21:21.
5   From *Holiness*.

All Scripture is God-breathed and is useful for teaching, rebuking, correcting

(2 Timothy 3:16 *NIV*)

People who know anything of our people, know perfectly well that they are utterly incapable of skilful deception [as was alleged]. Even infidel papers give them credit for incontrovertible sincerity. The next and most important slander concerning The Salvation Army, is that we set at nought the authority of the Holy Scripture. Allow me to quote from one sentence of our Catechism: "*What authority has the Bible with the Army?* While we hold that God does, by his Spirit, speak as directly to his people in this age as any other, still the Army does solemnly and most emphatically regard the Bible as the divine authorized standard by which all other professed revelations are to be tried; and, if any professed revelations speak and square not according to that standard, such revelations are to be rejected as having no truth in them. Whatever is contrary to the teaching of this book must be considered false and thrown overboard."[1] "To the law and to the testimony: if they speak not according to this word, it is because there is no light in them." – Isaiah viii. 20.

Of course our critics never quote that amongst their pretended extracts, because it would show the dirty business they are about, in trying to traduce the characters of people who not only believe in the Bible, but who *practise its precepts*. I think these remarks will apply equally to all the misrepresentations with respect to our little books, except perhaps I ought to refer to the slanderous assertion that we are opposed to marriages amongst our officers![2] We may well ask, what next?[3]

> Thank you for your word. Speak to me through my readings,
> that I may speak to others. Thank you for pages that live and breathe. Amen.

Cont/...

---

1 Doctrine No. 1 of The Salvation Army reads: "We believe that the Scriptures of the Old and New Testaments were given by inspiration of God, and that they only constitute the Divine rule of Christian faith and practice."
2 For many decades, Salvation Army officers were permitted to marry only other officers. This rule has now been relaxed in some territories, though not all, whereby officers are at liberty to marry Christians of any vocation or denomination.
3 From *The Salvation Army in Relation to The Church and State.*

THE ACCUSER OF OUR BROTHERS AND SISTERS,
WHO ACCUSES THEM... DAY AND NIGHT

(Revelation 12:10 *NIV*)

Cont/...

We answer this by simply pointing to recent facts, the marriage of our son[1] and about a score of officers within a few months. In judging of our instructions, however, on this point, please to bear in mind that we have, I should think, 200 women officers *not more than twenty*, and perhaps as many men of the same age, and you will see the absolute necessity, for their own sakes, for some oversight with respect to engagements. I believe the Wesleyans refuse to accept a candidate for ministry if he is engaged, and do not allow their young ministers to marry until their four years' probation has expired... We are accused of disregarding home ties, and sundering families. I answer that The Salvation Army has restored more profligate husbands and prodigal sons and daughters, and created more domestic bliss in one month, than most of our critics have done in a lifetime; if you doubt it, "Come and see." We do teach, however, that home ties, and all other ties, should be made, maintained and used for the glory of God and the salvation of men; and this we intend to go on teaching, however much our enemies may rage... Having learnt many new lessons in the five years' continuous labour since the Order Book was published, and having found by bitter experience how easy it was to put a false construction upon some of the sentences... we had resolved upon a careful revision, which was in progress at the very time when these recent attacks were made... I pray God to bring to a better spirit those who have undeservedly and bitterly maligned us, and thus, for a time at least, have "helped them that hate the Lord".[2,3]

God of truth, help me to remember where false accusations come from.
Give me the presence of mind to swat them away with contempt. Amen.

1   Bramwell Booth married Captain Florence Soper on 12 October 1882. This response to public criticism of The Salvation Army was published in 1883.
2   From 2 Chronicles 19:2, KJV.
3   From *The Salvation Army in Relation to The Church and State*.

Weep with those who weep
(Romans 12:15 *ESV*)

I do not suppose that you intended to reprove me in your last [letter]. Nevertheless, I felt the implied reproof, because it was so well deserved and, intended or not, I received it as a wound of a true friend.[1] I know I ought not, of all saints, or sinners either, to be depressed. I know it dishonours my Lord, grieves his Spirit, and injures me greatly, and I would fain hide from everybody to prevent their seeing it. But I cannot help it. I have struggled hard, more than anyone knows, for a long time against it. Sometimes I have literally held myself, head and heart and hands, and waited for the floods to pass over me. But now I appear to have lost the power of self-command to a great extent, and *weep I must*.

The doctors say, "Never mind. Regard it as a result of your affliction." But this does not satisfy me.[2]

I know there is grace to overcome. And yet, there seems much in the Bible to meet such a state. Well, at present I am under, under, under; and for this very reason I shrink from coming to you or going anywhere. I don't want to burden others.[3, 4]

Even the strongest of us, Lord, are fragile creatures. The human psyche is a complex mystery. Lord, for those afflicted by the horrible beast of depression, I pray your healing. Help those of us who watch as others suffer to resist the temptation of jumping in with counsel that might not help. Amen.

Cont/...

---

1 Proverbs 27:6.
2 Catherine Booth frequently toiled in the face of illness. Her health was not robust, and this appears to have led her into a season of depression.
3 From a letter to a friend.
4 From *Catherine Booth* by F. de L. Booth-Tucker.

HE LAY DOWN AND SLEPT

(1 Kings 19:5 *NASB*)

Cont/…

My dearest says, "Never mind all these rubs and storms. Let us fight through all, in order to save the world."

To this I say, "Amen!" But one must have the *strength* to fight. It is easier for some of us to fight than to lie wounded in the camp. I can neither fight nor run. I can only endure – oh, that I could always say with patience![1]

We are compassed with difficulties on every side.[2] Still there is so much to praise God for that I ought never to look at these troubles. Well, we shall pull through and get home! Then we will have a shout and a family gathering, and no mistake! Will we not?

I feel about these troubles just as I do about my own health, when I pray about it. I am met with: "Ye know not what ye ask."[3] I have such a sense of the wisdom and benevolence of God underlying every other feeling that I dare not go beyond.

"Nevertheless not my will, but thine, be done".[4, 5, 6]

Oh Lord, how easy it is to imagine you wish us to push on and on,
even when we are ill and exhausted. Help us to learn to rest instead!
My heartfelt prayers today are with those who feel they just can't go on.
May they know your help, and then your gradual, gentle restoration. Amen.

---

1 Army troubles and pressures, and ill health, had plunged Catherine Booth into depression. William Booth, too, struggled from time to time with this affliction.
2 From 2 Corinthians 4:8.
3 Matthew 20:22, KJV.
4 Luke 22:42, KJV.
5 From a letter to a friend.
6 From *Catherine Booth* by F. de L. Booth-Tucker.

Fish for people

(Matthew 4:19 *NIV*)

I said to a magistrate, a little while ago, who asked whether we could not give up the processions – "Oh dear, no! I would go to gaol, and die there, before I would give them up. We catch our grandest fish by the processions."

"But," said he, "We would give you a field to go in." "Oh! Thank you," I said, "but the men are not in the field. We are after *the people*, and we must go where the people are."

"Well," he said. "What are you going to do, supposing all the magistrates proclaim the towns?"

"Do?" I said. "Go on, to be sure."

"Suppose they put all your officers in prison?"

"Oh," I said. "We have plenty ready to come after them to fill their places. You try it; and when the prisons are full, then the English people will rise and ask why they are compelled to keep the people in gaol, and pay taxes for their support, for preaching the gospel." "But," he asked, "what will you say to the magistrates who condemn you?" "The old answer will do: 'Whether it be right to obey men rather than God, judge ye.' Didn't the magistrates come down on Paul and Silas, and did they not forbid them to speak any more in that Name? And what notice did Paul and Silas take of it? And so it must be with The Salvation Army."[1, 2, 3]

> Lord, maybe it should concern me more than it does that, often, the Church
> at large is ignored or regarded as irrelevant. Help us to rediscover that holy
> balance between legitimate protest and witness, and public disorder. Amen.

1   Salvation Army marches and open-air processions attracted huge amounts of opposition. Some of this was violent, resulting in public riots. Magistrates were largely unsympathetic to the Army's endeavours, regarding them as troublemakers. It was not uncommon for Salvationists to be sentenced to short spells in prison.
2   See Acts 4:19, KJV.
3   From *Catherine Booth* by F. de L. Booth-Tucker.

Of the many beautiful tributes paid to us by a most gracious public… perhaps the most correct is this: *Complete abandonment to the service of the man.* This, in large measure, is the cause of our success all over the world. When you come to think of it, The Salvation Army is a remarkable arrangement. It is remarkable in its construction. It is a great empire. An empire geographically unlike any other. It is an empire without a frontier. It is an empire made up of geographical fragments, parted from each other by vast stretches of railroad and immense sweeps of sea. It is an empire composed of a tangle of races, tongues, and colours, of types of civilization and enlightened barbarism such as never before in all human history gathered together under one flag. It is an Army, with its titles rambling into all languages, a soldiery spreading over all lands, a banner upon which the sun never goes down –with its head in the heart of a cluster of islands set in the grey, wind-blown northern seas, while its territories are scattered over every sea and under every sky.

The world has wondered what has been the controlling force holding this strange empire together. What is the electromagnetism governing its furthest atom as though it were at your elbow? What is the magic sceptre that compels this diversity of peoples to act as one man? What is the master passion uniting these multifarious pulsations into one heartbeat? Has it been a sworn-to signature attached to bond or paper? No; these can all too readily be designated "scraps" and be rent in twain. Has it been self-interest and worldly fame? No, for all selfish gain has had to be sacrificed upon the threshold of the contract. Has it been the bond of kinship, or blood, or speech? No, for under this banner the British master has become the servant of the Hindu, and the American has gone to lay down his life upon the veldts of Africa.

Cont/…

---

1   Evangeline Cory Booth (1865–1950), General of The Salvation Army, 1934–39, its first female General.

Cont/…

Has it been the bond of that almost supernatural force, glorious patriotism? No, not even this, for while we "know no man after the flesh",[1] we recognize our brother in all the families of the earth, and our General infused into the breasts of his followers the sacred conviction that the Salvationist's country is the world. What was it? What is it? Those ties created by a spiritual ideal. Our love for God demonstrated by our sacrifice for man. My father, in a private audience with the late King Edward, said: "Your Majesty, some men's passion is gold; some men's passion is art; some men's passion is fame; my passion is man!"[2] This was in our Founder's breast the white flame which ignited like sparks in the hearts of all his followers. *Man is our life's passion.* It is for man we have laid our lives upon the altar. It is for man we have entered into a contract with our God which signs away our claim to any and all selfish ends. It is for man we have sworn to our own hurt, and – my God thou knowest – when the hurt came, hard and hot and fast, it was for man we held tenaciously to the bargain. After the torpedoing of the *Aboukir*[3] two sailors found themselves clinging to a spar which was not sufficiently buoyant to keep them both afloat. Harry, a Salvationist, grasped the situation and said to his mate: "Tom, for me to die will mean to go home to Mother. I don't think it's quite the same for you, so you hold to the spar and I will go down; but promise me if you are picked up you will make my God your God and my people your people." Tom was rescued and told to a weeping audience in a Salvation Army hall the act of self-sacrifice which had saved his life, and testified to keeping his promise to the boy who had died for him.[4]

> Father, at this Christmas-time, I ask you to bless the unique ministry of
> The Salvation Army across the globe; musicians and singers who take to the
> streets with carols; officers, soldiers and volunteers who provide hot Christmas
> dinners for the lonely and vulnerable; those who give of their time to make up
> Christmas parcels for people who would otherwise receive nothing.
> God bless and use these Salvationist ministries! Amen.

1   See 2 Corinthians 5:16, KJV.
2   General William Booth was invited to Buckingham Palace in 1904.
3   HMS *Aboukir*, sunk by a German submarine on 22 September 1914, with the loss of 527 lives.
4   From *The War Romance of The Salvation Army.*

HE WAS DESPISED AND REJECTED

(Isaiah 53:3 *NIV*)

I would have given a trifle for you to have been with us yesterday: first, at the drawing-room meeting, where I tried to scrape together all my patience to meet and answer the old, time-worn objections to our measures, which one is so sick of hearing, to a respectable audience of Christians; and then, at night, in the midst of an excited audience, who grinned and groaned, and hooted so that anybody but Salvation Army soldiers would have given in and been beaten. We had a splendid congregation, however, of *just our sort*, mostly men, many of them young, full of the "blood and fire" of Hell. Many were disposed to listen, but about half were of the revolutionary type, and would not be calmed. The uproar was terrible but, just at the worst, the *Maréchale*[1] advanced into the middle of the hall, and, standing right in the midst of them, she mounted a form and pleaded like an apostle.[2]

Oh, it was a sublime sight, worth coming from England to see! There were a few desperadoes, ringleaders, who said awful things. One, with a face full of the Devil, hissed in rage inconceivable; bearing his arm and holding it aloft, he shrieked: "We will hear you if you will talk to us about anything else but Jesus, but we hate him; we will not have him; he is the cause of all our sorrows! I wish I had him here! I would pour a pail of cabbage-water over his head!" They shouted, *"Vive la Liberté!"* And when the *Maréchale* answered, "Amen!" they said, "Ah, we will have liberty, but no amens! No religion! We have had enough of that, we have had enough of Jesus!"[3]

Lord Jesus, have mercy.

---

1   Catherine Booth-Clibborn.
2   At the opening of the new Salvation Army hall in *Rue Oberkampff* in Paris.
3   From *Catherine Booth* by F. de L. Booth-Tucker.

December 28th

We are fools for Christ

(1 Corinthians 4:10 *NIV*)

The first sight of it appalled me. It was indeed a dome![1] As I looked upwards there appeared space enough to swallow any amount of sound that my poor voice could put into it. To make any considerable number of people hear me seemed impossible. On this point, however, I was greatly encouraged to learn at the conclusion of the first meeting that I had been distinctly heard in every portion of it by the 2,000 people present. I can never forget my feelings as I stood on the platform, and looked upon the people, realizing that among them there was no one to help me. When I commenced the Prayer Meeting, for which I should think quite 900 remained, Satan said to me, as I came down from the platform according to my usual custom, "You will never ask such people as these to come out and kneel down here. You will only make a fool of yourself if you do!" I felt stunned for the moment, but I answered, "Yes, I shall. I shall not make it any easier for them than for others. If they do not sufficiently realize their sins to be willing to come and kneel here and confess them, they are not likely to be of much use to the Kingdom of God!" Subsequent experience has confirmed this opinion. However, the Lord was better to me than my fears, for ten or twelve came forward, some of them handsomely dressed, and evidently belonging to the most fashionable circles.[2] The way was led by two old gentlemen, of seventy or more years of age. One of them said that he had sinned for many years against light and privilege, asking the Lord to save him, with all the simplicity of a little child. Others followed, until there was a goodly row of kneeling penitents. This was a great triumph in the midst of so many curious onlookers.[3]

> Lord God, you are indeed greater than our fears. Please help anyone
> who is fearful today, whatever their situation, to trust you. Amen.

---

1 'Catherine Booth was preaching in the Brighton Dome, East Sussex, England, in 1868. This was part of a spectacular suite of edifices erected by King George IV and could accommodate 3,000 people. Catherine booked the Dome because of its popularity with visitors to Brighton.
2 Brighton was something of a magnet for fashionable types.
3 From *Catherine Booth The Mother of The Salvation Army, Vol. I.*

AN ARMY WITH BILLOWING BANNERS
(Song of Solomon 6:10 *NLT*)

We are marching on! Some of our friends say, "Well, but could you not march without a flag?" Yes, we could, and we have marched a long time and a long way without one; but we can march better *with* one, and that is the reason we have one. All armies have banners, and we are an Army; we grew into one, and then we found it out, and called ourselves one. Every soldier of this Army is pledged to carry the standard of the cross into every part of the world, as far as he has opportunity. Our motto is: "The world for Jesus". We have all sworn fealty to the Lord Jesus Christ, and faithfulness to the Army, because it represents our highest conception of the work which he wants us to do.

The flag is a symbol, first, of our *devotion* to our great Captain in Heaven and to the great purpose for which his blood was shed – that he might redeem men and women from sin and death and Hell! When a soldier enlists in the service of the Queen he gives up, not a little of his time, or of his money, or a part of his strength, talents, or influence, but himself. So I trust everyone who shall pledge himself to this flag will resolve to give himself and herself – body, soul, and spirit; all he has, all he is, and all he can do – to be used up in the glorious service of his Master and King!... Our flag is emblematical of our faithfulness to our great trust... This flag is also an emblem of victory![1, 2, 3]

God of victory!

---

1   Catherine Booth was instrumental in designing the Salvation Army flag, which is rich in Trinitarian symbolism and meaning for Salvationists. The red centre of the flag represents the shed blood of Jesus Christ, the yellow star in the centre, the fire of the Holy Spirit, and the blue border, the absolute purity of God the Father. Flagpoles are usually topped with a steel cross intertwined with an "S". The "S" is engraved with another of the Army's mottos: "Blood and Fire". The first flag of the Salvation Army was presented to Coventry Corps, England, in 1878.
2   From an address to accompany the presentation of flags by Catherine Booth to some newly formed corps, Newcastle, England, 1879.
3   From *Catherine Booth The Mother of The Salvation Army, Vol. II.*

Let Justice Roll on Like a River
(Amos 5:24 *NIV*)

Allow me to intrude on your valuable time for a moment in order to call your attention to the perils of my daughter, Miss Booth, and her companions in Switzerland, which may not have been fully presented to you. Six months ago, after this illegal and groundless persecution commenced, Earl Granville[1] promised my husband that he would interfere but, although we have made two or three applications to his Lordship through parliamentary friends since then, so far as we can see, *nothing has been done!*

Now the authorities of Neuchatel are trying Miss Booth on a mere pretext, and we have reason to fear an entire miscarriage of justice. Miss Booth's imprisonment would probably help our cause more than anything else, but for the very delicate state of her health, consequent on the trying events of the last few months. I would not intrude on your much-needed privacy; but fearing that even a short imprisonment would cause a serious illness, or even fatal consequences, and thus terminate her Christ-like labours, I beg, with a mother's importunity, your timely interference… Our measures [The Salvation Army's] *have succeeded* in reaching multitudes of the worst classes, and the grace of God has reclaimed thousands of them from lives of open debauchery to temperance, industry, and religion. With deepest respect and unfeigned gratitude for all your hard service for humanity.[2, 3, 4]

> I pray for those groups and organizations that campaign for justice, whether in this country or overseas. Bless them as they lobby Members of Parliament on behalf of the voiceless. I pray too for victims of injustice. Amen.

---

1 Lord Granville, Liberal politician and Foreign Secretary.
2 In December, 1882, a handful of Salvationists entered Switzerland, but met with a hostile reception. Some were expelled, some were imprisoned, and others were left to the mercy of a brutal mob. Kate Booth and a Captain Becquet were imprisoned for their refusal to follow orders to cease their activities.
3 From a letter Catherine Booth wrote to the Right Honourable W. E. Gladstone, British Prime Minister, in 1883.
4 From *Catherine Booth* by F. de L. Booth-Tucker.

THE LAST ENEMY TO BE DESTROYED IS DEATH
(1 Corinthians 15:26 *NIV*)

Thy will be done; only let me be thine, whether suffering or in health, whether living or dying. (From Catherine Mumford's journal, aged seventeen.)

All our enemies have to be conquered by *faith*, not by realization, and is it not so with the last enemy, death? (To Commissioner Booth-Clibborn from her deathbed.)

Don't be concerned about your dying; only go on living well, and the dying will be all right. (From Catherine Booth's last message to Salvationists.)

No matter how advanced in holiness, every dying saint rests his soul on the blood of Christ. (From a public address.)

A denouncer of iniquity!... Thank God I have been that! That is what is wanted in the world today. (To a young officer, from her deathbed.)

Give me grace to cry in all life's conflicts and changes and temptations, and in death's final struggle as my Saviour did: "Father, glorify thyself." (From a letter to William Booth.)[1]

Catherine Booth, The Mother of The Salvation Army, was promoted to Glory on 4 October 1890 aged 61. Her passing, like her life, was an eloquent testimony to her unwavering faith in her Saviour. Surrounded by her loved ones, she slipped into eternity with words of Scripture and Salvation Army songs on her lips, and is interred with her beloved husband, General William Booth, at Abney Park Cemetery, north London.

To God be the glory!

---

1 · From *Catherine Booth* by Catherine Bramwell-Booth.

Booth, C. M., *Life and Death. Being Reports Of Addresses Delivered In London*. First published 1890, International Headquarters: 101, Queen Victoria Street, EC, London, UK. Publishing Offices: 98, 100 and 102, Clerkenwell Road, EC. Reprint 2015 in India by Facsimile Publishers, Delhi.

Booth, C., *Papers on Aggressive Christianity by Mrs General Booth*. Salvationist Publishing and Supplies, Ltd., London: Judd Street, King's Cross, WC1.

Booth, C., *Popular Christianity by The Late Mrs Booth*. The Salvation Army Book Department: London: 79 and 81 Fortress Road, NW. Simpkin, Marshall, Hamilton, Kent & Co. Ltd. London, EC. 1887.

Booth, Mrs, *Papers on Practical Religion*. International Headquarters: 101, Queen Victoria Street, EC, London, UK. 1889.

Booth, C., *Holiness: being an address delivered in St James' Hall, Piccadilly, London*. Headquarters – The Temple, Albert Street, Toronto.

Booth, C., *The Holy Ghost: an address*. Headquarters: Salvation Temple, Toronto.

Booth-Tucker, Commissioner F. de L., *The Life of Catherine Booth The Mother of The Salvation Army; Volume I*. Salvationist Publishing and Supplies Ltd., London: Judd Street, King's Cross, WC1 [*Third Edition*] 1924.

Booth-Tucker, Commissioner F. de L., *The Life of Catherine Booth The Mother of The Salvation Army; Volume II*. Salvationist Publishing and Supplies Ltd., London: Judd Street, King's Cross, WC1 [*Third Edition*] 1924.

Booth-Tucker, F. de L., *The Life of Catherine Booth The Mother of The Salvation Army. Volume I*. International Headquarters: 101, Queen Victoria Street, EC, London, UK. Publishing Offices: 98, 100 and 102, Clerkenwell Road, EC. 1893.

Booth-Tucker, F. de L., *The Short Life of Catherine Booth The Mother of The Salvation Army*. [Abridged from the original edition, 1893.] International Headquarters: 101, Queen Victoria Street, EC, London, UK. Publishing Offices: 98, 100 and 102, Clerkenwell Road, EC.

Bramwell-Booth, C., *Catherine Booth, The Story of Her Loves*. London: Hodder & Stoughton. First published 1970. Third impression 1971.

Duff, Lieut.-Colonel M., *The Warriors' Library. Edited by Bramwell Booth (1901). No. 1. Catherine Booth: A Sketch*. The Salvation Army Book Department. London: 100 Clerkenwell Road, EC. [3rd Edition].

Stead, W. T., *Catherine Booth*. James Nisbet & Co., Limited. 21, Berners Street, 1900.

Internet Sources

Booth, C., *The Catherine Booth Collection. Godliness, Highway of our God*
http://www.salvationfactory.org/catherine-booth-collection

Booth, E., Lutz, G., (Livingston) Hill, Mrs. *The War Romance of The Salvation Army.*
https://archive.org/details/warromanceofsalv00bootiala Published 1919.

https://en.wikipedia.org/wiki/Plymouth_Brethren

www.biblegateway.com online Bible search engine.

www.biblehub.com online Bible study suite regarding Bible references and translations.

CEV *Contemporary English Version*, Copyright © 1995 American Bible Society.

GNT *Good News Translation*, Copyright © 1976 American Bible Society.

KJV *King James Version* Text courtesy of https://www.kingjamesbibleonline.org

NASB *New American Standard Bible* Copyright © 1960, 1962, 1963, 1968, 1971, 1972, 1973, 1975, 1977, 1995 by The Lockman Foundation, La Habra, Calif.

NET *New English Translation Bible* copyright © 1996-2006 by Biblical Studies Press, L.L.C.

NIV *New International Version*, Copyright © 1973, 1978, 1984, 2011 by Biblica, Inc.

NLT *New Living Translation*, copyright ©1996, 2004, 2007. Used by permission of Tyndale House Publishers, Inc., Carol Stream, Illinois 60188.

ESV *English Standard Version* copyright © 2001 by Crossway Bibles, a publishing ministry of Good News Publishers.

WEB *World English Bible*, The World English Bible is a 1997 revision of the American Standard Version of the Holy Bible, first published in 1901.